Chronology of the United States

by
JOHN CLEMENTS

As you glance through this book, you will see at once that it is a handsome, colorful, and lavishly illustrated work, obviously designed and produced to please the eye. But when you pause to read it, you will discover that it is not only a stunning example of the art of book design, but also a unique contribution to the literature on the evolution of these United States. For what this book does, simply and succinctly, is capsulize and put into meaningful perspective all the key events in American history.

The concept and format are original and beautifully simple—each page (or two facing pages) presents a complete mini-history of one year, beginning with the founding of the Republic in 1789 and running to 1997. *In no other single source can* the citizen who wants a clear, concise grasp of American history . . . the student who wants a ready reliable reference . . . the writer, or the political, or economic analyst who wants background material . . . or the history buff who likes to browse through historical facts—*find so much vital information:*

- Dates and brief descriptions of major events—important moments in lives of prominent people—significant legislative actions—major political happenings
- Portraits of all the Presidents and Vice Presidents
- Brief biographies of all the Presidents
- Year by year maps of the states and territories—and year by year replicas of the flag
- Historic photographs and line drawings—900 in all over 400 in two-color reproduction
- And, on every yearly spread, the following: national business, economic and political data, gross national product—retail sales—bank resources—exports—imports—federal government expenditures—federal debt, population and a breakdown of congressional membership by party affiliation.

Should you want to find where to look for mention of a particular event or person—you simply consult the detailed index.

To discover the historical context or background of a particular event or person—you simply skim through the appropriate year-at-a-glance summaries.

And, should you want a balanced, readable, and graphic account of the growth of our country—you simply read the book page by page, letting it forge bits and pieces of information into a meaningful whole for you.

About the Author:

John Clements is author of the widely esteemed and highly successful *Taylor's Encyclopedia of Government Officials: Federal and State* and of *Clements' Encyclopedia of World Governments*. He is a writer, researcher, and lecturer whose fields of specialization are business and political affairs.

☆ ☆ ☆ ☆ ☆ ☆ ☆ ☆ ☆ ☆ ☆ ☆ ☆ ☆ ☆ ☆ ☆ ☆

United States of America

★ ★

Political Research, Inc.

Tegoland at Bent Tree
16850 Dallas Parkway
Dallas, Texas 75248

Chronology of the United States

by
JOHN CLEMENTS

Second Edition

© John Clements 1997

Library of Congress Catalog Card Number 70-175181

Published by
POLITICAL RESEARCH, INC.
DALLAS, TEXAS 75248
    U.S.A.

ISBN #0-07-011328-9

☆ ☆ ☆ ☆ ☆ ☆ ☆ ☆ ☆ ☆ ☆ ☆ ☆ ☆ ☆ ☆ ☆ ☆ ☆

Library of Congress Cataloging in Publication Data

Clements, John, date.
    Chronology of the United States

        1. U.S.—History—Chronology. I. Title
E174.5.C63   973   70-175181

ISBN 0-07-011328-9

☆ ☆

Political Research, Inc. is always dedicated to providing quality publications.

Political Research, Inc.

Tegoland at Bent Tree
16850 Dallas Parkway
Dallas, Texas 75248

Introduction

Few developments in history are more astonishing than the growth of the United States. A nation of less than four million in 1789 had grown to well over 200 million by 1970. A nation whose impact upon the outside world was marginal at the outset had become a superpower whose actions shaped the destiny of half the world by 1945.

It was a development mirrored in the steady growth of the federal government. With each administration there was an expansion of the national budget and an increase in the role of the government in the everyday life of Americans. It can safely be said that the federal role reflected the emergence of the American colossus.

The centrality of the federal government was established by George Washington. Jefferson and Jackson made of the Presidency a potent and at times dangerously powerful instrument. Lincoln, in leading the country safely through the Civil War, confirmed the preeminence of the federal government and the subordination of the states. In the aftermath of the fratricidal struggle, national policy provided the basis in law for the nation's emergence as the world's premier industrial power. From the "bully pulpit" of the Presidency, Theodore Roosevelt directed reform of the economy and of social conditions. It was a path that was subsequently followed by Woodrow Wilson, Franklin D. Roosevelt, Harry S Truman and Lyndon B. Johnson. Today, Americans look to Washington for security in health, employment, old age and countless other areas.

Again in the 20th century the Roosevelts, Wilson, Truman, Eisenhower, Kennedy, Johnson and Nixon have led the country into the international arena. Americans have learned to their pride and dismay that the United States has become an imperial power. Such power has made the world both tremble and look to it for security. It has also made Americans aware that the power they have created may one day be used at home. It is a reminder that mighty nations are as vulnerable to the power they possess as those beyond their borders.

The chronology that follows, traces all the aforementioned developments. It is a guide to the emergence of the United States as a world power. It is a handy reference work which traces president by president the significant developments that propelled a nation from the periphery to the center of global affairs. And it is a succinct summary of a history that for better or worse has irrevocably shaped the course of world history.

☆ ☆ ☆ ☆ ☆ ☆ ☆ ☆ ☆ ☆ ☆ ☆ ☆ ☆ ☆ ☆ ☆ ☆ ☆

James P. Shenton
Columbia University

Note to the Reader

The membership of Congress given for each year is that of the opening of the first session of the particular Congress. The following abbreviations are used:

AD	Administration
AM	Anti-Masonic
D	Democratic
DR	Democratic-Republican
F	Federalist
J	Jacksonian
NR	National Republican
O	Other
OP	Opposition
R	Republican
W	Whig
N/A	means "not available."

☆ ☆ ☆ ☆ ☆ ☆ ☆ ☆ ☆ ☆ ☆ ☆ ☆ ☆ ☆ ☆ ☆ ☆ ☆ ☆

Chronology
of the
United States

★ ★

JOHN CLEMENTS

1789 George Washington

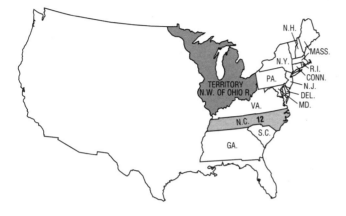

1st CONGRESS

SENATE	.... 26 Members
AD	 17
OP	 9
O	 0

HOUSE	.... 64 Members
AD	 38
OP	 26
O	 0

ESTIMATED
POPULATION
3,800,000

George Washington
1st President
1st Federalist

John Adams
1st Vice President
Federalist

UNITED STATES ECONOMY

GROSS NATIONAL PRODUCT	.... N/A
RETAIL SALES	.... N/A
BANK RESOURCES	.... N/A
EXPORTS	.... N/A
IMPORTS	.... N/A
FEDERAL GOVERNMENT EXPENDITURE	... $4,269,000
FEDERAL DEBT	.... N/A

George Washington

Birth	... Westmoreland County, VA, Feb. 22 (N.S.), 1732
Parents	.... Augustine and Mary Ball Washington
Married	.... Martha Dandridge Custis
Home	.... Mount Vernon, VA
Presidency	.... 1789 – 1797
Death	.... Mount Vernon, VA, Dec. 14, 1799

Events

January 7 • With the exception of New York, which failed to elect or appoint officials, presidential electors for the first presidential election are named directly by the people or by the state legislatures in the eleven states that have ratified the Constitution. (North Carolina, which is reluctant to approve the document without a bill of rights, and Rhode Island have yet to ratify the Constitution.)

January 23 • John Carroll founds Georgetown College (now Georgetown University), the first Catholic college in the United States.

February 4 • The presidential electors cast their ballots, and the election of senators and representatives is held in each state.

March 4 • The First Congress under the Constitution meets in New York but is unable to organize for lack of a quorum.

April 1 • The House of Representatives is organized: Frederick A. Muhlenberg (Pennsylvania) is elected speaker.

April 6 • The Senate elects John Langdon (New Hampshire) as temporary presiding officer, and the ballots cast by the presidential electors are counted. George Washington, having received sixty–nine votes, is unanimously elected president. John Adams, with thirty–four votes, is chosen vice president. (The remaining votes for vice president are scattered among several candidates.)

April 8 • The House begins deliberations.

April 11 • John Fenno founds the Federalist newspaper *Gazette of the United States* in New York. (It is moved to Philadelphia in 1790.)

April 30 • Washington is inaugurated on the balcony of Federal Hall, New York City; the oath is administered by Robert R. Livingston, chancellor of New York. In the hall's Senate chamber, the new president establishes a tradition by delivering an inaugural address. His speech, thought to have been written by James Madison, urges "the preservation of the sacred fire of liberty...entrusted to the hands of the American people."

May 7 • The first inaugural ball is held in honor of George Washington in New York.

May 12 • A number of workers, tradesmen, and political leaders form the Society of Tammany, which later becomes the Democratic machine of New York.

June 1 • The first congressional act, establishing the procedure for the time and manner of administering oaths for public office, is signed by President Washington.

July 4 • The first tariff bill, setting rates up to 15 percent, is adopted by Congress to raise revenue.

July 27 • The first executive department, the Department of Foreign Affairs, is created. It is headed by John Jay, who had served as secretary of foreign affairs under the Confederation; on September 11 it is renamed the Department of State.

August 7 • The War Department is created by Congress. On September 1, Henry Knox is named secretary of war.

September 2 • The Treasury Department is established, and Alexander Hamilton is named secretary of the treasury on September 11.

September 22 • Congress creates the office of postmaster general.

September 24 • Congress adopts the Federal Judiciary Act, which provides for the organization of the Supreme Court, thirteen district courts, and three circuit courts. It also creates the office of attorney general.

September 25 • Congress submits to the states 12 proposed amendments to the Constitution. Ten are eventually ratified by the states and become part of the Constitution as the Bill of Rights in 1791.

September 26 • Thomas Jefferson, Samuel Osgood and Edmund Randolph are named secretary of state, postmaster general, and attorney general, respectively. Since Jefferson is still serving as Minister to France,

John Jay, now named chief justice, continues to administer the Department of State until March 1790.

October • At a convention held in Philadelphia, the Protestant Episcopal Church is established separately from the Church of England. The Book of Common Prayer is revised to meet the requirements of the new church.

November 20 • New Jersey is the first state to ratify the Bill of Rights.

November 21 • Influenced by the submission of 12 proposed amendments to the states, North Carolina ratifies the Constitution. It is the 12th state to do so.

December 11 • A charter is granted to the University of North Carolina, which, in 1795, becomes the first state university to begin operations. (The University of Georgia, which was the first to receive a charter, does not begin instruction until 1801).

December 22 • North Carolina cedes its western lands to the United States, which accepts the cession on April 2, 1790. Commonly called the Southwest Territory, the "territory south of the River Ohio" will eventually become the state of Tennessee.

International and Cultural Events • The French Revolution begins with the fall of the Bastille. William H. Brown's *The Power of Sympathy*, the first American novel, urges the education of women.

The inauguration of George Washington.

1790 United States of America

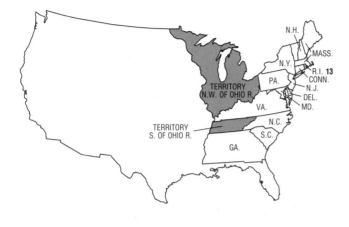

ESTIMATED
POPULATION
3,929,000

1st CONGRESS		
SENATE	....	26 Members
AD	....	17
OP	....	9
O	....	0
HOUSE	....	64 Members
AD	....	38
OP	....	26
O	....	0

George Washington
1st President
1st Federalist

John Adams
1st Vice President
Federalist

UNITED STATES ECONOMY

GROSS NATIONAL PRODUCT	.... N/A
RETAIL SALES	.... N/A
BANK RESOURCES	.... N/A
EXPORTS	.... $29,000,000
IMPORTS	.... $30,000,000
FEDERAL GOVERNMENT EXPENDITURE	.. $ 4,260,000
FEDERAL DEBT	.... N/A

Events

January 14 • Hamilton presents to the House of Representatives the first report on the public credit, which shows a foreign debt of $11,710,378, a domestic national debt of $44,414,085 and state debts of $25,000,000. To put public finance on a firm basis, he suggests that the federal government fund the foreign and domestic national debts at par and also assume

$21,500,000 of the states' debts. The proposals are opposed by those who have been forced to sell their securities at greatly reduced prices and by the southern states, which have already contracted to pay their debts. In the original vote in the House on April 12, the plan to assume the states' debts is rejected.

February 11 • The first petition for the abolition of slavery is sent to Congress by the Society of Friends.

March 1 • The Census Act is passed by Congress making the United States the first nation to provide, by law, for a periodic count of its citizens. The first census, completed on August 1, shows a total population of 3,929,625, including 59,557 free blacks and 697,624 slaves.

March 26 • Congress adopts a Naturalization Act, which sets a residency requirement of two years for prospective citizens.

April 10 • Congress passes the Patent Act, establishing a board with authority to grant protection to inventors through exclusive rights to their inventions for a period of time. The Patent Office is opened on July 31.

April 17 • Bejamin Franklin dies in Philadelphia at the age of 84.

May 29 • The Convention of Rhode Island ratifies the Constitution by a majority of two votes. George Washington calls this action by the 13th state "this happy event, which unites under the general government, all the states which were originally confederated."

May 31 • Washington signs the Copyright Act, which protects books, maps, and plays for two consecutive fourteen-year periods.

July 10 • In a compromise designed to obtain southern support for the assumption of state debts, the House of Representatives votes to establish the permanent national capital along the Potomac River. The president is to choose the 10-mile-square district. Meanwhile, Philadelphia, the northern choice for the permanent capital, is to serve as the temporary capital until 1800.

July 26 • The House of Representatives approves the assumption by the federal government of the states' debts.

August 4 • Congress approves the funding of the national debt at par. Bonds bearing six percent interest are subsequently issued.

August 10 • Captain Robert Gray arrives in Boston, ending the first trip to be made around the world in an American ship.

August 15 • John Carroll is consecrated in England as the first Roman Catholic bishop in the United States. His see is established in Baltimore.

September 25 • The Massachusetts General Court repeals the state's excise law "in consequence of the assumption of the state debts by the United States."

United States of America 1790

October 18 • U.S. troops under the command of General Josiah Harmar are defeated near present-day Fort Wayne, Indiana, by the forces of Miami chief The Little Turtle. The episode inaugurates five years of warfare in the Northwest Territory.

December 6 • Congress meets in Philadelphia.

December 14 • Hamilton, in a report to the House of Representatives, urges the creation of a national bank.

December 16 • The Virginia resolutions, which were drawn up by Patrick Henry, take strong exception to the assumption provisions, claiming that there is no constitutional basis for the federal government's assuming the debts of the states.

December 21 • The first United States cotton mill, established by Samuel Slater, begins production in Pawtucket, Rhode Island.

International and Cultural Events • Great Britain and Spain adopt the Nootka South Convention, which fortifies British claims in the dispute with the United States over the Oregon country. The Scottish-born cabinetmaker Duncan Phyfe opens a shop in New York. Royall Tyler, later chief justice of the Vermont Supreme Court, publishes the text of *The Contrast*, the first professionally produced (1787) comedy written by an American.

President George Washington confers with Thomas Jefferson and Alexander Hamilton.

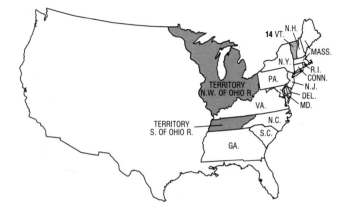

2nd CONGRESS

SENATE	....	29 Members
F	....	16
DR	....	13
O	....	0

HOUSE	....	70 Members
F	....	37
DR	....	33
O	....	0

ESTIMATED
POPULATION
4,056,000

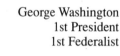

George Washington
1st President
1st Federalist

John Adams
1st Vice President
Federalist

UNITED STATES ECONOMY

GROSS NATIONAL PRODUCT	....	N/A
RETAIL SALES	....	N/A
BANK RESOURCES	....	N/A
EXPORTS	....	$29,000,000
IMPORTS	....	$37,000,000
FEDERAL GOVERNMENT EXPENDITURE	..	$ 4,269,500
FEDERAL DEBT	....	N/A

Events

January 10 • Vermont ratifies the Constitution. On March 4, it is admitted to the Union as the 14th state.

January 28 • At the request of Congress (April 15, 1790), Hamilton reports on the establishment of a mint.

February 25 • President Washington, after much deliberation on constitutional questions, signs the bill creating the charter for the first Bank of the United States. At this time, the Jeffersonian theory of strict constructionism and the Hamiltonian theory of implied powers emerge as alternate philosophies of constitutional interpretation.

March 3 • Congress enacts a law taxing distilled spirits in order to raise revenue. Known as the "whisky tax," it arouses the opposition of farmers whose income depends on distilling their grain. The farmers are supported by several state legislatures, which adopt resolutions against the new law.

March 30 • President Washington issues a proclamation designating the boundary of the District of Columbia. Within its borders are two communities: Georgetown, Maryland, and Alexandria, Virginia.

May–June • Madison and Jefferson endeavor to obtain support from anti-Federalists in New York and New England for their opposition to the administration. Later, the anti-administration forces coalesce in the Republican (Democratic-Republican) party, while adherents of the administration come to constitute the Federalist party.

July 4 • The newly created Bank of the United States begins a subscription for funds.

September 29 • An act of the Pennsylvania General Assembly authorizes the incorporation of a company to build a canal between the Schuylkill and Susquehanna Rivers.

October 31 • With the encouragement of Madison, Philip Freneau founds the *National Gazette*, an anti-administration newspaper, in Philadelphia.

The Bill of Rights.

United States of America 1791

December 5 • Hamilton submits his report on manufactures to Congress.

December 12 • The main office of the first Bank of the United States opens its doors in Philadelphia.

December 15 • The Bill of Rights, consisting of the first 10 amendments to the Constitution of the United States, takes effect.

International and Cultural Events • France becomes a constitutional monarchy. George Hammond is appointed first British Minister to the United States. Britain reinforces its claim to Nootka Sound territory by sending George Vancouver to explore the area. Thomas Paine publishes the first part of *The Rights of Man*.

THE BILL OF RIGHTS

The First Ten Amendments
to
the Constitution of the United States

ARTICLE I
Freedom of Religion, of Speech, and of the Press; Right of Petition

Congress shall make no law respecting an establishment of religion, or prohibiting the free exercise thereof; or abridging the freedom of speech, or of the press; or the right of the people peaceably to assemble, and to petition the Government for a redress of grievances.

ARTICLE II
Right to Keep Arms

A well regulated Militia, being necessary to the security of a free State, the right of the people to keep and bear Arms, shall not be infringed.

ARTICLE III
Quartering of Soldiers in Private Houses

No Soldier shall, in time of peace be quartered in any house, without the consent of the Owner, nor in time of war, but in a manner to be prescribed by law.

ARTICLE IV
Search Warrants

The right of the people to be secure in their persons, houses, papers, and effects, against unreasonable searches and seizures, shall not be violated, and no Warrants shall issue, but upon probable cause, supported by Oath or affirmation, and particularly describing the place to be searched, and the persons or things to be seized.

ARTICLE V
Criminal Proceedings

No person shall be held to answer for a capital, or otherwise infamous crime, unless on a presentment or indictment of a Grand Jury, except in cases arising in the land or naval forces, or in the Militia, when in actual service in time of War or public danger, nor should any person be subject for the same offense to be twice put in jeopardy of life or limb; nor shall be compelled in any criminal case to be a witness against himself, nor be deprived of life, liberty, or property, without due process of law; nor shall private property be taken for public use, without just compensation.

ARTICLE VI
Criminal Proceedings (continued)

In all criminal prosecutions, the accused shall enjoy the right to a speedy and public trial, by an impartial jury of the State and district wherein the crime shall have been committed, which district shall have been previously ascertained by law, and to be informed of the nature and cause of the accusation; to be confronted with the witnesses against him; to have compulsory process for obtaining witnesses in his favor, and to have the Assistance of Counsel for his defense.

ARTICLE VII
Jury Trial in Civil Cases

In Suits at common law, where the value in controversy shall exceed twenty dollars, the right of trial by jury shall be preserved, and no fact tried by a jury, shall be otherwise re-examined in any Court of the United States, than according to the rules of the common law.

ARTICLE VIII
Excessive Punishments

Excessive bail shall not be required, nor excessive fines imposed, nor cruel and unusual punishments inflicted.

ARTICLE IX
Unenumerated Rights of the People

The enumeration in the Constitution, of certain rights, shall not be construed to deny or disparage others retained by the people.

ARTICLE X
Powers Reserved to states

The powers not delegated to the United States by the Constitution, nor prohibited by it to the States, are reserved to the States respectively, or to the people.

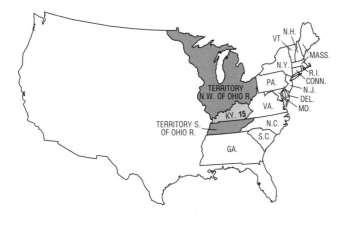

2nd CONGRESS

SENATE .... 29 Members
F 16
DR 13
O 0

ESTIMATED
POPULATION
4,194,000

HOUSE .... 70 Members
F 37
DR 33
O 0

George Washington
1st President
1st Federalist

John Adams
1st Vice President
Federalist

UNITED STATES ECONOMY

GROSS NATIONAL PRODUCT .... N/A
RETAIL SALES .... N/A
BANK RESOURCES .... N/A
EXPORTS $32,000,000
IMPORTS $40,000,000
FEDERAL GOVERNMENT EXPENDITURE .. $ 2,080,000
FEDERAL DEBT $77,228,000

Events

January 12 • Thomas Pinckney is appointed the first minister to Great Britain; the Senate confirms Gouverneur Morris as minister to France.

February 21 • Congress adopts the Presidential Succession Act. If the president and vice president are unable to act because of death, resignation, disability, or removal, the succession passes to the president pro tempore of the Senate and then, if that office is vacant, to the speaker of the House.

April 2 • Congress enacts a law establishing a mint in Philadelphia and a decimal system of coinage. The ratio of silver to gold is set at 15 to one.

May 8 • The Militia Act, necessitated by Indian trouble in the Northwest Territory, empowers states to call up men between 18 and 45 years of age.

May 11 • Captain Robert Gray discovers the Columbia River, which he names for his ship. Continuing around the world for a second time, he arrives in Boston on July 20, 1793.

May 17 • The New York Stock Exchange is founded.

June 1 • Kentucky, a slave state, is admitted to the Union as the 15th state.

August 21 • As opposition to the excise tax on whisky increases in the South and in western Pennsylvania, a convention meets in Pittsburgh to discuss measures to circumvent it. The delegates adopt a number of strongly worded resolutions.

September 29 • President Washington, reacting to the Pittsburgh resolutions, issues a proclamation emphasizing that the tax will be collected according to law and warning against interference.

October 10 • The Virginia Senate, in passing a bill that provides for the appointment of electors to choose a president and vice president of the United States, devise a system whereby the state is divided into districts. Qualified voters are to elect representatives to a general assembly that will meet at the district courthouse on the first Monday in November in every fourth year to vote for an elector. Each elector should be allowed seven cents per mile for traveling expenses and $1.67 for attendance.

October 13 • The cornerstone of the White House is laid in Washington, D.C.

November 1 • A general election is held to choose presidential electors. On December 5, Washington is re-elected president (132 electoral votes), and Adams is re-elected vice president (77 votes).

November 5 • The second session of the Second Congress meets in Philadelphia.

International and Cultural Events • Invaded by Prussia and Austria, France proclaims itself a republic. Louis XV is confined in the old house of the Knights Templar. He goes on trial in December. The Swedish king Gustavus III is murdered by a Swedish aristocrat. Denmark becomes the first nation to abolish the slave trade. In Great Britain, Mary Wollstonecraft publishes *Vindication of the Rights of Women.*

United States of America 1793

Events

January 23 • After a crisis in land and stock speculation, resolutions questioning Hamilton's management of the Treasury are submitted to Congress.

February 12 • The first Fugitive Slave Act is passed by Congress.

February 28 • The House of Representatives defeats nine resolutions of censure against Hamilton.

March 4 • Washington begins his second term as president of the United States and Adams his second term as vice president.

April 8 • Edmond Charles Édouard Genêt (Citizen Genêt), French minister to the United States, arrives in Charleston, South Carolina. While on his way to Philadelphia, he commissions privateers for action against British shipping.

April 22 • Washington issues a proclamation of neutrality on the part of the United States in the war between France and Great Britain and warns United States citizens not to take part in the conflict.

May 18 • Citizen Genêt tardily reports to and is received by President Washington.

June 5 • Jefferson informs Genêt that he must stop commissioning privateers and engaging in other warlike activities. Genêt agrees to do so, but still sends out another privateer.

June 8 • Great Britain begins the seizure of American and other neutral vessels laden with cargo bound for France.

July 31 • Jefferson submits his resignation as secretary of state, effective in December.

August 23 • President Washington asks for the recall of Citizen Genêt because of his undiplomatic actions in the United States. (However, the Jacobins are now in control of the French government, and Genêt's successor brings an order for his arrest. Genêt then requests political asylum; remaining in the United States, he becomes an American citizen.)

September 18 • The cornerstone for the Capitol designed by William Thornton is laid by President Washington in the city bearing his name.

October 7 • General Anthony Wayne moves into Ohio Indian country with 2,600 troops.

October 28 • Eli Whitney applies for a patent on a cotton gin.

December 31 • Secretary of State Jefferson resigns his post and begins to construct an opposition party. He is succeeded as secretary of state by Edmund Randolph on January 2, 1794.

International and Cultural Events • American opinion is divided when France declares war on Great Britain,

ESTIMATED POPULATION 4,332,000	3rd CONGRESS
	SENATE .... 30 Members
	F 17
	DR 13
	O 0
	HOUSE .... 105 Members
	DR 57
	F 48
	O 0

George Washington
1st President
1st Federalist

John Adams
1st Vice President
Federalist

UNITED STATES ECONOMY

GROSS NATIONAL PRODUCT	N/A
RETAIL SALES	N/A
BANK RESOURCES	N/A
EXPORTS	$43,000,000
IMPORTS	$42,000,000
FEDERAL GOVERNMENT EXPENDITURE	$ 4,482,000
FEDERAL DEBT	$80,359,000

Spain and The Netherlands. Louis XVI and Marie Antoinette are guillotined. France orders confiscation of neutral vessels carrying goods to its enemies. American coastal shipping is affected by British orders-in-council directing confiscation of neutral ships carrying French West Indian goods. French engineer Claude Chappe invents the semaphore, a visual telegraph permitting rapid communication over long distances.

1794 United States of America

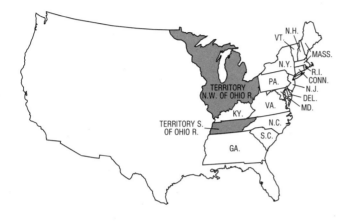

3rd CONGRESS

SENATE . . . . 30 Members
F 17
DR 13
O 0

HOUSE . . . . 105 Members
DR 57
F 48
O 0

ESTIMATED
POPULATION
4,469,000

George Washington
1st President
1st Federalist

John Adams
1st Vice President
Federalist

UNITED STATES ECONOMY

GROSS NATIONAL PRODUCT . . . . N/A
RETAIL SALES . . . . N/A
BANK RESOURCES . . . . N/A
EXPORTS $55,000,000
IMPORTS $46,000,000
FEDERAL GOVERNMENT EXPENDITURE . . $ 6,991,000
FEDERAL DEBT $78,427,000

Events

January 3 • James Madison, in response to the British orders-in-council, introduced seven commercial resolutions in the House of Representatives. Designed to penalize countries discriminating against American commerce and to reimburse Americans for any losses due to foreign measures not in accordance with the "law of nations," they arouse much discussion. Only one resolution comes to a vote, and none are adopted.

February • Sir Guy Carleton, the British governor of Lower Canada, promises the return of Indian lands in the Northwest Territory in exchange for Indian aid in a war with the United States.

March 5 • The 11th Amendment, limiting federal judicial authority over the states, is submitted to the states by Congress.

April 19 • John Jay, chief justice of the United States, is confirmed as an envoy to negotiate a treaty with Great Britain.

May 1 • The first trade union in the United States, the Federal Society of Journeymen Cordwainers, is established in Philadelphia, Pennsylvania.

May 8 • The Post Office Department is created.

May 27 • James Monroe is appointed minister to France.

June 5 • The Neutrality Act is adopted. Under its provisions, American citizens may not enter the service of foreign powers, and foreign armed ships may not be provisioned and fitted out in United States ports.

July • As the federal government proceeds to collect the excise tax on distilled spirits, the Whiskey Rebellion erupts in western Pennsylvania.

August 7 • Washington issues a proclamation ordering participants in the Whiskey Rebellion to disband. He also calls up a militia force of 12,000 men from Pennsylvania and nearby states.

August 20 • General Anthony Wayne decisively defeats a force of 2,000 Indians in the Battle of Fallen Timbers in northwestern Ohio. In October, he builds Fort Wayne at the head of the Maumee River.

September 24 • As the rebels fail to disband, Washington orders the militia to put down the Whiskey Rebellion. The presence of the substantial force is sufficient to induce the rebels to return home, and the rebellion ends without bloodshed.

November 19 • Jay's Treaty is signed in London by representatives of the United States and Great Britain, but its terms do not become known in the United States until March 1795. The chief American advantage in the treaty is a promise by the British to withdraw from their military posts in the Northwest Territory by June 1, 1796. The British also make certain trade concessions, and other problems are to be referred for settlement to joint commissions. However, the British refuse to alter their position on neutral shipping and other sensitive issues.

International and Cultural Events • Robespierre is guillotined. Kosciusko leads an unsuccessful bid for Polish independence. Thomas Paine publishes *The Age of Reason*. Joseph Priestly settles in the United States after a British mob sacks his laboratory.

United States of America 1795

Events

January 2 • Timothy Pickering is appointed secretary of war.

January 29 • The Naturalization Act is passed. It requires five years' residence in the United States before citizenship may be granted.

January 31 • Secretary of the Treasury Alexander Hamilton resigns. Oliver Wolcott, Jr., is named to replace him.

February 7 • Ratification of the 11th Amendment is completed with its passage by the state of North Carolina. President Adams will declare the amendment adopted in a message to Congress dated January 8, 1798.

March 3 • Land in Ohio is granted to the French inhabitants of Gallipolis, who had been induced to emigrate in 1790 by false claims by the Scioto Company of Boston, which had represented the region as settled and cultivated.

April • Thomas Pinckney, minister to Great Britain, is sent to Spain as a special commissioner.

May 1 • Under an act of Congress in 1794 the United States flag is given 15 stars and 15 stripes in recognition of the admission of Vermont (1791) and Kentucky (1792).

June 24 • The Senate ratifies Jay's Treaty after a lengthy debate in which the Federalists generally favor, and the Democratic-Republicans generally oppose, ratification. A particularly controversial article on West Indian trade is suspended from the treaty. The treaty is then sent to President Washington for his signature (affixed August 14).

August 3 • Twelve Indian tribes sign the Treaty of Greenville with the United States. Lines are drawn in Ohio separating Indian lands in the Northwest Territory from lands intended for white settlement.

August 19 • Secretary of State Edmund Randolph, resigns as a result of charges of corruption later shown to have been unfounded. Timothy Pickering replaces him on December 10.

September 5 • The United States signs a treaty agreeing to pay tribute to the Algerian pirates.

October 27 • The Treaty of San Lorenzo is signed in Madrid by representatives of the United States and Spain. The treaty, better known as Pinckney's Treaty, provides for the free navigation of the entire Mississippi River. Spain recognizes the southern and western boundaries of the United States as, respectively, the 31st parallel and the Mississippi River.

December 7 • The first session of the Fourth Congress opens in Philadelphia.

December 15 • The Senate rejects the appointment of

4th CONGRESS

SENATE	....	32 Members
F	....	19
DR	....	13
O	....	0
HOUSE	....	106 Members
F	....	54
DR	....	52
O	....	0

ESTIMATED POPULATION
4,607,000

George Washington
1st President
1st Federalist

John Adams
1st Vice President
Federalist

UNITED STATES ECONOMY

GROSS NATIONAL PRODUCT	.... N/A
RETAIL SALES	.... N/A
BANK RESOURCES	.... N/A
EXPORTS	.... $72,000,000
IMPORTS	.... $85,000,000
FEDERAL GOVERNMENT EXPENDITURE	.. $ 7,540,000
FEDERAL DEBT	.... $80,748,000

John Rutledge as chief justice of the United States because of the negative position on Jay's Treaty that he adopted in a speech made prior to his appointment.

International and Cultural Events • A new French Constitution sets up a five-man Directory. Yazoo land grants by a corrupt Georgia legislature scandalize the nation. The new legislature's attempt to rescind these grants is declared unconstitutional by the Supreme Court in *Fletcher v. Peck* (1810).

1796 United States of America

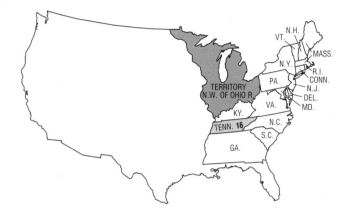

4th CONGRESS

SENATE .... 32 Members
F 19
DR 13
O 0

HOUSE .... 106 Members
F 54
DR 52
O 0

**ESTIMATED
POPULATION
4,745,000**

George Washington
1st President
1st Federalist

John Adams
1st Vice President
Federalist

UNITED STATES ECONOMY

GROSS NATIONAL PRODUCT .... N/A
RETAIL SALES .... N/A
BANK RESOURCES .... N/A
EXPORTS $94,000,000
IMPORTS $97,000,000
FEDERAL GOVERNMENT EXPENDITURE .. $ 5,727,000
FEDERAL DEBT $83,762,000

Events

January • In a case brought before the House of Representatives, Robert Randall is charged with attempting to coerce members in behalf of Great Lakes traders. The House resolves that any attempt to influence the conduct of the House or its members, on subjects pertaining to legislative functions by motives other than the public good, is in contempt of the House.

February 29 • President Washington promulgates Jay's Treaty. The United States and France are on the verge of war.

March 8 • In *Hylton v. United States*, the first Supreme Court test case on a congressional act, the constitutionality of the carriage tax voted in 1794 is upheld.

April 30 • Despite strong Democratic-Republican opposition, the House of Representatives votes in favor of an appropriation to carry out Jay's Treaty.

May 18 • Congress adopts the Land Act, which calls for the division of public land into townships (six miles square) and one-half of the townships into 640-acre sections. The land is to be sold at auction for a minimum price of $2 per acre.

June 1 • Tennessee, a slave state, is admitted to the Union as the 16th state.

July 11 • Captain Moses Porter arrives at Detroit with an advanced unit of U.S. troops to take possession of the fort and settlement from the British. About noon, the Stars and Stripes replaces the Union Jack as the flag flying above the French-founded settlement.

August 22 • James Monroe is replaced as minister to France by Charles C. Pinckney.

August 22 • Fort Michilimackinac, a British frontier post, is evacuated in compliance with Jay's Treaty.

September 17 • Washington's Farewell Address is published in the *Daily American Advertiser* in Philadelphia. The address, never actually delivered, deals with Washington's reasons for not wishing to run for a third term and also gives words of advice to the country, warning against permanent alliances.

October 29 • The Yankee sailing ship *Otter* enters Monterey Bay. It is the first American ship to enter Californian waters.

November 4 • A treaty with Tripoli is signed to end the seizure of American ships and the imprisonment of American sailors. The humiliating terms of the treaty force the United States to pay ransom money, large commissions and annual tribute.

December 7 • In the third presidential election, John Adams (Federalist) receives 71 electoral votes and is elected president; Thomas Jefferson (Democratic-Republican) receives 68 electoral votes and is elected vice president. Thomas Pinckney (Federalist) receives 59 votes, and Aaron Burr (Democratic-Republican), 30 votes.

International and Cultural Events • In February, France declares that Jay's Treaty with Great Britain annuls all United States treaties with France. In July, it claims the right to search and capture all neutral ships bound for British ports. Edward Jenner develops a smallpox vaccination. Gilbert Stuart is commissioned by Martha Washington to paint from life the Athenaeum head of her husband.

John Adams 1797

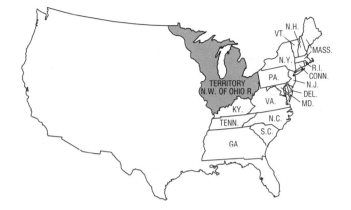

Events

February 27 • Timothy Pickering, secretary of state, reports on the damage caused by France to American commerce. The French government, which considers that Jay's Treaty has made the United States subservient to Great Britain, has been unwilling to receive Charles C. Pinckney as minister since his arrival in France in December 1796.

March 4 • John Adams is inaugurated as the second president of the United States. Thomas Jefferson becomes vice president.

March 10 • The frigate *United States*, the first American naval vessel, is launched at Philadelphia.

May 15 • The French-American crisis causes President Adams to convene the first special session of Congress. At issue is the expulsion of the U.S. minister to France, Charles C. Pinckney, continuing measures for defense and a negotiated settlement of the dispute.

May 31 • The president appoints Charles C. Pinckney, Elbridge Gerry and John Marshall as members of a commission to obtain a treaty of friendship and commerce with France. On October 8, they are received by Foreign Minister Talleyrand.

June 24 • To help defend the nation in case of war with France, Congress adopts a bill providing that an 80,000-man militia be in a state of constant preparedness.

June 26 • Charles Newbold receives a patent for a cast-iron plow, but he is unable to convince farmers that it will not contaminate the soil.

July 8 • The Senate expels Senator William Blount on conspiracy charges, alleging that Blount, with British support, planned a filibustering expedition against the Spanish in Louisiana and Florida.

August 28 • A treaty with Tunis is signed by the United States. It guarantees protection for Americans at a cost even higher than that imposed by the treaty with Tripoli.

September 7 • The U.S. frigate *Constellation* is launched at Baltimore, Maryland.

October 18 • Three agents of Talleyrand demand, as a condition for negotiating a treaty with the United States, a large loan and a "gift" to Talleyrand of $240,000. Since the commissioners refer to the agents as X, Y, and Z in their reports, the incident subsequently becomes known as the XYZ Affair. Popular tradition attributes to Pinckney a ringing rejection of the bribe scheme: "Millions for defense but not one cent for tribute."

October 21 • The U.S.S. *Constitution*, later known as "Old Ironsides," is launched at Boston.

International and Cultural Events • The final partition of Poland is completed. Napoleon is selected to command the invasion of Great Britain. Austrian composer Franz Schubert is born.

5th CONGRESS

SENATE	.... 32 Members
F	 20
DR	 12
O	 0
HOUSE	.... 106 Members
F	 58
DR	 48
O	 0

ESTIMATED
POPULATION
4,883,000

John Adams
2nd President
2nd Federalist

Thomas Jefferson
2nd Vice President
Democratic-Republican

UNITED STATES ECONOMY

GROSS NATIONAL PRODUCT	.... N/A
RETAIL SALES	.... N/A
BANK RESOURCES	.... N/A
EXPORTS	.... $79,000,000
IMPORTS	.... $90,000,000
FEDERAL GOVERNMENT EXPENDITURE	.. $ 6,134,000
FEDERAL DEBT	.... $82,064,000

John Adams

Birth	...Braintree (later Quincy), MA, Oct. 19 (O.S.), 1735
Parents	.... John and Susanna Boylston Adams
Married	.... Abigail Smith
Home	.... Quincy, MA
Presidency	.... 1797 – 1801
Death	.... Quincy, MA, July 4, 1826

1798 United States of America

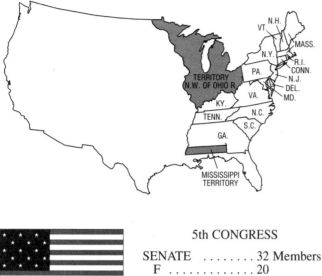

5th CONGRESS

SENATE .... 32 Members
F 20
DR 12
O 0

HOUSE .... 106 Members
F 58
DR 48
O 0

ESTIMATED
POPULATION
5,021,000

John Adams
2nd President
2nd Federalist

Thomas Jefferson
2nd Vice President
Democratic-Republican

UNITED STATES ECONOMY

GROSS NATIONAL PRODUCT .... N/A
RETAIL SALES .... N/A
BANK RESOURCES .... N/A
EXPORTS $83,000,000
IMPORTS $84,000,000
FEDERAL GOVERNMENT EXPENDITURE ... $ 7,677,000
FEDERAL DEBT $79,229,000

Events

January 8 • The 11th Amendment to the Constitution is adopted. It bars suits against a state by citizens of another state or of a foreign state.

January 17 • The United States commissioners to France restate the position of their government on French interference with American shipping, but the French

response, on March 18, is unsatisfactory, and negotiations end.

April 3 • The commissioners' dispatches on the XYZ Affair are made public when President Adams sends them to Congress. Anti-French sentiment rises.

April 7 • An act of Congress creates the Mississippi Territory. The boundaries of the territory are extended in 1804 and 1812.

April 30 • President Adams signs into law a bill establishing the Department of the Navy and the Office of Secretary of the Navy. Prior to this action, the secretary of war was responsible for naval affairs.

May 21 • Benjamin Stoddert is appointed secretary of the newly created Department of the Navy.

June 18 • In a warlike atmosphere, the first of four Alien and Sedition Acts is adopted. Aliens must now reside 14 years rather than five years, in the United States before they may become citizens.

June 25 • The Alien Act is adopted. Under its provisions, the president may deport aliens whom he considers dangerous. The act expires in 1800.

July 6 • The Alien Enemies Act is adopted. It permits the president to arrest, imprison or banish subjects of a country with which the United States is at war. On July 7, Congress repeals the treaties of 1778 with France.

July 14 • The Sedition Act is adopted. It forbids various antigovernment actions, including publication of false or malicious statements.

August • Eli Whitney devises a jig to guide tools and thus make possible interchangeable parts.

November 16 • The Kentucky legislature adopts resolutions, drawn up by Thomas Jefferson, that contend that the Alien and Sedition Acts are unconstitutional and that the states have the right to determine such. On December 24, Virginia adopts similar resolutions, drafted by James Madison.

International and Cultural Events • Napoleon wins the Battle of the Pyramids. Wordsworth and Coleridge launch English romanticism with *Lyrical Ballads*. In the United States, Charles Brockden Brown, precursor of Hawthorne, publishes *Wieland*.

ARTICLE XI
Suits against States

The Judicial power of the United States shall not be construed to extend to any suit in law or equity, commenced or prosecuted against one of the United States by Citizens of another State, or by Citizens or Subjects of any Foreign State.

(Adopted in 1798)

United States of America 1799

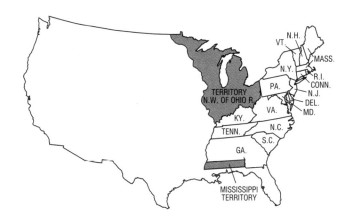

Events

January 30 • Congress adopts the Logan Act, which prohibits the private conduct of diplomatic regotiations. (In 1798, George Logan, a Quaker, had engaged in peace discussions with Talleyrand.)

February 9 • In a naval engagement off Nevis in the West Indies, the French frigate *L'Insurgente* is captured by the U.S.S. *Constellation*.

February 18 • President Adams, who unlike a number of other Federalists desires to avoid outright war with France, appoints William Vans Murray as minister to France.

February • Indignant over a federal property tax imposed by Congress in July 1798, farmers in Bucks and Northhampton counties, Pennsylvania, rebel under the leadership of John Fries. After federal troops put down the rebellion, Fries is twice tried and convicted of treason. Sentenced to be hanged, he is pardoned by President Adams.

May 5 • Talleyrand is informed of President Adams's decision to reopen negotiations with France.

June 15 • New Hampshire legislators issue their own set of "Resolutions," refuting the previous year's resolutions by their counterparts in Kentucky and Virginia.

October 16 • President Adams sends Oliver Ellsworth and William R. Davie to join William Vans Murray as members of a commission to bring peace between the United States and France.

November 22 • The Kentucky Resolutions reaffirm those of 1798, adding the "nullification" is the remedy for

	6th CONGRESS
SENATE	.... 32 Members
F	 19
DR	 13
O	 0
HOUSE	.... 106 Members
F	 64
DR	 42
O	 0

ESTIMATED POPULATION 5,159,000

John Adams
2nd President
2nd Federalist

Thomas Jefferson
2nd Vice President
Democratic-Republican

UNITED STATES ECONOMY

GROSS NATIONAL PRODUCT	.... N/A
RETAIL SALES	.... N/A
BANK RESOURCES	.... N/A
EXPORTS	...........................$111,000,000
IMPORTS	...........................$ 96,000,000
FEDERAL GOVERNMENT EXPENDITURE	..$ 9,666,000
FEDERAL DEBT	......................$ 78,409,000

constitutional infractions.

December 14 • George Washington dies at Mount Vernon, eulogized as "first in war, first in peace, and first in the hearts of his countrymen."

International and Cultural Events • The Russian-American Company is granted Alaskan monopoly by the czar. Napoleon becomes first consul.

Congress Hall and the New Theater on Chestnut Street, Philadelphia, Pennsylvania.

15

6th CONGRESS

SENATE .... 32 Members
F 19
DR 13
O 0

HOUSE .... 106 Members
F 64
DR 42
O 0

ESTIMATED
POPULATION
5,297,000

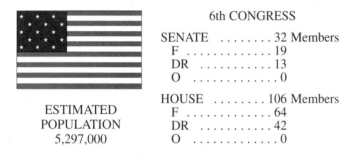

John Adams
2nd President
2nd Federalist

Thomas Jefferson
2nd Vice President
Democratic-Republican

UNITED STATES ECONOMY

GROSS NATIONAL PRODUCT .... N/A
RETAIL SALES .... N/A
BANK RESOURCES .... N/A
EXPORTS $107,000,000
IMPORTS $108,000,000
FEDERAL GOVERNMENT EXPENDITURE ..$ 10,786,000
FEDERAL DEBT ....$ 82,976,000

Events

January 6 • Congress abolishes imprisonment for debt, stipulating that a debtor take an oath of poverty.
January 10 • A treaty negotiated with Tunis, one of the Barbary States, is ratified by the United States government.
February 1 • The U.S.S. *Constellation* fights the French frigate *La Vengeanc*e to a draw.
March 8 • American peace commissioners are received

by Napoleon, but little progress is made in ending the quasi war with France.
April 4 • The Federal Bankruptcy Act, covering traders and merchants, is adopted.
April 24 • The Library of Congress is created by an act of Congress.
May 7 • Congress divides the Northwest Territory, designating the eastern portion as the Northwest Territory and the western as Indiana Territory.
May 10 • The Land Act of 1800 (Harrison Land Act) is adopted. Minimum purchases of 320 acres may be made. New district land offices are created. Credit provisions lead to speculation.
May 23 • James T. Callender's seditious libel trial opens in Richmond, Virginia. Widely regarded as the most famous of the Sedition Act cases, it pitted the strength of the Virginia Democratic-Republicans, who paid for Callender's defense costs and provided legal council against Judge Samuel Chase, a Federalist. A jury will eventually find Callender guilty and sentence him to nine months in the Richmond jail.
June • The federal government is moved from Philadelphia to Washington.
August 30 • A timely warning by a slave alerts Virginia state and local officials to a planned slave revolt in and around Richmond. Gabriel, who along with 36 followers will later be hanged, had planned to seize the state capitol and arsenal.
September 30 • The United States commissioners to France sign a convention that effectively ends the Franco-American naval war. Whereas the commissioners have taken the position that France owes the United States compensation for the seizure of ships and cargoes and that the treaties of 1778 should be annulled, the convention suspends the treaties and leaves all questions of compensation to future negotiations. This is not satisfactory to the United States Senate, which ratifies the convention with the proviso that the treaties in fact be abrogated. On December 21, 1801, after the United States has agreed to the French demand that claims under the treaties be withdrawn, the convention goes into effect.
November 17 • Congress meets in Washington, D.C., for the first time.
December 3 • In the presidential election Vice President Jefferson and Aaron Burr (New York) are the Democratic-Republican nominees for president and vice president, respectively. The Federalist candidates are President Adams and Charles C. Pinckney (South Carolina).
International and Cultural Events • France secretly acquires Louisiana from Spain. Robert Owen builds a model factory at New Lanark, Scotland. Parson Weems publishes a "biography" of Washington; a later edition adds the cherry-tree fable. John Chapman (Johnny Appleseed) sows a trail of apple seeds from Pennsylvania to present-day Ohio.

Thomas Jefferson 1801

Events

January 20 • John Marshall is named chief justice of the United States.

February 11 • The ballots of the electors in the presidential election of December 3, 1800, are counted. Aaron Burr and Thomas Jefferson each receive 73 votes; John Adams has 65; Charles C. Pinckney 64; and John Jay, one. On February 17, Jefferson is elected president and Burr vice president in a House election.

February 27 • The Judiciary Act is adopted. The number of Supreme Court justices is reduced from six to five, 16 circuit courts are established, and the number of court officials is increased.

March 3 • President Adams, on his last day in office, appoints Federalists to the new court positions (the "midnight judges"). A conflict over these appointments leads to *Marbury v. Madison* (1803).

March 4 • Jefferson is inaugurated president in Washington, and power passes to the Democratic-Republicans. He calls for reduced government spending, recognition of states' rights, intellectual tolerance and no "entangling alliances."

May 14 • The pasha of Tripoli, one of the Barbary States, declares war on the United States because of his dissatisfaction with United States tribute payments.

August 7 • Presbyterian minister Barton W. Stone begins a two-week revival meeting at Cane Ridge, Kentucky. The revival, which drew an estimated crowd of 25,000 people, marked the height of the Great Revival in the United States.

October 16 • Robert R. Livingston, newly appointed minister to France, sails for Europe.

December 8 • Because of President Jefferson's distaste for ceremony, he delivers his annual message to Congress in writing, setting a precedent continued by his successors until 1913.

International and Cultural Events • J.H. Pestalozzi, Swiss educator, publishes his influential *How Gertrude Teaches Her Children*. Robert Fulton builds the first submarine, the *Nautilus*, in France.

Original Senate wing of the Capitol in Washington, completed in 1801.

ESTIMATED POPULATION
5,486,000

7th CONGRESS

SENATE . . . . 31 Members
   DR 18
   F 13
   O 0

HOUSE . . . . 105 Members
   DR 69
   F 36
   O 0

Thomas Jefferson
3rd President
1st Democratic-Republican

Aaron Burr
3rd Vice President
Democratic-Republican

UNITED STATES ECONOMY

GROSS NATIONAL PRODUCT . . . . N/A
RETAIL SALES . . . . N/A
BANK RESOURCES . . . . N/A
EXPORTS $134,000,000
IMPORTS $132,000,000
FEDERAL GOVERNMENT EXPENDITURE . .$ 9,395,000
FEDERAL DEBT . . . .$ 83,038,000

Thomas Jefferson	
Birth	Shadwell, Goochland (now Albemarle) County, VA, Apr. 13, 1743
Parents	Peter and Jane Randolph Jefferson
Married	Martha Wayles Skelton
Home	Monticello, near Charlottesville, VA
Presidency	1801 – 1809
Death	Monticello, VA, July 4, 1826

1802 United States of America

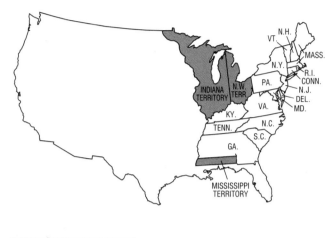

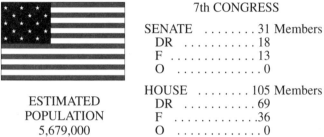

7th CONGRESS

SENATE .... 31 Members
DR 18
F 13
O 0

HOUSE .... 105 Members
DR 69
F 36
O 0

ESTIMATED
POPULATION
5,679,000

Thomas Jefferson
3rd President
1st Democratic-Republican

Aaron Burr
3rd Vice President
Democratic-Republican

UNITED STATES ECONOMY

GROSS NATIONAL PRODUCT	N/A
RETAIL SALES	N/A
BANK RESOURCES	N/A
EXPORTS	$98,000,000
IMPORTS	$91,000,000
FEDERAL GOVERNMENT EXPENDITURE	$ 7,862,000
FEDERAL DEBT	$80,713,000

Events

January 8 • President Jefferson asks Congress to repeal the Judiciary Act of 1801, which he considers a partisan Federalist measure. The act is repealed on March 8.

January 29 • The president names John James Beckley as the first librarian of Congress.

February 6 • Congress authorized the president to employ naval power in the conflict with Tripoli, thereby implying the existence of a state of war.

March 16 • Congress passes a bill creating the United States Military Academy.

April 24 • For approximately $1.2 million and the eastern part of the South Carolina cession of 1787, Georgia cedes to the United States its claim to lands lying west of the Chattahoochee River. In an attempt to end the Yazoo controversy, the federal government will try for years to set aside five million acres, or the proceeds from the sale of that land, for the disposition of Yazoo land warrants but will be continually frustrated in its efforts by the legislative actions of Virginian John Randolph. Randolph's absence from the House in 1814 will provide the government with the opportunity to resolve the dispute.

April 29 • The Judiciary Act of 1802 is adopted. Under its provisions, the Supreme Court once again consists of six justices. Each of them is to preside over a circuit court; the separate circuit courts are abolished. In addition, the Supreme Court is limited to one term a year.

April 30 • An act of Congress enables the residents of the Northwest Territory (Ohio) to choose delegates to a convention empowered to draft a state constitution. On November 29, the constitution of Ohio is completed and approved by the delegates.

May 3 • Washington is incorporated as a city by an act of Congress; its mayor is to be appointed by the president.

July 4 • The United States Military Academy opens at West Point, New York.

August 11 • The United States and Spain sign a convention providing for commissioners to settle claims of the citizens of both countries.

October 16 • Although Louisiana has belonged to France since October 1800, Napoleon's government has left the province under Spanish administration. Now the Spanish governor abolishes the right, enjoyed by United States citizens since 1795, of depositing goods shipped down the Mississippi at New Orleans, where they are transferred to oceangoing ships. This infringement, as well as other restrictions upon the commercial rights of American seamen and traders, contributes to President Jefferson's decision to purchase New Orleans from France.

December 6 • The second session of the Seventh Congress convenes. In his annual message, President Jefferson reiterates his concern for governmental economy.

International and Cultural Events • The Treaty of Amiens creates peace between France and Great Britain, temporarily relieving American ships from trade restraints. Napoleon sends his brother-in-law, General Leclerc, to re-establish French authority in Haiti, where the insurrectionary leader Toussaint L'Ouverture is captured by trickery (he dies in prison in France). Daniel Webster writes *The Rights of Neutral Nations in Time of War.*

United States of America 1803

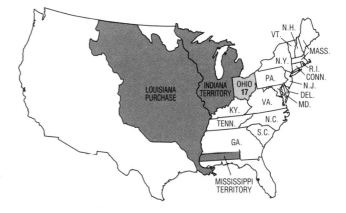

Events

January 12 • President Jefferson appoints James Monroe envoy extraordinary to France to purchase New Orleans and, if possible, Florida.

February • In *Marbury v. Madison*, the Supreme Court holds a law of Congress to be unconstitutional. Writing for a unanimous court, Chief Justice John Marshall states that "it is emphatically the province and duty of the judicial department to say what the law is." The case, the first to be so decided, sets a precedent.

March 1 • Ohio, a free state, enters the Union as the 17th state.

April 12 • Monroe reaches Paris. Meanwhile, the French have concluded that, in view of the impending resumption of hostilities with Great Britain, it is in their interest to sell Louisiana to the United States. On April 11, Talleyrand informs Minister Robert R. Livingston that France is ready to sell all of Louisiana. Although this is far more than Livingston and Monroe have been instructed to purchase, they enter into negotiations with the French and complete arrangements for the purchase.

April 19 • Spanish officials once again grant American traders the right of deposit at the port of New Orleans.

May 2 • Livingston and Monroe sign a treaty and two conventions, dated as of April 30, for the purchase of Louisiana. The price of the territory itself is $11,250,000; in addition, the United States is to assume the claims of American citizens against France, amounting to $3,750,000. With the acquisition of Louisiana, the United States is extended to twice its former size, although the boundaries of the territory are defined ambiguously in the treaty, and it is not clear whether or not they incorporate West Florida and portions of Texas.

May 23 • Commodore Edward Preble is placed in command of a squadron sent to the Mediterranean Sea in the war against Tripoli.

June 7 • Governor William Henry Harrison of Indiana Territory signs a treaty with nine Indian tribes for the cession of land around Vincennes. A second treaty is signed on August 7.

August 17 • Captain John Whistler arrives on the site of present-day Chicago, Illinois, with an infantry company from Fort Detroit and commences the construction of Fort Dearborn.

August 31 • Meriwether Lewis and William Clark, sent on an exploring expedition by President Jefferson, begin their journey on the Ohio River.

October 20 • The United States Senate ratifies the treaty for the purchase of Louisiana by a vote of 24 to seven.

October 31 • Tripoli captures the United States frigate *Philadelphia*, which had run onto a reef.

	8th CONGRESS	
ESTIMATED POPULATION 5,872,000	SENATE .... 34 Members	
	DR 25	
	F 9	
	O 0	
	HOUSE .... 141 Members	
	DR 102	
	F 39	
	O 0	

Thomas Jefferson
3rd President
1st Democratic-Republican

Aaron Burr
3rd Vice President
Democratic-Republican

UNITED STATES ECONOMY

GROSS NATIONAL PRODUCT	N/A
RETAIL SALES	N/A
BANK RESOURCES	N/A
EXPORTS	$88,000,000
IMPORTS	$80,000,000
FEDERAL GOVERNMENT EXPENDITURE	$7,852,000
FEDERAL DEBT	$77,055,000

December 9 • Congress proposes the adoption of the 12th Amendment, calling for the separate election of the president and vice president.

December 20 • French officials turn over Louisiana to the United States in a ceremony at New Orleans.

International and Cultural Events • Renewal of war between Great Britain and France creates new problems for American shipping. John James Audubon begins the scientific observation and banding of birds on his estate near Philadelphia.

1804 United States of America

ESTIMATED
POPULATION
6,065,000

8th CONGRESS

SENATE .... 34 Members
  DR 25
  F 9
  O 0

HOUSE .... 141 Members
  DR 102
  F 39
  O 0

Thomas Jefferson
3rd President
1st Democratic-Republican

Aaron Burr
3rd Vice President
Democratic-Republican

UNITED STATES ECONOMY

GROSS NATIONAL PRODUCT .... N/A
RETAIL SALES .... N/A
BANK RESOURCES .... N/A
EXPORTS $114,000,000
IMPORTS $102,000,000
FEDERAL GOVERNMENT EXPENDITURE ..$ 8,719,000
FEDERAL DEBT ....$ 86,427,000

Events

January 5 • Democratic-Republican supporters of President Jefferson in the House of Representatives begin an investigation of Justice Samuel Chase of the Supreme Court, a Federalist whose decisions on the bench have angered the president. On March 12, the House votes to impeach Chase on the grounds of improper conduct in two trials.

February 16 • Sailing a ketch into Tripoli harbor, naval Lieutenant Stephen Decatur and his men manage to board and destroy the captured *Philadelphia*.

March 26 • An act of Congress creates the Territory of Orleans from the southern portion of the Louisiana Purchase. The rest is established as the District (later Territory) of Louisiana.

March 26 • The Land Act of 1804 is adopted, having been ratified by the legislatures of 13 of the 17 states. Under its provisions, quarter sections may be purchased, and the minimum cash payment is set at $1.64 per acre.

April 25 • Vice President Burr, running for the governorship of New York as part of a separatist movement led by Federalist extremists of New England, is defeated because of the influence of Alexander Hamilton.

April 29 • Commodore Preble captures two Tripolitan ships.

May 14 • Lewis and Clark and their party leave St. Louis, proceeding westward by boat up the Missouri River.

July • Aaron Burr, provoked by his defeat in the New York election and reacting to a press report of a remark made by Hamilton about Burr's character, challenges Hamilton to a duel. When the duel is fought in Weehawken, New Jersey, on July 11, Hamilton is mortally wounded. He dies the following day.

August-September • Commodore Preble leads five attacks on Tripoli in which the city is heavily bombarded.

August 13 • Governor Harrison of Indiana Territory purchases the claims of the Delaware Indians to land between the Wabash and Ohio Rivers.

August 18 and 27 • Governor Harrison signs treaties with the Indians at Vincennes for the cession of land north of the Ohio River and south of the tract around Vincennes ceded on June 7, 1803.

September 25 • The 12th Amendment to the Constitution is adopted. It provides for separate electoral ballots for the president and vice president.

October 1 • William C.C. Claiborne takes up his post as governor of the Territory of Orleans, inaugurating territorial government at New Orleans.

October 27 • Lewis and Clark establish winter quarters at the Mandan Indian villages near the present-day Bismarck, North Dakota.

November 3 • Governor Harrison of Indiana Territory negotiates a treaty with the Fox and Sauk Indians for the cession of five million acres of land in what is now Wisconsin in return for a promise of the Indians' right to remain.

December 5 • In the presidential election, President Jefferson is re-elected, receiving 162 electoral votes to 14 for Charles C. Pinckney, his Federalist opponent. George Clinton (New York) is elected vice president.

International and Cultural Events • The Napoleonic Code, which as modified and amended is still the basic law in France and served as a model for Louisiana state law, is promulgated. Napoleon is crowned emperor of the French.

ARTICLE XII

Election of President and Vice President

The Electors shall meet in their respective states, and vote by ballot for President and Vice-President, one of whom, at least, shall not be an inhabitant of the same state with themselves; they shall name in their ballots the person voted for as President, and in distinct ballots the person voted for as Vice-President, and they shall make distinct lists of all persons voted for as President, and of all persons voted for as Vice-President, and of the number of votes for each, which lists they shall sign and certify, and transmit sealed to the seat of the government of the United States, directed to the President of the Senate; — The President of the Senate shall, in the presence of the Senate and House of Representatives, open all the certificates and the votes shall then be counted; — The person having the greatest number of votes for President, shall be the President, if such number be a majority of the whole number of Electors appointed; and if no person have such majority, then from the persons having the highest numbers not exceeding three on the list of those voted for as President, the House of Representatives shall choose immediately, by ballot, the President. But in choosing the President, the votes shall be taken by states, the representation from each state having one vote; a quorum for this purpose shall consist of a member or members from two-thirds of the states, and a majority of all the states shall be necessary to a choice. And if the House of Representatives shall not choose a President whenever the right of choice shall devolve upon them, before the fourth day of March next following, then the Vice-President shall act as President, as in the case of the death or other constitutional disability of the President. — The person having the greatest number of votes as Vice-President, shall be the Vice-President, if such number be a majority of the whole number of Electors appointed, and if no person have a majority, then from the two highest numbers on the list, the Senate shall choose the Vice-President; a quorum for the purpose shall consist of two-thirds of the whole number of Senators, and a majority of the whole number shall be necessary to a choice. But no person constitutionally ineligible to the office of President shall be eligible to that of Vice-President of the United States.

(Adopted in 1804, superseding Article II, Section l, Paragraph 3)

Meriwether Lewis and William Clark holding a council with the Indians.

1805 United States of America

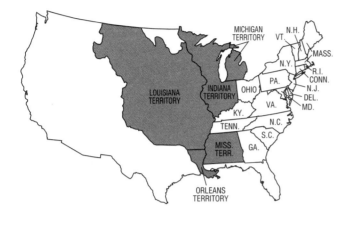

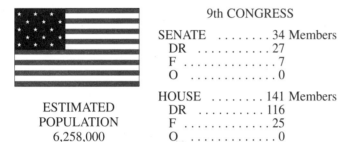

9th CONGRESS

SENATE .... 34 Members
DR 27
F 7
O 0

HOUSE .... 141 Members
DR 116
F 25
O 0

ESTIMATED
POPULATION
6,258,000

Thomas Jefferson
3rd President
1st Democratic-Republican

George Clinton
4th Vice President
Democratic-Republican

UNITED STATES ECONOMY

GROSS NATIONAL PRODUCT .... N/A
RETAIL SALES .... N/A
BANK RESOURCES .... N/A
EXPORTS $134,000,000
IMPORTS $144,000,000
FEDERAL GOVERNMENT EXPENDITURE ..$ 10,506,000
FEDERAL DEBT ....$ 82,312,000

Events

January 2 • The Senate opens impeachment proceedings against Justice Chase. His acquittal on March 1 discourages potential impeachment action against other Federalist judges. Although other Supreme Court justices will face threats of impeachment, Chase will remain the only Supreme Court justice ever impeached by the House of Representatives.

January 11 • Michigan Territory is formed from part of Indiana Territory.

January • William Dunbar and Dr. George Hunter re-turn to Natchez, Mississippi, completing a scientific expedition, begun in October 1804 at the request of President Jefferson, to the Red River of the South and the Quachita.

March 2 • An act of Congress regularizes the land system in Louisiana Territory, to which the standard pattern of townships and sections is to be applied.

March 3 • By an act of Congress, the District of Louisiana is renamed Louisiana Territory, and St. Louis is designated its capital. Congress also places in the legislation official confirmation of French and Spanish Louisiana land grants.

March 4 • President Jefferson is inaugurated for his second term. He calls for federal public works.

April 7 • Lewis and Clark and their party leave the Mandan villages, where they have wintered, and travel up the Missouri River. On April 26, they reach the mouth of the Yellowstone River, and on June 13, the Great Falls of the Missouri. At Three Forks, where they arrive on July 25, they name the three rivers. Proceeding up the Jefferson, they soon find it unnavigable. They then strike out overland and cross the continental divide via Lemhi Pass. After acquiring horses from the Snake Indians, they move north to the Bitterroot Valley and then west over difficult country. Reaching the Clearwater River on October 7, they make canoes in which they float down the river to the Snake River, from which the enter the Columbia River on October 17. On November 7, they sight the Pacific Ocean. They winter at Fort Clatsop, near present-day Astoria, Oregon.

Zebulon Pike, from a painting by Charles Willson Peale.

April 26 • William Eaton, United States consul in Tunis, seizes the port of Derna with a small force that he had led overland from Egypt. Participation by a small Marine detachment in this Tripolitan War victory is remembered in the "to the shores of Tripoli" phrase of the corps' hymn.

May • A group of philanthropists in New York founds the Free School Society, subsequently renamed the Public School Society.

May 1 • Virginia enacts a law requiring all freed slaves to leave the state. Anyone refusing to leave faces imprisonment or deportation.

June 4 • The war with Tripoli ends with the signing of a treaty of peace. The United States agrees to pay $60,000 to ransom the *Philadelphia's* crew, but the annual tribute to Tripoli is discontinued.

June 11 • A fire, allegedly ignited in a barn, destroys most of the town of Detroit, Michigan. The following year, Congress will grant Detroit residence 10,000 acres of land on which they will rebuild their town.

July 23 • American shipping is hard hit when a stratagem by which it had eluded Great Britain's "Rule of 1756" is thwarted. Reversing an earlier decision, a British court rules that a cargo brought by the U.S. ship *Essex* from Spain to Salem and then reshipped to Havana was never meant for the neutral United States port. The British seize many U.S. ships.

August 9 • Lieutenant Zebulon Pike leaves St. Louis to explore the sources of the Mississippi River. He returns on April 30, 1806.

International and Cultural Events • Lord Nelson decisively defeats the combined French and Spanish fleets at the battle of Trafalgar: "England expects every man to do his duty." The first daily newspaper, *El Diario de Mexico* is published in Mexico. Egypt gains its independence from the Ottoman Empire.

Monticello, the home of Thomas Jefferson near Charlottesville, Virginia.

9th CONGRESS

SENATE .... 34 Members
DR 27
F 7
O 0

HOUSE .... 141 Members
DR 116
F 25
O 0

ESTIMATED
POPULATION
6,451,000

Thomas Jefferson
3rd President
1st Democratic-Republican

George Clinton
4th Vice President
Democratic-Republican

UNITED STATES ECONOMY

GROSS NATIONAL PRODUCT .... N/A
RETAIL SALES .... N/A
BANK RESOURCES .... N/A
EXPORTS $148,000,000
IMPORTS $155,000,000
FEDERAL GOVERNMENT EXPENDITURE ..$ 9,804,000
FEDERAL DEBT ....$ 75,723,000

Events

February 12 • The Senate adopts a resolution condemning British seizures of American cargo and seamen. This and other protests against the violation of neutral rights are disregarded by Great Britain.

March 29 • Congress passes a bill authorizing the construction of the Cumberland Road, which is to connect Maryland with the Ohio River at Wheeling. It eventually reaches Vandalia, Illinois.

April 18 • As British measures against American shipping continue, Congress adopts the Non-Importation Act, which forbids the imporation of various British goods. Designed to become effective November 15, it is suspended by President Jefferson on December 19.

May • A jury in Philadelphia, Pennsylvania, finds a group of journeymen boot- and shoe-makers guilty of a criminal conspiracy to raise their wages. The trial sets the legal precedent for how courts will view labor union cases in the United States for the next four decades.

June 15 • Lewis and Clark start to cross the Rocky Mountains on their journey back to St. Louis. After the crossing, the party divides into three small groups.

July 15 • Lieutenant Pike leaves Fort Bellefontaine at the head of an expedition to explore the Southwest. The party reaches New Mexico, where it is captured by Spanish soldiers. It is escorted to United States territory by July 1, 1807.

July 15 • Clark reaches the Yellowstone River and descends the river to its junction with the Missouri River.

August • Aaron Burr attempts to carve an independent empire out of the West, but whether he intended to detach Louisiana from the Union or to lead filibusters against Spanish territory (New Spain) is never established.

August • The Brethren, a group of five Williams College students, form the first foreign missionary service in the United States.

September 23 • Lewis and Clark reach St. Louis, bringing their expedition to a successful conclusion.

October 21 • Congress adopts an act "establishing rules and articles of government of the armies of the United States."

November 27 • President Jefferson, who has been informed of Burr's plans, issues a proclamation advising American citizens not to join expeditions directed against Spanish territory.

December 31 • In London, James Monroe and William Pinckney negotiate a treaty to protect American ships. President Jefferson (March 1807) considers it too weak to be submitted to the Senate.

December 31 • With profits declining, traders and trappers south and west of the upper Great Lakes organize the Michilimackinac Company. To ease the competition between itself and its new rival, the North West Company, a British concern established around 1784, will agree to abandon its trading posts lying between Sault Ste. Marie, Michigan, and La Pointe, Wisconsin. Profits, however, do not improve.

International and Cultural Events • Reacting to the British blockade of the continent, Napoleon issues the Berlin Decree, declaring a blockade of the British Isles, though he lacks ships to enforce it. John Howard Payne, United States playwright prodigy, presents his *Julia, or The Wanderer* at New York's fashionable Park Theater.

United States of America 1807

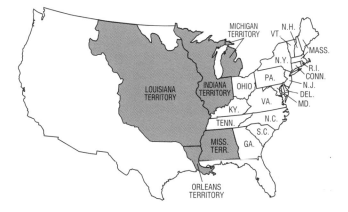

Events

February 19 • Aaron Burr is arrested for forming an expedition against Spanish territory. On March 30, he is arraigned in the United States circuit court in Richmond, Virginia, over which Chief Justice Marshall is presiding. On June 24, he will be indicted for treason.

June 22 • After the captain of the U.S.S. *Chesapeake*, at sea off Norfolk, Virginia, refuses to allow a search for four supposed British deserters, the British ship *Leopard* fires on the American vessel, killing several seamen. The British then remove the four men from the *Chesapeake*.

July 2 • In reply to the warlike act against the *Chesapeake*, President Jefferson orders British warships to leave the territorial waters of the United States. By this and other means of peaceful coercion he hopes to avoid outright war.

August 3 • Burr's trial for treason begins. On September 1, he is acquitted. Because he faces prosecution in several states for treason and the murder of Hamilton, he then leaves for Europe, where he remains in exile until 1812.

August 17 • Robert Fulton's steamboat *Clermont* begins its New York-Albany-New York voyage. The trip takes five days; running time is 62 hours.

December 22 • President Jefferson signs the Embargo Act, which prohibits American vessels from sailing for foreign ports and foreign vessels from taking goods from American ports. The measure is extremely unpopular in states with maritime trading interests, particularly those in New England, where the economy is gravely affected.

International and Cultural Events • A British order-in-council prohibits any ships from engaging in the coastal trade of France or its allies. Later, new orders-in-council prohibit any ships from trading with European ports barring British ships. Vessels wishing to trade with an open European port must be cleared at a British port. Napoleon's Milan Decree orders the seizure of any ship complying with the British blockade. Portugal's John VI

10th CONGRESS	
SENATE	34 Members
DR	28
F	6
O	0
HOUSE	142 Members
DR	118
F	24
O	0

ESTIMATED
POPULATION
6,644,000

Thomas Jefferson
3rd President
1st Democratic-Republican

George Clinton
4th Vice President
Democratic-Republican

UNITED STATES ECONOMY

GROSS NATIONAL PRODUCT	N/A
RETAIL SALES	N/A
BANK RESOURCES	N/A
EXPORTS	$162,000,000
IMPORTS	$167,000,000
FEDERAL GOVERNMENT EXPENDITURE	$ 8,354,000
FEDERAL DEBT	$ 69,218,000

Robert Fulton's *Clermont,* the first successful steam-propelled ship.

flees a Napoleonic invasion and establishes the capital of the Portuguese empire in Rio de Janeiro. Boston's leading citizens found the Athenaeum, a subscription library and museum that becomes a meeting place for men of letters. The British government abolishes the slave trade throughout the British empire. The first United States scientific agency, the U.S. Coast Survey, is established.

10th CONGRESS	
SENATE	.... 34 Members
DR	 28
F	 6
O	 0
HOUSE	.... 142 Members
DR	 118
F	 24
O	 0

ESTIMATED
POPULATION
6,838,000

Thomas Jefferson
3rd President
1st Democratic-Republican

George Clinton
4th Vice President
Democratic-Republican

UNITED STATES ECONOMY

GROSS NATIONAL PRODUCT	.... N/A
RETAIL SALES	.... N/A
BANK RESOURCES	.... N/A
EXPORTS	.... $55,000,000
IMPORTS	.... $71,000,000
FEDERAL GOVERNMENT EXPENDITURE	.. $ 9,932,000
FEDERAL DEBT	.... $65,196,000

Events

January 1 • A congressional bill (March 2, 1807) barring the importation of slaves into the United States comes into force, but it provides that smuggled slaves are to be turned over to the state concerned to be sold.

January 9 • The Embargo Act of 1807 is broadened by the adoption of a new Embargo Act. A third act is adopted on March 12. The three measures are only partially effective, for smugglers are active on the land frontiers and the Great Lakes. Moreover, ships that were not in American ports when the acts were adopted continue to trade in foreign ports without returning home.

April 6 • The American Fur Company, which has been organized by John Jacob Astor, is incorporated in New York. Within two decades, the company comes to control the entire fur trade of the country.

April 17 • American ships in European ports are subject to seizure after Napoleon's Bayonne Decree declares them either violators of the Embargo Acts or disguised British ships. The Bayonne Decree causes American ship owners to lose $10 million in ships and cargoes.

May 6 • The *Phoenix*, a steamship that has been designed by John Stevens, is the first steam-propelled vessel to make an ocean voyage, proceeding from Hoboken, New Jersey, to Philadelphia.

July 12 • The first newspaper west of the Mississippi River, the *Missouri Gazette*, is published in St. Louis.

October • Great Britain sends George Rose as an emissary to the United States to resolve the controversy over the attack by the *Leopard* on the *Chesapeake* in 1807. The British offer reparations, but final settlement is delayed until 1811.

November 10 • The Osage Treaty is signed. Under its terms, the Osage, a southern Sioux tribe, cede nearly all of present-day Missouri and Arkansas north of the Arkansas River. The treaty is ratified by the United States on April 28, 1810. The Osage subsequently relocate to Oklahoma, near the Arkansas River.

December 7 • In the presidential election, James Madison, the choice of the Democratic-Republican caucus in Congress after President Jefferson decides not to seek a third term, is elected president. He receives 122 electoral votes to 47 for Charles C. Pinckney (Federalist) and six for Vice President George Clinton, the candidate of anti-embargo eastern Democratic-Republicans. (James Monroe, chosen by disaffected southern Democratic-Republicans as their candidate, has withdrawn his name from the race.) Clinton, who has also run again for vice president, is re-elected, receiving 113 electoral votes to 47 for Rufus King, his Federalist opponent. However, the Federalist increase their representation in Congress.

International and Cultural Events • Joseph Bonaparte is installed on the Spanish throne. Beethoven's Fifth Symphony is played for the first time. The first recorded duel between congressmen—George W. Campbell, a Democratic-Republican from Tennessee, and Barent Gardenier, a Federalist from New York—is fought.

James Madison 1809

Events

January 9 • The Enforcement Act is adopted. It authorizes the seizure of any goods that are suspected of being intended for shipment abroad in violation of the Embargo Acts. The act arouses great resentment.

February 20 • In *United States v. Peters*, the Supreme Court rules that a state does not have the power to set aside an order that has been issued by a federal court.

February 23 • Jonathan Trumbull, the governor of Connecticut, condemns the Embargo Acts as unconstitutional. Other New England officials and legislatures also register their adamant opposition to these measures, and widespread talk of nullification is present.

March 1 • President Jefferson signs the Non-Intercourse Act, which repeals the Embargo Acts and again permits Americans to engage legally in foreign trade. This authorization does not extend to Great Britain and France, but the president is empowered to restore trade relations with either nation provided it rescinds the orders and decrees that have injured neutral commerce.

March 1 • Illinois Territory is created from the western portion of Indiana Territory.

March 4 • James Madison is inaugurated president.

April 19 • Relying on an agreement with David Erskine, the British minister to Washington, that Great Britain will revoke its orders-in-council against neutral shipping on June 10, President Madison proclaims the restoration of trade relations with Great Britain, which, however, repudiates Erskine.

August 9 • President Madison, reacting to the annulment of the agreement with Erskine, proclaims the reinstatement of the Non-Intercourse Act vis-a-vis Great Britain.

September 30 • Governor William Henry Harrison signs the Treaty of Fort Wayne, by which the Indians of western Indiana cede three tracts of land adjoining earlier cessions along the Wabash River to the United States.

December 25 • Doctor Ephraim McDowell performs the first successful ovarian operation in the world at his home in Danville, Kentucky. Without the use of anesthesia, he removes a 22-pound, six-ounce ovarian tumor from Mrs. Jane Crawford.

International and Cultural Events • Napoleon annexes the Papal States and imprisons Pius VII. Lamarck's *Philosophie zoologique* anticipates Darwin. Washington Irving publishes his satirical *A History of New York*.

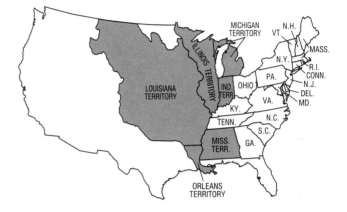

11th CONGRESS

SENATE	34 Members
DR	28
F	6
O	0
HOUSE	142 Members
DR	94
F	48
O	0

ESTIMATED
POPULATION
7,031,000

James Madison
4th President
2nd Democratic-Republican

George Clinton
4th Vice President
Democratic-Republican

UNITED STATES ECONOMY

GROSS NATIONAL PRODUCT	N/A
RETAIL SALES	N/A
BANK RESOURCES	N/A
EXPORTS	$88,000,000
IMPORTS	$76,000,000
FEDERAL GOVERNMENT EXPENDITURE	. . $10,281,000
FEDERAL DEBT	$57,023,000

James Madison

Birth	Port Conway, VA, Mar. 15, 1751
Parents	James and Eleanor Rose Conway Madison
Married	Dolley Payne Todd
Home	Montpellier (now Montpelier), VA
Presidency	1809 – 1817
Death	Montpellier, VA, June 28, 1836

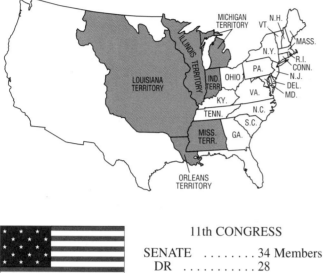

11th CONGRESS

SENATE .... 34 Members
DR 28
F 6
O 0

HOUSE .... 142 Members
DR 94
F 48
O 0

ESTIMATED
POPULATION
7,224,000

James Madison
4th President
2nd Democratic-Republican

George Clinton
4th Vice President
Democratic-Republican

UNITED STATES ECONOMY

GROSS NATIONAL PRODUCT	N/A
RETAIL SALES	N/A
BANK RESOURCES	N/A
EXPORTS	$117,000,000
IMPORTS	$110,000,000
FEDERAL GOVERNMENT EXPENDITURE	$ 8,157,000
FEDERAL DEBT	$ 53,173,000

Events

March 16 • In *Fletcher v. Peck*, the Supreme Court rules for the first time that a state law is unconstitutional. In its unanimous decision, the Court declared that a 1796 Georgian law had impaired contractual obligations by its rescission of the 1795 Yazoo land sale.

March 23 • United States ships entering French-controlled ports may be seized and sold according to Napoleon's Rambouillet Decree. Published on May 14, it is retroactive to May 20, 1809.

May 1 • As a replacement for the Non-Intercourse Act of 1809, Congress adopts Macon's Bill No. 2, which has been proposed by Representative Nathaniel Macon of North Carolina. The new law legalizes trade with both France and Great Britain. It also provides that if one of the two powers ceases restricting neutral shipping by March 3, 1811, the president is authorized to prohibit trade with the other unless it too abolishes its restrictions within three months.

June 23 • John Jacob Astor establishes the Pacific Fur Company, which, in April 1811, founds Astoria at the mouth of the Columbia River.

July 12 • The trial of members of a cordwainers' union who have used a strike to advance their demands opens in New York. Their conviction and fines for illegal conspiracy are a blow to early unionism.

August 5 • The Duc de Cadore, minister of foreign affairs for France, is advised by Napoleon to tell the United States minister in Paris that the decrees issued against neutral commerce will be rescinded after November 1 if the British orders-in-council are also rescinded. That same day, however, Napoleon issues the Trianon Decree, whereby United States ships that entered French-controlled ports between May 20, 1809, and May 1, 1810, are to be confiscated.

September 26 • Americans residing in western Spanish West Florida, the possession of which has been in dispute since the Louisiana Purchase, seize the Baton Rouge fort and declare the independence of the area between the Mississippi and Pearl Rivers, calling it the Republic of West Florida. On October 27, President Madison proclaims the annexation of the area, which is incorporated into Orleans Territory (and so becomes part of the state of Louisiana in 1812).

November 2 • President Madison, who has been led to believe by the United States minister's account of the Duc de Cadore's assurances that the French decrees against neutral shipping have actually been rescinded, issues a proclamation stating that trade with Great Britain will be halted if the British orders-in-council are not rescinded within three months. On March 2, 1811, all trade relations with Great Britain are accordingly suspended. Meanwhile, the French continue to seize American ships.

International and Cultural Events • Friedrich Krupp founds the fortune of the German armament family when he opens a small steel mill in Essen. In Boston, Massachusetts, the first regular orchestra in the United States, the Boston Philharmonic Society, is founded by Johann Christian Gottlieb Graupner. The orchestra will disband in 1824.

United States of America 1811

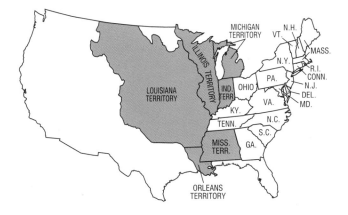

Events

February 20 • The Senate votes against rechartering the Bank of the United States, and its charter duly expires on March 4.

April 2 • James Monroe is named secretary of state.

April 12 • A small group of settlers, partners and employees of the Pacific Fur Company establish the first permanent American settlement in the Pacific Northwest (Fort Astoria) near the mouth of the Columbia River.

May 16 • The United States frigate *President* engages the British corvette *Little Belt*, which it erroneously believes is a frigate that has impressed an American. Nine on the corvette are killed.

July 31 • The people of Vincennes in Indiana Territory, alarmed by the confederacy being formed by the Shawnee Tecumseh and his brother, known as The Prophet, urge Governor William Henry Harrison to attack the Indian village on Tippecanoe Creek.

September 11 • The first steamboat to be launched in the interior of the country, the *New Orleans*, leaves Pittsburgh. It travels the Ohio and Mississippi, arriving at New Orleans on January 12, 1812.

September 26 • Governor Harrison leaves Vincennes with 1,000 men for Tippecanoe Creek. Meanwhile, Chief Tecumseh has gone south to secure an alliance with the Creek Indians. Early on November 7, while camping a mile from the Indian village, the American force is attacked by the Indians, who are led by The Prophet. The Indians are driven off after a fierce battle, and Harrison

William Henry Harrison, hero of the battle of Tippecanoe.

	12th CONGRESS	
SENATE	.... 36 Members	
DR	 30	
F	 6	
O	 0	
HOUSE	.... 144 Members	
DR	 108	
F	 36	
O	 0	

ESTIMATED
POPULATION
7,460,000

James Madison
4th President
2nd Democratic-Republican

George Clinton
4th Vice President
Democratic-Republican

UNITED STATES ECONOMY

GROSS NATIONAL PRODUCT	.... N/A
RETAIL SALES	.... N/A
BANK RESOURCES	.... N/A
EXPORTS	...........................$114,000,000
IMPORTS	...........................$ 78,000,000
FEDERAL GOVERNMENT EXPENDITURE	..$ 8,058,000
FEDERAL DEBT	.....................$ 48,006,000

destroys their village. The hostilities add to the influence of the so-called War Hawks in Congress, young men elected in 1810. Among them are Henry Clay, the new speaker of the House of Representatives, and John C. Calhoun.

December 16 • A severe earthquake affects about one million square miles in the Ohio and Mississippi valleys. At New Madrid, Missouri, and other places the course of the Mississippi River is changed.

International and Cultural Events • George III is declared insane, and the prince of Wales becomes the prince regent. Luddites riot in Great Britain.

1812 United States of America

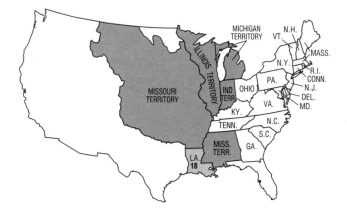

12th CONGRESS	
SENATE	36 Members
DR	30
F	6
O	0
HOUSE	144 Members
DR	108
F	36
O	0

ESTIMATED
POPULATION
7,700,000

James Madison
4th President
2nd Democratic-Republican

George Clinton
4th Vice President
Democratic-Republican

UNITED STATES ECONOMY

GROSS NATIONAL PRODUCT	N/A
RETAIL SALES	N/A
BANK RESOURCES	N/A
EXPORTS	$75,000,000
IMPORTS	$96,000,000
FEDERAL GOVERNMENT EXPENDITURE	$20,281,000
FEDERAL DEBT	$45,210,000

Events

February 11 • Massachusetts governor Elbridge Gerry signs a bill into law redistricting Essex County. The strange salamander-like shapes of the districts give rise to the term "gerrymandering."

April 1 • President Madison asks Congress to approve a 60-day embargo; a 90-day embargo is authorized on April 4.

April 10 • The United States is informed by Great Britain that, since French decrees against neutral commerce have not actually been rescinded, British orders-in-council remain in force.

April 20 • Vice President George Clinton dies. He is the first vice president to die in office.

April 30 • Louisiana is admitted to the Union as the 18th state.

May 14 • The eastern region of West Florida is formally incorporated into the Mississippi Territory. The United States had claimed this area, lying between the Mississippi and Perdido rivers, as part of the Louisiana Purchase.

May 18 • A congressional caucus of southern Democratic-Republicans nominates President Madison for re-election and Elbridge Gerry (Massachusetts) for vice president.

June 1 • President Madison sends a war message to Congress, citing injuries to trade and impressment. A War Hawk majority, whose real interests lie in expansionism, declares war on Great Britain on June 18. Meanwhile, too late to affect the issue, the British suspend the orders-in-council as of June 23.

June 4 • Louisiana Territory is renamed Missouri Territory.

June 26 • Governor Caleb Strong of Massachusetts proclaims a fast to protest the war. On August 5, he denies the federal government's request for militia, as has Governor John Cotton Smith of Connecticut (July 2).

July 17 • The United States post on Mackinac Island is surrendered to the British.

August 15 • Indians massacre the American garrison evacuating Fort Dearborn (present-day Chicago).

August 16 • After leading an abortive expedition into Canada, General William Hull surrenders Detroit to the British.

August 19 • The U.S.S. *Constitution* defeats and sinks the British frigate *Guerriere*.

October 13 • An American force under General Stephen Van Rensselaer is defeated after crossing the Niagara River into Canada.

November • The British blockade the Delaware and Chesapeake bays.

December 2 • In the presidential election, Madison is re-elected, receiving 128 electoral votes to 89 for De Witt Clinton, chosen by anti-war Democratic-Republicans and Federalists. Gerry is elected vice president by a vote of 131 to 86 for Jared Ingersoll, his Federalist opponent. Federalist representation in Congress is substantially increased.

International and Cultural Events • Napoleon's Grande Armee, some 500,000 strong, invades Russia in June. Decimated by hunger, it retreats from ruined Moscow in October.

United States of America 1813

Events

January 22 • An American force moving toward Detroit is defeated at Frenchtown.

March 4 • President Madison is inaugurated for his second term.

March 11 • President Madison formally accepts an offer by Alexander I of Russia to mediate the war between the United States and Great Britain. The British will formally reject the offer in July.

April 27 • An American force that has crossed Lake Ontario from Sackets Harbor, New York, seizes York (now Toronto). Zebulon Pike is among those killed. All the public buildings are burned.

May 27 • The British extend their blockade to the Gulf Coast and to eastern ports as far north as New York. Long Island Sound is included on November 19.

May 27 • The British evacuate Fort Erie and Fort George, near the New York border.

May 28-29 • A British force lands at Sackets Harbor and is driven off.

June 1 • The British frigate *Shannon* disables and seizes the U.S.S. *Chesapeake*. Mortally wounded, Captain James Lawrence of the *Chesapeake* tells his crew, "Don't give up the ship."

June 6 • An American force is defeated at Stoney Creek, near Hamilton, Upper Canada (Ontario).

August 2 • The garrison of Fort Stephenson, in western Ohio, repels a British attack.

August 30 • Upper Creek Indians attack Fort Mims, near Mobile, in the first engagement of the Creek War. Many of the defenders are massacred.

September 5 • Secretary of War John Armstrong goes to Sackets Harbor, from which he plans a two-pronged drive on Montreal to be led by General James Wilkinson from Sackets Harbor and General Wade Hampton from Plattsburg.

September 7 • The earliest known use of the phrase "Uncle Sam" is printed in an anonymous editorial in the Troy (New York) *Post*.

September 10 • A naval force assembled at Put-in-Bay on Lake Erie, under the command of Captain Oliver Hazard Perry, defeats a British force under Captain Robert H. Barclay in the decisive battle of Lake Erie. Perry sends a message to General William Henry Harrison: "We have met the enemy and they are ours." On September 18, the British evacuate Detroit.

October 5 • General Harrison defeats the British and Indians in the battle of the Thames at Moravian Town, Upper Canada. Chief Tecumseh is killed in the battle, and the British lose Indian support.

October 25 • General Hampton fights the British at Chateaugay, Lower Canada (Quebec), but then returns

13th CONGRESS	
SENATE	.........36 Members
DR	27
F	9
O	0
HOUSE	........180 Members
DR	112
F	68
O	0

ESTIMATED
POPULATION
7,939,000

James Madison
4th President
2nd Democratic-Republican

Elbridge Gerry
5th Vice President
Democratic-Republican

UNITED STATES ECONOMY

GROSS NATIONAL PRODUCT	.................N/A
RETAIL SALES	.............................N/A
BANK RESOURCES	.........................N/A
EXPORTS	...........................$45,000,000
IMPORTS	...........................$30,000,000
FEDERAL GOVERNMENT EXPENDITURE	..$31,682,000
FEDERAL DEBT	.......................$55,963,000

to Plattsburg. General Wilkinson, after a defeat at Chrysler's Farm on November 11, also gives up the projected drive on Montreal.

December 10 • An American force burns Newark in Upper Canada before it leaves nearby Fort George. On December 18, the British take Fort Niagara, and on December 29-30, they burn Buffalo.

International and Cultural Events • Napoleon is defeated at the Battle of the Nations (October).

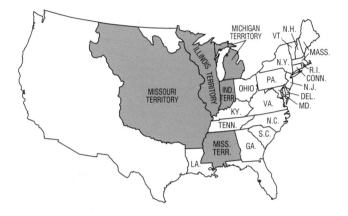

13th CONGRESS

SENATE . . . . .36 Members
DR 27
F 9
O 0

HOUSE . . . . 180 Members
DR 112
F 68
O 0

ESTIMATED
POPULATION
8,179,000

James Madison
4th President
2nd Democratic-Republican

Elbridge Gerry
5th Vice President
Democratic-Republican

UNITED STATES ECONOMY

GROSS NATIONAL PRODUCT . . . . N/A
RETAIL SALES . . . . N/A
BANK RESOURCES . . . . N/A
EXPORTS . . . .$ 11,000,000
IMPORTS . . . .$ 20,000,000
FEDERAL GOVERNMENT EXPENDITURE . .$ 34,721,000
FEDERAL DEBT . . . .$ 81,488,000

Events

January • President Madison accepts a proposal by Lord Castlereagh to engage in peace negotiations and appoints Henry Clay, Jonathan Russell, John Quincy Adams, and James A. Bayard to serve on a peace commission. Their appointment is confirmed by the Senate on January 18, as is that of a fifth commissioner, Albert Gallatin, on February 8.

March 27 • In the last major battle of the Creek War, Tennessee militia, led by Generals Andrew Jackson and John Coffee, defeat the Indians at Horseshoe Bend in what is now Alabama.

April 15 • The Embargo and Non-Importation acts are repealed. The acts were extremely unpopular in New England.

April 25 • The British extend the blockade of the United States coast to New England.

July 5 • After crossing the Niagara River into Upper Canada and taking Fort Erie, an American force led by Major General Jacob Brown and Brigadier General Winfield Scott is victorious in the battle of the Chippewa.

July 22 • The Wyandot, Seneca, Delaware, Shawnee and Miami Indians make their peace with the United States in the Treaty of Greenville.

July 25 • General Brown engages the British in a hard-fought but indecisive battle at Lundy's Lane, near Niagara Falls.

August 8 • Anglo-American peace negotiations open in Ghent. Each side seeks an advantage as news of the changing course of the war arrives.

August 9 • The Creeks sign the Treaty of Fort Jackson, ceding their lands in southern Georgia and eastern Mississippi Territory to the United States.

August 19 • A British force lands at Benedict, Maryland, and moves toward Washington. After defeating an American force at Bladensburg, it seizes Washington, D.C., and in reprisal for the damage at York, on August 24-25 burns the White House, the Capitol and other public buildings.

August 27 • President Madison returns to the smoky ruins of what was Washington, D.C.

September 11 • Captain Thomas Macdonough, commanding an American squadron on Lake Champlain, wins a decisive victory.

September 13-14 • Heavy casualties and an unsuccessful bombardment of Fort McHenry induce the British to give up their effort to take Baltimore. Watching the bombardment, Francis Scott key writes "The Star Spangled Banner."

October 14 • Congress authorizes the purchase of former president Jefferson's personal library (approximately 7,000 books) to replace the books destroyed when the British burned the Library of Congress.

December 24 • The United States and Great Britain sign a treaty of peace at Ghent. No territorial changes take place, and other issues are either unresolved or postponed.

International and Cultural Events • Paris falls to the Allies in March. Napolean abdicates and is exiled to Elba. Talleyrand skillfully represents France at the Congress of Vienna. In Waltham, Massachusetts, Francis Cabot Lowell builds the world's first power-operated factory for the conversion of raw cotton into cloth.

United States of America 1815

Events

January 1 • A British force led by General Sir Edward Pakenham, which had landed at Lake Borgne, to the east of New Orleans, on December 14, is held off by the artillery of the American defenders of the city, who are led by General Andrew Jackson.

January 5 • A convention of disaffected New England Federalists, which has been meeting in Hartford in secret session to consider revision of the United States Constitution, ends with the adoption of resolutions designed to limit the power of the federal government and increase that of the states. When it becomes known that the unpopular war has already ended, the convention is derided.

January 8 • A reinforced British force attacks Jackson's carefully prepared positions near New Orleans, suffering heavy casualties. The American victory in the battle of New Orleans comes two weeks after the Treaty of Ghent, news of which does not reach the United States until February 11.

January 20 • President Madison, citing problems with its provisions, vetoes a bill chatering a second national bank.

February 11 • Word of the signing of the Treaty of Ghent arrives in the United States.

February 15 • The Senate ratifies the Treaty of Ghent. With its proclamation by President Madison on February 17, the War of 1812 ends.

February 16 • The first American railroad charter is issued to John Stevens of New Jersey. The railroad, which was never built, is to run from Trenton to New Brunswick.

March 3 • The House of Representatives votes for a standing army of 10,000 men, or one-half the number requested by the president.

March 3 • An act of Congress approves the dispatch of a punitive expedition against Algiers, which has taken advantage of the War of 1812 to harass American shipping.

May • First issue of Boston's *North American Review* is available; under the editorship of Jared Sparks (1824-1830), it achieves permanent national importance.

May 10 • Captain Stephen Decatur, with a fleet of 10 ships, leaves New York for Algiers. On June 17, he captures the Algerian flagship, and two days later, he takes a second ship. On June 30, the dey is compelled to sign a treaty abolishing tribute payments and to free American prisoners.

July 3 • Great Britain and the United States sign a commercial convention. Each agrees to abolish duties discriminating against the other, and the United States is allowed to trade with the East Indies.

July 26 • Tunis signs a treaty with Decatur in which it agrees to respect American shipping. The exaction of

tribute comes to an end.

August 5 • Captain Decatur secures a treaty from Tripoli similar to those with Algiers and Tunis.

December 4 • President Madison urges Congress to authorize a public works program; it helps to strengthen the federal government.

International and Cultural Events • Returning from Elba, Napolean is defeated at Waterloo and exiled to St. Helena.

ESTIMATED
POPULATION
8,419,000

14th CONGRESS

SENATE .... 36 Members
  DR 25
  F 11
  O 0

HOUSE .... 182 Members
  DR 117
  F 65
  O 0

James Madison
4th President
2nd Democratic-Republican

Vice President
None

UNITED STATES ECONOMY

GROSS NATIONAL PRODUCT .... N/A
RETAIL SALES .... N/A
BANK RESOURCES .... N/A
EXPORTS $81,000,000
IMPORTS $96,000,000
FEDERAL GOVERNMENT EXPENDITURE .. .$32,708,000
FEDERAL DEBT $99,834,000

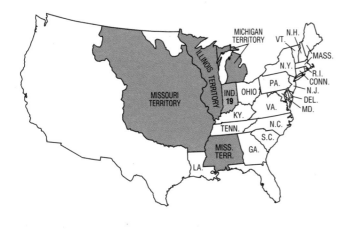

14th CONGRESS

SENATE . . . . 36 Members
  DR 25
  F 11
  O 0

HOUSE . . . . 182 Members
  DR 117
  F 65
  O 0

ESTIMATED
POPULATION
8,659,000

James Madison
4th President
2nd Democratic-Republican

Vice President
None

UNITED STATES ECONOMY

GROSS NATIONAL PRODUCT . . . . N/A
RETAIL SALES . . . . N/A
BANK RESOURCES . . . . N/A
EXPORTS $105,000,000
IMPORTS $163,000,000
FEDERAL GOVERNMENT EXPENDITURE . . $ 30,587,000
FEDERAL DEBT $127,335,000

Events

January 11 • John C. Calhoun introduces a bill in Congress to establish a second Bank of the United States, for which the need has become increasingly apparent since the first Bank of the United States went out of existence in 1811. With the support of Speaker Henry Clay, the bill is adopted by the House of Representatives on March 14, after much debate, and by the Senate on April 10. Like the old bank, the new one is chartered for 20 years. Capital is set at $35 million, and the federal government is to receive a $1.5 million bonus from the bank.

March 16 • A caucus of Democratic-Republicans in Congress nominates James Monroe (Virginia) for president; he receives 65 votes to 54 for William H. Crawford. Daniel D. Tompkins (New York) is the candidate for the vice presidency.

March 20 • In *Martin v. Hunter's Lessee*, the Supreme Court holds that the Judiciary Act of 1789 empowers it to review decisions by state courts.

April • Partly in response to the enormous influence that the British trappers and traders held over the Indians in the upper Great Lakes and northern plains area, Congress passed a law banning foreign citizens from the American fur trade. Congress' action will clear the territory of highly experienced trappers and allow men, such as John Jacob Astor, to create fur trading empires in the Great Plains and upper Great Lakes regions.

April 27 • With the support of John C. Calhoun and Henry Clary, the Tariff Act of 1816 is adopted. Under its provisions, duties designed to protect so-called infant industries are levied on pig iron, wool and cotton textiles, leather, paper, and other goods. Rates vary from 15 to 30 percent ad valorem.

May 10 • A United States post, Fort Howard, is established at Green Bay, a center of the fur trade in the Illinois Territory (now Wisconsin).

June • Delegates to a convention meeting in Corydon, Indiana Territory, draw up a constitution for a state government as authorized by Congress.

July 9 • W.L. Lovely concludes an agreement with the Cherokees for the cession to the United States of land in what is now northern Alabama.

July 27 • United States forces invade Spanish Florida and raze Fort Apalachicola, a former British fort where the Seminole Indians have been harboring slaves escaping from the United States.

December 4 • In the presidential election Monroe is elected president, receiving 183 electoral votes to 34 for Rufus King, his Federalist opponent. Tompkins is elected vice president. Federalist representation in Congress is reduced.

December 11 • Indiana, a free state, is admitted to the union as the 19th state.

December 13 • The Provident Institution for Savings, the first savings bank to begin operations in the United States, is chartered in Boston.

International and Cultural Events • The American Colonization Society is founded to promote emancipation by settling freedmen in Africa. Blacks in Philadelphia establish the independent African Methodist Episcopal Church.

James Monroe 1817

Events

January 7 • The second Bank of the United States is opened for business in Phildelphia.

February 8 • Congress adopts a bill, sponsored by John C. Calhoun, to use the $1.5 million bonus from the Bank of the United States, as well as profits from the government's one-fifth share of the bank's stock, to finance such public works as canals and roads. The bill is vetoed by President Madison, who believes it would be wrong to use federal funds for this purpose without amending the Constitution.

February 20 • On this date, the federal government began accepting either legal tender or bank notes redeemable in specie as payment of public dues. This congressional directive, authored by Daniel Webster of New Hampshire, forces state banks to resume specie payments. The contraction of note issues that also results will be partially responsible for the Panic of 1819.

March 1 • An act of Congress authorizes the people of Mississippi to hold a convention to draft a constitution and prepare the territory for state government.

March 4 • Monroe is inaugurated president.

April 28-29 • An agreement is concluded in Washington by Richard Rush, acting secretary of state, and Sir Charles Bagot, minister to the United States from Great Britain, to restrict the number of naval ships of the two nations that are stationed on the Great Lakes.

May • President Monroe begins a tour of the Northeast and Middle West. Both Democratic-Republicans and Federalists welcome him in such a friendly fashion that a newspaper in Boston says that the nation is entering an "Era of Good Feelings." This name has since been applied to Monroe's administrations, in which nationalism obscures sectional differences.

July 4 • The state of New York begins work on the Erie Canal to connect the Hudson River at Albany with Lake Erie at Buffalo.

September 27 • Title to four million acres of Indian land in northwestern Ohio passes by treaty to the United States.

November • The First Seminole War begins. Raids by Seminole Indians along the border between Georgia and Florida are countered by United States troops, who follow the Indians into Spanish territory. On December 26, General Andrew Jackson is placed in command of the American force.

December 10 • Mississippi, a slave state, is admitted to the union as the 20th state. The eastern part of Mississippi Territory has been organized as Alabama Territory (1817).

International and Cultural Events • The British economist David Ricardo anticipates Marx in *Principles of Political Economy and Taxation.*

15th CONGRESS

SENATE .... 44 Members
  DR 34
  F 10
  O 0

HOUSE .... 183 Members
  DR 141
  F 42
  O 0

ESTIMATED POPULATION
8,899,000

James Monroe
5th President
3rd Democratic-Republican

Daniel D. Tompkins
6th Vice President
Democratic-Republican

UNITED STATES ECONOMY

GROSS NATIONAL PRODUCT .... N/A
RETAIL SALES .... N/A
BANK RESOURCES .... N/A
EXPORTS $103,000,000
IMPORTS $113,000,000
FEDERAL GOVERNMENT EXPENDITURE ..$ 21,844,000
FEDERAL DEBT $123,492,000

James Monroe

Birth .... Westmoreland County, VA, Apr. 28, 1758
Parents .... Spence and Elizabeth Jones Monroe
Married .... Eliza Kortright
Home .... Ash Lawn, near Charlottesville, VA
Presidency .... 1817 – 1825
Death .... New York, NY, July 4, 1831

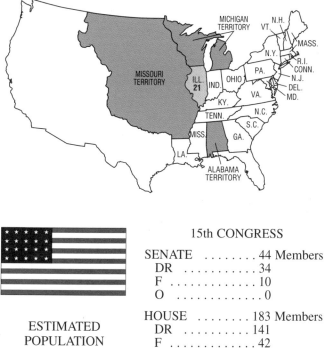

15th CONGRESS

SENATE .... 44 Members
DR 34
F 10
O 0

HOUSE .... 183 Members
DR 141
F 42
O 0

ESTIMATED
POPULATION
9,139,000

James Monroe
5th President
3rd Democratic-Republican

Daniel D. Tompkins
6th Vice President
Democratic-Republican

UNITED STATES ECONOMY

GROSS NATIONAL PRODUCT .... N/A
RETAIL SALES .... N/A
BANK RESOURCES .... N/A
EXPORTS $116,000,000
IMPORTS $141,000,000
FEDERAL GOVERNMENT EXPENDITURE ..$ 19,825,000
FEDERAL DEBT $103,467,000

Events

January 6 • General Jackson writes President Monroe that he will secure Florida for the United States in two months' time if he receives word that its acquisition is desirable. Although the president does not answer the letter, Jackson anticipates his instructions and attacks into Florida.

March 18 • Congress adopts a law providing pensions for veterans of the Revolutionary War.

April 4 • President Monroe signs a bill regularizing the design of the flag of the United States, which henceforth is to have thirteen alternate red and white stripes and, on a blue field, a white star for each state admitted to the Union.

April 7 • General Jackson captures St. Marks, Florida, where he arrests Alexander Arbuthnot, a Scottish trader charged with assisting the Seminoles. Arbuthnot and Robert Ambrister, an English trader similarly charged, are court-martialed and, on April 29, executed. On May 24, Jackson captures Pensacola. These actions are condemned by cabinet members and by House and Senate committees, but Jackson has popular support, and he is not censured.

April 20 • A new tariff bill is adopted. Scheduled reductions in textile duties are postponed, and duties on manufactured iron goods are increased.

June 20 • The Connecticut General Assembly abolishes property requirements for voting. It is the first eastern state to do so.

August 27 • The first steamboat on the upper Great Lakes, the 330-ton *Walk-in-the-Water*, arrives at Detroit on its maiden voyage.

October 19 • Governor Isaac Shelby of Kentucky and General Andrew Jackson negotiate a treaty with the Chickasaw that opens up western Kentucky to settlement. The Chickasaw agree to surrender their lands between the Mississippi River and the northern part of the Tennessee River in return for a $20,000 annuity lasting 15 years. The acquisition of this seven million acre tract will become known as the "Jackson Purchase."

October 20 • The northwestern boundary of the United States, which because of the ambiguity of the Treaty of Paris has been in dispute with Great Britain since 1783, is determined by a convention signed in London by representatives of the two countries. The boundary line is drawn from the Lake of the Woods westward along the 49th parallel to the continental divide. The Oregon country, to the west, is to be left open to the nationals and ships of both countries for a 10-year period (subsequently extended indefinitely). In addition, the commercial convention of 1815 is renewed, and an agreement is reached on the Newfoundland fisheries.

November 28 • Secretary of State John Quincy Adams notifies Spain that if it cannot control the Indians in Florida, it should turn over the area to the United States.

December 3 • Illinois, a free state, is admitted to the Union as the 21st state. Contrary to the provisions of the Northwest Ordinance, its northern boundary has been established at 43°30′N.

International and Cultural Events • The painter Washington Allston returns to settle in Boston after an amazingly successful career in England, where he had studied under Benjamin West.

United States of America 1819

Events

January • The curtailment of credit following a period of inflated prices and land speculation causes a financial panic that lasts throughout the year. The policies of the Bank of the United States are blamed by many in the hard-hit South and West.

February 2 • In ruling in *Dartmouth College v. Woodward* that a private corporation's charter cannot be impaired by a state legislature, the Supreme Court encourages *laissez faire* by freeing business corporations from state control.

February 13 • James Tallmadge of New York introduces an amendment to the Missouri enabling bill that would prohibit slavery in the future state. The House will pass the amendment a few days later. The Senate, however, will refuse to follow the lead of the House.

February 18 • The House of Representatives rejects an amendment, offered by John W. Taylor of New York, to the bill organizing Arkansas Territory that would bar the future importation of slaves.

February 22 • Secretary of State Adams and Luis de Onis, Spanish minister in Washington, sign a treaty whereby Spain, influenced in part by Andrew Jackson's expedition, cedes East Florida to the United States and renounces any claims to West Florida, which had been annexed by the United States between 1810 and 1812. The treaty also fixes the disputed boundary between United States and Spanish territory in the West. The line runs north from the Gulf of Mexico along the Sabine River. Turning west along the Red River, it continues to the 100th meridian, then north to the Arkansas River, which it follows to the river's source. The line then runs north to the 42d parallel and west to the Pacific Ocean. The United States agrees to be responsible for $5 million worth of claims by American citizens against Spain. Although the United States Senate ratifies the treaty two days later, Spain delays, and new ratifications are exchanged on February 22, 1821.

March 2 • Arkansas Territory is created from part of Missouri Territory, effective July 4.

March 6 • In *M'Culloch v. Maryland*, the Supreme Court upholds federal sovereignty and the doctrine of implied powers by ruling that states cannot tax an agency of the federal government, such as the Bank of the United States. "The power to tax is the power to destroy," it says.

May 24 - June 20 • The *Savannah* makes the first transatlantic steamship voyage.

September 24 • The United States signs the Treaty of Saginaw with the Chippewa Indians, who thereby cede land around Saginaw Bay and other areas in what is now Michigan.

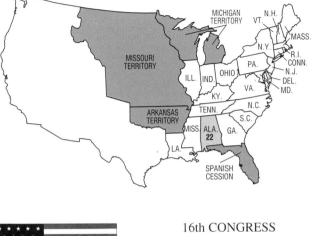

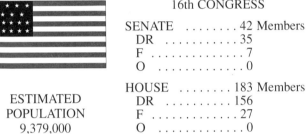

16th CONGRESS	
SENATE .... 42 Members	
DR 35	
F 7	
O 0	
HOUSE .... 183 Members	
DR 156	
F 27	
O 0	

ESTIMATED
POPULATION
9,379,000

James Monroe
5th President
3rd Democratic-Republican

Daniel D. Tompkins
6th Vice President
Democratic-Republican

UNITED STATES ECONOMY

GROSS NATIONAL PRODUCT .... N/A
RETAIL SALES .... N/A
BANK RESOURCES .... N/A
EXPORTS ....$ 91,000,000
IMPORTS $105,000,000
FEDERAL GOVERNMENT EXPENDITURE ..$ 21,464,000
FEDERAL DEBT ....$ 95,530,000

December 8 • Maine, which has voted for separation from Massachusetts, petitions Congress for statehood. Massachusetts had agreed to this course of action for its District of Maine the preceeding June.

December 14 • Alabama, a slave state, is admitted to the Union as the twenty-second state.

International and Cultural Events • After defeating the Spanish at Boyacá, Simón Bolívar is elected president of Gran Colombia.

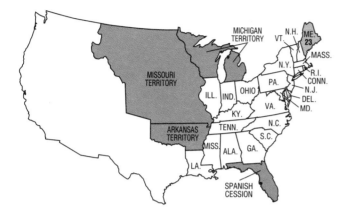

16th CONGRESS

SENATE	42 Members
DR	35
F	7
O	0
HOUSE	183 Members
DR	156
F	27
O	0

ESTIMATED
POPULATION
9,618,000

James Monroe
5th President
3rd Democratic-Republican

Daniel D. Tompkins
6th Vice President
Democratic-Republican

UNITED STATES ECONOMY

GROSS NATIONAL PRODUCT	N/A
RETAIL SALES	N/A
BANK RESOURCES	N/A
EXPORTS	$ 84,000,000
IMPORTS	$ 84,000,000
FEDERAL GOVERNMENT EXPENDITURE	$ 18,261,000
FEDERAL DEBT	$ 91,016,000

Events

January 3 • The House of Representatives passes a bill calling for the admission of Maine to the Union. Since Maine is a free state, its admission would upset the hitherto equal balance between free and slave states (eleven of each in 1820). On February 16, the Senate adopts a bill combining the admission of Maine as a free state and Missouri as a slave state. The next day, it adopts

a compromise amendment, proposed by Senator Jesse B. Thoms of Illinois, that would couple admission of Missouri as a slave state with a provision barring slavery in the rest of the Louisiana Purchase north of 36°30´N.

March 1 • The House of Representatives passes a bill for the admission of Missouri as a free state. The next day, however, it accepts the Senate bill as amended by Senator Thomas, and on March 3, the so-called Missouri Compromise is adopted. On March 6, Congress passes a bill enabling the residents of Missouri to draft a constitution.

March 15 • Maine is admitted to the Union as the 23rd state.

April 24 • The Land Act of 1820 is adopted. Under its provisions, public land may no longer be sold for credit. Although cash must now be paid, the minimum price is lowered to $1.25 per acre. A minimum of 80 acres must be purchased.

May 15 • A bill proclaiming the foreign trade in slaves to be piracy is adopted by Congress. Any United States citizens who import slaves are subject to the death penalty.

June 6 • An expedition headed by Major Stephen H. Long leaves Pittsburgh on a journey to explore the region south of the Missouri River. It reaches Colorado, passing through plains that Long names the Great American Desert.

July 19 • The Missouri constitutional convention adopts a clause barring free blacks and mulattoes from the future state.

December 6 • President Monroe is re-elected, receiving 231 electoral votes to one for John Quincy Adams. Three abstentions are recorded. Vice President Tompkins is also re-elected.

Henry Clay.

United States of America 1821

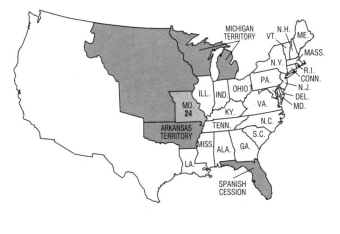

Events

January • Benjamin Lundy begins publishing the *Genius of Universal Emancipation*, an antislavery monthly, in Mount Pleasant, Ohio.

January 17 • The government of New Spain (Mexico) grants land in Texas to an American, Moses Austin, for the establishment of a colony. Austin dies in July, and his grant is taken up by his son, Stephen F. Austin, who later establishes a colony in the lower Brazos River area.

March 2 • Congress approves a bill resolving the dispute that had arisen with the 1820 adoption of a discriminatory clause by the Missouri Territory constitutional convention. The new compromise, which has been devised by Speaker Henry Clay, requires the Missouri General Assembly to promise that the state constitution will not be employed to authorize the curtailment of the rights of citizens of the United States. On June 6, the general assembly gives Congress the required assurances.

March 5 • President Monroe is inaugurated for his second term after postponing the ceremonies from the previous day, a Sunday.

April 15 • Present Monroe selects General Andrew Jackson to be the U.S. commissioner and governor of the territories of East and West Florida.

May • The first high school in the United States, the English Classical School, opens in Boston. In 1824, its name is changed to English High School.

May 31 • The first Roman Catholic cathedral to be built in the United States is dedicated in Baltimore.

June 1 • Emma Hart Willard establishes the first collegiate-level school for women in the United States (the Waterford Academy for Young Ladies) in Waterford, New York.

July 1 • Governor Jackson takes official possession of Florida. Since no territorial government has as yet been organized, he acts in a capacity resembling that of a military governor.

August 10 • Missouri is admitted to the Union as the 24th state. The United States now is composed of 12 slave and 12 free states.

November 10 • A new constitution is adopted in New York state. It eliminates most property requirements for voting. By an amendment adopted in 1826, the franchise is extended to all white males.

November 16 • William Becknell, a trader from Arrow Rock, Missouri, arrives in Santa Fe after a journey with pack horses from Franklin, Missouri. This route he pioneered becomes known as the Santa Fe Trail; over the years, it is followed by hundreds of wagon trains. Becknell and other Amerians prosper in the Santa Fe trade.

	17th CONGRESS
	SENATE .... 48 Members
	DR 44
	F 4
	O 0
ESTIMATED	HOUSE .... 183 Members
POPULATION	DR 158
9,939,000	F 25
	O 0

James Monroe
5th President
3rd Democratic-Republican

Daniel D. Tompkins
6th Vice President
Democratic-Republican

UNITED STATES ECONOMY

GROSS NATIONAL PRODUCT .... N/A
RETAIL SALES .... N/A
BANK RESOURCES .... N/A
EXPORTS .... $ 76,000,000
IMPORTS .... $ 72,000,000
FEDERAL GOVERNMENT EXPENDITURE ..$ 15,811,000
FEDERAL DEBT .... $ 89,987,000

International and Cultural Events • Napoleon dies on St. Helena. Simón Bolívar defeats the Spaniards at Carabobo. Augustin de Iturbide announces Mexico's independence from Spain. Czar Alexander I extends Russia's Pacific Coast claim as far south as 51°N, which overlaps the boundaries of the Oregon country. Michael Faraday discovers electromagnetic rotation. James Fenimore Cooper publishes *The Spy*.

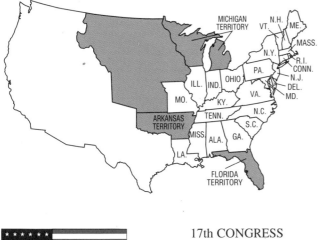

James Monroe
5th President
3rd Democratic-Republican

Daniel D. Tompkins
6th Vice President
Democratic-Republican

17th CONGRESS

SENATE . . . . 48 Members
DR 44
F 4
O 0

HOUSE . . . . 183 Members
DR 158
F 25
O 0

ESTIMATED
POPULATION
10,268,000

UNITED STATES ECONOMY

GROSS NATIONAL PRODUCT . . . . N/A
RETAIL SALES . . . . N/A
BANK RESOURCES . . . . N/A
EXPORTS . . . .$ 83,000,000
IMPORTS . . . .$ 92,000,000
FEDERAL GOVERNMENT EXPENDITURE . . .$ 15,000,000
FEDERAL DEBT . . . .$ 93,547,000

Events

March 8 • With the achievement of independence by several republics in Latin America, President Monroe sends Congress a message stating that these nations merit recognition by the United States. On May 4, Congress appropriates funds for the establishment, at the president's discretion, of diplomatic missions in independent Latin American nations.

March 20 • William Henry Ashley advertises in the *Missouri Republican* of St. Louis for young men willing to participate in an expedition up the Missouri River. With the ensuing formation of the Rocky Mountain Fur Company, large parts of the West are explored and mapped by its employees.

March 30 • An act of Congress permits the formation of a territorial government in Florida.

April 29 • Congress adopts a bill providing for a system of tolls to furnish funds for repairing the Cumberland Road. On May 4, the bill is vetoed by President Monroe, who believes that the federal government does not have constitutional authority to enforce the bill's provisions.

May 30 • A black informer discloses a plan, devised by Denmark Vesey, a free black of Charleston, South Carolina, to seize the city on June 16. Convicted in a trial, Vesey and 35 others are executed. Thirty-four blacks are sent out of South Carolina, and four white men are jailed.

June 19 • The United States extends recognition to the Republic of Gran Colombia. On December 12, recognition is extended to Mexico.

July 20 • Andrew Jackson is nominated for the presidency by the Tennessee General Assembly. The nomination is the first of several nominations by state legislatures.

September 3 • The Sauk and Fox Indians sign a treaty that allows them to live and hunt on land ceded to the United States government.

November 18 • Henry Clay is nominated for the presidency by the Kentucky General Assembly.

International and Cultural Events • Brazil becomes independent of Portugal.

Preisdent James Monroe, at the globe, with his advisors discussing the Monroe Doctrine. Secretary of State John Quincy Adams, at left, played a key role.

United States of America 1823

Events

January 27 • The United States extends recognition to Argentina and Chile.

February 18 • Augustín I (Agustín de Iturbide), Emperor of Mexico, confirms to Stephen F. Austin the grant of Texas land made by the government of New Spain to his father.

March 3 • Congress passes a bill authorizing the building of lighthouses and harbor improvements.

July 17 • In reply to Czar Alexander's decree of 1821, Secretary of State Adams tells the Russian minister to Washington that the United States will not consent to any Russian claims to territory in North America and that new European colonies may not be established in the Americas.

August 20 • Disturbed by the possibility of French intervention to reconquer the former Spanish colonies in South America, George Canning, foreign secretary of Great Britain, asks Richard Rush, United States minister to London, whether the United States government would be interested in joining Great Britain in a declaration opposing European intervention in the Americas. Rush makes a report to Washington.

September 4 • Voters in the Michigan Territory elect Father Gabriel Richard non-voting delegate to the U.S. House of Representatives. The first Roman Catholic priest to sit in Congress, he served until 1825.

September 10 • The Champlain Canal, connecting the Hudson River with Lake Champlain, opens to commercial traffic.

November 7 • At a cabinet meeting, Secretary Adams opposes any joint declaration with Great Britain on the question of European intervention in the New World. He prefers a declaration by the United States alone. Eventually his views win over President Monroe. (In October, Canning had obtained from the French ambassador in London assurances that France had no intention of acquiring former Spanish colonies.)

December 2 • President Monroe presents his annual message to Congress, which includes passages on foreign affairs that come to be known as the Monroe Doctrine. He states that "the American continents, by the free and independent condition which they have assumed and maintain, are henceforth not to be considered as subjects for future colonization by any European powers." Moreover, "we should consider any attempt" on the part of the allied powers (that is, the Holy Alliance) "to extend their system to any portion of this hemisphere as dangerous to our peace and safety." The United States "could not view any interposition for the purpose of oppressing [the new nations], or controlling in any other manner their destiny, by any European power, in any other light than as the manifestation of an unfriendly disposition toward the United States."

International and Cultural Events • Deputized by the Holy Alliance, French forces restore Ferdinand VII to absolute power in Spain. He revokes the Constitution. The English mathematician Charles Babbage proposes a calculation machine.

18th CONGRESS

SENATE	....	48 Members
DR	....	44
F	....	4
O	....	0
HOUSE	....	213 Members
DR	....	187
F	....	26
O	....	0

ESTIMATED POPULATION 10,596,000

James Monroe
5th President
3rd Democratic-Republican

Daniel D. Tompkins
6th Vice President
Democratic-Republican

UNITED STATES ECONOMY

GROSS NATIONAL PRODUCT	.... N/A
RETAIL SALES	.... N/A
BANK RESOURCES	.... N/A
EXPORTS	............................$ 89,000,000
IMPORTS	............................$ 87,000,000
FEDERAL GOVERNMENT EXPENDITURE	..$ 14,707,000
FEDERAL DEBT	........................$ 90,876,000

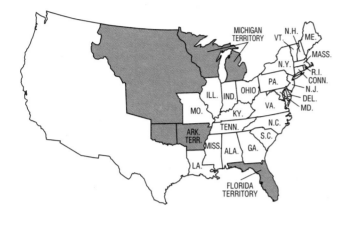

18th CONGRESS

SENATE	.... 48 Members
DR	 44
F	 4
O	 0

ESTIMATED
POPULATION
10,924,000

HOUSE	.... 213 Members
DR	 187
F	 26
O	 0

James Monroe
5th President
3rd Democratic-Republican

Daniel D. Tompkins
6th Vice President
Democratic-Republican

UNITED STATES ECONOMY

GROSS NATIONAL PRODUCT	.... N/A
RETAIL SALES	.... N/A
BANK RESOURCES	.... N/A
EXPORTS	.... $ 90,000,000
IMPORTS	.... $ 90,000,000
FEDERAL GOVERNMENT EXPENDITURE	..$ 20,327,000
FEDERAL DEBT	.... $ 90,270,000

Events

February 14 • A small minority of Democratic-Republican members of Congress caucus and nominate Secretary of the Treasury William H. Crawford for president.

February 15 • At a political gathering in Boston, Secretary of State John Quincy Adams is nominated for president.

March 2 • In *Gibbons v. Ogden*, the Supreme Court rules that a monopoly granted by the state of New York for steam navigation between New York and New Jersey does not prevent the holder of a federal license granted under the authority of a congressional law concerning coastal trade from engaging in such interstate trade. The commerce clause of the Constitution, broadly interpreted, empowers Congress to regulate navigation within state lines.

March 4 • Andrew Jackson is nominated for president by a convention meeting in Harrisburg, Pennsylvania.

April 17 • The United States and Russia sign a treaty setting the dividing line between Russian and American claims on the Pacific Coast at 54°40´N.

April 30 • Congress adopts a general survey bill, which is favored by members from the Middle West and the West. Under its provisions, the president may have surveys made for canals and roads and estimates of their costs drawn up.

April 30 • Congress appropriates $10,000 for the surveying of a road between Detroit and Chicago, the Great Sauk Trail.

May 22 • The Tariff Act of 1824 is adopted. Rates on woolen and cotton manufactures are raised to 33.3 percent, and duties are levied on previously untaxed goods, including glass, linen, silk, and lead. The chief advocate of the new law is Henry Clay. In a speech delivered in Congress on March 30-31, he proposes what he calls his "American System," which would be based on the development of a home market through improvements and protectionism.

May 26 • The United States extends recognition to the Empire of Brazil.

September • Reverend Benton Pixey, his wife Lucia and their two children establish a mission among the Osage at their village on the west bank of the Neosho River. The first mission in what is now Kansas, it was under the auspices of the United Foreign Missionary Society.

September 11 • A political meeting in Philadelphia endorses Henry Clay's candidacy for the presidency.

October 3 • The United States and Gran Colombia sign a treaty of amity and commerce.

December 1 • In the presidential election, Andrew Jackson receives 99 electoral votes; John Quincy Adams, 84; William H. Crawford, 41; and Henry Clay, 37. Since none of the candidates has a majority, the House of Representatives has the task of choosing from the top three candidates. John C. Calhoun is elected vice president.

December • James Bridger, who had been with Ashley in 1822, discovers the Great Salt Lake.

International and Cultural Events • France's new king, Charles X, combats liberalism. Joseph Aspdin gets a British patent for portland cement.

John Quincy Adams 1825

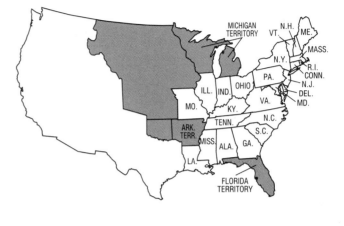

Events

January 3 • Robert Owens purchases land in Indiana on which he will found a utopian community called New Harmony. It lasts two years.

February 9 • With the support of Henry Clay, who has been eliminated from the contest, John Quincy Adams is elected president by the House of Representatives, voting by states. Adams receives 13 votes to seven for Andrew Jackson and four for William H. Crawford. By this time, the Democratic-Republican party has split between the followers of Jackson, who are called Democratic-Republicans, and those of Adams and Clay, who are known as National Republicans.

February 12 • At Indian Springs, Geogia, representatives from only eight of 56 Creek villages agree to cede their lands in Georgia to the United States in exchange for land west of the Mississippi River. Most Creeks will refuse to honor the treaty and seek redress from the nation's leaders.

February • On the recommendation of John C. Calhoun, President Monroe adopts an official policy of removing the Indians still living east of the Mississippi River to lands in the West.

March 3 • Congress authorizes the surveying of a road linking the Missouri River and New Mexico.

March 4 • Adams is inaugurated president.

July 4 • Construction of the Cumberland Road is resumed, extending it westward through Ohio.

August 19 • Chiefs of the Chippewa, Iowa, Potawatomi, Sauk and Fox, Sioux, and Winnebago tribes sign a treaty in Prairie due Chien, in what is now Wisconsin, fixing the boundaries between their lands. The meeting was arranged by the federal government at the request of the Chippewa and Sioux, who wish to end an enmity of long standing.

October • The general assembly of Tennessee nominates Jackson for president in 1828.

October 26 • The Erie Canal connects Buffalo and Albany. Linking the Hudson River and Lake Erie, it promotes the commercial rise of New York.

December 6 • In his annual message to Congress, President Adams advocates a national program of internal improvements.

December 7 • The marquis de Lafayette completes a 16-month visit to the United States. Arriving in New York on August 16, 1824, at the invitation of President Monroe, he will travel throughout the United States, being received everywhere with tremendous enthusiasm. He stays with Jefferson at Monticello, visits battle sites, and lays the cornerstone of the Bunker Hill Monument.

International and Cultural Events • Boston carpenters strike for a 10-hour day. In Britain, workers younger than 16 are restricted to a 12-hour day. Czar Nicholas I crushes the Decembrist demands for a constitution.

	19th CONGRESS
SENATE	.... 46 Members
AD	 26
J	 20
O	 0
HOUSE	.... 202 Members
AD	 105
J	 97
O	 0

ESTIMATED
POPULATION
11,252,000

John Quincy Adams
6th President
4th Democratic-Republican

John C. Calhoun
7th Vice President
Democratic-Republican

UNITED STATES ECONOMY

GROSS NATIONAL PRODUCT	.... N/A
RETAIL SALES	.... N/A
BANK RESOURCES	.... N/A
EXPORTS	.... $112,000,000
IMPORTS	.... $106,000,000
FEDERAL GOVERNMENT EXPENDITURE	.. $ 18,857,000
FEDERAL DEBT	.... $ 83,788,000

John Quincy Adams

Birth	...... Braintree (now Quincy), MA, July 11, 1767
Parents	.... John and Abigail Smith Adams
Married	.... Louisa Catherine Johnson
Home	.... Quincy, MA
Presidency	.... 1825 – 1829
Death	.... Washington, D.C., Feb. 23, 1848

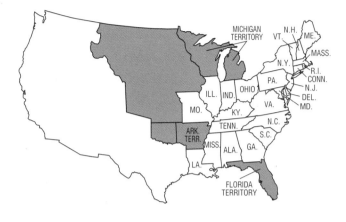

19th CONGRESS

SENATE .... 46 Members
AD 26
J 20
O 0

HOUSE .... 202 Members
AD 105
J 97
O 0

ESTIMATED
POPULATION
11,580,000

John Quincy Adams
6th President
4th Democratic-Republican

John C. Calhoun
7th Vice President
Democratic-Republican

UNITED STATES ECONOMY

GROSS NATIONAL PRODUCT .... N/A
RETAIL SALES .... N/A
BANK RESOURCES .... N/A
EXPORTS $91,000,000
IMPORTS $95,000,000
FEDERAL GOVERNMENT EXPENDITURE ..$17,036,000
FEDERAL DEBT $81,054,000

Events

January 11 • In response to a message from President Adams dated December 26, 1825, proposing the sending of two delegates to an inter-American Congress to be held in Panama at the urging of Simón Bolívar, the Senate Committee on Foreign Relations withholds its approval. However, on March 14, after heated debate, the Senate passes a bill appropriating funds for the delegates, and on March 25, the House of Representatives follows suit. In actual fact, neither of the appointed delegates attends the Panama Congress: one dies on the way, and the other arrives too late.

January 24 • The Creek Indians sign the Treaty of Washington, ceding to the United States lands in western Georgia, which are to be vacated by January 1, 1827.

February 13 • The American Temperance Society is founded in Boston by a group of men who have been influenced by the preaching of Lyman Beecher.

February 17 • Unwilling to accept the land cession changes contained in the Treaty of Washington, Governor George M. Troop of Georgia calls up the state militia to prevent the arrival of federal troops in the western part of the state. President Adams had ordered the troops into the area to prevent Georgia from surveying the ceded territory.

April 8 • Henry Clay and John Randolph fight a duel as a result of Randolph's reiteration of charges of a "corrupt bargain," whereby Clay helped Adams win the Presidency with the understanding that he would be appointed secretary of state.

May 2 • The United States extends recognition to the Republic of Peru, which had declared its independence from Colombia.

July 4 • On the 50th anniversary of the Declaration of Independence, two former presidents and signers of the Declaration die. First was Thomas Jefferson at Monticello, Virginia, and later that day, John Adams at Quincy, Massachusetts.

August 22 • Jedediah Strong Smith leaves the Great Salt Lake at the head of an expedition to California. Traveling through the Cajon Pass, he reaches the Pacific coast in November, completing a pioneer overland journey. After spending the winter in southern California, he returns to Utah by a more northerly route and then goes back to California. In 1828, he moves up the coast to Oregon, and the next year, he travels in the Rocky Mountains to what is now Wyoming.

September • The disappearance of a former Mason of Batavia, New York, who had disclosed secrets of the order, arouses feeling against Freemasonry in the state and leads to the formation of the Anti-Masonic party, the earliest American third party.

October 7 • The Quincy Tramway, the first railroad in the United States, is completed in Massachusetts. Three miles long, it is used to haul granite for the Bunker Hill Monument from a quarry.

November • In the midterm elections, the Jacksonians win a majority in both houses of Congress.

International and Cultural Events • Cooper publishes *The Last of the Mohicans*. Under the editorship of Shadrach Penn, the Louisville *Advertiser* becomes the first daily newspaper west of the Allegheny Mountains.

United States of America 1827

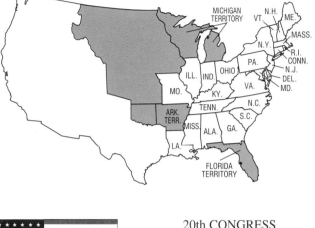

Events

February 2 • In *Martin v. Mott*, the Supreme Court rules that the president has constitutional authority to call out the state militia and place it in federal service when he deems it necessary to do so. This authority cannot be contravened by state officials.

February 10 • The House of Representatives approves a bill that would increase substantially duties on woolen textiles. When the bill comes before the Senate, however, southern opposition plus a tie-breaking vote by Vice President Calhoun result in its defeat on February 28.

February 28 • The Baltimore & Ohio Railroad receives a charter from the state of Maryland. On March 8, it also receives a charter from Virginia.

May 8 • A site is selected for Cantonment Leavenworth (later Fort Leavenworth) in what is now Kansas. The post is established to provide military protection for the rapidly increasing trade along the Santa Fe Trail to the West.

May 14 • Farmers and manufacturers meet in Philadelphia to discuss the declining wool market.

June 19 • Joel R. Poinsett is recalled as United States minister to Mexico after he has become involved in a Masonic dispute with political overtones. He has favored the York rite over the Scottish rite.

July 26 • At New Echota, Georgia, the Cherokees adopt a constitution modeled after the U.S. Constitution. It establishes a bicameral legislature, a plural executive and a judiciary.

July 30 - August 3 • With the failure of Congress to adopt the new protectionist tariff bill, protectionists hold a convention in Harrisburg, Pennsylvania. Some 100 delegates assembled from 13 states present their views. Their recommendations include higher duties on iron goods, textiles, flax and hemp.

August 6 • The United States and Great Britain agree to renew their commercial treaty of 1818 and to continue their joint occupation of the Oregon country.

October 10 • The physicist Joseph Henry, in a paper read before the Albany Institute, discusses the results of his early experiments in electromagnetism, which will lead to the development of the telegraph.

November 15 • The Creek Indians sign a treaty ceding to the United States all their lands in Georgia not covered by the Treaty of Washington of 1826.

December 24 • The recommendations of the Harrisburg Convention are presented to the new Congress, but with the Jacksonians in control, they are not accepted.

International and Cultural Events • The German physicist Georg Ohm formulates Ohm's law. *Freedom's Journal*, the first black newspaper, is issued in New York. James Audubon publishes the first folio of his monumental *The Birds of America*. Edgar Allen Poe publishes his first book of poetry. In February, *Mardi Gras* is celebrated for the first time in New Orleans. Sarah Hale publishes the first anti-slavery novel, *Northwood*. Massachusetts enacts the first American high school law.

ESTIMATED POPULATION 11,909,000	20th CONGRESS
	SENATE .... 48 Members
	J 28
	AD 20
	O 0
	HOUSE .... 213 Members
	J 119
	AD 94
	O 0

John Quincy Adams
6th President
4th Democratic-Republican

John C. Calhoun
7th Vice President
Democratic-Republican

UNITED STATES ECONOMY

GROSS NATIONAL PRODUCT	N/A
RETAIL SALES	N/A
BANK RESOURCES	N/A
EXPORTS	$98,000,000
IMPORTS	$90,000,000
FEDERAL GOVERNMENT EXPENDITURE ..	$16,193,000
FEDERAL DEBT	$73,987,000

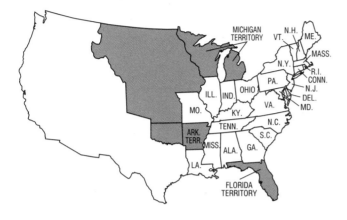

20th CONGRESS

SENATE	....	48 Members
J	....	28
AD	....	20
O	....	0
HOUSE	....	213 Members
J	....	119
AD	....	94
O	....	0

ESTIMATED
POPULATION
12,237,000

John Quincy Adams
6th President
4th Democratic-Republican

John C. Calhoun
7th Vice President
Democratic-Republican

UNITED STATES ECONOMY

GROSS NATIONAL PRODUCT	.... N/A
RETAIL SALES	.... N/A
BANK RESOURCES	.... N/A
EXPORTS	.... $84,000,000
IMPORTS	.... $97,000,000
FEDERAL GOVERNMENT EXPENDITURE	.. $16,395,000
FEDERAL DEBT	.... $67,457,000

Events

January 31 • The Committee on Manufactures of the House of Representatives, which is controlled by Jacksonians, introduces a tariff bill providing for excessively high duties on a wide variety of goods, including raw materials, in a complicated scheme devised to injure President Adams's standing with all sections of the country. It is believed that the president will be held responsible for the expected defeat of the bill. Although no one likes the bill and the Jacksonian majority defeats proposed amendments, the protectionists vote for the bill in the absence of something better, as do some Jacksonians. The bill is adopted by the House on April 23 and by the Senate on May 13. President Adams signs the Tariff Act of 1828 on May 19. The new law arouses widespread protests and becomes known as the Tariff of Abominations.

July 4 • Ceremonies are held to inaugurate construction of the Baltimore & Ohio Railroad.

October 16 • The Delaware and Hudson Canal, running from Honesdale, Pennsylvania, to Kingston, New York, is opened to traffic.

December 3 • In the presidential election, Andrew Jackson is elected president, receiving 178 electoral votes to 83 for John Quincy Adams. John C. Calhoun is re-elected vice president, receiving 171 electoral votes as Jackson's running mate.

December 19 • The general assembly of South Carolina, in a series of eight resolutions, questions the constitutionality of the Tariff Act of 1828, which it condemns as unfair and burdensome. Supplementing the resolutions is an unsigned essay, "South Carolina Exposition and Protest," written by Vice President Calhoun. In it Calhoun, the former nationalist, advocates nullification of federal laws deemed unconstitutional by a state convention.

December 30 • The general assembly of Georgia adopts resolutions against the Tariff Act of 1828.

The Boston waterfront from the South Boston Bridge in 1828.

Andrew Jackson 1829

Events

February 4-5 • The legislatures of Virginia and Mississippi adopt resolutions questioning the constitutionality of the Tariff Act of 1828.

March 2 • With the financial aid of Thomas H. Perkins, Dr. John Dix Fisher incorporates in South Boston the Perkins Institute and Massachusetts School for the Blind, the first such school in the United States.

March 4 • Jackson is inaugurated president. In his inaugural address, Jackson stresses states' rights and the need to limit governmental expenditures, but he slights other economic matters. He takes counsel with private advisers, who soon become known as his "Kitchen Cabinet."

August 25 • The Mexican government rejects a proposal by President Jackson to purchase Texas.

September 15 • The Guerrero Decree abolishes slavery in the Republic of Mexico.

December 8 • In his annual message to Congress, President Jackson is critical of the constitutional basis and operations of the Bank of the United States.

International and Cultural Events • Robert Peel's Catholic Emancipation bill allows Catholics to sit in Parliament. His new London police force is popularly known as Peelers or Bobbies. Greece gains its independence from the Ottoman Empire.

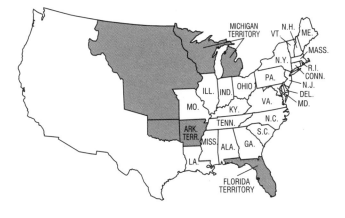

	21st CONGRESS	
	SENATE	48 Members
	D	26
	NR	22
	O	0
ESTIMATED	HOUSE	213 Members
POPULATION	D	139
12,565,000	NR	74
	O	0

Andrew Jackson
7th President
1st Democrat

John C. Calhoun
7th Vice President
Democrat

UNITED STATES ECONOMY

GROSS NATIONAL PRODUCT	N/A
RETAIL SALES	N/A
BANK RESOURCES	N/A
EXPORTS	$83,000,000
IMPORTS	$83,000,000
FEDERAL GOVERNMENT EXPENDITURE	$15,203,000
FEDERAL DEBT	$58,421,000

Andrew Jackson

Birth	Waxhaw, SC, Mar. 15, 1767
Parents	Andrew and Elizabeth Hutchinson Jackson
Married	Rachel Donelson Robards
Home	The Hermitage, near Nashville, TN
Presidency	1829 – 1837
Death	The Hermitage, near Nashville, TN, June 8, 1845

The New York waterfront.

21st CONGRESS

SENATE .... 48 Members
D 26
NR 22
O 0

HOUSE .... 213 Members
D 139
NR 74
O 0

ESTIMATED
POPULATION
12,901,000

Andrew Jackson
7th President
1st Democrat

John C. Calhoun
7th Vice President
Democrat

UNITED STATES ECONOMY

GROSS NATIONAL PRODUCT .... N/A
RETAIL SALES .... N/A
BANK RESOURCES .... N/A
EXPORTS $86,000,000
IMPORTS $79,000,000
FEDERAL GOVERNMENT EXPENDITURE ..$15,143,000
FEDERAL DEBT $48,565,000

Events

January 13 • The Senate opens debate on a resolution introduced on December 29, 1829, by Samuel A. Foot of Connecticut, proposing that the federal government temporarily limit the sale of public lands. Opposition to the resolution is based on two grounds: the alleged eastern endeavor to impede western growth, cited in a speech by Thomas Hart Benton of Missouri on January 18, and the need to defend the rights of the states from federal encroachment, expressed by Robert Y. Hane of South Carolina on January 19. Daniel Webster takes up the challenge to the Union. In a debate with Hayne that continues until January 27, he contends that the people, through the Constitution, established a national government with sovereign powers.

April 6 • The Church of Jesus Christ of Latter-day Saints (Mormons) is organized by Joseph Smith and five other men in Fayette, New York.

May 27 • President Jackson vetoes the Maysville Road bill on the ground that the route is confined to one state, Kentucky, and is not linked to other improvements. By making his objections specific, he retains the support of people who favor internal improvements in general.

May 28 • President Jackson signs the Indian Removal Act, which authorizes him to resettle eastern Indians, exchanging their lands east of the Mississippi River for new lands in the West.

May 29 • The Preemption Act of 1830 is adopted. Under its provisions, anyone who had cultivated public land in the previous year is permitted to buy a maximum of 160 acres at $1.25 per acre. The act, which is renewed in succeeding years, protects squatters from speculators and claim jumpers.

July 15 • The Sioux, Sauk, Fox and other Indians of the upper Mississippi Valley sign a treaty at Prairie du Chien, Wisconsin, ceding land in what are now Iowa, Missouri and Minnesota to the United States.

August 4 • James Thompson, a civil engineer, plats the town of Chicago, Illinois.

August 28 • The "Tom Thumb," the first locomotive built in the United States, runs on track recently laid by the Baltimore and Ohio Railroad. Peter Cooper is the locomotive's designer and builder.

September 27 • The Choctaw Indians cede to the United States the remainder of their lands east of the Mississippi River, amounting to almost eight million acres, by the Treaty of Dancing Rabbit Creek. They receive in exchange land in what is now Oklahoma.

October 5 • Negotiations between Secretary of State Martin Van Buren and Sir Charles Vaughan, British minister in Washington, have resulted in the reopening of trade with the British West Indies.

December 25 • At the formal opening of the South Carolina Railroad, the locomotive "Best Friend of Charleston" takes well-wishers on a short ride. The "Best Friend" is the first locomotive to pull a train of cars in regular service in the United States.

International and Cultural Events • France's July Revolution ends the rule of Charles X; Louis-Philippe becomes the "Citizen King." Venezuela and Ecuador separate from Gran Colombia. Mexico closes Texas to settlement by Americans.

United States of America 1831

Events

January 1 • The abolitionist William Lloyd Garrison begins publishing the newspaper the *Liberator* in Boston.

February 15 • Vice President Calhoun, whose criticism of President Jackson's actions during the First Seminole War has been brought to the president's attention, has the letters that were exchanged at the time between Jackson and officials in Washington published in a pamphlet.

March 18 • In *Cherokee Nation v. Georgia*, the Supreme Court rules that the Cherokees, who have sought an injunction against the state of Georgia to prevent it from applying its laws to their territory, do not constitute a foreign nation and thus cannot institute a suit in the Court.

April • President Jackson's difficulties with Vice President Calhoun are intensified by a division within the cabinet over the status of Mrs. John H. Eaton, wife of the secretary of war, whom Mrs. Calhoun and the wives of other cabinet members consider immoral and refuse to accept socially. Secretary of State Van Buren, a widower who has supported the president and Mrs. Eaton resolves the crisis by resigning himself. Eaton resigns on April 7, and Van Buren's resignation is accepted on April 11. By August 8, all the other cabinet members, except the postmaster general, have also been replaced.

July 4 • The United States and France sign a treaty, negotiated in Paris by Minister William C. Rives, for the settlement of spoliation claims dating from the Napoleonic wars. France is to pay $5 million, and the United States $300,000.

July 4 • James Monroe, the sixth president of the United States, dies in New York City.

August 21 • Nat Turner, a radical slave-preacher, leads a slave uprising in Southampton County, Virginia, in which almost 60 whites are killed. Turner and 12 of his followers are executed; about 100 other blacks are killed during the search for the rebels.

August - September • Cyrus Hall McCormick's new mechanical reaper is used in harvesting. He patents it in 1834.

September 26 • The Anti-Masonic party convenes in Baltimore. It nominates William Wirt for president and Amos Ellmaker for vice president. This is the first national party nominating convention to take place.

November • Having returned saddened, slandered and defeated from a stormy presidency, John Quincy Adams is surprised when he is elected to the U.S. House of Representatives from his old district of Quincy. He will be re-elected every two years until his death in 1848.

December • The Virginia House of Delegates begins debating the merits of slavery in the commonwealth. By the time the debates end in January 1832, the assembly will have defeated various motions on the issue, includ-

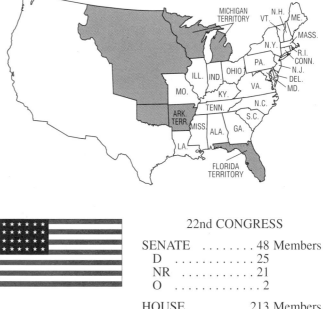

Andrew Jackson
7th President
1st Democrat

John C. Calhoun
7th Vice President
Democrat

22nd CONGRESS

SENATE	.... 48 Members
D	 25
NR	 21
O	 2
HOUSE	.... 213 Members
D	 141
NR	 58
O	 14

ESTIMATED
POPULATION
13,321,000

UNITED STATES ECONOMY

GROSS NATIONAL PRODUCT	.... N/A
RETAIL SALES	.... N/A
BANK RESOURCES	.... N/A
EXPORTS	...........................$ 97,000,000
IMPORTS	...........................$112,000,000
FEDERAL GOVERNMENT EXPENDITURE	..$ 15,248,000
FEDERAL DEBT	.....................$ 39,123,000

ing a proposal calling on Virginia to fund colonization projects for free blacks

December 12 • The National Republican party convenes in Baltimore. It nominates Henry Clay (Kentucky) for president and John Sergeant (Pennsylvania) for vice president.

International and Cultural Events • The *Beagle* sails with Charles Darwin to survey the South American coast. Dr. Samuel F. Smith writes "America," setting it to the tune of "God Save the King."

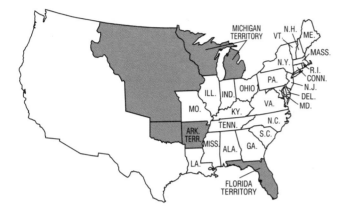

ESTIMATED
POPULATION
13,742,000

22nd CONGRESS

SENATE .... 48 Members
D 25
NR 21
O 2

HOUSE .... 213 Members
D 141
NR 58
O 14

Andrew Jackson
7th President
1st Democrat

John C. Calhoun
7th Vice President
Democrat

UNITED STATES ECONOMY

GROSS NATIONAL PRODUCT .... N/A
RETAIL SALES .... N/A
BANK RESOURCES .... N/A
EXPORTS $101,000,000
IMPORTS $112,000,000
FEDERAL GOVERNMENT EXPENDITURE ..$ 17,298,000
FEDERAL DEBT ....$ 24,322,000

Events

January 9 • The Bank of the United States, which has been under attack in the West because of its conservative policies, applied to Congress for a renewal of its charter, although the expiration date is four years hence.

March 3 • In *Worcester v. Georgia*, the Supreme Court rules that a Georgia law applying to the Cherokee Nation is unconstitutional, since only the federal government has jurisdiction in Indian territories.

April 6 - August 2 • Chief Black Hawk leads some of the Sauk and Fox Indians in what becomes known as the Black Hawk War. The Indians attempt to recover ceded lands in Illinois and Wisconsin, but are decisively defeated. On August 27, Black Hawk is captured, and the Potawatomi and Winnebago, allies of the Sauk and Fox with whom Black Hawk has sought shelter, are later compelled to cede land in northern Illinois.

May 9 • Seminole Indians sign a treaty with the United States at Payne's Landing, Florida. It sets terms for the exchange of Seminole lands in Florida for new lands in the West.

May 21 • The Democratic party (formerly the Democratic-Republican party) convenes in Baltimore. It nominates President Jackson for re-election and Martin Van Buren for vice president.

June • A cholera epidemic strikes first in New York. By October, it has spread to New Orleans. Thousands of people die.

July 10 • President Jackson vetoes a bill, passed by Congress on July 3, that would have renewed the charter of the Bank of the United States. Henry Clay's support of the bank in the presidential campaign costs him votes.

July 13 • Henry Schoolcraft, commanding an exploring party, discovers the source of the Mississippi River at Lake Itasca, Minnesota.

July 14 • The Tariff Act of 1832 is adopted. Although it is more moderate than the act of 1828, the changes are of benefit mainly to the northeastern states, and the South is dissatisfied.

November 24 • In South Carolina, where opposition to the protective tariff is particularly strong, a state convention adopts an ordinance that nullifies the tariff acts of 1828 and 1832. On November 27, the state legislature adopts measures to enforce the ordinance, including military preparations.

December 5 • In the presidential election, President Jackson is re-elected, receiving 219 electoral votes to 49 for Clay and seven for Wirt; John Floyd (Virginia) receives 11 votes from South Carolina. Van Buren is elected vice president (189 electoral votes).

December 10 • President Jackson issues a proclamation in which he tells the people of South Carolina that states cannot secede from the Union. South Carolina legislators reply defiantly.

December 12 • Vice President Calhoun is elected to the Senate from South Carolina. He resigns as vice president on December 28.

International and Cultural Events • Giuseppe Mazzini founds the Young Italy society to fight for Italian unification. Samuel Morse, inspired by Andre Ampere, begins work on his telegraph.

United States of America 1833

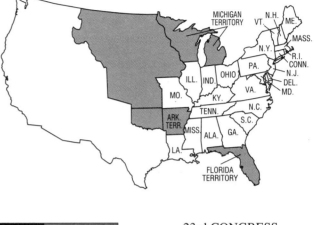

Events

January 1 • *Knickerbocker Magazine* is published for the first time. Until 1859, when it ceases publication, the magazine is one of the most popular literary publications in the country.

January 16 • Taking up the challenge to federal authority posed by the nullification ordinance adopted in South Carolina, President Jackson asks Congress to adopt a force bill to enable him to carry out the provisions of the tariff acts of 1828 and 1832.

February 12 • A new tariff bill devised by Henry Clay, which represents a compromise with the southern position, is introduced in the House of Representatives. Meanwhile, word of its preparation having reached South Carolina, the nullification ordinance is suspended on January 21. Congress adopts the tariff and force bills on March 1; the president signs both bills the next day.

February 16 • In *Barron v Baltimore*, the U.S. Supreme Court rules that the Bill of Rights is binding only on the federal government, not on state governments.

March 2 • A resolution of the House of Representatives approves the continued use of the Bank of the United States for the deposit of government funds. However, President Jackson is determined to have the deposits withdrawn, and on April 3, Attorney General Roger B. Taney states that this is lawful.

March 4 • President Jackson is inaugurated for his second term.

March 15 • The South Carolina Convention rescinds the nullification ordinance. On March 18, however, it adopts an ordinance nullifying the force bill.

April 1-13 • American settlers in Texas, meeting in convention in San Felipe de Austin, vote in favor of separating Texas from Mexico.

June 1 • Because Secretary of the Treasury Louis McLane is unwilling to remove the government deposits from the bank, President Jackson names him secretary of state and William J. Duane secretary of the treasury.

September 10 • President Jackson informs the cabinet that the government will remove its deposits from the Bank of the United States on October 1. Secretary Duane is as reluctant as McLane had been to take the required action, and on September 23, Attorney General Taney becomes secretary of the treasury in his stead.

September 26 • Secretary Taney orders the transfer of the first lot of government funds to a state bank in Philadelphia. During the next three months, funds are deposited in various other state banks.

December 3 • President Jackson informs Congress in his annual message that he was justified in removing deposits from the Bank of the United States because of

	23rd CONGRESS
SENATE	48 Members
D	20
NR	20
O	8
HOUSE	260 Members
D	147
AM	53
O	60

ESTIMATED
POPULATION
14,162,000

Andrew Jackson
7th President
1st Democrat

Martin Van Buren
8th Vice President
Democrat

UNITED STATES ECONOMY

GROSS NATIONAL PRODUCT	N/A
RETAIL SALES	N/A
BANK RESOURCES	N/A
EXPORTS	$101,000,000
IMPORTS	$119,000,000
FEDERAL GOVERNMENT EXPENDITURE	$ 23,018,000
FEDERAL DEBT	$ 7,012,000

its partisan position in the elections of 1832.

December 6 • The American Anti-Slavery Society is founded in Philadelphia.

December 26 • Henry Clay asks the Senate to censure President Jackson and the Treasury.

International and Cultural Events • In New York a General Trades Union links organized labor (until the Panic of 1837). Oberlin College becomes the first coeducational college.

1834 United States of America

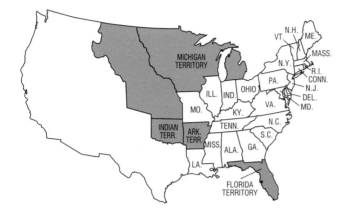

23rd CONGRESS

SENATE . . . . 48 Members
D 20
NR 20
O 8

HOUSE . . . . 260 Members
D 147
AM 53
O 60

ESTIMATED
POPULATION
14,582,000

Andrew Jackson
7th President
1st Democrat

Martin Van Buren
8th Vice President
Democrat

UNITED STATES ECONOMY

GROSS NATIONAL PRODUCT . . . . N/A
RETAIL SALES . . . . N/A
BANK RESOURCES $419,000,000
EXPORTS $116,000,000
IMPORTS $140,000,000
FEDERAL GOVERNMENT EXPENDITURE . .$ 18,628,000
FEDERAL DEBT . . . .$ 4,760,000

Events

January 3 • Stephen F. Austin, who has gone to Mexico City to present the Texan settlers' resolution for separation from Mexico, is arrested by the Mexican government and imprisoned for eight months.

January 29 • President Jackson issues orders for the dispatch of troops to a construction site on the Chesapeake and Ohio Canal, where violence has

occurred after the calling of a strike for a closed shop. This is the first such use of federal troops.

March 28 • The Senate approves the resolutions, introduced by Henry Clay in December 1833, censuring President Jackson and the Treasury for the removal of federal funds from the Bank of the United States. (In 1837, the resolution concerning the president is removed from the Senate's journal.)

April • Parties and groups opposed to the Jackson administration begin to come together to form a new party, which becomes known as the Whig party. It includes adherents of the National Republican and Anti-Masonic parties, proponents of states' rights who have supported John C. Calhoun's stand on nullification, and Democrats opposed to the president regarding the bank issue. Its most prominent leaders are Clay and Daniel Webster.

April 4 • The House of Representatives adopts four resolutions in support of the president's actions in removing deposits from the bank.

June 15 • Fur trader Nathaniel J. Wyeth establishes Fort Hall, Idaho, which becomes an important stopping point on the Oregon Trail.

June 24 • As opposition to President Jackson's policies persist, the Senate withholds confirmation of the appointment of Roger B. Taney as secretary of the treasury.

June 28 • The Second Coinage Act is adopted. The ratio of silver to gold is changed from 15 to one to almost 16 to one, which undervalues silver and causes a shortage of coins.

July 4 • Rioting between groups favoring and opposing the abolition of slavery occurs in New York.

October 28 • In accordance with the provisions of the Treaty of Payne's Landing of 1832, the federal government orders the Seminoles to leave Florida.

November 1 • The Philadelphia and Trenton Railroad is completed.

November 10 • The first public lands in Wisconsin go on sale at the government land office in Mineral Point.

December 1 • Abraham Lincoln takes his seat for the first time in the Illinois House of Representatives. Lincoln had lost his first bid for the office in 1832.

December 2 • In his annual message to Congress, President Jackson calls attention to the failure of France to pay the first installment due on the spoliation agreement of 1831 and requests authorization for reprisals.

International and Cultural Events • Carlists wage a civil war in Spain. The Zollverein is formed by merging customs unions in north and south Germany. George Bancroft publishes the first volume of his *History of the United States.*

United States of America 1835

Events

January • Legislative caucuses in Massachusetts and Tennessee nominate, respectively, Daniel Webster and Hugh L. White for president as part of a Whig strategy to present several candidates in the hope of preventing a Democratic majority and thus transferring the election to the House of Representatives.

January 30 • The president is unharmed in an assassination attempt by Richard Lawrence.

April 25 • France appropriates funds to pay the spoliation claims but demands that President Jackson explain his 1834 call for reprisals. He refuses to do so (December).

May 20 • The Democratic party convenes in Baltimore. It nominates Vice President Van Buren for president and Richard M. Johnson (Kentucky) for vice president.

July 6 • Chief Justice John Marshall dies. On December 28, Roger B. Taney is named to succeed him, but because of opposition in the Senate, he is not confirmed until March 15, 1836.

July 29 • A mob burns abolitionist literature impounded by the Charleston, South Carolina, post office. In Boston, abolitionist William Lloyd Garrison is mobbed on October 21.

October 29 • Radical New York Democrats form the Equal Rights (Locofoco) party.

November • Resistance by the Seminole Indians of Florida to removal to the West causes the Second Seminole War, which lasts until 1843. The Seminoles are led by Osceola until his capture in 1837.

December 15 • President Antonio Lopez de Santa Anna of Mexico promulgates a unitary constitution, thus abrogating the local rights of the Texans.

December 16 • The Anti-Masonic party convenes in Harrisburg, Pennsylvania. It nominates William Henry Harrison (Ohio) for president and Francis Granger (New

The attempted assassination of President Jackson.

24th CONGRESS		
SENATE	. . . .	52 Members
D	. . . .	27
W	. . . .	25
O	. . . .	0
HOUSE	. . . .	243 Members
D	. . . .	145
W	. . . .	98
O	. . . .	0

ESTIMATED POPULATION 15,003,000

Andrew Jackson
7th President
1st Democrat

Martin Van Buren
8th Vice President
Democrat

UNITED STATES ECONOMY

GROSS NATIONAL PRODUCT	. . . . N/A
RETAIL SALES	. . . . N/A
BANK RESOURCES	. . . . $498,000,000
EXPORTS	. . . . $132,000,000
IMPORTS	. . . . $166,000,000
FEDERAL GOVERNMENT EXPENDITURE	. . $ 17,573,000
FEDERAL DEBT	. . . . $ 38,000

York) for vice president. General Harrison is also endorsed by Pennsylvania Whigs.

December 29 • By the Treaty of New Echota, the Cherokee Indians exchange their lands east of the Mississippi River for new land in Indian Territory, to which they are moved by 1838.

International and Cultural Events • Alexis de Tocqueville's *Democracy in America* is published. Samuel Colt patents a revolving breech pistol.

1836 United States of America

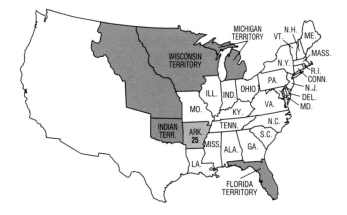

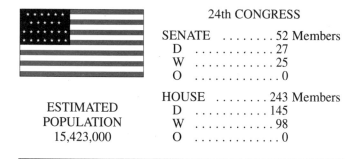

24th CONGRESS

SENATE .... 52 Members
D 27
W 25
O 0

ESTIMATED
POPULATION
15,423,000

HOUSE .... 243 Members
D 145
W 98
O 0

Andrew Jackson
7th President
1st Democrat

Martin Van Buren
8th Vice President
Democrat

UNITED STATES ECONOMY

GROSS NATIONAL PRODUCT .... N/A
RETAIL SALES .... N/A
BANK RESOURCES $622,000,000
EXPORTS $141,000,000
IMPORTS $209,000,000
FEDERAL GOVERNMENT EXPENDITURE .. $ 30,868,000
FEDERAL DEBT .... $ 38,000

Events

January • James G. Birney founds the antislavery newspaper *Philanthropist* in New Richmond, Ohio.
February 23 - March 6 • A large Mexican force under General Santa Anna besieges the Alamo at San Antonio, Texas. The 187 Texan and American defenders are finally overwhelmed and killed.
March 1 • The Bank of the United States is transformed

into a Pennsylvania state bank.
March 1-2 • Texans meeting in convention at Washington, Texas, declare their independence from Mexico and draft a constitution.
March 11 • The Senate adopts the practice of hearing and rejecting abolitionist petitions, but the House, on May 26, passes a "gag" resolution over the objections of John Quincy Adams.
March 17 • Texans adopt a Constitution that legalizes slavery in the new republic.
April 20 • Wisconsin Territory is formed from the western portion of Michigan Territory.
April 21 • Sam Houston, commander of the Texan forces, defeats and captures Santa Anna in the battle of San Jacinto.
April 27-28 • The first antislavery convention in the United States is reportedly held just outside the town of Granville, Ohio, by the approximately 192 delegates of the Ohio Anti-slavery Society. Granville officials had prohibited the society from holding its convention in their town.
May 10 • President Jackson announces that the United States has received four payments due from France on the spoilation claims. Viscount Palmerston, the British foreign secretary, had been responsible for mediating the dispute between France and the United States.
June 15 • Arkansas, a slave state, is admitted to the Union as the 25th state.
June 23 • The Deposit Act (Surplus Revenue Act) is adopted. In addition to providing for the designation of one or more deposit banks in each state, it stipulates that any surplus revenue of the national government exceeding $5 million be distributed among the several states.
June 28 • James Madison, the fifth president of the United States, dies at his Virginia home, Montpelier.
July 11 • At the president's order, the Treasury requires that public land be paid for in specie.
September • Dr. Marcus Whitman arrives in the Oregon country at the head of the first group with women to make the overland journey.
October 22 • Houston is sworn in as president of the Republic of Texas.
December 7 • In the presidential election, Van Buren is elected president, receiving 170 electoral votes to 73 for Harrison, 26 for White and 14 for Webster. Willie P. Mangum (North Carolina) receives 11 votes from South Carolina. The vice-presidential contest does not produce a majority for any of the four candidates, and on February 8, 1837, the Senate decides in favor of Richard M. Johnson, the Democratic nominee.
International and Cultural Events • Louis Napoleon is exiled to the United States after the failure of a military coup in Strasbourg. Ralph Waldo Emerson's anonymously published "Nature" sets forth some basic concepts of American transcendentalism.

Martin Van Buren 1837

Events

January 26 • Michigan, a free state, is admitted to the Union as the 26th state.

February • In *New York v. Miln*, the Supreme Court rules that a state may require incoming ships engaged in interstate or foreign trade to supply data on their passengers despite the constitutional power of Congress to regulate such trade.

February 12 • Mobs demonstrating against high prices ransack flour warehouses in New York.

March 1 • Congress adopts a bill to rescind the Specie Circular of July 11, 1836, but President Jackson pocket-vetoes it.

March 3 • President Jackson recognizes the Republic of Texas (Congress had recommended this step in July 1836).

March 3 • An act of Congress increases the number of justices of the Supreme Court to nine.

March 4 • President Jackson has his Farewell Address published. He urges the various sections of the country to place the Union above local interests.

March 4 • Van Buren is inaugurated president.

March - May • Economic difficulties that have developed during the Jackson administration worsen to produce the Panic of 1837. The Specie Circular of July 1836, coupled with the withdrawal of funds from depository banks to be distributed to the states under the Surplus Revenue Act and the calling of loans by hard-pressed creditors in Great Britain, has served to shrink credit after a period of land speculation and inflation. On May 10, the banks of New York cease to make payments in specie; most other American banks follow suit. Economic distress, marked by substantial unemployment, continues until 1843.

August 4 • The government of Texas asks the United States to annex the republic. The request is refused on August 25, largely because of a desire to avoid the slavery question.

September 5 • President Van Buren asks a special session of Congress to consider a specie currency and government depositories for federal funds. Congress merely authorizes the issuance of $10 million in Treasury notes.

November 7 • Elijah P. Lovejoy, an Illinois publisher of an abolitionist paper, is killed by a mob.

December 19 • The House of Representatives, at the insistence of southern members, adopts an even stricter "gag rule" than the one it had adopted the previous year. The rule, which will be renewed each year until 1844, requires all petitions or papers concerning slavery to be laid on the table.

International and Cultural Events • Victoria ascends the British throne. Horace Mann issues his first *Annual Report* on Massachusetts public education.

25th CONGRESS

SENATE	.... 52 Members
D	 30
W	 18
O	 4

HOUSE	.... 239 Members
D	 108
W	 107
O	 24

ESTIMATED
POPULATION
15,843,000

Martin Van Buren
8th President
2nd Democrat

Richard M. Johnson
9th Vice President
Democrat

UNITED STATES ECONOMY

GROSS NATIONAL PRODUCT	.... N/A
RETAIL SALES	.... N/A
BANK RESOURCES	.... $707,000,000
EXPORTS	.... $133,000,000
IMPORTS	.... $161,000,000
FEDERAL GOVERNMENT EXPENDITURE	.. $ 37,243,000
FEDERAL DEBT	.... $ 337,000

Martin Van Buren	
Birth	.... Kinderhook, NY, Dec. 5, 1782
Parents	.... Abraham and Maria Hoes Van Buren
Married	.... Hannah Hoes
Home	.... Kinderhook, NY
Presidency	.... 1837 – 1841
Death	.... Kinderhook, NY, July 24, 1862

25th CONGRESS

SENATE . . . . 52 Members
D 30
W 18
O 4

HOUSE . . . . 239 Members
D 108
W 107
O 24

ESTIMATED
POPULATION
16,264,000

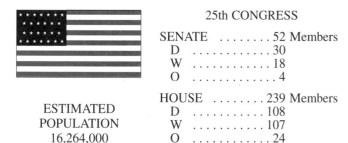

Martin Van Buren
8th President
2nd Democrat

Richard M. Johnson
9th Vice President
Democrat

UNITED STATES ECONOMY

GROSS NATIONAL PRODUCT . . . . N/A
RETAIL SALES . . . . N/A
BANK RESOURCES $682,000,000
EXPORTS $128,000,000
IMPORTS $135,000,000
FEDERAL GOVERNMENT EXPENDITURE . .$ 33,865,000
FEDERAL DEBT . . . .$ 3,308,000

Events

January 5 • Reacting to the destruction by Canadian militia of the *Caroline*, a vessel used in the Niagara River by American sympathizers to supply rebels against British rule in Canada, President Van Buren issues a proclamation of neutrality.

February 14 • Despite the adoption of a new gag rule by the House of Representatives on December 19, 1837,

John Quincy Adams presents 350 antislavery petitions to the House.

May 21 • Congress rescinds the Specie Circular of July 11, 1836.

May 29 • American sympathizers with the Canadian rebels burn the Canadian ship *Sir Robert Peel* in the St. Lawrence River.

June 12 • An act of Congress establishes Iowa Territory, which is formed from the western portion of Wisconsin Territory.

July 7 • Congress declares railroads legal carriers of the mail.

August 13 • Banks in New York resume payments in specie. This step is followed by other banks, but in 1839, Pennsylvania banks suspend specie payments again. Other banks follow suit, and full resumption of specie payments is not achieved until 1842.

August 18 • Captain Charles Wilkes begins a four-year exploring and scientific expedition to investigate the Pacific and Antarctic oceans. The six ships under his command gather much valuable information.

October • The Cherokee Indians still remaining in Georgia are removed by federal troops and dispatched westward along the "Trail of Tears."

October 12 • The Republic of Texas formally withdraws its request for annexation.

November 21 • President Van Buren issues a second proclamation of neutrality. By the end of the year, border incidents with Canada have almost ceased.

December 3 • Joshua Giddings, an Ohio Whig, takes his seat in the House of Representatives and becomes the first avowed abolitionist in Congress.

December 11 • The House of Representatives adopts a new gag rule. It repeats this procedure at each new session until 1844.

International and Cultural Events • The *Great Western* initiates steamship service between New York and Bristol. Reforms demanded by British Chartists include manhood suffrage.

Fashionable dress for fall and winter.

United States of America 1839

Events

January • A dispute over the frontier between Maine and New Brunswick, which has persisted since 1783, when the boundary was inadequately defined in the Treaty of Paris, comes to a head with the appointment by the Maine Legislature of Rufus McIntire as a land agent empowered to expel Canadian lumbermen from the Aroostook area. On February 12, Canadian authorities arrest McIntire. The militia of Maine and New Brunswick are mobilized in what becomes known as the Aroostook War. Congress approves the raising of a force of 50,000 and allocates $10 million, but before any blood is shed, General Winfield Scott, as President Van Buren's emissary, concludes a truce with New Brunswick. By agreement with Great Britain, the frontier is to be determined by a boundary commission. The present line is confirmed by treaty in 1842.

January 12 • Anthracite coal is used successfully to smelt iron in Mauch Chunk, Pennsylvania.

November 13 • Abolitionists of moderate views form the Liberty party at a convention held in Warsaw, New York. The delegates nominate James G. Birney (Kentucky), a former slaveowner, for president and Thomas Earle (Pennsylvania) for vice president.

December 4 • The Whig party convenes in Harrisburg, Pennsylvania. It nominates William Henry Harrison (Ohio) for president and a former states' rights Democrat, John Tyler (Virginia), for vice president. Harrison, the victor of the battle of Tippecanoe, is chosen

	26th CONGRESS
	SENATE . . . . 50 Members
	D 28
	W 22
	O 0
ESTIMATED	HOUSE . . . . 242 Members
POPULATION	D 124
16,684,000	W 118
	O 0

Martin Van Buren
8th President
2nd Democrat

Richard M. Johnson
9th Vice President
Democrat

UNITED STATES ECONOMY

GROSS NATIONAL PRODUCT . . . . N/A
RETAIL SALES . . . . N/A
BANK RESOURCES $702,000,000
EXPORTS $135,000,000
IMPORTS $188,000,000
FEDERAL GOVERNMENT EXPENDITURE . . $ 26,899,000
FEDERAL DEBT . . . .$ 10,434,000

because Henry Clay's views have made him too many political enemies.

International and Cultural Events • The Chinese prohibition of opium imports leads to the Opium War. France recognizes the Republic of Texas. William Talbot and Louis Daguerre publish their separate photographic methods. Charles Goodyear perfects rubber vulcanization, which he patents in 1844.

The inauguration of President Martin Van Buren in the Old House Chamber of the Capitol

57

26th CONGRESS

SENATE .... 50 Members
D 28
W 22
O 0

HOUSE .... 242 Members
D 124
W 118
O 0

ESTIMATED
POPULATION
17,120,000

Martin Van Buren
8th President
2nd Democrat

Richard M. Johnson
9th Vice President
Democrat

UNITED STATES ECONOMY

GROSS NATIONAL PRODUCT .... N/A
RETAIL SALES .... N/A
BANK RESOURCES $658,000,000
EXPORTS $160,000,000
IMPORTS $134,000,000
FEDERAL GOVERNMENT EXPENDITURE .. $ 24,318,000
FEDERAL DEBT .... $ 3,573,000

Events

January 19 • The Wilkes Expedition sights the continent of Antarctica. The discovery is commemorated in the sector later named Wilkes Land in the captain's honor.

March 31 • President Van Buren establishes a 10-hour day for workingmen employed on public works of the federal government.

April 1 • The Liberty party holds a national convention in Albany, New York, at which it confirms the presidential slate of James G. Birney and Thomas Earle, nominated in November 1839.

May 5 • The Democratic party convenes in Baltimore. It nominates President Van Buren for re-election but does not choose a vice president. The convention adopts a platform favoring a strict construction of the Constitution and opposing federal expenditures for public works.

July 4 • President Van Buren signs the Independent Treasury Act, which provides for the creation of government depositories (subtreasuries) for federal funds and the use of specie for all government transactions by June 30, 1843. Passage of the act over strong Whig opposition is made possible by the support of states' rights Democrats.

November–December • Alexander McLeod, A Canadian deputy sheriff, is charged in New York with the death of an American during the destruction of the *Caroline* in 1838. Held for trial over a British protest, he is acquitted in October 1841.

November 13 • Great Britain establishes diplomatic relations with the Republic of Texas. The two countries sign a commercial treaty.

December 2 • In the presidential election, Harrison is elected president, receiving 234 electoral votes to 60 for Van Buren. Tyler is elected vice president, and the Whigs gain control of both houses of Congress.

International and Cultural Events • Queen Victoria marries Albert of Saxe-Cogurg-Botha. The social theorist Pierre-Joseph Proudhon asks *What Is Property?* Richard Henry Dana, Jr., publishes *Two Years before the Mast.*

Pro-Harrison cartoon depicting Kinder & Co. (Van Buren) robbing the U.S. Treasury.

Harrison/Tyler 1841

Events

March 4 • William Henry Harrison is inaugurated president. His cabinet, appointed on March 5 and 6, includes Daniel Webster as secretary of state.

March 9 • In the *Amistad* case, the Supreme Court upholds a decision of a lower court and rules that 53 blacks mutineers be freed. The Africans, who were being transported in a Spanish slave ship in 1839, had mutinied and then were taken into custody by a United States warship.

April 4 • Succumbing to pneumonia, President Harrison dies in Washington. John Tyler becomes the first vice president to succeed to the presidency in this manner.

April 9 • President Tyler states that he intends to be guided by traditional strict-construction principles in setting government fiscal policy.

June 7 • Henry Clay proposes repealing the Independent Treasury Act and establishing a government bank, increasing tariff rates, and distributing funds from the sale of public lands to the states. The act is repealed on August 13.

August 6 • Congress adopts a Whig-sponsored bill to create a new bank called the Fiscal Bank of the United States; the bill is vetoed by President Tyler on August 16.

August 19 • A short-lived uniform bankruptcy law goes into effect. During the three years that it remains on the books, more than 33,730 people voluntarily declare bankruptcy.

September 3 • A second bank bill, designed to meet some of President Tyler's objections to the first bill, is adopted by Congress, but it too is vetoed on September 9. All cabinet members but Webster resign.

September 4 • The Distribution-Preemption Act is adopted. It provides that public land may be purchased at the minimum price after settlement. Although land sale proceeds are to be distributed to the states, this provision is to be rescinded if tariff rates exceed 20 percent (it is rescinded in 1842).

International and Cultural Events • British claim sovereignty over Hong Kong. Brook farm, an American experiment in communal living, attracts such men as Nathaniel Hawthorne and Charles A. Dana.

27th CONGRESS

SENATE . . . . 52 Members
W 28
D 22
O 2

ESTIMATED
POPULATION
17,733,000

HOUSE . . . . 241 Members
W 133
D 102
O 6

William Henry Harrison
9th President
1st Whig

John Tyler
10th Vice President
Whig

UNITED STATES ECONOMY

GROSS NATIONAL PRODUCT . . . . N/A
RETAIL SALES . . . . N/A
BANK RESOURCES $608,000,000
EXPORTS $136,000,000
IMPORTS $148,000,000
FEDERAL GOVERNMENT EXPENDITURE . .$ 26,566,000
FEDERAL DEBT . . . .$ 5,251,000

William Henry Harrison
Birth . . Berkeley, Charles City County, VA, Feb. 9, 1773
Parents . . . . Benjamin and Elizabeth Bassett Harrison
Married . . . . Anna Symmes
Home . . . . North Bend, near Cincinnati, OH
Presidency 1841
Death . . . . Washington, D.C., Apr. 4, 1841

John Tyler
Birth . . Greenway, Charles City County, VA, Mar. 29, 1790
Parents . . . . John and Mary Armistead Tyler
Married . . . . Letitia Christian; Julia Gardiner
Home . . . . . . Sherwood Forest, Charles City County, VA
Presidency . . . . 1841 – 1845
Death . . . . Richmond, VA, Jan. 18, 1862

1842 United States of America

27th CONGRESS

SENATE .... 52 Members
W 28
D 22
O 2

HOUSE .... 241 Members
W 133
D 102
O 6

ESTIMATED
POPULATION
18,345,000

John Tyler
10th President
2nd Whig

Vice President
None

UNITED STATES ECONOMY

GROSS NATIONAL PRODUCT .... N/A
RETAIL SALES .... N/A
BANK RESOURCES $472,000,000
EXPORTS $119,000,000
IMPORTS $119,000,000
FEDERAL GOVERNMENT EXPENDITURE . . $ 25,206,000
FEDERAL DEBT .... $ 13,594,000

Events

January • In *Prigg v. Commonwealth of Pennsylvania*, the Supreme Court rules that a Pennsylvania law forbidding the seizure of fugitive slaves is unconstitutional and that enforcement of the Federal Fugitive Slave Act of 1793 is entirely a federal responsibility. Subsequently personal liberty laws are adopted in northern states.

March 23 • The House of Representatives censures Representative Joshua R. Giddings of Ohio for having presented resolutions opposing slavery and the shipment of slaves in the coastal trade. He resigns his seat but is re-elected in April.

March 30 • The Tariff Act of 1842, raising rates to the level of the Tariff Act of 1832, is adopted.

March 31 • Henry Clay resigns his seat in the Senate to concentrate on improving Whig prospects.

April 18 • Thomas W. Dorr is elected governor of Rhode Island by supporters of a state constitution adopted in 1841 by men disfranchised under the royal charter of 1663, which the state has used as its constitution. Adherents of the old charter re-elect Samuel W. King as governor, and the general assembly calls out the militia to remove the government set up by Dorr in the northwestern part of the state. King asks President Tyler for assistance, but Dorr's supporters are easily dispersed without it. In 1844, Dorr is sentenced to life imprisonment, but he is freed the next year. In 1843, the state adopts a new constitution with liberalized suffrage.

June–October • John C. Frémont leads an exploring expedition to the Rocky Mountains in southern Wyoming.

August 9 • The Webster-Ashburton Treaty, negotiated by the secretary of state and Lord Ashburton for Great Britain, is signed in Washington. The disputed boundary between Maine and New Brunswick is established on the present line by a compromise, and minor adjustments are made to the west. The United States is assured possession of the Mesabi Range, in what is now Minnesota. On August 20, the treaty is ratified by the Senate.

September 11 • An invading Mexican army captures San Antonio, Texas. Hostilities end in 1843 with a truce arranged by the British Minister to Texas.

October 20 • Commodore Thomas ap C. Jones, believing the United States to be at war with Mexico, seizes Monterey, California, but soon leaves.

December 30 • President Tyler states in a message to Congress that the United States will look with disfavor upon the attempt by any power to control the Hawaiian Islands. In 1843, a United States diplomatic representative is sent to Hawaii.

International and Cultural Events • Treaty of Nanking ends the Opium War and opens China to trade. P.T. Barnum opens his American Museum in New York. Chief Justice Lemuel Shaw of the Massachusetts Supreme Court hands down the first judicial decision in the United States upholding the right of workmen to strike, maintain a closed shop and organize labor unions. The case, *Commonwealth of Massachusetts v. Hunt*, rejects the judicial view that labor unions are illegal criminal conspiracies.

United States of America 1843

Events

January • Dorothea Lynde Dix publishes a paper, addressed to the Massachusetts General Court, on the harsh treatment of the insane. Her investigations in the United States and Europe lead to substantial reforms.

May • John C. Frémont's second expedition leaves Missouri. After crossing the Rocky Mountains and exploring the valleys of the Snake and Columbia rivers, the party turns south and then crosses into California via the Carson Pass. From Sutter's Fort, it proceeds down the San Joaquin Valley and then east along the Spanish Trail. It reaches Missouri in July 1844.

May 8 • Daniel Webster resigns as secretary of state. On July 24, he is succeeded by Able P. Upshur.

May 22 • Approximately 1,000 settlers leave Independence, Missouri, for Oregon. Their journey marks the beginning of a large migration westward.

July 5 • American settlers in the Oregon country approve a constitution for a provisional government.

July 12 • Mormon leader Joseph Smith pronounces polygamy a devinely sanctioned practice.

August 14 • The Second Seminole War ends. Almost all the Seminoles have been removed from Florida.

August 23 • President Santa Anna states that Mexico would consider the annexation of Texas by the United States an act of war.

October 16 • Secretary of State Upshur tells Issac Van Zandt, minister of Texas in Washington, that his government is ready to discuss annexation. However,

28th CONGRESS

SENATE .... 54 Members	
W 28	
D 25	
O 1	

ESTIMATED
POPULATION
18,957,000

HOUSE .... 222 Members	
D 142	
W 79	
O 1	

John Tyler
10th President
2nd Whig

Vice President
None

UNITED STATES ECONOMY

GROSS NATIONAL PRODUCT .... N/A
RETAIL SALES .... N/A
BANK RESOURCES $393,000,000
EXPORTS $101,000,000
IMPORTS .... $ 81,000,000
FEDERAL GOVERNMENT EXPENDITURE .. $ 11,858,000
FEDERAL DEBT .... $ 32,743,000

President Sam Houston is reluctant to reopen the question while northern opposition might prevent Senate ratification of an annexation treaty.

International and Cultural events • Great Britain attempts to annex the Kingdom of Hawaii. Oliver Wendell Holmes publishes his controversial *The Contagiousness of Puerperal Fever*.

The Frémont expedition reaches the Rocky Mountains.

28th CONGRESS

SENATE .... 54 Members
W 28
D 25
O 1

HOUSE .... 222 Members
D 142
W 79
O 1

ESTIMATED
POPULATION
19,569,000

John Tyler
10th President
2nd Whig

Vice President
None

UNITED STATES ECONOMY

GROSS NATIONAL PRODUCT .... N/A
RETAIL SALES .... N/A
BANK RESOURCES $427,000,000
EXPORTS $126,000,000
IMPORTS $126,000,000
FEDERAL GOVERNMENT EXPENDITURE ..$ 22,338,000
FEDERAL DEBT .... $ 23,462,000

Events

January 16 • Secretary of State Upshur asks the United States representative in Texas to assure President Houston that an annexation treaty would have the approval of the required two-thirds majority of the United States Senate.

March 6 • Following the death of Upshur in an accident on February 28, John C. Calhoun is appointed secretary of state.

April 12 • A treaty for the annexation of Texas, negotiated by Secretary Calhoun, is signed in Washington. It is submitted to the Senate by President Tyler on April 22.

May • Growing conflict between Protestants and Catholics leads to violence in Philadelphia. The disorder continues until July.

May 1 • The Whig party convenes in Baltimore. It nominates Henry Clay (Kentucky) for president and Theodore Frelinghuysen (New Jersey) for vice president.

May 27 • The Democratic party convenes in Baltimore. It nominates James Knox Polk (Tennessee) for president and George M. Dallas (Pennsylvania) for vice president. The party platform calls for the annexation of Texas and the acquisition of the entire Oregon country: "Fifty-four Forty or Fight."

May 27 • Democrats supporting President Tyler also convene in Baltimore. Although on May 30 he accepts their nomination, he withdraws his candidacy on August 20 and supports Polk.

June 8 • Because of antislavery sentiment, the Senate refuses to ratify the Texas annexation treaty.

June 20 • Samuel F.B. Morse is granted a patent for the telegraph he demonstrated on May 24.

June 27 • Amid growing anti-Mormon sentiment, an angry mob forces its way into the Hancock County jail at Carthage, Illinois, and kills Mormon leader Joseph Smith and his brother, Hyrum.

July 1 and 27 • In two letters Clay, who had opposed the annexation of Texas, states that he favors it under certain conditions. This stand loses him antislavery support in the North.

July 3 • Caleb Cushing negotiates a treaty opening five Chinese ports to American ships.

September 19 • By chance, William Austin Burt, a government surveyor, discovers outcroppings of iron ore near present-day Negaunee, Michigan. The discovery confirmed the existence of large quantities of iron ore in the state.

December 3 • The House of Representatives rescinds the gag rule on antislavery petitions.

December 4 • In the presidential election, Polk is elected president, receiving 170 electoral votes to 105 for Clay, his Whig opponent. Clay's loss of New York's 36 electoral votes because of the defection of antislavery Whigs to Birney proves decisive. Dallas is elected vice president.

December 12 • Anson Jones becomes president of Texas, succeeding Houston.

International and Cultural Events • In Great Britain, a new Factory Act limits the daily working hours of women and of children younger than 13 to 12 and six and one-half hours, respectively.

James Knox Polk 1845

Events

January 23 • A congressional act appoints the Tuesday following the first Monday in November as election day in all states for presidential elections.

February 20 • President Tyler vetoes a bill barring the Treasury from paying for ships that he has ordered. On March 3, for the first time, Congress overrides a presidential veto.

February 28 • As requested by President Tyler in his annual message of December 2, 1844, Congress adopts a joint resolution for the annexation of Texas. This procedure bypasses the requirement of a two-thirds vote of the Senate to ratify a treaty. The resolution authorizes the president to negotiate a new treaty with Texas that could be approved by either procedure, but he does not exercise this option. The resolution is approved on March 1.

March • Mexico and Texas begin discussions leading to Mexican recognition of Texas' independence. These discussions end when Texas learns of the congressional annexation resolution. On March 28, Mexico severs diplomatic relations with the United States.

March 3 • Florida, a slave state, is admitted to the Union as the 27th state.

March 4 • Polk is inaugurated president.

May • The third Frémont expedition to the west begins.

May 28 • President Polk orders General Zachary Taylor, commander of United States forces stationed in Louisiana, to be ready to enter Texas if it is invaded by Mexico. On June 15, Taylor is ordered to the Rio Grande, but he halts near Corpus Christi on July 31.

June 8 • Former president Andrew Jackson dies at his Tennessee home, the Hermitage.

July 4 • A convention in Texas approves annexation to the United States.

October 10 • The U.S. Naval Academy at Fort Severn, Annapolis, Maryland, is formally opened.

December 2 • President Polk, in his annual message to Congress, claims all of Oregon. He also opposes any European interference in North America.

December 16 • The Mexican government refuses to receive John Slidell, sent by President Polk to discuss the boundary of Texas and the sale of California and New Mexico, because of political repercussions from the disclosure of his mission.

December 29 • Texas is admitted to the Union as the 28th state.

International and Cultural Events • Friedrich Engels publishes *The Condition of the Working Classes in England*. Edgar Allan Poe wins fame with *The Raven and Other Poems*. Baseball is codified by Alexander Cartwright.

29th CONGRESS

SENATE	.... 56 Members
D	 31
W	 25
O	 0

HOUSE	.... 226 Members
D	 143
W	 77
O	 6

ESTIMATED
POPULATION
20,182,000

James Knox Polk
11th President
3rd Democrat

George M. Dallas
11th Vice President
Democrat

UNITED STATES ECONOMY

GROSS NATIONAL PRODUCT	.... N/A
RETAIL SALES	.... N/A
BANK RESOURCES	.... $434,000,000
EXPORTS	.... $135,000,000
IMPORTS	.... $138,000,000
FEDERAL GOVERNMENT EXPENDITURE	.. $ 22,937,000
FEDERAL DEBT	.... $ 15,925,000

James Knox Polk

Birth	.... Mecklenburg County, NC, Nov. 2, 1795
Parents	.... Samuel and Jane Knox Polk
Married	.... Sarah Childress
Home	.... Nashville, TN
Presidency	.... 1845 – 1849
Death	.... Nashville, TN, June 15, 1849

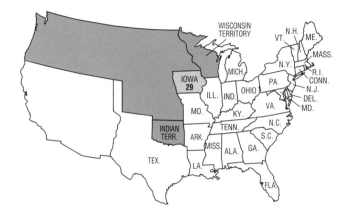

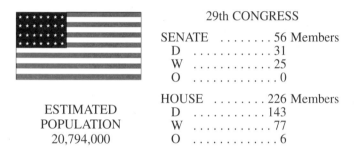

29th CONGRESS

SENATE .... 56 Members
D 31
W 25
O 0

HOUSE .... 226 Members
D 143
W 77
O 6

ESTIMATED
POPULATION
20,794,000

James Knox Polk
11th President
3rd Democrat

George M. Dallas
11th Vice President
Democrat

UNITED STATES ECONOMY

GROSS NATIONAL PRODUCT .... $ N/A
RETAIL SALES .... $ N/A
BANK RESOURCES $456,000,000
EXPORTS $133,000,000
IMPORTS $143,000,000
FEDERAL GOVERNMENT EXPENDITURE .. $ 27,767,000
FEDERAL DEBT .... $ 15,550,000

Events

January 5 • A resolution calling for an end to the Anglo-American occupation of the Oregon country is introduced in the House of Representatives. During the debate reference is made to the "manifest destiny" of the United States to expand over the continent (the phrase had first appeared in a periodical in July 1845).

January 12 • John Slidell's report of the Mexican position is received in Washington. The next day, the president sends orders to General Taylor to move to the Rio Grande.

January 27 • John C. Frémont and his party arrive in Monterey, California. He remains in the area until March 9, when the local authorities force him to move north.

February 6 • Slidell reports that the Mexican government, now headed by General Mariano Paredes, has adopted a rigid position. After the Mexican authorities again decline to receive him, he returns to the United States in late March.

February 11 • Under the leadership of Brigham Young, Mormons living in Illinois begin the hazardous journey to the Great Salt Lake (Utah).

March 28 • Acting on orders from President Polk, General Zachary Taylor relocates his troops from the Nueces River to the left bank of the Rio Grande. Across the river at Matamoros, Mexican troops are hastily constructing a fort, as are the Americans.

April 12 • The commander of the Mexican forces at Matamoros, General Pedro de Ampudia, warns General Taylor to withdraw peacefully from the area or suffer the consequences.

April 23 • Congress adopts a joint resolution to end the Anglo-American occupation of Oregon. President Polk signs the resolution on April 27, and on May 21, he notifies Great Britain that the agreement for joint occupation will be terminated a year later. Great Britain has already expressed interest in fixing the Oregon boundary at 49°N, but President Polk insists that the formal proposal be made by the British.

April 24 • A Mexican force crosses the Rio Grande west of Matamoros. The next day, it attacks and captures a scouting party sent out by General Taylor.

April 25 • President Polk drafts a message asking Congress to declare war against Mexico, citing Mexican president General Mariano Paredes' refusal to receive U.S. representative John Slidell. Events will force Polk to rewrite the message.

April 26 • General Taylor informs Washington of the skirmish, saying that "hostilities may now be considered as commenced." President Polk will receive the dispatch on May 9.

May 3 • Mexican forces besiege Fort Texas. On May 8, on his way to relieve the fort, Taylor defeats the Mexicans at Palo Alto. The next day, he is victorious at Resaca de la Palma and lifts the siege.

May 9 • Upon the receipt of dispatches, Frémont turns south again. Meanwhile, on April 17, Thomas O. Larkin, United States consul in Monterey, receives word of his appointment (October 17, 1845) as an agent to convince the Californians to join the United States.

May 11 • Having received news of the fighting near the Rio Grande, President Polk asks Congress to issue a declaration of war with Mexico. It does so the next day; on May 13, he signs the declaration.

May–June • Blockades of Mexican ports on the Pacific Ocean and the Gulf of Mexico are ordered, and Colonel Stephen W. Kearny is instructed to take Santa Fe and, later, to move on California. The war, which is popular in the West, is bitterly opposed by antislavery forces in the North.

May 18 • General Taylor crosses the Rio Grande and enters the evacuated city of Matamoros.

June 6 • A proposed treaty on the Oregon boundaries, which has been drafted by the British government, is received in Washington. The boundary is drawn westward along the 49th parallel and then curves around Vancouver Island, reaching the Pacific Ocean through Juan de Fuca Strait. President Polk submits the draft treaty to the Senate, which ratifies it on June 15. This compromise permits the administration to pursue the Mexican War without concern for the northern border.

June 14 • American settlers in California take control of Sonoma and proclaim the Republic of California, known as the Bear Flag Republic from the flag they raise. Frémont arrives on June 25 and is placed in command by the settlers on July 5.

July 7 • Commodore John D. Sloat, commander of the United States naval expedition on the Pacific Coast, lands a detachment at Monterey and takes possession of California for the United States. On July 9, his subordinates occupy San Francisco and Sonoma.

August 6 • The Independent Treasury Act is adopted. It restores the system in effect in 1840-1841 under a previous act.

August 8 • The House of Representatives passes a bill appropriating $2 million to be used in peace negotiations with Mexico, that is, to help acquire territory. The bill has been amended by what becomes known as the Wilmot Proviso. Introduced by Representative David Wilmot of Pennsylvania, it would prohibit slavery in any territory acquired from Mexico. The Senate adjourns without acting on the bill.

August 10 • The Smithsonian Institution is established by act of Congress.

August 13 • A force under Commodore Robert F. Stockton, who has succeeded Sloat, occupies Los Angeles. On August 17, Stockton proclaims California's annexation by the United States.

August 15 • Colonel Kearny's expeditionary force arrives in Las Vegas, where he proclaims the annexation of New Mexico by the United States. On August 18, he takes Santa Fe.

September 20-25 • General Taylor, who has advanced into Mexico after ascending the Rio Grande, begins an assault on the city of Monterrey on September 20. It requires four days of hard fighting before the Mexican defenders surrender on September 24 (formally on September 25). After an armistice ending on November 13, Taylor takes Saltillo (November 16).

September 22 • José María Flores leads a revolt of Mexican Californians against United States rule. They retake San Diego and Los Angeles and within a week are in control of southern California. Flores takes office as governor on September 29.

October • Under orders from Kearny, Colonel Alexander W. Doniphan leaves Santa Fe on an expedition to Chihuahua. He takes El Paso on December 27.

December 6 • Kearny, who reached California on November 25, defeats Mexican troops in San Pascual on December 6. On December 12, he occupies San Diego.

December 12 • The United States charge d' affaires in Bogotá, Benjamin A. Bidlack, signs a commercial treaty with the government of New Granada (Colombia). The United States receives transit rights across the Isthmus of Panama and guarantees New Granadan sovereignty over the isthmus.

December 28 • Iowa, a free state, is admitted to the Union as the 29th state.

International and Cultural Events • Second failure of the Irish potato crop; in the next six years, more than 1.5 million Irish emigrate to the United States. At the Massachusetts General Hospital, ether is first used for surgery. Elias Howe is granted a sewing machine patent. Herman Melville publishes *Typee*, tale of Polynesia.

The earliest known photographic image of the Capitol taken about 1846. Later the dome will be replaced and the wings extended.

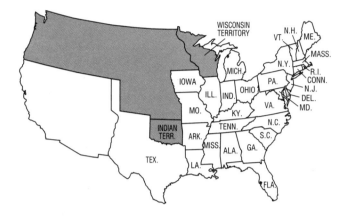

30th CONGRESS

SENATE .... 58 Members
D 36
W 21
O 1

HOUSE .... 227 Members
W 115
D 108
O 4

ESTIMATED
POPULATION
21,406,000

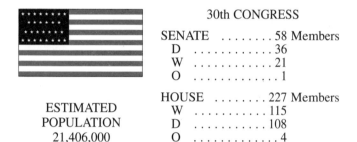

James Knox Polk
11th President
3rd Democrat

George M. Dallas
11th Vice President
Democrat

UNITED STATES ECONOMY

GROSS NATIONAL PRODUCT .... N/A
RETAIL SALES .... N/A
BANK RESOURCES $458,000,000
EXPORTS $181,000,000
IMPORTS $178,000,000
FEDERAL GOVERNMENT EXPENDITURE .. $ 57,281,000
FEDERAL DEBT .... $ 38,827,000

Events

January 3 • General Winfield Scott orders the assignment of 9,000 men in General Taylor's force to a planned assault on Veracruz. Taylor is to halt his advance.

January 10 • General Kearny and Commodore Stockton capture Los Angeles. On January 13, the remaining Mexican belligerents in California sign the Treaty of Cahuenga with Captain Frémont.

January 16 • Commodore Stockton, believing that he, rather than General Kearny, is empowered to establish a civil government in California, appoints Frémont as governor.

February 5 • General Taylor, who has aired his differences with the administration in a letter published in a New York newspaper on January 22, moves west without informing Scott. General Santa Anna, who has been elected president of Mexico (December 1846), moves his forces north from San Luis Potosi. The two armies meet in battle near Buena Vista on February 22 and February 23; Taylor wins a decisive victory. Thereafter, the war in the north remains quiescent.

February 13 • Acting on new orders, General Kearny sets up a new government in Monterey, but Frémont, in Los Angeles, still insists he is governor.

February 15 • The House of Representatives adopts an appropriations bill for negotiations with Mexico. Like the 1846 bill, it has been amended to include the Wilmot Proviso. In the Senate, however, support for the proviso is insufficient, and on March 1, an appropriations bill is passed without it. The House, in turn, approves the Senate bill on March 3.

February 19 • Senator John C. Calhoun, in the debate on the Wilmot Proviso, presents four resolutions in which he defends the right of states to make their own decisions on slavery and denies the power of Congress to require prospective states to agree to special conditions. The states each have rights in the territories, which they own jointly.

February 19 • A relief party from California reaches the Donner party, which has been stranded on the eastern slope of the Sierra Nevadas all winter. Rescuers are surprised to discover evidence of cannibalism. It will take rescuers several trips before they can lead all the survivors out of the mountains. Of the 87 people who left Missouri in the late spring of 1846, only 47 survived.

February 28 • Moving south from El Paso, Colonel Doniphan defeats a Mexican army at Sacramento. The next day, he occupies the city of Chihuahua.

March 3 • Congress authorizes the first U.S. postage stamps. On July 1, a five cent Benjamin Franklin stamp and a 10 cent George Washington stamp will go on sale for the first time.

March 9 • General Scott's expeditionary force lands near Veracruz. The city, besieged by land and sea, surrenders on March 27.

April 8 • Scott leaves Veracruz in the direction of Mexico City. At Cerro Gordo, he defeats a Mexican force under Santa Anna on April 18. Jalapa falls the next day, and Puebla on May 15.

May 31 • After appointing Richard B. Mason governor of California, General Kearny leaves for

Washington with Captain Frémont and Commodore Stockton.

July • Brigham Young leads the Mormons to the valley of the Great Salt Lake, where he founds Deseret (present-day Utah).

August 20 • United States forces take Contreras and Churubusco, near Mexico City. Santa Anna asks for an armistice, and on August 24, the armistice of Tacubaya takes effect.

August 27 • Nicholas P. Trist, special emissary of President Polk, and Mexican representatives engage in peace discussions that end in failure on September 6. The next day, the armistice ends.

September 8 • General Scott's troops fight the Mexicans at Molino del Rey, and on September 12-13, they take Chapultepec. On September 13-14, they enter Mexico City.

September 16 • Santa Anna, who has withdrawn from Mexico City before the entrance of United States troops, resigns as president. Removed from his army command on October 7, he leaves Mexico. On November 11, Pedro María Anaya is elected to succeed him.

September 16 • General Scott issues General Order No. 20, establishing military rule in Mexico.

November 22 • Trist receives word from the Mexican government that it is prepared to negotiate peace terms. Although he has been recalled to Washington, he agrees on December 4 to enter into negotiations.

December 12 • Fearful that a European nation might take possession of the Isthmus of Panama, the Republic of New Granada (Colombia) opens negotiations with the U.S. minister, Benjamin A. Bidlack. On December 12, the two parties sign a commercial agreement by which the United States guarantees the sovereignty of New Granada and the neutrality of the isthmus. In return, New Granada grants the United States right of way across the isthmus. The Senate ratifies the treaty in June 1848.

International and Cultural Events • Liberia is proclaimed an independent republic. Henry Ward Beecher begins his ministry at the Plymouth Congregational Church in Brooklyn and makes its pulpit a sounding board for leading issues. New Hampshire legalizes the 10-hour work day.

General Taylor with some of his staff at Monterrey.

1848 United States of America

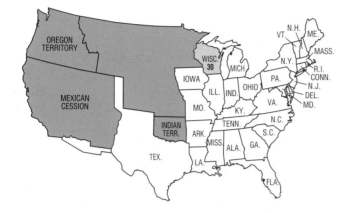

30th CONGRESS

SENATE . . . . 58 Members
D 36
W 21
O 1

HOUSE . . . . 227 Members
W 115
D 108
O 4

ESTIMATED
POPULATION
22,018,000

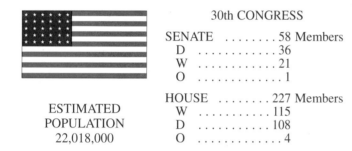

James Knox Polk
11th President
3rd Democrat

George M. Dallas
11th Vice President
Democrat

UNITED STATES ECONOMY

GROSS NATIONAL PRODUCT . . . . N/A
RETAIL SALES . . . . N/A
BANK RESOURCES $512,000,000
EXPORTS $174,000,000
IMPORTS $188,000,000
FEDERAL GOVERNMENT EXPENDITURE . .$ 45,377,000
FEDERAL DEBT . . . .$ 47,045,000

Events

January 24 • While building a sawmill for John Augustus Sutter, James W. Marshall discovers gold about 40 miles up the American River from Sutter's Fort (present-day Sacramento), California.

February 2 • The United States and Mexico sign the Treaty of Guadalupe Hidalgo, which ends the Mexican War. Besides giving up its claims to Texas north of the Rio Grande, Mexico cedes its provinces of California and New Mexico, for which the United States agrees to pay $15 million and assume $3,250,000 in American claims against Mexico. The treaty is ratified on March 10 by a vote of 38 to 14.

May 22 • The Democratic party convenes in Baltimore. It nominates General Lewis Cass (Michigan) for president and General William O. Butler (Kentucky) for vice president.

May 29 • Wisconsin, a free state, is admitted to the Union as the 30th state.

June 7 • The Whig party convenes in Philadelphia. It nominated General Zachary Taylor for president and Millard Fillmore (New York) for vice president.

July 18-19 • Elizabeth Cady Stanton calls a women's rights convention in Seneca Falls, New York.

August 9 • The Free-Soil party, composed of antislavery Democrats and Whigs and supporters of the Liberty party, convenes in Buffalo. It nominates former president Van Buren for president.

August 14 • President Polk signs a bill organizing Oregon Territory with a ban on slavery. The bill had caused great wrangling in Congress, especially when northerners attempted to tie Oregon to the issue of slavery and the newly acquired Mexican territories. Southern members eventually relented and allowed Oregon Territory to be formed without slavery because it was located north of the Missouri Compromise line.

November 7 • In the presidential election, Taylor is elected president, receiving 163 electoral votes to 127 for Cass, his Democratic opponent. It is the first time that all states vote on the same day.

December 5 • President Polk verifies reports of gold in California in his message to Congress.

International and Cultural Events • Paris, Vienna, Venice, Berlin, and Warsaw are shaken by rebellion. Marx and Engels issue the *Communist Manifesto.*

General Winfield Scott enters Mexico City at the head of his troops.

Zachary Taylor 1849

Events

January 22 • Forty-seven southerners sign an "Address of the Southern Delegates." Written by Senator John C. Calhoun, it lists numerous northern acts of aggression against southern rights, including preventing slavery in the territories and failure to help in the capture of fugitive slaves.

February 28 • The *California* arrives at San Francisco with the first gold seekers from the East. During the summer, thousands of "forty-niners" make the overland journey by wagon train.

March 3 • An act of Congress establishes the Department of the Interior.

March 3 • President Polk signs an act creating Minnesota Territory.

March 5 • Taylor is inaugurated president.

June 15 • Former president James K. Polk dies in Nashville, Tennessee.

October 13 • A convention meeting in Monterey adopts a state constitution for California; slavery is forbidden. Once the constitution is ratified, a new state government takes office on December 20.

December 4 • In his message to the new Congress, President Taylor asks that California be admitted to the Union, but southern members are hostile to the recommendation, because slave states would then be outnumbered. Meanwhile, a deeply divided House is unable to elect a speaker until December 22.

International and Cultural Events • Hungarian independence following Louis Kossuth's 1848 revolution is suppressed by Austria. Henry David Thoreau publishes "Civil Disobedience." Amelia Bloomer begins a reform of women's clothing.

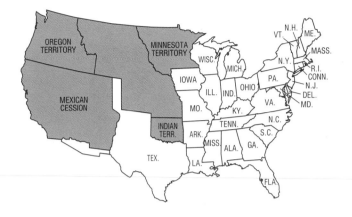

31st CONGRESS	
SENATE	. . . . 62 Members
D	 35
W	 25
O	 2
HOUSE	. . . . 230 Members
D	 112
W	 109
O	 9

ESTIMATED
POPULATION
22,631,000

Zachary Taylor
12th President
3rd Whig

Millard Fillmore
12th Vice President
Whig

UNITED STATES ECONOMY

GROSS NATIONAL PRODUCT	. . . . N/A
RETAIL SALES	. . . . N/A
BANK RESOURCES	. . . .$479,000,000
EXPORTS	. . . .$166,000,000
IMPORTS	. . . .$173,000,000
FEDERAL GOVERNMENT EXPENDITURE	. .$ 45,052,000
FEDERAL DEBT	. . . .$ 63,062,000

Gold seekers in California.

Zachary Taylor	
Birth	Montebello, VA, Nov. 24, 1784
Parents	Richard and Mary Strother Taylor
Married	Margaret Mackall Smith
Home	Baton Rouge, LA
Presidency	1849 – 1850
Death	Washington, D.C., July 9, 1850

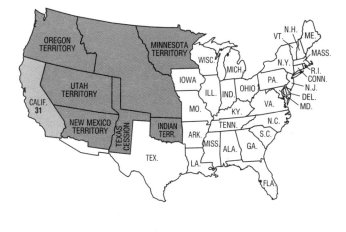

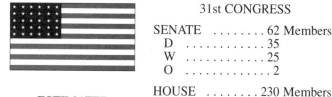

31st CONGRESS

SENATE .... 62 Members
D 35
W 25
O 2

HOUSE .... 230 Members
D 112
W 109
O 9

ESTIMATED
POPULATION
23,261,000

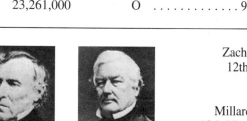

Zachary Taylor
12th President
3rd Whig

Millard Fillmore
12th Vice President
Whig

UNITED STATES ECONOMY

GROSS NATIONAL PRODUCT .... N/A
RETAIL SALES .... N/A
BANK RESOURCES $532,000,000
EXPORTS $135,000,000
IMPORTS $174,000,000
FEDERAL GOVERNMENT EXPENDITURE .. $ 39,543,000
FEDERAL DEBT .... $ 63,453,000

Millard Fillmore

Birth .... Locke, NY, Jan. 7, 1800
Parents .... Nathaniel and Phoebe Millard Fillmore
Married ... Abigail Powers; Caroline Carmichael McIntosh
Home .... Buffalo, NY
Presidency .... 1850 – 1853
Death .... Buffalo, NY, Mar. 8, 1874

Events

January 29 • Alarmed by the growing hostility between North and South and the danger it poses for the Union, Henry Clay offers to the Senate a group of resolutions that he hopes will form a valid compromise. He recommends that California be admitted to the Union as a free state, in accordance with its wishes, and that no reference be made to slavery in organizing other parts of the Mexican cession. The slave trade, but not slavery itself, should be barred in the District of Columbia. The return of fugitive slaves should be facilitated. With regard to Texas, the boundary with New Mexico should be redrawn, the United States government should assume the debt contracted by the Republic of Texas, and the state should cease to claim Mexican territory.

February 5-6 • The great debate on these resolutions is opened by Clay, who pleads with both sides to support the compromise in the interest of the Union and cautions the South not to consider secession as a solution to its problems. The most effective speech in favor of the resolutions is that of Daniel Webster, delivered on March 7, in which he puts the preservation of the Union before all other considerations. The compromise is opposed by antislavery men, such as William H. Seward, and by southern partisans. John C. Calhoun's speech in defense of southern rights is read for him on March 4 (he dies on March 31).

March 12 • California requests that it be admitted to the Union.

April 18 • The Senate refers the resolutions to a select committee, which, on May 8, recommends an omnibus bill on California, the territories, and the Texas–New Mexico boundary and a second bill barring the slave trade in the District of Columbia.

April 19 • The Clayton-Bulwer Treaty, negotiated by Secretary of State John M. Clayton and Sir Henry Bulwer for Great Britain, is signed in Washington. It provides for joint control and protection of the projected isthmian canal.

May 25 • Unwilling to wait for Congress, residents of what will become the New Mexico Territory form their own state government, banning slavery in the process. Congress does not recognize their actions.

June 3-12 • Southern leaders hold a convention in Nashville to discuss slavery and southern rights. Secessionists are outnumbered, and moderate views prevail. The delegates adopt, among others, a resolution advocating the extension of the 36°30´ line of the Missouri Compromise to the Pacific Ocean.

June 17 • A fire aboard the *Griffith*, a steamship on Lake Erie, kills 300 people.

United States of America 1850

July 9 • President Taylor dies, and (July 10) Vice President Fillmore is sworn in as president.

July 25 • Gold is discovered in the Oregon Territory along the Rogue River (southwestern Oregon).

September 6 • Congress adopts the first of five measures constituting what is called the Compromise of 1850. The Texas and New Mexico Act, which is signed by President Fillmore on September 9, provides for the organization of New Mexico Territory and the adjustment of its boundary with Texas. States formed from the territory are to make their own constitutional provisions regarding slavery. The Utah Act, also signed on September 9, creates a territory in the same way as New Mexico Territory.

September 7 • A bill admitting California to the Union as a free state (the 31st state) is adopted. It is signed by President Fillmore on September 9.

September 12 • Congress adopts the Fugitive Slave Act. Signed by President Fillmore on September 18, it authorizes the imposition of fines, imprisonment, and the assessment of civil damages in cases of interference with the capture of fugitive slaves. In the North, states adopt new personal liberty laws, and individuals aid the underground railroad.

September 17 • Congress adopts a bill forbidding all trade in slaves within the District of Columbia. It is signed by the president on September 20.

September 28 • Flogging is abolished as a punishment in the U.S. Navy.

November 11-18 • A second convention is held in Nashville. The few delegates who attend maintain that the South has a constitutional right to secede. A more typical attitude is that of a state convention in Georgia, which, on December 10, declares that Georgia wishes to remain in the Union, although it will secede if the compromise is violated.

International and Cultural Events • Count Cavour, architect of Italian unification, is appointed to the Piedmontese Cabinet. Wordsworth dies, and Tennyson is made Great Britain's poet laureate. Hawthorne publishes *The Scarlet Letter*. Jenny Lind, the "Swedish Nightingale," debuts at the Castle Garden Theater in New York City.

Daniel Webster addressing the Senate.

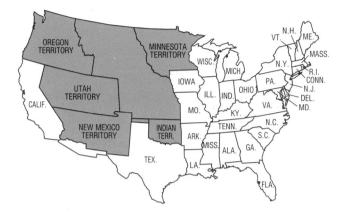

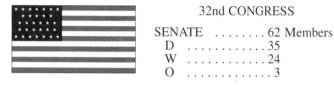

32nd CONGRESS

SENATE .... 62 Members
D 35
W 24
O 3

HOUSE .... 233 Members
D 140
W 88
O 5

ESTIMATED
POPULATION
24,086,000

Millard Fillmore
13th President
4th Whig

Vice President
None

UNITED STATES ECONOMY

GROSS NATIONAL PRODUCT .... N/A
RETAIL SALES .... N/A
BANK RESOURCES $597,000,000
EXPORTS $170,000,000
IMPORTS $211,000,000
FEDERAL GOVERNMENT EXPENDITURE .. $ 47,709,000
FEDERAL DEBT .... $ 68,305,000

Events

March 3 • An act of Congress authorizes the coinage of silver three-cent pieces. At the same time a three-cent postal rate is adopted.

April 25 • President Fillmore issues a proclamation warning against filibustering expeditions against Cuba, in which annexationists from the South have participated to stimulate a rebellion against Spanish rule.

May 19 • The first train on the Erie Railroad, which runs for 483 miles between Piermont, New York, and Lake Erie, arrives at terminus in Dunkirk.

June 5 • Harriet Beeher Stowe's novel *Uncle Tom's Cabin* begins appearing serially in the *National Era* of Washington. In 1852, it is published as a book, and by the next year, more than a million copies have been sold. Its critical picture of slavery does much to influence public opinion in the North.

July 23 • Sioux Indians sign the Treaty of Traverse des Sioux with representatives of the United States government. They agree to cede their lands in northern Iowa and southern Minnesota.

August 16 • Fifty-one American Southerners captured in an unsuccessful filibustering expedition are executed in Havana. Others, sent to Spain, are freed after Congress appropriates $25,000 for riot damage to the Spanish consulate in New Orleans.

September 18 • The first issue of the *New York Daily Times* is published by Henry J. Raymond. The present name, *The New York Times*, is adopted in 1857.

November • The Hungarian patriot Louis Kossuth, hero of the unsuccessful Hungarian revolution of 1848 against the Hapsburgs, receives a warm welcome on a visit to the United States.

December • In *Cooley v. Board of Wardens of the Port of Philadelphia*, the U.S. Supreme Court rules that states may regulate commerce that is local in nature.

December 24 • A fire in the Library of Congress destroys about 35,000 volumes, including a large part of the library that Thomas Jefferson donated in 1815.

International and Cultural Events • Louis Napoleon's coup d'état forces the revision of France's Constitution. The London Exposition's Crystal Palace shows the architectural potential of iron and glass. Herman Melville publishes *Moby Dick*.

At an antislavery meeting in Boston, Wendell Phillips speaks against the fugitive slave act.

United States of America 1852

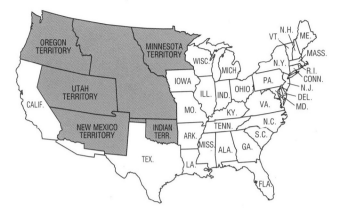

Events

January • George N. Sanders publishes in the *Democratic Review* the first of a series of articles on "Young America," a movement in the Democratic party espoused by such younger men as Stephen A. Douglas. (The term, in a more general sense, has been in use since the 1840s to denote a romantic nationalistic movement whose adherents support the contemporary liberal revolutions in Europe.) Sanders advocates assistance to European republicans, expansion of the United States and free trade.

January • President Fillmore approves the dispatch of an expedition to Japan, to be headed by Commodore Matthew C. Perry, for the purpose of opening the country, which has been almost entirely barred to foreigners since the early 17th century. Perry is to try to obtain assistance for American sailors shipwrecked in Japanese waters, facilities for reprovisioning American merchant vessels and permission to trade in specified Japanese ports. He sails with four ships on November 24.

March 19 • Ohio enacts the first labor law in the United States for the purpose pf protecting children and women in factories. The law establishes a 10-hour workday for children younger than 18 and for women. It further declares that in the absence of a contract stipulating the length of the workday, the workday is to be 10 hours. Legislators, however, failed to incorporate enforcement procedures into the law, an omission that most employers quickly notice. The Ohio Bureau of Labor Statistics will report in 1878 that most Ohio employers are unaware that the law even exists.

June 1 • The Democratic party convenes in Baltimore. It nominates Franklin Pierce (New Hampshire) for president and William R. King (Alabama) for vice president. Its platform supports the Compromise of 1850.

June 16 • The Whig party convenes in Baltimore. It nominates General Winfield Scott (New Jersey) for president and William A. Graham (North Carolina) for vice president. Like the Democrats, the Whigs support the Compromise of 1850. Henry Clay, its architect, dies in Washington on June 29.

August 11 • The Free-Soil party convenes in Pittsburgh. It nominates John P. Hale (New Hampshire) for president and George W. Julian (Indiana) for vice president. Its platform opposes the Compromise of 1850.

October 24 • After resigning as secretary of state, Daniel Webster dies in Marshfield, Massachusetts.

November 2 • In the presidential election, Pierce is elected president, receiving 254 electoral votes to 42 for Scott, his Whig opponent. King is elected vice president. Both the Whigs and the Free-Soilers have lost ground. After the election, the American party begins to gather strength.

32nd CONGRESS

SENATE	....	62 Members
D	....	35
W	....	24
O	....	3
HOUSE	....	233 Members
D	....	140
W	....	88
O	....	5

ESTIMATED POPULATION
24,911,000

Millard Fillmore
13th President
4th Whig

Vice President
None

UNITED STATES ECONOMY

GROSS NATIONAL PRODUCT	.................N/A
RETAIL SALES	.............................N/A
BANK RESOURCES	..........................N/A
EXPORTS	...........................$620,000,000
IMPORTS	...........................$155,000,000
FEDERAL GOVERNMENT EXPENDITURE	..$207,000,000
FEDERAL DEBT	......................$ 66,199,000

Founded in 1849 as a secret society, it becomes known as the Know-Nothing party because of its members' professed ignorance of its affairs. Appealing to nativist prejudice, the party opposes both Catholics and foreigners. Its influence reaches its peak in 1854 and 1855.

International and Cultural Events • A plebescite makes France an empire again; Louis Napoleon is now Napoleon III. Victor Emmanuel II of Sardinia appoints Count Cavour his prime minister.

1853 Franklin Pierce

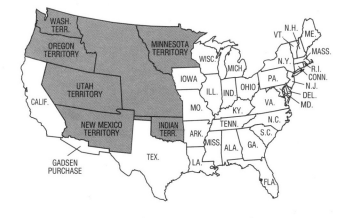

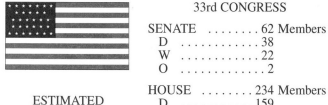

33rd CONGRESS

SENATE	.... 62 Members
D	 38
W	 22
O	 2

HOUSE	.... 234 Members
D	 159
W	 71
O	 4

ESTIMATED POPULATION
25,736,000

Franklin Pierce
14th President
4th Democrat

William R.D. King
13th Vice President
Democrat

UNITED STATES ECONOMY

GROSS NATIONAL PRODUCT	.... N/A
RETAIL SALES	.... N/A
BANK RESOURCES	.... $577,000,000
EXPORTS	.... $190,000,000
IMPORTS	.... $264,000,000
FEDERAL GOVERNMENT EXPENDITURE	.. $ 48,184,000
FEDERAL DEBT	.... $ 59,805,000

Franklin Pierce

Birth	.... Hillsboro, NH, Nov. 23, 1804
Parents	.... Benjamin and Anna Kendrick Pierce
Married	.... Jane Means Appleton
Home	.... Concord, NH
Presidency	.... 1853 – 1857
Death	.... Concord, NH, Oct. 8, 1869

Events

February 21 • The Coinage Act of 1853 is adopted. It establishes a subsidiary silver system by reducing the silver content of coins smaller than the dollar. In addition, $3 gold pieces may now be minted.

March 2 • An act of Congress creates Washington Territory from the northern portion of Oregon Territory.

March 4 • Pierce is inaugurated president. In his inaugural address, he promises to support the Compromise of 1850. He also promises to add more territory to the United States through peaceful means.

March 4 • Congress appropriates $150,000 for an extensive survey of possible transcontinental railroad routes. The War Department will conduct the survey.

April 18 • Suffering from tuberculosis when elected vice president, William Rufus Devine King dies.

May 19 • James Gadsden is instructed to settle with Mexico a dispute over the southern boundary of New Mexico Territory, which has persisted since the signing of the Treaty of Guadalupe Hidalgo in 1848. The acquisition of additional territory by the United States will facilitate a projected railroad route.

July 8 • Commodore Perry's expedition to Japan reaches Yedo Bay (Tokyo Bay). On July 14, he presents to Japanese officials a letter from President Fillmore to the emperor. To allow time for a reply, Perry leaves Japanese waters until early 1854.

December 30 • Gadsden and the Mexican government sign a treaty whereby Mexico sells to the United States land comprising the southernmost areas of what are now New Mexico and Arizona, thus establishing the present United States–Mexico boundary. The treaty is ratified by the Senate on June 29, 1854, after the purchase price has been reduced to $10 million.

International and Cultural Events • Napoleon III weds Eugénie de Montijo. Baron Haussmann begins the replanning that leads to present-day Paris.

Reception at the White House during Pierce's administration.

United States of America 1854

Events

January 4 • Having attempted unsuccessfully since 1850 to organize a new Nebraska territory, Senator Stephen A. Douglas introduces a bill that he hopes will dilute Southern opposition sufficiently to permit passage. The question of slavery is to be decided on the basis of popular sovereignty. On January 23, Douglas reports a second bill, which provides for two territories, Kansas and Nebraska. Since reliance on popular, or squatter, sovereignty abrogates the Missouri Compromise, which bans all slavery north of 36°30′, antislavery leaders are aroused and, on January 24, issue the "Appeal of the Independent Democrats."

February 28 • Spanish officials in Havana seize and fine the United States packet *Black Warrior* when they find a mistake in its papers. The United States minister to Spain, Pierre Soulé, inflates the incident, but Spain apologizes in 1855.

February 28 • Opponents of the Kansas-Nebraska bill, meeting in Ripon, Wisconsin, propose the creation of a new party, the Republican party.

March 31 • After returning to Japan in February with his fleet increased to seven ships, Commodore Perry induces the Japanese government to sign the Treaty of Kanagawa. The treaty, which is promulgated on June 22, 1855, permits American vessels to trade in Hakodate and Shimoda and also obtains facilities for shipwrecked American sailors and the provisioning of ships.

April 26 • Eli Thayer founds the Massachusetts Emigrant Aid Society in order to encourage antislavery settlers to go to Kansas. The society, renamed the New England Emigrant Aid Company in 1855, is responsible for settling about 2,000 people.

May 26 • The Kansas-Nebraska Act, creating two new territories, is adopted by Congress. It is signed by President Pierce on May 30.

June 5 • A treaty extending reciprocal fishing privileges and providing for substantial duty-free imports between the United States and Canada is signed in Washington. The United States annuls it in 1866.

July 6 • Antislavery Michigan men meet in Jackson and assume the name Republican party; they demand that the Fugitive Slave and Kansas-Nebraska acts be repealed. Other state conventions are held on July 13.

October 9 • The United States ministers to Spain, Great Britain and France meet in Ostend, Belgium, to draw up a plan for the acquisition of Cuba by purchase or by force. Sent to Washington as a diplomatic dispatch on October 18, the plan becomes known as the Ostend Manifesto.

November 29 • Kansas residents and a large number of so-called Border Ruffians (Missourians who cross into the territory to vote illegally) go to the polls. With the

	33rd CONGRESS	
	SENATE	62 Members
	D	38
	W	22
	O	2
ESTIMATED	HOUSE	234 Members
POPULATION	D	159
26,561,000	W	71
	O	4

Franklin Pierce
14th President
4th Democrat

Vice President
None

UNITED STATES ECONOMY

GROSS NATIONAL PRODUCT	N/A
RETAIL SALES	N/A
BANK RESOURCES	.$795,000,000
EXPORTS	.$214,000,000
IMPORTS	.$289,000,000
FEDERAL GOVERNMENT EXPENDITURE . .	.$ 58,045,000
FEDERAL DEBT	.$ 42,244,000

help of the Missourians' votes, proslavery candidate John W. Whitfield wins the election for non-voting delegate to Congress. Whitfield defeated his free-state opponents, J.A. Wakefield and R.P. Flenneken, by a vote of 2,258 to 248 and 305, respectively.

International and Cultural Events • The Crimean War victory at Balaklava is celebrated in Tennyson's "Charge of the Light Brigade." Thoreau publishes *Walden; or, Life in the Woods.*

1855 United States of America

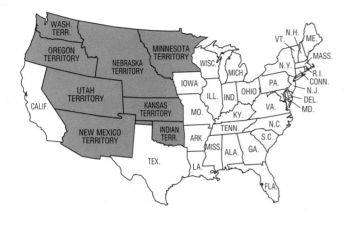

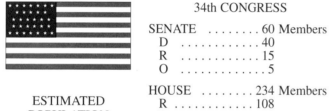

34th CONGRESS

SENATE .... 60 Members
D 40
R 15
O 5

HOUSE .... 234 Members
R 108
D 83
O 43

ESTIMATED
POPULATION
27,386,000

Franklin Pierce
14th President
4th Democrat

Vice President
None

UNITED STATES ECONOMY

GROSS NATIONAL PRODUCT	N/A
RETAIL SALES	N/A
BANK RESOURCES	$817,000,000
EXPORTS	$193,000,000
IMPORTS	$258,000,000
FEDERAL GOVERNMENT EXPENDITURE	$ 59,743,000
FEDERAL DEBT	$ 35,588,000

Events

March 3 • The Ostend Manifesto is published. Spain is indignant, and antislavery northerners charge the administration with attempting to enlarge slave territory. Secretary of State William L. Marcy disavows the manifesto.

March 30 • In elections held under the threats of about 5,000 Border Ruffians, armed invaders from Missouri, a proslavery territorial legislature is chosen in Kansas.

May 21 • Massachusetts enacts a personal liberty law, which is designed to prevent the enforcement of the federal Fugitive Slave Act. The legislature earlier justified its action by declaring that the law violated the 10th Amendment.

July 2 • The territorial legislature of Kansas, whose election Governor Andrew H. Reeder has allowed to stand for fear of further violence, meets in Pawnee. In Pawnee and Shawnee Mission, where it meets on July 16, it adopts proslavery laws.

July 31 • President Pierce dismisses Governor Reeder on charges of speculating in Kansas land. In fact, his removal on this pretext makes it possible to install proslavery advocate Wilson Shannon.

August 4 • President Pierce names Townsend Harris as consul general to Japan.

September 5 • Antislavery Kansas settlers, meeting in Big Springs, refuse to recognize the proslavery legislature and urge that Kansas be admitted to the Union as a free state. Meanwhile, the settlers form a Free-State party.

October • William Walker, a filibuster from Tennessee, becomes dictator of Nicaragua with the support of local politicians and of American financiers attempting to seize control of the Accessory Transit Company from Cornelius Vanderbilt. His actions are condemned by President Pierce on December 8.

October 1 • John W. Whitfield, elected as delegate to Congress from Kansas Territory in 1854, is re-elected by the votes of proslavery men. On October 9, former Governor Reeder is elected to the same post by Free-State men.

October 23–November 12 • A Convention is held in Topeka by Free-State men. It adopts a constitution forbidding slavery as well as a separate ordinance barring all blacks from Kansas.

November 26–December 7 • As hostility between Free-State and proslavery forces mounts in Kansas, clashes occur on the Wakarusa River. An attack on Lawrence by proslavery men with assistance from Missourians is averted when Governor Shannon ends the "Wakarusa War."

December 15 • Voters in Kansas Territory approve both the Topeka Constitution and the ordinance barring blacks from the territory.

International and Cultural Events • Alexander II becomes czar of Russia. David Livingstone discovers Victoria Falls on the Zambezi River. Walt Whitman publishes *Leave of Grass.* America sings "Listen to the Mocking Bird."

United States of America 1856

Events

January 15 • Free-State voters in Kansas Territory elect a governor, Charles Robinson, and a legislature. On January 24, President Pierce informs Congress that he considers this action rebellious.

February 11 • As open conflict becomes imminent in what soon is known as "Bleeding Kansas," the president calls on the armed contestants to disperse.

February 22 • The American (Know-Nothing) party convenes in Philadelphia. It nominates former president Millard Fillmore for president and Andrew J. Donelson (Tennessee) for vice president. They are also nominated by the Whig party, which convenes in Baltimore on September 17.

March 17 • Senator Douglas introduces a bill providing for the admission of Kansas as a state after a new constitutional convention is held. Republicans want Kansas admitted under the Topeka Constitution. On May 19, Senator Charles Sumner, Republican of Massachusetts, makes a speech, called "The Crime against Kansas," in which he savagely denounces the supporters of slavery, among them Senator Andrew P. Butler of South Carolina. Three days later, Butler's cousin, Representative Preston S. Brooks, beats Sumner with a stick as he sits in the Senate, injuring him so severely that he does not recover until late in 1859.

May 21 • Proslavery Kansans and Border Ruffians attack and loot Lawrence, killing one man. On May 24-25, John Brown and a small band murder five proslavery men at Pottawotamie Creek.

June 2 • The Democratic party convenes in Cincinnati. It nominates James Buchanan (Pennsylvania) for president and John C. Breckinridge (Kentucky) for vice president.

June 17 • The Republican party convenes in Philadelphia. It nominates Colonel John C. Frémont (California) for president and William L. Dayton (New Jersey) for vice president.

July 3 • The House of Representatives votes for the admission of Kansas under the Topeka Constitution, but this act is unacceptable to the Senate, and Congress adjourns on August 30 without taking action.

August 18 • Governor Shannon resigns. John W. Geary, appointed to succeed him on September 9, forstalls an attack on Lawrence on September 15, and the fighting ends.

September • Construction crews, which at their peak totaled 10,000 men, finish work on the Illinois Central Railroad. Measuring 705.5 miles in length, it is the longest railroad in the world to date.

November 4 • In the presidential election, Buchanan is elected president, receiving 174 electoral votes to 114 for Frémont and eight for Fillmore. Breckinridge is elected vice president.

International and Cultural Events • Richard Burton sets out to find the Nile's source. Henry Bessemer invents a steelmaking process. *Harper's Weekly* begins publication in New York. Frederick Douglass, a former slave who will eventually become an advisor to President Lincoln, publishes his autobiography, *My Bondage, My Freedom.*

34th CONGRESS	
SENATE	. . . . 60 Members
D	 40
R	 15
O	 5
HOUSE	. . . . 234 Members
R	 108
D	 83
O	 43

ESTIMATED POPULATION
28,212,000

Franklin Pierce
14th President
4th Democrat

Vice President
None

UNITED STATES ECONOMY

GROSS NATIONAL PRODUCT . . . . N/A
RETAIL SALES . . . . N/A
BANK RESOURCES $880,000,000
EXPORTS $266,000,000
IMPORTS $310,000,000
FEDERAL GOVERNMENT EXPENDITURE . .$ 69,571,000
FEDERAL DEBT . . . .$ 31,974,000

1857 James Buchanan

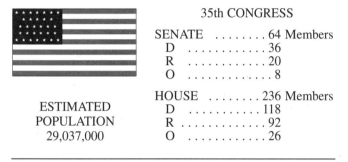

(map of the United States with territories and states labeled)

![U.S. flag]

35th CONGRESS

SENATE	....	64 Members
D	....	36
R	....	20
O	....	8
HOUSE	....	236 Members
D	....	118
R	....	92
O	....	26

ESTIMATED POPULATION
29,037,000

James Buchanan
15th President
5th Democrat

John C. Breckinridge
14th Vice President
Democrat

UNITED STATES ECONOMY

GROSS NATIONAL PRODUCT	.... N/A
RETAIL SALES	.... N/A
BANK RESOURCES	.... $953,000,000
EXPORTS	.... $279,000,000
IMPORTS	.... $348,000,000
FEDERAL GOVERNMENT EXPENDITURE	.. $ 67,796,000
FEDERAL DEBT	.... $ 28,701,000

James Buchanan

Birth	.... Near Mercersburg, PA, Apr. 23, 1791
Parents	.... James and Elizabeth Speer Buchanan
Home	.... Wheatland, near Lancaster, PA
Presidency	.... 1857 – 1861
Death	..... Wheatland, near Lancaster, PA, June 1, 1868

Events

January 12–February 14 • The proslavery territorial legislature of Kansas holds a session in Lecompton. It passes a bill providing for a constitutional convention, but not for ratification of the constitution by the people. Vetoed by Governor Geary, the bill is then repassed.

March 3 • The Tariff Act of 1857 is adopted. It lowers the average duty to 20 percent ad valorem.

March 4 • Governor Geary resigns. On March 24, he is succeeded by Robert J. Walker.

March 4 • Buchanan is inaugurated president .

March 6 • In the Dred Scott case, the Supreme Court rules that Scott, a slave from Missouri who had sued to obtain his freedom, is not a citizen with the constitutional right to sue in a federal court. The fact that he had lived for a short time in the free state of Illinois and for four years in Wisconsin Territory, from which the Missouri Compromise barred slavery, does not make him free under Missouri law. Moreover, the Court holds that the Missouri Compromise is unconstitutional. Northerners condemn the decision.

May 1 • William Walker, his rule in Nicaragua brought to an end by the armies of other Central American countries and the opposition of Cornelius Vanderbilt, whose transisthmian concession Walker had transferred to other interests, surrenders to the United States Navy and leaves the country. When he returns to Nicaragua in November with a new expedition, the U.S. Navy ousts him and sends him back to the United States. A third expedition, to Honduras in 1860, ends in his death.

June 18 • Japan agrees to permit United States ships to trade in Nagasaki.

August 24 • The Panic of 1857 begins with the failure of a branch of the Ohio Life Insurance and Trust Company. Many banks and businesses fail, but by 1859, conditions improve.

October 5 • The Free-State party wins a majority of the seats in the Kansas territorial legislature.

October 19–November 8 • The Lecompton Convention drafts a proslavery constitution for Kansas.

December 8 • President Buchanan asks Congress for troops to quell an alleged Mormon rebellion in Utah. The "Mormon War" will end in compromise.

International and Cultural Events • Giuseppe Garibaldi works for Italian unification under Victor Emmanuel II. The Sepoy rebellion threatens British control of India. John O'Mahony forms the Fenian movement in New York. Elisha Otis's first passenger elevator clears the way for skyscrapers. Members of the Cambridge, Massachusetts, "Saturday Club" launch a new magazine, the *Atlantic Monthly*. James Russell Lowell will serve as the magazine's first editor.

United States of America 1858

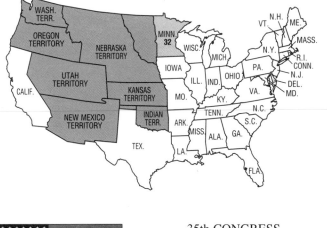

Events

January 4 • The Lecompton Constitution, approved on December 21, 1857, in a vote in which the choice lay between accepting the document with its slavery clause intact or without the clause but with property rights in existing slaves maintained, is presented in a new election, called by the Free-State legislature. Free-State adherents, who had declined to participate in the first election, now have a third alternative: outright rejection of the constitution. Proslavery men do not vote, and the constitution is rejected by a vote of 10,224 to 162.

February 2 • President Buchanan, in a message to Congress, recommends the admission of Kansas under the Lecompton Constitution, that is, as a slave state. Although Stephen A. Douglas and other northern Democrats express bitter opposition to this procedure, the Senate, on March 23, approves a bill incorporating the president's recommendation.

April 1 • The House of Representatives amends the Kansas bill to provide for a new popular vote on the Lecompton Constitution. Because this would not be acceptable to the Senate, Representative William H. English of Indiana offers a compromise that is adopted by Congress on April 30 and signed by the president on May 4. The law provides for a new vote on the constitution, with acceptance bringing statehood and large land grants. However, it is rejected on August 2 by a vote of 11,300 to 1,788.

May 11 • Minnesota, a free state, is admitted to the Union as the 32nd state.

June 16 • Abraham Lincoln, addressing a Republican state convention in Springfield, Illinois, that has endorsed him for the United States Senate, makes a strong antislavery speech in which he says, "'A house divided against itself cannot stand.' I believe this government cannot endure permanently half slave and half free."

July 24 • Lincoln challenges Senator Douglas, the Democratic candidate in the Illinois contest, to meet him in a series of debates. The first debate is held in Ottawa, Illinois, on August 21, and the seventh and last in Alton on October 15. Lincoln presents his views on the immorality of slavery, while Douglas defends popular sovereignty. Republican candidates for the legislature win a greater number of votes than their opponents, but outdated districting produces a Democratic majority, which re-elects Douglas.

July 29 • Japan and the United States agree to enter into diplomatic relations.

October 9 • The first stagecoach belonging to the Overland Mail Company, a John Butterfield and William G. Fargo company, reaches St. Louis, Missouri. It took the

35th CONGRESS	
SENATE .... 64 Members	
D 36	
R 20	
O 8	
HOUSE .... 236 Members	
D 118	
R 92	
O 26	

ESTIMATED
POPULATION
29,862,000

James Buchanan
15th President
5th Democrat

John C. Breckinridge
14th Vice President
Democrat

UNITED STATES ECONOMY

GROSS NATIONAL PRODUCT .... N/A
RETAIL SALES .... N/A
BANK RESOURCES $849,000,000
EXPORTS $251,000,000
IMPORTS $263,000,000
FEDERAL GOVERNMENT EXPENDITURE . .$ 74,185,000
FEDERAL DEBT .... $ 44,913,000

Concord coach 23 days and four hours to travel the distance between San Francisco, California, and St. Louis.

Fall • The discovery of gold on Cherry Creek in Kansas Territory (90 miles from Pike's Peak) starts a second gold rush west.

International and Cultural Events • Jews may now sit in Parliament; after the Sepoy rebellion, the East India Company loses its powers to the crown. Cyrus W. Field lays the first Atlantic cable.

SENATE . . . . 66 Members
D 36
R 26
O 4

HOUSE . . . . 237 Members
R 114
D 92
O 31

ESTIMATED
POPULATION
30,687,000

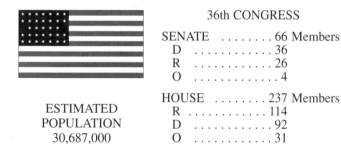

James Buchanan
15th President
5th Democrat

John C. Breckinridge
14th Vice President
Democrat

UNITED STATES ECONOMY

GROSS NATIONAL PRODUCT . . . . N/A
RETAIL SALES . . . . N/A
BANK RESOURCES $983,000,000
EXPORTS $278,000,000
IMPORTS $331,000,000
FEDERAL GOVERNMENT EXPENDITURE . . $ 69,071,000
FEDERAL DEBT . . . . $ 58,498,000

Events

February 14 • Oregon, a free state, is admitted to the Union as the 33rd state.

March 7 • In *Albleman v. Booth*, the Supreme Court rules that state courts may not issue writs of habeas corpus to free federal prisoners and that the Fugitive Slave Act of 1850 is constitutional.

May 12 • The Southern Commercial Convention, meeting in Vicksburg, Mississippi, calls for the repeal of laws barring trade in foreign slaves.

June • The Comstock Lode is discovered near present-day Virginia City, Nevada. This silver strike, the first major one of its kind in the United States, increases the "gold fever" gripping the country.

October 4 • The people of Kansas Territory ratify an antislavery constitution drawn up at Wyandotte.

October 16 • As part of a plan to free slaves, John Brown leads an armed raid on Harper's Ferry, Virginia (now West Virginia), seizing the federal armory and arsenal. He receives no support, however, and on October 18, he is captured by Colonel Robert E. Lee, commanding a force of United States Marines. Convicted of treason and criminal conspiracy, he is hanged at Charlestown on December 2.

November 22 • Great Britain returns the Bay Islands to Honduras. In 1860, it relinquishes its protectorate over the Mosquito Coast of Nicaragua. By these steps, the British remove causes for recrimination by the United States in the isthmian area.

December 14 • Georgia adopts a law prohibiting the manumission of slaves in wills or deeds.

December 19 • In his annual address to Congress, President Buchanan tells members that the foreign slave traffic will be stopped.

International and Cultural Events • Work is begun on the Suez Canal. Charles Darwin publishes *Origin of Species*, and J. S. Mill *On Liberty*. First American oil well is drilled near Titusville, Pennsylvania, by Edwin L. Drake. "Dixie," written by Dan Decatur Emmett, is first sung publicly in New York City in April.

President James Buchanan and members of his cabinet. From left to right: Secretary of the Interior Jacob Thompson; Secretary of State Lewis Cass; Secretary of War John B. Floyd; President Buchanan; Secretary of the Treasury Howell Cobb; Secretary of the Navy Isaac Toucey; Postmaster General Joseph Holt; and Attorney General Jeremiah S. Black.

United States of America 1860

Events

February 2 • Senator Jefferson Davis presents resolutions on slavery based on the extreme southern position. He maintains that slavery cannot be prohibited in the territories and, indeed, should be protected there. In the same vein, he states that it is unconstitutional to attack the practice of slavery in the slave states and that states should not interfere with each other's institutions. The Senate approves the resolution on May 24.

February 27 • In a speech at Cooper Union in New York, Abraham Lincoln is conciliatory toward the South but firm on the question of slavery in the territories.

April 3 • The Pony Express begins its 18 months of existence with the dispatch of the first rider west from St. Joseph, Missouri. With about 200 stations linking St. Joseph and San Francisco, California, the Pony Express eventually becomes too costly to operate. The completion of the transcontinental telegraph in October 1861 will doom the express.

April 23 • The Democratic party convenes in Charleston, South Carolina. On April 30, after the convention refuses to adopt an extreme pro-slavery platform, the delegates from eight southern states leave. On May 3, the convention adjourns without making a nomination.

May 9 • The Constitutional Union party is formed in Baltimore by former adherents of the American and Whig parties. The new party nominates John Bell (Tennessee) for president and Edward Everett (Massachusetts) for vice president.

May 16 • The Republican party convenes in Chicago. It nominates Abraham Lincoln (Illinois) for president and Hannibal Hamlin (Maine) for vice president.

June 18 • The Democratic party reconvenes in Baltimore. It nominates Stephen A. Douglas (Illinois) for president and Herschel V. Johnson (Georgia) for vice president.

June 28 • The southern Democrats who left the Charleston Convention convene in Baltimore. They nominate Vice President John C. Breckinridge for president and Joseph Lane (Oregon) for vice president.

November 6 • In the presidential election, Lincoln is elected president. He receives 180 electoral votes to 72 for Breckinridge, 39 for Bell, and 12 for Douglas.

December 3 • In his annual message to Congress, President Buchanan says that the federal government cannot legally use force to bar secession.

December 20 • A state convention called after Lincoln's election meets in Columbia, South Carolina, and votes to secede from the United States.

December 26 • Under the cover of darkness, Major Robert Anderson, commander of the federal forts in Charleston harbor, moves his force from Fort Moultrie to

	36th CONGRESS
	SENATE .... 66 Members
	D 36
	R 26
	O 4
ESTIMATED	HOUSE .... 237 Members
POPULATION	R 114
31,513,000	D 92
	O 31

James Buchanan
15th President
5th Democrat

John C. Breckinridge
14th Vice President
Democrat

UNITED STATES ECONOMY

GROSS NATIONAL PRODUCT	N/A
RETAIL SALES	N/A
BANK RESOURCES	$ 1,000,000,000
EXPORTS	$ 316,000,000
IMPORTS	$ 354,000,000
FEDERAL GOVERNMENT EXPENDITURE ..$	63,131,000
FEDERAL DEBT	$ 64,844,000

the more defensible Fort Sumter.

December 27 • In the first overt act of the upcoming war, South Carolina troops occupy Fort Moultrie and Castle Pinckney.

December 30 • South Carolina troops seize the federal arsenal at Charleston.

International and Cultural Events • Garibaldi's Red Shirts take Sicily and Naples. The prince of Wales, later Edward VII, tours the United States and Canada.

81

1861 Abraham Lincoln

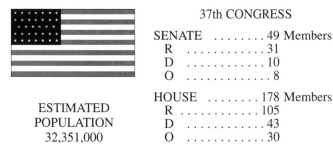

37th CONGRESS

SENATE . . . . 49 Members
R 31
D 10
O 8

HOUSE . . . . 178 Members
R 105
D 43
O 30

ESTIMATED
POPULATION
32,351,000

Abraham Lincoln
16th President
1st Republican

Hannibal Hamlin
15th Vice President
Republican

UNITED STATES ECONOMY

GROSS NATIONAL PRODUCT . . . . N/A
RETAIL SALES . . . . N/A
BANK RESOURCES . . . .$ 1,016,000,000
EXPORTS . . . .$ 205,000,000
IMPORTS . . . .$ 289,000,000
FEDERAL GOVERNMENT EXPENDITURE . .$ 66,547,000
FEDERAL DEBT . . . .$ 90,582,000

Abraham Lincoln	
Birth	Near Hodgenville, KY, Feb. 12, 1809
Parents	Thomas and Nancy Hanks Lincoln
Married	Mary Todd
Home	Springfield, IL
Presidency	1861 – 1865
Death	Washington, D.C., Apr. 15, 1865

Events

January 3 • The Delaware General Assembly, a slave state, votes unanimously not to secede.

January 3 • Georgia takes over Fort Pulaski. On January 24, it seizes the federal arsenal in Augusta.

January 4 • Alabama takes over the arsenals at Mount Vernon, Fort Gaines and Fort Morgan.

January 6 • Florida takes over the federal arsenal in Apalachicola.

January 9 • Mississippi adopts an ordinance of secession. Similar ordinances are adopted by Florida on January 10, Alabama on January 11, Georgia on January 10, Louisiana on January 26, and Texas on February 1. The Texas ordinance is approved by popular vote on February 23.

January 9 • A ship sent by President Buchanan to supply Fort Sumter is forced to leave when it is fired upon in Charleston harbor.

January 10 • Louisiana seizes the federal barracks and arsenal in Baton Rouge.

January 29 • Kansas, a free state, is admitted to the Union as the 34th state.

February 4 • Delegates from Alabama, Florida, Georgia, Louisiana, Mississippi and South Carolina meet in convention in Montgomery, Alabama. On February 8, they form a provisional government of the Confederate States of America, and the next day, they elect Jefferson Davis (Mississippi) provisional president and Alexander H. Stephens (Georgia) vice president. Davis is inaugurated in Montgomery on February 18. Texas joins the Confederacy on March 2, and on March 11, the delegates adopt a permanent constitution that is similar to the U.S. Constitution except for its emphasis on states' rights and its protection of slavery.

February 4 • A peace convention, summoned by the general assembly of Virginia, is held in Washington under the chairmanship of former president Tyler. Delegates from 21 northern and southern states approve a compromise plan to restore the Union, but it proves unsatisfactory.

February 8 • Arkansas takes over the federal arsenal in Little Rock.

February 16 • Texas takes over the federal arsenal in San Antonio. Two days later, all federal posts in the state are yielded by General David E. Twiggs.

February 28 • Colorado Territory is created by an act of Congress, which on March 2 also creates Dakota and Nevada territories.

March 2 • The Morill Tariff Act is adopted. Duties are increased by as much as 10 percent in order to protect American manufactures.

March 4 • Lincoln is inaugurated president. In his inaugural address, Lincoln states that the Union is perpetual and cannot be dissolved by an act of secession. He assures the South that it will not be attacked and that federal power will be used only to possess the property of the government.

March 4 • A state convention in Missouri votes against secession.

April 6 • Having reluctantly decided that the garrison holding out at Fort Sumter must be resupplied, President Lincoln informs the governor of South Carolina that he is sending a relief expedition with provisions only. On April 11, however, General Pierre G.T. Beauregard, in charge of Confederate forces in Charleston, asks the commander of the fort, Major Robert Anderson, to surrender. Although Major Anderson refuses to do so, he says that his food supplies will soon run out. The Confederate authorities decide not to wait and, on April 12, open fire. After being bombarded from shore for more than 30 hours, the garrison surrenders on April 13. The garrison suffered no casualties during the bombardment.

April 15 • President Lincoln issues a proclamation asking the states for 75,000 volunteers to combat an insurrection. The Civil War begins.

April 17 • Influenced by President Lincoln's proclamation, Virginia secedes from the Union. Its example is followed by Arkansas on May 6, Tennessee on May 7, and North Carolina on May 20.

April 19 • Southern ports are blockaded by a presidential proclamation.

April 19 • A secessionist mob stones U.S. troops in Baltimore, killing four. They are the first casualties of the war.

May 13 • Great Britain declares its neutrality in the ongoing civil conflict. Southerners had hoped that it would enter the war on their side.

May 20 • The general assembly of Kentucky adopts a resolution of neutrality.

May 21 • Richmond, Virginia, becomes the capital of the Confederacy.

May 25 • John Merryman, a secessionist from Baltimore, is imprisoned in Fort McHenry. Chief Justice Taney issues a writ of habeas corpus, which the commander of the fort refuses to honor on the ground that he has presidential authorization not to do so. Taney gives his opinion that only Congress can suspend habeas corpus. Although Lincoln maintains his position, he subsequently obtains congressional authorization.

June 11–19 • The people of western Virginia form a Unionist government at a convention in Wheeling.

July 21 • A Union force commanded by General Irvin McDowell, advancing toward Richmond, attacks a Confederate force under General Beauregard at Manassas Junction, Virginia. In the ensuing First Battle of Bull Run, Beauregard, aided by a force led by General Joseph E. Johnston and a valiant stand by General Thomas J. Jackson (henceforth known as Stonewall Jackson), defeats the Union force, which retreats in disorder to Washington.

July 24 • Major General George B. McClellan is named to replace General McDowell. On November 1, he becomes general-in-chief of the Union Army.

August 5 • Congress adopts an income tax.

August 16 • President Lincoln prohibits all trade with the states that have seceded.

August 30 • In St. Louis, Major General Frémont, commander of the Western Department, orders the emancipation of rebel slaves. Lincoln countermands this order; Frémont is transferred.

November 8 • Two Confederate commissioners are taken from the British steamship *Trent* by a United States naval vessel, causing a diplomatic incident. On December 26, their release is ordered.

December 20 • The Joint Committee on the Conduct of the War is established by Congress at the instigation of critics of the administration.

International and Cultural Events • The Kingdom of Italy is proclaimed under Victor Emmanuel II. Czar Alexander II emancipates the serfs. Modern psychiatric theory is foreshadowed in Oliver Wendell Holmes's *Elsie Venner*. After "Dixie," introduced in 1859 by the Northern minstrel Dan Emmett, is played at Jefferson Davis' inauguration, it becomes identified with the Confederacy.

The bombardment of Fort Sumter.

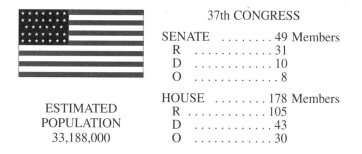

37th CONGRESS

SENATE .... 49 Members
R 31
D 10
O 8

HOUSE .... 178 Members
R 105
D 43
O 30

ESTIMATED
POPULATION
33,188,000

Abraham Lincoln
16th President
1st Republican

Hannibal Hamlin
15th Vice President
Republican

UNITED STATES ECONOMY

GROSS NATIONAL PRODUCT .... N/A
RETAIL SALES .... N/A
BANK RESOURCES .... $ 1,012,000,000
EXPORTS .... $ 180,000,000
IMPORTS .... $ 189,000,000
FEDERAL GOVERNMENT EXPENDITURE ..$ 474,762,000
FEDERAL DEBT .... $ 524,178,000

Events

January 15 • Edwin M. Stanton is named secretary of war.

February • Residents living in the far western counties of Virginia, which comprised the area of the "Restored Government" of Virginia, ratify a constitution for their proposed state.

February 6 • As the first step in a campaign against Confederate positions in the Mississippi Valley, Union forces led by General Ulysses S. Grant and Commodore Andrew J. Foote take Fort Henry on the Tennessee River.

February 8 • As part of the blockade against the Confederacy, General Ambrose E. Burnside seizes Roanoke Island, North Carolina. On March 14, he takes New Bern.

February 13–16 • General Grant besieges Fort Donelson on the Cumberland River and forces its surrender. Nashville, Tennessee, left unprotected, falls to the Union on February 25.

March 9 • The Union low-decked ironclad *Monitor*—"a Yankee cheesbox on a raft"—and the Confederate ironclad *Virginia* (the former USS *Merrimack*) duel at Hampton Roads, Virginia. The *Virginia* is forced to withdraw.

March 11 • President Lincoln removes General McClellan from overall command, but leaves him as commander of the Army of the Potomac.

March 15–April 7 • Union land and naval forces besiege the heavily fortified Island No. 10 in the Mississippi River, forcing its surrender.

April 4 • The Peninsular Campaign begins when General McClellan's Army of the Potomac, which has been transported to Fort Monroe, Virginia, moves on Yorktown, aiming to take Richmond.

April 6-7 • General Albert Sidney Johnston's Confederate troops, joined by Beauregard's, attack Grant's position at Pittsburg Landing, Tennessee. In the ensuing battle of Shiloh, the Union forces are hardpressed until General Don Carlos Buell arrives with reinforcements. The Confederate troops then withdraw to Corinth, Mississippi. Both sides suffer very heavy casualties; General Johnston is killed.

April 11 • To help blockade Savannah, Georgia, Union forces take Fort Pulaski.

April 16 • An act of Congress provides for compensated emancipation in the District of Columbia.

April 26 • Union forces take Fort Macon, North Carolina.

May 1 • New Orleans falls to Union forces after a squadron commanded by Admiral David G. Farragut breaches its defenses.

May 4 • McClellan's forces take Yorktown. Advancing to White Horse, they establish a base on May 14. Expected reinforcements do not arrive because a daring campaign led by Stonewall Jackson in the Shenandoah Valley alarms Washington.

May 10 • Union forces take Norfolk, Virginia.

May 15 • The Department of Agriculture is created.

May 20 • President Lincoln signs the Homestead Act, which enables any adult head of a household to acquire 160 acres of surveyed land after living on it for five years and paying a nominal fee.

May 31-June 1 • A Confederate force led by General

Joseph E. Johnston attacks McClellan in the inconclusive but costly battle of Fair Oaks (Seven Pines).

June 1 • General Robert E. Lee is named to command the Confederate Army of Northern Virginia.

June 19 • An act of Congress prohibits slavery in United States territories.

June 25–July 1 • General Lee attacks McClellan's forces in a series of hard-fought encounters known as the Seven Days' Battles. McClellan withdraws to Harrison's Landing on the James River.

July 1 • The secession of Southern states having made a northern route possible, Congress passes the Pacific Railway Act. The act authorizes the construction of the transcontinental track from both ends. The Union Pacific Railroad is to build westward from Nebraska, and the Central Pacific Railroad is to build eastward from California. They will eventually meet in Utah.

July 2 • President Lincoln signs the Morrill Act, which provides public land grants to support state agricultural and mechanical colleges.

July 11 • General Henry W. Halleck is named general-in-chief of the Union Army.

August 9 • General Jackson defeats units of General John Pope's advancing Union forces at Cedar Mountain, Virginia.

August 29–30 • In the Second Battle of Bull Run, General Lee defeats General Pope's forces, which retreat toward Washington.

September 15 • A Confederate force under General Jackson seizes Harper's Ferry.

September 17 • An advance into Maryland by General Lee is repulsed by Union forces under General McClellan in the costly battle of Antietam, fought near Sharpsburg. Both sides suffered more than 10,000 casualties, making it the bloodiest single-day of fighting in the entire war.

September 22 • President Lincoln issues the Preliminary Emancipation Proclamation, ordering the freeing of all slaves in those areas in rebellion on January 1, 1863.

October 8 • General Buell defeats a Confederate force under General Braxton Bragg at Perryville, Kentucky. The bloodiest battle fought in Kentucky, the battle of Perryville stops the Confederate advances into the state.

November 7 • President Lincoln replaces General McClellan, who has delayed in pursuing Lee, with General Ambrose E. Burnside.

December 13 • Attacking General Lee's forces at Fredericksburg, Virginia, General Burnside loses so many men that he is forced to withdraw.

International and Cultural Events • Otto von Bismarck, shaper of the future German empire, becomes premier of Prussia. Richard J. Gatling—his name has given us the word *gat*—demonstrates his multiple-firing gun. James McNeill Whistler's painting *The White Girl* is a Paris sensation.

The Second Battle of Bull Run.

1863 United States of America

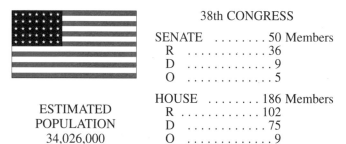

ESTIMATED
POPULATION
34,026,000

38th CONGRESS

SENATE	.... 50 Members
R	 36
D	 9
O	 5

HOUSE	.... 186 Members
R	 102
D	 75
O	 9

Abraham Lincoln
16th President
1st Republican

Hannibal Hamlin
15th Vice President
Republican

UNITED STATES ECONOMY

GROSS NATIONAL PRODUCT	.... N/A
RETAIL SALES	.... N/A
BANK RESOURCES	...................$ 1,209,000,000
EXPORTS	...........................$ 186,000,000
IMPORTS	............................$ 243,000,000
FEDERAL GOVERNMENT EXPENDITURE	..$ 714,741,000
FEDERAL DEBT	......................$ 1,119,774,000

Events

January 1 • President Lincoln issues the Emancipation Proclamation, stating that all slaves in those areas that are still in rebellion are now free.

January 2 • The battle of Murfreesboro, begun on December 31, 1862, ends in a Union victory and the retreat of General Bragg from central Tennessee.

January 25 • President Lincoln transfers command of

the Army of the Potomac from General Burnside to General Joseph Hooker.

February 6 • Secretary of State William H. Seward rejects an offer by Emperor Napoleon III, received on February 3, to mediate the war.

February 24 • Arizona Territory is created by an act of Congress.

February 25 • The National Bank Act is adopted. It creates the Office of Comptroller of the Currency and, with amendments of June 3, 1864, sets up a national banking system that lasts until the Federal Reserve System in 1913.

March 3 • Congress creates Idaho Territory.

March 3 • The National Academy of Sciences is established by an act of Congress.

March 3 • An act of Congress provides for the conscription of men aged 20 to 45 (if married, to 35) for service in the Union Army. A man may discharge his liability by paying $300 or by obtaining a substitute.

April 2 • Food riots erupt in Richmond. Although they planned only to loot grocery stores, hundreds of hungry women soon begin pillaging jewelry stores and other shops within a 10 block area. Only after Confederate president Jefferson Davis threatens to shoot the looters does the rioting stop.

May 2–4 • General Lee's Army of Northern Virginia defeats General Hooker's Army of the Potomac at Chancellorsville, Virginia. Stonewall Jackson, severely wounded, dies on May 10.

May 19 • General Grant, who has moved his army down the west side of the Mississippi River and has approached the Confederate strongpoint of Vicksburg, Mississippi, from the south, now attacks the city. Repulsed, he makes another unsuccessful attack on May 22 and then besieges the Confederate defenders. Vicksburg surrenders on July 4.

June 3 • General Lee begins a drive north toward Pennsylvania. A corps commanded by General Richard S. Ewell defeats the garrison at Winchester on June 15 and nears Harrisburg by June 29.

June 20 • West Virginia is admitted to the Union as the 35th state.

June 28 • President Lincoln replaces General Hooker with General George G. Meade.

July 1–3 • The battle of Gettysburg takes place when units of Lee's and Meade's forces meet in the town on June 30. By the end of three days of fighting, Lee, who has lost 20,000 men, is forced to withdraw. The battle is the turning point of the war.

July 9 • General Nathaniel P. Banks takes Port Hudson, Louisiana, the last Confederate strongpoint on the Mississippi.

July 13–16 • Mobs rioting in New York against the draft cause many deaths and extensive property damage.

United States of America 1863

September 9 • General Bragg withdraws from Chattanooga, which is threatened by the Union Army of the Cumberland, led by General William S. Rosecrans.

September 19–20 • Pursuing Bragg, Rosecrans encounters a reinforced Confederate force 10 miles south of Chattanooga. In the ensuing battle of Chickamauga, only the firm stand of General George H. Thomas permits a Union retreat to Chattanooga.

October 16 • President Lincoln places the Union armies in the West under the command of General Grant, who replaces Rosecrans with Thomas.

November 19 • President Lincoln delivers a memorable address at the dedication of a national cemetery in Gettysburg:

> Four score and seven years ago our fathers brought forth on this continent, a new nation, conceived in Liberty, and dedicated to the proposition that all men are created equal.
>
> Now we are engaged in a great civil war, testing whether that nation, or any nation so conceived, and so dedicated, can long endure. We are met on a great battle-field of that war. We have come to dedicate a portion of that field, as a final resting place for those who here gave their lives that that nation might live. It is altogether fitting and proper that we should do this.
>
> But, in a large sense, we can not dedicate—we can not consecrate—we can not hallow—this ground. The brave men, living and dead, who struggled here, have consecrated it far above our poor power to add or detract. The world will little note, nor long remember, what we say here, but it can never forget what they did here. It is for us, the living, rather to be dedicated here to the unfinished work which they who fought here have, thus far, so nobly advanced. It is rather for us to be here dedicated to the great task remaining before us—that from these honored dead we take increased devotion to that cause for which they gave the last full measure of devotion; that we here highly resolve that these dead shall not have died in vain; that this nation, under God, shall have a new birth of freedom; and that government of the people, by the people, for the people, shall not perish from the earth.

November 23–25 • The Army of the Cumberland, to which Grant has sent reinforcements under General Hooker and General William T. Sherman, attacks Bragg's Army of Tennessee in the battle of Chattanooga. Driven from Lookout Mountain and Missionary Ridge, the Confederate forces withdraw into Georgia.

December 3 • With the Union victory at Chattanooga, General James Longstreet, who has been besieging Knoxville, also withdraws, leaving Tennessee under Union control.

December 8 • President Lincoln issues a proclamation setting forth a conciliatory Reconstruction plan. It includes pardon for rebels who take a loyalty oath and recognition of a state government that is formed by 10 percent of the 1860 voters who take the oath and legislate emancipation.

International and Cultural Events • Ferdinand Lassalle, state socialism theorist, forms Germany's first worker's political party; it evolves into the Social Democratic party.

The Battle of Gettysburg.

1864 United States of America

38th CONGRESS

SENATE .... 50 Members
R 36
D 9
O 5

HOUSE .... 186 Members
R 102
D 75
O 9

ESTIMATED
POPULATION
34,863,000

Abraham Lincoln
16th President
1st Republican

Hannibal Hamlin
15th Vice President
Republican

UNITED STATES ECONOMY

GROSS NATIONAL PRODUCT .... $ N/A
RETAIL SALES .... $ N/A
BANK RESOURCES .... $ 973,000,000
EXPORTS .... $ 144,000,000
IMPORTS .... $ 316,000,000
FEDERAL GOVERNMENT EXPENDITURE .. $ 865,323,000
FEDERAL DEBT .... $ 1,815,831,000

Events

March 9 • General Grant is promoted to the rank of lieutenant general and put in overall command of Union forces.

April 8 • A campaign up the valley of the Red River toward Shreveport, Louisiana, by a Union force under General Banks is halted by Confederate troops at Sabine Crossroads. Banks withdraws to the Mississippi River.

May 4 • General Sherman, in command of an army of 110,000 men, leaves Chattanooga on a march toward Atlanta. His advance is opposed by General Joseph E. Johnston, who with about 60,000 men can afford only delaying actions. On June 27 at Kenesaw Mountain, however, he thwarts an attack by Sherman. On July 17, as Sherman nears Atlanta, Johnston is replaced by General John B. Hood.

May 5–6 • The armies of General Grant and General Lee fight the Battle of the Wilderness, in northern Virginia. Casualties are heavy, and the outcome is inconclusive. The Battle of the Wilderness pitted Lee for the first time against an opponent willing to press forward despite the cost. Union casualties in the battle are 18,000; Confederate, 10,800.

May 8–12 • Grant's and Lee's forces renew their battles at Spotsylvania Court House. Union losses are heavy, but Grant is determined to wear Lee down.

May 26 • Montana Territory is created by an act of Congress.

June 3 • In the battle of Cold Harbor, Grant makes an unsuccessful and costly attack on Lee's position. The battle of Cold Harbor marks Lee's last great victory in the field.

June 5 • Major General David Hunter defeated at Piedmont, Virginia, Confederate forces under the commands of Brigadier Generals John G. Imboden and William E. "Grumble" Jones. The Union victory opens the Shenandoah Valley, which has become an important agricultural region for the Confederacy, to attack for the first time during the war.

June 7 • The National Union (Republican) party convenes in Baltimore. It nominates President Lincoln for re-election and Andrew Johnson (Tennessee), a War Democrat, for vice president.

June 15–18 • Grant fails in an attempt to take the rail junction of Petersburg, south of Richmond. He then lays siege to the city.

June 19 • The confederate raider *Alabama*, which has destroyed or captured more than 60 United States ships, is sunk in the English Channel by the USS *Kearsarge*.

June 30 • The Morrill Tariff Act of 1861 is amended to increase duties. Congress also increases excise and income taxes.

July 2 • Congress adopts the Wade-Davis bill, embodying a Radical Republican plan for the Reconstruction of the south. President Lincoln, who prefers his own more conciliatory plan, pocket-vetoes the bill.

July 2–13 • Confederate troops under General Jubal A. Early raid Maryland.

July 4 • An act of Congress permits the immigration of contract labor.

United States of America 1864

August 5–23 • After forcing his way through the mined approaches to Mobile Bay, Admiral Farragut overcomes the Confederate defenses and blockades Mobile.

August 29 • The Democratic party convenes in Chicago. It nominates General George B. McClellan for president and George H. Pendleton (Ohio) for vice president. The platform includes a demand that the war be ended. McClellan rejects this plank.

September 1 • With the failure of two attacks on General Sherman's forces in July and the cutting of supply lines on August 31, General Hood is forced to withdraw his forces from Atlanta. Sherman enters the city on September 2. Radical Republicans, who had been contemplating a new presidential nominee, decide to support President Lincoln.

September 19 • General Early is defeated at Winchester, Virginia, by the Union Army of the Shenandoah, led by Philip H. Sheridan. Three days later, Early is defeated at Fisher's Hill.

October 19 • In Sheridan's absence, Early attacks the Union troops at Cedar Creek. Surprised, they are almost routed when Sheridan returns to lead them to victory. Early is driven from the Shenandoah Valley, to which Sheridan lays waste in order to deny its supplies to the Confederates.

October 31 • Nevada is admitted to the Union as the 36th state.

November 8 • In the presidential election, Lincoln is re-elected, receiving 212 electoral votes to 21 for McClellan, his Democratic opponent. Andrew Johnson is elected vice president.

November 16 • After ordering the destruction of everything in Atlanta that might be of use to the Confederates, General Sherman sets out with 62,000 men on a "march to the sea." On its way, the army confiscates or destroys all supplies and installations and causes random destruction over a width of 60 miles. Arriving at Savannah on December 10, Sherman forces its surrender on December 22.

December 6 • President Lincoln appoints Salmon P. Chase, former secretary of the treasury, as chief justice of the U.S. Supreme Court, succeeding Roger B. Taney, who died on October 12.

December 15–16 • A Union force under General Thomas, left by Sherman to defend Tennessee, routs General Hood's army in the hills to the south of Nashville.

International and Cultural Events • With the aid to French troops, the conservative opposition to President Benito Juárez installs Archduke Maximilian of Austria as emperor of Mexico. The International Workingmen's Association (First International) is organized in London by Karl Marx. Pius IX issues the *Syllabus errorum*, in which he condemns liberalism, socialism and rationalism.

General Sherman's march to the sea.

1865 Lincoln/Johnson

39th CONGRESS

SENATE .... 52 Members
R 42
D 10
O 0

HOUSE .... 191 Members
R 149
D 42
O 0

ESTIMATED
POPULATION
35,701,000

Abraham Lincoln
16th President
1st Republican

Andrew Johnson
16th Vice President
Democrat

UNITED STATES ECONOMY

GROSS NATIONAL PRODUCT .... N/A
RETAIL SALES .... N/A
BANK RESOURCES .... $ 1,357,000,000
EXPORTS .... $ 137,000,000
IMPORTS .... $ 239,000,000
FEDERAL GOVERNMENT EXPENDITURE .. $ 1,297,555,000
FEDERAL DEBT .... $ 2,677,929,000

Andrew Johnson	
Birth	Raleigh, NC, Dec. 29, 1808
Parents	Jacob and Mary McDonough Johnson
Married	Eliza McCardle
Home	Greenville, TN
Presidency	1865 – 1869
Death	Near Carter Station, TN, July 31, 1875

Events

January 15 • Fort Fisher, North Carolina, is captured by Union land and sea forces.

January 16 • General Sherman's army begins a campaign that takes it northward through South Carolina and North Carolina. Columbia (February 17) and other cities and towns in South Carolina are partially burned.

February 1 • Congress proposes the adoption of the 13th Amendment, forbidding slavery.

February 3 • President Davis sends Vice President Stephens, John A. Campbell, and Robert M.T. Hunter to meet President Lincoln aboard a Union ship in Hampton Roads, Virginia. Since the southerners require the North to acknowledge the independence of the Confederacy, the conference is unsuccessful.

February 18 • Charleston, South Carolina, evacuated by its Confederate defenders as Sherman's drive continues, is occupied by Union forces.

March 3 • An act of Congress creates the Freedmen's Bureau to aid former slaves, helping them obtain jobs, schooling, land and medical care.

March 4 • President Lincoln is inaugurated for his second term. In his inaugural address, he again urges a conciliatory course: "With malice toward none; with charity for all; with firmness in the right, as God gives us to see the right, let us strive on to finish the work we are in; to bind up the nation's wounds; to care for him who shall have borne the battle, and for his widow and his orphan—to do all which may achieve and cherish a just and lasting peace, among ourselves, and with all nations."

March 19–20 • General Sherman drives General Johnston back at Bentonville, North Carolina. The next day, he occupies Goldsboro.

March 25 • General Grant repulses an attack by General Lee at Fort Steadman, near Petersburg. An April attack at Five Forks also fails. The next day, Lee is forced to evacuate both Petersburg and Richmond.

April 7 • Lee, whose diminished army is almost encircled by pursuing Union forces, receives a proposal from General Grant that he surrender.

April 9 • Lee and Grant, meeting at Appomattox Court House, arrange the surrender of Lee's army. Officers and men are free to go home, the officers with their sidearms and all with privately owned horses or mules.

April 12 • The formal surrender of Lee's force at Appomattox Court House takes place. Brigadier General Joshua L. Chamberlain received the surrender. Major General John B. Gordon's Second Corps led the way through the column of Union troops lining the Richmond Stage Road.

April 14 • While watching a play at Ford's Theater in Washington, President Lincoln is shot in the head by John Wilkes Booth. At the same time, Secretary Seward is gravely wounded at his home in a related assassination attempt.

April 15 • Lincoln dies. Vice President Johnson is sworn in as his successor.

April 18 • General Johnston surrenders to General Sherman. The instrument of surrender, which includes broad political concessions that Sherman has not been impowered to make, is rejected in Washington and a new document, similar to that drawn up at Appomattox, is signed on April 26.

April 26 • Booth, caught after escaping to Virginia, refuses to surrender and dies from a gunshot. On July 7, four people convicted of complicity in the assassination are hanged in Washington.

May 4 • General Richard Taylor surrenders all other Confederate forces east of the Mississippi River to General Edward R.S. Canby.

May 26 • General Edmund Kirby-Smith surrenders the Confederate forces west of the Mississippi River to General Canby. The war has cost the lives of 359,000 Union and 258,000 Confederate soldiers.

May 29 • President Johnson, who has espoused Lincoln's conciliatory plan of Reconstruction, issues a proclamation, offering amnesty to former Confederates who take a loyalty oath. Taking advantage of the interim before the assembly of the new Congress, he extends recognition to four new state governments established by Lincoln and arranges for the formation of new governments for the rest of the former Confederate states.

November 22–29 • The Mississippi legislature adopts laws on vagrancy, labor service, and the like, constituting the first of the black codes devised in the South to regulate the status of blacks.

December 4 • The Joint Committee on Reconstruction is created by Congress. Opposing President Johnson's actions, it rejects the credentials of senators and representatives newly elected in the former Confederate states.

December 18 • The 13th Amendment to the Constitution is adopted.

International and Cultural Events • Extending Louis Pasteur's germ theory (1861), Joseph Lister introduces antiseptic surgery in England. Leo Tolstoy begins publication of *War and Peace*. George M. Pullman patents a railway sleeping car.

ARTICLE XIII

Section 1. Neither slavery nor involuntary servitude, except as a punishment for crime whereof the party shall have been duly convicted, shall exist within the United States, or any place subject to their jurisdiction.

Secton 2. Congress shall have power to enforce this article by appropriate legislation.

(Adopted in 1865)

The Grand Review, held in Washington in May 1865.

1866 United States of America

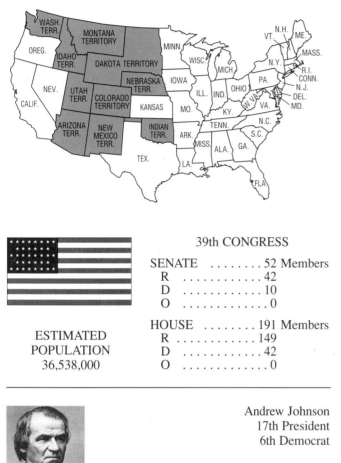

Events

February 12 • Secretary Seward sends a note to the French government demanding that it remove its army from Mexico.

February 19 • Congress adopts a bill to broaden the powers of the Freedmen's Bureau. Under its provisions, anyone charged with interfering with the civil rights of freedmen would be subject to a military trial. Vetoed by President Johnson on constitutional grounds, the bill is adopted on July 16.

April 9 • The Civil Rights Act, which had been vetoed by President Johnson for interfering with the rights of the states, is adopted by Congress. All native-born individuals, except untaxed Indians, are citizens with equal rights regardless of race.

June 1 • Militant Fenians, members of an anti-British Irish society, enter Canada from Buffalo. After defeating a force of militia, they return to the United States and are temporarily imprisoned.

June 13 • Congress adopts the Fourteenth Amendment, which stipulates that requirements for United States citizenship cover African Americans and prohibits former officeholders who engaged in the rebellion from holding office. No state can be restored to the Union without ratifying the amendment.

June 20 • The Joint Committee on Reconstruction declares that Reconstruction is strictly a congressional responsibility. Ex-Confederate states are not to be represented in Congress.

July • The United States begins constructing Fort Phil Kearny, on the Bozeman Trail, in Wyoming. Attacks on the fort by angry Indians mark the start of the First Sioux War. On December 21, Captain William Fetterman and a party of 80 men are killed by the Sioux.

July 1 • Congress levies a 10 percent tax on all state bank notes. States will quickly remove their money from circulation, the main aim of the act.

July 19 • Tennessee ratifies the 14th Amendment; on July 24, it is restored to the Union.

July 27 • A permanent transatlantic cable is completed.

July 30 • Riots erupt in New Orleans, Louisiana, over the placement of black male suffrage in the state's constitution. In the violence that ensues, 48 blacks are killed and at least 160 others are injured.

August 14–16 • The National Union Convention is held in Philadelphia in an effort to consolidate support for the president's position on Reconstruction. However, the Radical Republicans are successful in the midterm elections.

August 20 • A national labor organization, the National Labor Union, is established in Baltimore.

November 20 • The Grand Army of the Republic, a national organization of Union veterans, holds its first national encampment in Indianapolis.

December • In *Ex parte Milligan*, the Supreme Court rules that civilians may not be tried by a military commission in areas outside a theater of war where civil courts are open.

International and Cultural Events • The Austro-Prussian War paves the way for the North German Confederation. Alfred Nobel invents dynamite. With *The Black Crook*, musical comedy is born in New York.

United States of America 1867

Events

January 8 • Congress extends the suffrage to black males living in Washington, D.C. Although President Johnson vetoes the bill, Congress, as it will do so often, overrides Johnson's veto.

January 31 • Congress extends the suffrage to all males older than 21 living in the territories.

March 1 • Nebraska is admitted to the Union as the 37th state.

March 2 • The initial Reconstruction Act is adopted over the veto of President Johnson. The former Confederacy, with the exception of Tennessee, is organized into five military districts. New state governments are to be formed by constitutional conventions chosen by an electorate that includes blacks but not former Confederates excluded under the 14th Amendment.

March 2 • The Tenure of Office Act is adopted over President Johnson's veto. The president must obtain Senate approval to remove from office any official whose appointment required Senate approval.

March 2 • Congress adopts the Command of the Army Act, which stipulates that military orders must be channeled through the commander of the U.S. Army, General Grant.

March 23 • Since none of the affected states have taken steps to call constitutional conventions, Congress adopts the first supplementary Reconstruction Act. Under its provisions, the commanders of the various military districts are to arrange for the registration of voters.

March 30 • A treaty whereby the United States purchases Alaska from Russia for $7.2 million is signed in Washington. It is ratified by the Senate on April 9.

April–May • In *Georgia v. Stanton* and *Mississippi v. Johnson*, the Supreme Court rules that it lacks jurisdiction to bar enforcement of the Reconstruction Acts.

May • The Ku Klux Klan, a secret organization that intimidates blacks and others in the interest of white supremacy in the South, is formally constituted in Nashville. The organization as such is disbanded in 1869, but individuals carry on in the same vein thereafter.

July 19 • Congress adopts the second supplementary Reconstruction Act, which gives the military commanders greater power over state officials.

August 12 • President Johnson suspends Secretary of War Edwin M. Stanton from office for acting in league with the Radical Republicans.

August 28 • The United States acquires the Midway Islands.

December 4 • A secret order of farmers, the National Grange of the Patrons of Husbandry, is founded in Washington. It will seek to control railroad rates and middlemen.

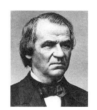

Andrew Johnson
17th President
6th Democrat

Vice President
None

40th CONGRESS	
SENATE	........53 Members
R	42
D	11
O	0
HOUSE	........192 Members
R	143
D	49
O	0

ESTIMATED
POPULATION
37,376,000

UNITED STATES ECONOMY

GROSS NATIONAL PRODUCT	..........$ 6,710,000,000
RETAIL SALES	...............................N/A
BANK RESOURCES	...................$ 1,674,000,000
EXPORTS	............................$ 280,000,000
IMPORTS	............................$ 396,000,000
FEDERAL GOVERNMENT EXPENDITURE	..$ 357,543,000
FEDERAL DEBT	.......................$ 2,650,168,000

International and Cultural Events • The British North America Act establishes Canada as a federation and a dominion. Karl Marx publishes volume 1 of *Das Kapital*. Garibaldi's march on Rome is stopped by French and papal forces. French troops leave Mexico; Maximilian is tried and executed. Imprisoned since May 1865, Jefferson Davis is released on bail; federal prosecution is dropped in 1869.

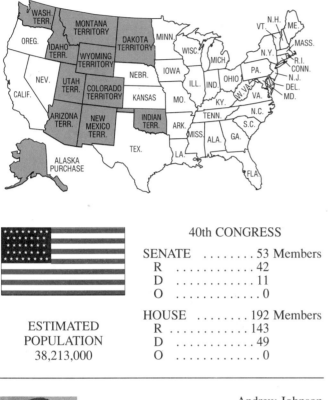

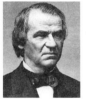

40th CONGRESS

SENATE .... 53 Members
R 42
D 11
O 0

HOUSE .... 192 Members
R 143
D 49
O 0

ESTIMATED
POPULATION
38,213,000

Andrew Johnson
17th President
6th Democrat

Vice President
None

UNITED STATES ECONOMY

GROSS NATIONAL PRODUCT ....$ 6,710,000,000
RETAIL SALES .... N/A
BANK RESOURCES ....$ 1,736,000,000
EXPORTS ....$ 269,000,000
IMPORTS ....$ 327,000,000
FEDERAL GOVERNMENT EXPENDITURE ..$ 2,583,446,000
FEDERAL DEBT .... N/A

Events

February 21 • President Johnson, who has reinstated Secretary Stanton on January 13, dismisses him with the object of providing a test case on the constitutionality of the Tenure of Office Act.

February 24 • The House of Representatives adopts a resolution that impeaches President Johnson on 11 articles, nine of which concern the Tenure of Office Act.

March 11 • Congress adopts the third supplementary Reconstruction Act, which provides that a state constitution may be adopted by majority vote without considering the number of registered voters.

March 13 • The impeachment trial of President Johnson opens with Chief Justice Chase presiding. Counsel for the president, who is not present, contending that the Tenure of Office Act is unconstitutional. In voting on one article on May 16, the Senate divides 35 to 19 for conviction, or one vote less than the two-thirds majority required. A vote on two other articles on May 28 produces the same totals. The trial will adjourn with the acquittal of the president.

April • The First Sioux War ends with the Treaty of Fort Laramie. The United States government agrees to abandon the forts it has built on the Bozeman Trail and to furnish food and other supplies. The Indians are to cease attacking whites. Land east of the Big Horn Mountains and north of the North Platte River is stated to be Indian territory.

May 21 • The Republican party convenes in Chicago. It nominates General Ulysses S. Grant for president and Schuyler Colfax (Indiana) for vice president.

June 22–25 • Alabama, Arkansas, Florida, Georgia, Louisiana, North Carolina and South Carolina, which have formed new governments under the Reconstruction Acts, are readmitted to the Union.

June 25 • An act of Congress sets an eight-hour day for federally employed laborers and mechanics.

July 4 • The Democratic party convenes in New York. It nominates Horatio Seymour (New York) for president and Francis P. Blair (Missouri) for vice president.

July 25 • Wyoming Territory is created by act of Congress.

July 28 • The 14th Amendment to the Constitution is adopted.

July 28 • The Burlingame Treaty between the United States and China is signed in Washington. Its provisions include free immigration from each country to the other.

September • Military government is reimposed on Georgia after the legislature expels blacks.

November 3 • In the presidential election, Grant is elected president, receiving 214 electoral votes to 80 for Seymour, his Democratic opponent.

International and Cultural Events • Disraeli becomes British prime minister. C. L. Sholes and two friends get a patent for a typewriter. Louisa May Alcott publishes volume 1 of *Little Women*.

ARTICLE XIV

Civil Rights; Apportionment of Representatives;
Political Disabilities; Public Debt

Section 1. All persons born or naturalized in the United

States, and subject to the jurisdiction thereof, are citizens of the United States and of the State wherein they reside. No State shall make or enforce any law which shall abridge the privileges or immunities of citizens of the United States; nor shall any State deprive any person of life, liberty, or property, without due process of law; nor deny to any person within its jurisdiction the equal protection of the laws.

Section 2. Representatives shall be apportioned among the several States according to their respective numbers, counting the whole number of persons in each State, excluding Indians not taxed. But when the right to vote at any election for the choice of electors for President and Vice President of the United States, Representatives in Congress, the Executive and Judicial officers of a State, or the members of the Legislature thereof, is denied to any of the male inhabitants of such State, being twenty-one years of age, and citizens of the United States, or in any way abridged, except for participation in rebellion, or other crime, the basis of representation therein shall be reduced in the proportion which the number of such male citizens shall bear to the whole number of male citizens twenty-one years of age in such State.

Section 3. No person shall be a Senator or Representative in Congress, or elector of President and Vice President, or hold any office, civil or military, under the United States, or under any State, who, having previously taken an oath, as a member of Congress, or as an officer of the United States, or as a member of any State legislature, or as an executive or judicial officer of any State, to support the constitution of thc Unitcd Statcs, shall have engaged in insurrection or rebellion against the same, or given aid or comfort to the enemies thereof. But Congress may by a vote of two-thirds of each House, remove such disability.

Section 4. The validity of the public debt of the United States, authorized by law, including debts incurred for payment of pensions and bounties for services in suppressing insurrection or rebellion, shall not be questioned. But neither the United States nor any State shall assume or pay any debt or obligation incurred in aid of insurrection or rebellion against the United States, or any claim for the loss or emancipation of any slave; but all such debts, obligations and claims shall be held illegal and void.

Section 5. The Congress shall have power to enforce, by appropriate legislation, the provisions of this article.

(Adopted in 1868)

Impeachment charges are brought against Andrew Johnson.

1869 Ulysses S. Grant

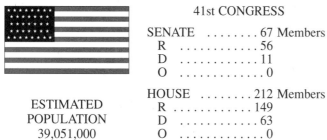

41st CONGRESS

SENATE .... 67 Members
R 56
D 11
O 0

HOUSE .... 212 Members
R 149
D 63
O 0

ESTIMATED
POPULATION
39,051,000

Ulysses S. Grant
18th President
2nd Republican

Schuyler Colfax
17th Vice President
Republican

UNITED STATES ECONOMY

GROSS NATIONAL PRODUCT ....$ 6,710,000,000
RETAIL SALES .... N/A
BANK RESOURCES ....$ 1,736,000,000
EXPORTS ....$ 275,000,000
IMPORTS ....$ 418,000,000
FEDERAL GOVERNMENT EXPENDITURE ..$ 322,865,000
FEDERAL DEBT ....$ 2,545,111,000

Ulysses S. Grant	
Birth	Point Pleasant, OH, Apr. 27, 1822
Parents	Jesse and Hannah Simpson Grant
Married	Julia Dent
Home	Galena, IL
Presidency	1869 – 1877
Death	Mount McGregor, NY, July 23, 1885

Events

January 14 • The Johnson-Clarendon Convention is concluded to settle Anglo-American claims, including those arising from the damage done to United States shipping during the Civil War by the *Alabama* and other Confederate raiders constructed or outfitted in Great Britain. It fails of ratification in the Senate on April 13.

January 19 • Susan B. Anthony is elected president of the American Equal Rights Association.

February 2 • Improving on John Deere's original round-blade plow, James Oliver patents the chilled iron plow. With a removable cutting edge of tempered steel, the plow will allow farmers to break the hard prairie sod.

February 24 • The Morrill Tariff Act is revised to increase customs duties.

February 27 • Congress proposes the adoption of the Fifteenth Amendment, guaranteeing every citizen the right to vote without regard to race or previous condition of servitude.

March 4 • Grant is inaugurated president.

March 18 • Congress adopts the Public Credit Act, which stipulates that government debts be paid in gold.

May–August 29 • John Wesley Powell leads an exploring party on a hazardous journey down the Colorado River. With funds appropriated by Congress, he makes three more trips down the river (1871, 1874, 1875).

May 10 • The tracks of the Union Pacific and Central Pacific railroads are connected at Promontory, Utah, thus completing the first transcontinental railway route.

May 15 • Elizabeth Cady Stanton is elected president of the National Women Suffrage Association.

September 1 • At a convention held in Chicago the Prohibition party is formed.

September 24 • A scheme devised by James Fisk and Jay Gould to corner gold results this day in a panic called Black Friday. The two financiers have had the assistance of Abel Rathbone Corbin, President Grant's brother-in-law, in an attempt to prevent any action by the federal government. The price has risen from 135 to 162 before Secretary of the Treasury George S. Boutell sells $4 million worth of gold, driving the price down and ending the scheme.

December 10 • A law adopted in Wyoming Territory extends the suffrage to women. It is the first such law passed in the United States.

December 22 • An act of Congress makes Georgia's readmission to the Union conditional on its ratification of the 15th Amendment.

International and Cultural Events • Hudson's Bay Company territory is sold to Canada by governmental order. The Suez Canal is opened. Dmitri Mendeleyev formulates his periodic law of elements. Mark Twain publishes *The Innocents Abroad*.

United States of America 1870

Events

January 26 • Following the adoption of a new constitution and ratification of the 15th Amendment, Virginia is restored to the Union.

February 7 • In *Hepburn v. Griswold*, the first of the Legal Tender cases, the Supreme Court rules that Treasury notes issued under the Legal Tender Acts of 1862 and 1863 could not constitutionally be made legal tender by the acts for debts contracted before their adoption.

February 23 • Mississippi is readmitted to the Union on the same conditions as Virginia.

March 30 • The 15th Amendment to the Constitution is adopted. It provides for black suffrage.

March 31 • Texas is readmitted to the Union on the same conditions as Virginia and Mississippi.

May 25–27 • Fenian raids over the Canadian border from Vermont and New York are thwarted by United States and Canadian authorities.

May 31 • Congress adopts the Ku Klux Klan Act of 1870, which is designed to enforce the 15th Amendment.

June 21–22 • The Department of Justice is created by an act of Congress to accommodate the growing responsibilities of the attorney general.

June 30 • The Senate refuses to approve a treaty, submitted by President Grant on January 10, for the annexation of the Dominican Republic by the United States.

July 14 • The Tariff Act of 1870 is adopted. Rates are lowered slightly, and duties are removed from some commodities.

July 14 • Secretary of State Hamilton Fish declares, in a memorandum, the the Monroe Doctrine implies that the territory of one European power in the Western Hemisphere may not be transferred to another European power.

July 15 • Georgia is restored to the Union for the second time. It is the last state to be readmitted.

August 1 • Women vote for the first time in the United States in an election in Utah Territory.

December 5 • The third session of the 41st Congress convenes with representatives of all the states present for the first time since 1860.

International and Cultural Events • Napoleon III is deposed after his defeat and capture at Sedan in the Franco-Prussian War. John D. Rockefeller organizes the Standard Oil Company of Ohio. John and Isaiah Hyatt patent celluloid.

ARTICLE XV
Right of Suffrage

Section 1. The right of citizens of the United States to vote shall not be denied or abridged by the United States

41st CONGRESS

ESTIMATED
POPULATION
39,905,000

SENATE .... 67 Members
R 56
D 11
O 0

HOUSE .... 212 Members
R 149
D 63
O 0

Ulysses S. Grant
18th President
2nd Republican

Schuyler Colfax
17th Vice President
Republican

UNITED STATES ECONOMY

GROSS NATIONAL PRODUCT .... $ 6,710,000,000
RETAIL SALES .... N/A
BANK RESOURCES .... $ 1,781,000,000
EXPORTS .... $ 377,000,000
IMPORTS .... $ 436,000,000
FEDERAL GOVERNMENT EXPENDITURE .. $ 309,654,000
FEDERAL DEBT .... $ 2,436,453,000

or by any State on account of race, color or previous condition of servitude.

Section 2. The Congress shall have power to enforce this article by appropriate legislation.

(Adopted in 1870)

1871 United States of America

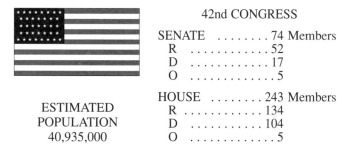

ESTIMATED
POPULATION
40,935,000

42nd CONGRESS

SENATE .... 74 Members
R 52
D 17
O 5

HOUSE .... 243 Members
R 134
D 104
O 5

Ulysses S. Grant
18th President
2nd Republican

Schuyler Colfax
17th Vice President
Republican

UNITED STATES ECONOMY

GROSS NATIONAL PRODUCT ....$ 6,710,000,000
RETAIL SALES .... N/A
BANK RESOURCES ....$ 2,003,000,000
EXPORTS ....$ 428,000,000
IMPORTS ....$ 520,000,000
FEDERAL GOVERNMENT EXPENDITURE ..$ 292,177,000
FEDERAL DEBT ....$ 2,322,052,000

Events

January 19 • General George Stoneman begins a winter campaign against the Apache Indians, who have harassed whites in Arizona Territory.

February 28 • The Supplementary Enforcement Act is adopted to enforce the 15th Amendment. Elections in several former Confederate states are put under federal supervision.

March 3 • An act of Congress ends the practice of concluding treaties with Indian tribes. Hereafter less formal agreements are made.

March 4 • President Grant appoints the writer and editor George W. Curtis as chairman of the Commission on Civil Service Reform, created by act of Congress on March 3. The commission lasts until 1875, when Curtis, whose report on suggested reforms has not been implemented, resigns.

April 20 • Congress adopts the Ku Klux Klan Act of 1871, which gives the president the power to suspend the writ of habeas corpus and to use military force to quell disturbances and to enforce the 14th Amendment in the south.

April 30 • More than 100 Apache Indians are killed by a mob at Camp Grant, Arizona. Sporadic fighting with Apaches will continue for 15 years.

May 1 • In *Knox v. Lee* and *Parker v. Davis*, the Supreme Court, which now includes two new members appointed by the president, reverses its decision in *Hepburn v. Griswold* and rules that the Legal Tender Acts of 1862 and 1863 are constitutional.

May 8 • After successful diplomatic negotiations conducted by Secretary Fish, the Treaty of Washington is concluded with Great Britain. It provides for the settlement of fishing and boundary disputes and the arbitration of the *Alabama* claims. A mixed commission in Halifax is to consider Canadian and United States fishing privileges, and the question of the boundary line in Juan de Fuca Strait is referred to the emperor of Germany. Five arbitrators, appointed by Brazil, Great Britain, Italy, Switzerland and the United States, are to settle the claims.

July 8 • *The New York Times* begins publishing an exposé of a ring led by William Marcy Tweed that has corrupted the government of New York City, robbing the city of sums estimated at from $30 million to $200 million. Arrested on civil charges (October 26) and on criminal charges (December 16), Tweed will be convicted in 1873.

October 8 • On Sunday evening, fires erupt on both sides of Green Bay. At Peshtigo, a lumbering community of 1,700, the suddenness of the fires catch many people off guard. More than 800 people die in the town; 400 more in the surrounding area. The fires destroy more than 2,000 square miles of virgin forest.

October 8–9 • A devastating fire destroys a large part of Chicago. About 300 people die and property damage is estimated at $200 million.

International and Cultural Events • France cedes Alsace-Lorraine to Germany; the provisional government of the Third Republic (1871-1940) suppresses the Paris Commune. Henry M. Stanley finds David Livingstone in Africa for the New York *Herald.*

United States of America 1872

Events

February 2 • To standardize when Americans elect a president, Congress changes the date of the presidential election to the first Tuesday after the first Monday in November, effective in 1876.

February 17 • Chieftains in the Somoan Islands grant the United States the right to establish a naval station at Pago Pago, but the treaty is not ratified by the Senate.

February 22 • In an opera house in Columbus, Ohio, delegates attend the first national convention of the National Prohibition party. They select James Black of Pennsylvania as their party's presidential nominee.

March 1 • Yellowstone National Park is created in Wyoming by act of Congress.

May 1 • The Liberal Republican party convenes in Cincinnati. It nominates Horace Greeley (New York) for president and B. Gratz Brown for vice president.

May 22 • Congress adopts the Amnesty Act, which removes restrictions from all but a few hundred former Confederates, thereby permitting them to hold office.

June 5 • The Republican party convenes in Philadelphia. It nominated President Grant for re-election and Henry Wilson for vice president.

June 6 • The Tariff Act of 1872 is adopted. Duties on manufactures are cut by 10 percent.

July 9 • The Democratic party convenes in Baltimore. It nominates Greeley and Brown, the Liberal Republican candidates.

September 3 • The "Straight" Democrats convene in Louisville. They nominate Charles O'Conor (New York) for president and John Quincy Adams II (Massachusetts) for vice president.

September 4 • The New York *Sun* states that Vice President Colfax and others have received stock from the Crédit Mobilier, a company used to siphon profits from the Union Pacific Railroad.

September 14 • The United States is awarded $15.5 million by the *Alabama* claims tribunal.

September 25 • The Liberal Colored Republicans convene in Louisville. They nominate Greeley and Brown, the Liberal Republican candidates.

October 21 • Emperor William I, arbitrating the dispute over the British Columbia-Washington territory boundary, awards the San Juan Islands to the United States.

November 5 • In the presidential election, Grant is re-elected, receiving 286 electoral votes to 66 for Greeley. Greeley dies on November 29, and 63 electors pledged to him cast their votes for other candidates: Thomas A. Hendricks, 42; B. Gratz Brown, 18; Charles J. Jenkins, two; David Davis, one.

42nd CONGRESS

SENATE	....	74 Members
R	....	52
D	....	17
O	....	5
HOUSE	....	243 Members
R	....	134
D	....	104
O	....	5

ESTIMATED POPULATION
41,972,000

Ulysses S. Grant
18th President
2nd Republican

Schuyler Colfax
17th Vice President
Republican

UNITED STATES ECONOMY

GROSS NATIONAL PRODUCT	..........$ 7,580,000,000
RETAIL SALES	.... N/A
BANK RESOURCES	....................$ 2,145,000,000
EXPORTS	............................$ 428,000,000
IMPORTS	............................$ 627,000,000
FEDERAL GOVERNMENT EXPENDITURE	..$ 277,518,000
FEDERAL DEBT	.......................$ 2,209,991,000

International and Cultural Events • The Three Emperors' League is formed by the rulers of Germany, Russia and Austria-Hungary. Modoc Indians refuse to return to the Klamath Reservation; the Modoc War with federal troops ends in 1873 with the hanging of Chief Kintpuash. Feminist Victoria Claflin Woodhull and black leader Frederick Douglass head the People's party national ticket. Thomas A. Edison perfects a telegraph transmitter-receiver.

43rd CONGRESS

SENATE .... 73 Members
R 49
D 19
O 5

HOUSE .... 300 Members
R 194
D 92
O 14

ESTIMATED
POPULATION
43,006,000

Ulysses S. Grant
18th President
2nd Republican

Henry Wilson
18th Vice President
Republican

UNITED STATES ECONOMY

GROSS NATIONAL PRODUCT ....$ 7,580,000,000
RETAIL SALES .... N/A
BANK RESOURCES ....$ 2,731,000,000
EXPORTS ....$ 505,000,000
IMPORTS ....$ 642,000,000
FEDERAL GOVERNMENT EXPENDITURE ..$ 290,345,000
FEDERAL DEBT ....$ 2,151,210,000

Events

February 12 • Congress adopts the Coinage Act of 1873, which discontinues coinage of the standard silver dollar and thus establishes the single gold standard. The law becomes a political issue as new silver discoveries are made in the West.

February 27 • After investigating the Crédit Mobilier scandal, the House of Representatives censures two of its members, James Brooks and Oakes Ames.

March 1 • Since 1867, Christopher L. Sholes has been working on various models of his typewriter, securing a patent for one in 1868. On March 1, Sholes signs a contract with E. Remington & Sons (the gun manufacturer), who will market the typewriter under the company's name. Within a few years, the Remington typewriter will revolutionize the business world.

March 3 • The salaries of the president, members of Congress, justices of the Supreme Court, and other officials are substantially increased by an act of Congress. Faced with widespread opposition, Congress, in January 1874, repeals all provisions of the law except those relating to the president and the justices.

March 3 • The Timber Culture Act is adopted. An individual may obtain 160 acres of timberland provided he maintains 40 acres of the land properly.

March 3 • The Coal Lands Act is adopted. Under its provisions, coal-bearing land in the public domain is offered for sale at $10 to $20 per acre. An individual may purchase 160 acres, and a group of people 320 acres.

March 4 • President Grant is inaugurated for his second term. Henry Wilson becomes vice president.

April 14 • In the Slaughter-House cases the Supreme Court rules that the Fourteenth Amendment was adopted to bar states from interfering with the rights of blacks as United States citizens, not to protect property rights, which in the cases under review had been adversely affected by a slaughtering monopoly created by the Louisiana legislature.

Fall • The first public kindergarten in the United States opens at the Des Peres School in St. Louis, Missouri. Susan Elizabeth Bow, with the aid of two apprentices and one paid assistant, will teach 68 students the first semester.

September 18 • The bankruptcy of Jay Cooke and Company, a prominent banking concern, brings to an end an inflationary period of excessive expansion. The ensuing Panic of 1873 is accompanied by widespread business failures and general economic distress, under the impact of which the National Labor Union, formed in 1866, collapses.

October 31 • The *Virginius*, a filibustering ship flying the United States flag without proper authority, is captured by a Spanish warship while transporting arms to rebels in Cuba. Spanish officials in Santiago execute 53 people. On November 29, Secretary Fish obtains $80,000 in damages for the families of the Americans who are among those killed.

International and Cultural Events • An economic crisis grips Europe. A National Convention of Colored Persons petitions Congress for civil rights. Joseph F. Glidden's improved barbed wire begins a transformation of western rangeland.

United States of America 1874

Events

April 14 • Congress adopts a bill to increase the amount of legal tender notes (greenbacks) in circulation permanently to $400 million. The bill is vetoed by President Grant on April 22, and on June 10, Congress adopts a new bill increasing the amount temporarily to $383 million.

April–May • An attempt by a defeated candidate to oust Governor Elisha Baxter of Arkansas, a Republican supported by Democrats, ends on May 15, when President Grant recognizes Baxter.

July • Swarms of hungry Rocky Mountain locusts, or grasshoppers, descended on the Plains states. The grasshoppers, which at times blot out the sun, devour everything in sight, even the clothes off people's backs. Relief in the form of money, supplies and seeds comes from people across the country.

July 4 • James B. Eads's steel arch bridge across the Mississippi River at St. Louis is completed. It is the first such bridge across the river.

September 14 • The White League of New Orleans fights the police to oust the Republican government of William P. Kellogg. Although the Democrats claim he was defeated in the governor's race, he is reinstated by federal troops on September 17.

November 18–20 • At a convention held in Cleveland, delegates assembled from 17 states organize the Women's Christian Temperance Union.

November 25 • A conference held in Indianapolis at the

	43rd CONGRESS	
	SENATE .... 73 Members	
	R 49	
	D 19	
	O 5	
ESTIMATED	HOUSE .... 300 Members	
POPULATION	R 194	
44,040,000	D 92	
	O 14	

Ulysses S. Grant
18th President
2nd Republican

Henry Wilson
18th Vice President
Republican

UNITED STATES ECONOMY

GROSS NATIONAL PRODUCT ....$ 7,580,000,000	
RETAIL SALES .... N/A	
BANK RESOURCES ....$ 2,891,000,000	
EXPORTS ....$ 569,000,000	
IMPORTS ....$ 567,000,000	
FEDERAL GOVERNMENT EXPENDITURE ..$ 302,634,000	
FEDERAL DEBT ....$ 2,159,933,000	

call of the Indiana Granger party forms the Greenback party to push for currency inflation.

December 7 • The president's annual message to Congress favors the resumption of specie payments.

International and Cultural Events • Domestic reform and a strong foreign policy mark Disraeli's new ministry. The Methodist Episcopal camp meeting in Chautauqua, New York, adds secular subjects.

The Wells, Fargo & Company express office in Virginia City, Nevada.

1875 United States of America

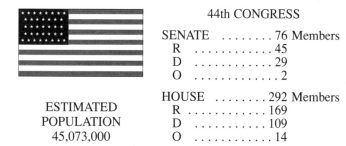

	44th CONGRESS	
	SENATE .... 76 Members	
	R 45	
	D 29	
	O 2	
ESTIMATED	HOUSE .... 292 Members	
POPULATION	R 169	
45,073,000	D 109	
	O 14	

Ulysses S. Grant
18th President
2nd Republican

Henry Wilson
18th Vice President
Republican

UNITED STATES ECONOMY

GROSS NATIONAL PRODUCT	$ 7,580,000,000
RETAIL SALES	N/A
BANK RESOURCES	$ 3,205,000,000
EXPORTS	$ 499,000,000
IMPORTS	$ 533,000,000
FEDERAL GOVERNMENT EXPENDITURE ...	$ 274,623,000
FEDERAL DEBT	N/A

Events

January 14 • An act of Congress calls for the resumption of payments in specie on or before January 1, 1879, and a decrease in the amount of greenbacks in circulation to $300 million.

January 30 • The United States signs a treaty of commercial reciprocity with Hawaii. Sugar and other Hawaiian products are to be imported into the United States duty-free, and no Hawaiian territory is to be acquired by another power. The treaty is ratified by the Senate on March 18.

March 1 • The Civil Rights Act, proposed originally by Senator Sumner, is adopted. Under its provisions, all citizens, regardless of race, are guaranteed equal enjoyment of such public facilities as conveyances, inns and restaurants. None may be excluded from jury service. In 1883, the Supreme Court finds the act unconstitutional.

March 3 • The Tariff Act of 1875 is adopted. Under its provisions the level of rates is raised generally to the pre-1870 level.

March 4 • Former president Andrew Johnson takes his seat in the United States Senate. He will serve until his death on July 31.

April 27 • Archbishop John McCloskey, the first American Roman Catholic cardinal, is invested in St. Patrick's Cathedral, New York.

May 1 • Public attention having been drawn by the *St. Louis Democrat* to a scandal involving United States revenue officials and whisky distillers (the so-called Whisky Ring), Secretary of the Treasury Benjamin H. Bristow begins an official investigation. On May 10, more than 200 people are indicted on charges of conspiring to deprive the federal government of liquor taxes. On December 9, the president's private secretary, Gen. Orville E. Babcock, is also indicted (he is subsequently acquitted through Grant's efforts).

May 17 • Jockey Oliver Lewis rides Aristides to victory in the first running of the Kentucky Derby.

September 1 • A murder is committed by the "Molly Maquires," a secret miners' union that has engaged in violence since 1862. Convictions in the case lead to the breakup of the group.

October–December • Sioux Indians, angered by an influx of gold prospectors into the Black Hills, which have been guaranteed to the Sioux by the Treaty of Fort Laramie, begin to leave their reservations despite being forbidden to do so. Government supplies have not been received, and they need to hunt to survive. The Indians' refusal to return the reservation leads to the Second Sioux War.

November 22 • Ill during most of his vice presidency, Henry Wilson dies.

December 15 • The House of Representatives adopts a resolution against a third term to forestall any attempt by Grant to run for re-election.

International and Cultural Events • Great Britain acquires control of the Suez Canal by purchasing the Egyptian Khedive's interest. Mary Baker Eddy publishes *Science and Health*, in which the principles of Christian Science are laid down.

United States of America 1876

Events

March 2 • The House of Representatives votes to impeach Secretary of War William W. Belknap, who is charged with having taken a bribe from a trading post operator in the Indian Territory. He resigns that same day, on August 1, he is acquitted at a Senate trial because many senators doubt their authority to try a former official.

March 7 • Alexander Graham Bell receives a patent for a telephone.

March 27 • In *United States v. Reese*, the Supreme Court rules that "the 15th Amendment does not confer the right of suffrage upon anyone."

May 10–October • The Centennial Exposition, commemorating the centennial of American independence, is held in Philadelphia. Many new machines are shown.

May 17 • The Prohibition party convenes in Cleveland. It nominates General Green Clay Smith for president and Gideon T. Stewart for vice president.

May 18 • The Greenback party convenes in Indianapolis. It nominates Peter Cooper for president and Samuel F. Carey for vice president.

June 16 • The Republican party convenes in Cincinnati. It nominates Rutherford B. Hayes (Ohio) for president and William A. Wheeler (New York) for vice president.

June 25 • As part of the drive against the Sioux Indians, Lieutenant Colonel George A. Custer leads a force of the Seventh Cavalry to the Little Bighorn River in Montana Territory, where he encounters a force under Chiefs Sitting Bull and Crazy Horse. Custer divides his command into three sections. His own section is cut off by the Sioux, and Custer and 264 of his men are killed.

June 27 • The Democratic party convenes in St. Louis. It nominates Samuel J. Tilden (New York) for president and Thomas A. Hendricks (Indiana) for vice president.

August 1 • Colorado is admitted to the Union as the 38th state.

September–December • United States troops defeat various Sioux bands. Sitting Bull retreats into Canada. In 1877, Crazy Horse surrenders.

October 6 • The American Library Association is organized at a meeting in Philadelphia.

November 7 • In the presidential election, Tilden receives 184 undisputed electoral votes to 163 undisputed votes for Hayes. However, the Republicans insist that the electoral votes of Florida, Louisiana, Oregon, and South Carolina are in dispute; if all of these are awarded to Hayes, Tilden will have one vote less than a majority. On December 6, each of the four states present two sets of votes.

December 12 • Henry William Blair, a Republican from New Hampshire, introduces a prohibition amendment in the House of Representatives. It is the first time that such an amendment is introduced.

International and Cultural Events • Porfirio Diaz seizes power in Mexico. John Hopkins University is the first American educational institution to emphasize graduate studies. Mark Twain publishes *The Adventures of Tom Sawyer*. Baseball's National League is established. In New York City, Frederick Law Olmstead, landscape architect, completes one of his most famous projects, Central Park.

	44th CONGRESS
SENATE	.... 76 Members
R	 45
D	 29
O	 2
HOUSE	.... 292 Members
R	 169
D	 109
O	 14

ESTIMATED
POPULATION
46,107,000

Ulysses S. Grant
18th President
2nd Republican

Vice President
None

UNITED STATES ECONOMY

GROSS NATIONAL PRODUCT	..........$ 7,580,000,000
RETAIL SALES	...............................N/A
BANK RESOURCES	..................$ 3,183,000,000
EXPORTS	...........................$ 526,000,000
IMPORTS	...........................$ 461,000,000
FEDERAL GOVERNMENT EXPENDITURE	..$ 265,101,000
FEDERAL DEBT	......................$ 2,130,846,000

1877 Rutherford B. Hayes

45th CONGRESS

SENATE .... 76 Members
R 39
D 36
O 1

HOUSE .... 293 Members
D 153
R 140
O 0

ESTIMATED
POPULATION
47,141,000

Rutherford B. Hayes
19th President
3rd Republican

William A. Wheeler
19th Vice President
Republican

UNITED STATES ECONOMY

GROSS NATIONAL PRODUCT ....$ 9,180,000,000
RETAIL SALES .... N/A
BANK RESOURCES ....$ 3,204,000,000
EXPORTS ....$ 590,000,000
IMPORTS ....$ 451,000,000
FEDERAL GOVERNMENT EXPENDITURE ..$ 241,334,000
FEDERAL DEBT ....$ 2,107,760,000

Rutherford B. Hayes

Birth .... Delaware, OH, Oct. 4, 1822
Parents .... Rutherford and Sophia Birchard Hayes
Married .... Lucy Webb
Home .... Fremont, OH
Presidency .... 1877 – 1881
Death .... Fremont, OH, Jan. 17, 1893

Events

January 29 • Congress establishes an Electoral Commission composed of 15 members of the Senate, House of Representatives and Supreme Court, of whom seven are Republicans and seven Democrats. The fifteenth member is scheduled to be Justice David Davis, an independent, but since he has been elected to the Senate, a Republican is chosen in his place. The new member, who at first supports Tilden, joins the other Republicans to form a majority for assigning (February 9-28) all the disputed votes to Hayes, who on March 2 is declared to be elected.

March 1 • In the Granger cases, a group of cases involving state regulation of railroads and other private businesses, the Supreme Court rules that states have the power to set rates in the public interest and that businesses so regulated are not deprived of their rights under the due-process clause of the 14th Amendment.

March 3 • The Desert Land Act permits individuals to purchase 640 acres at 25 cents per acre if they agree to irrigate the land in three years.

March 5 • Hayes is inaugurated president.

April 24 • Reconstruction ends with the withdrawal of federal troops from Louisiana, the last southern state to have had a Radical Republican government. This withdrawal and the appointment (March 5) of a southerner to the cabinet are the price for southern acquiescence to Hayes' election.

June–October • The southern Nez Percé Indians, led by Chief Joseph, wage a war with the United States troops sent to remove them from a reservation in Oregon. They win several engagements but fail to reach the Canadian border, surrendering to General Nelson A. Miles at Bear Paw Mountain, in Montana Territory. The survivors are sent to a reservation in Oklahoma, where many die.

June 14 • Flag Day is celebrated across the country for the first time on the 100th anniversary of the first U.S. flag.

July 17 • Angered by wage cuts, Baltimore & Ohio Railroad workers call a strike that soon spreads to other lines. After violent clashes with state militia in West Virginia and Pennsylvania, the strikers are quelled by federal troops. The strike is the first great strike in U.S. history.

November 23 • A joint fisheries commission, set up in Halifax by the Treaty of Washington of 1871, decides that the United States owes Great Britain $5.5 million for fishing privileges in Canadian waters over a 12-year period.

International and Cultural Events • Queen Victoria is proclaimed Empress of India. The Russo-Turkish War follows anti-Turkish uprisings in Europe. Edison patents a phonograph. George B. Selden builds a two-cycle gasoline-operated vehicle.

United States of America 1878

Events

January • The Knights of Labor, an industrial union founded in Philadelphia in 1869, adopts a constitution as a national organization.

January 17 • A treaty with Samoan chieftains gives the United States a naval base at Pago Pago.

February 22 • At a convention held in Toledo, Ohio, the Greenback Labor party is formed from Greenback and other elements. It favors such inflationary measures as the issuance of new greenbacks and the discontinuance of specie payments, as well as restrictions on the immigration of Chinese and limitations on required hours of work.

February 28 • Congress adopts the Bland-Allison Act over the veto of President Hayes. Under its provisions, the secretary of the treasury must purchase $2 million to $4 million worth of silver each month for coinage into standard silver dollars. The measure is a compromise between the views of sound-money advocates and proponents of the free coinage of silver, who include both inflationists and western silver producers.

May 31 • An act of Congress provides that outstanding greenbacks, amounting to some $347 million, continue permanently as currency.

June 3 • The Timber Cutting Act permits a settler to procure for himself free timber from public land. The Timber and Stone Act authorizes the sale of nonagricultural land in the Far West at $2.50 an acre in parcels of 160 acres or less.

June 11 • An act of Congress establishes a government for the District of Columbia that consists of three commissioners, two being residents appointed by the president and one an army engineer.

July 11 • Wishing to reform the civil service, President Hayes suspends from office Alonzo B. Cornell, naval officer, and Chester A. Arthur, collector of customs of the port of New York. Because of the Tenure of Office Act, he has been unable to dismiss the two officials, who owe their posts to Rescoe Conkling, Republican boss of New York state, and have the support of Radical Republicans in the Senate. Later, the new Senate approves his own appointees.

September–January 1879 • United States troops subdue the Cheyenne Indians in the Dull Knife campaign in Wyoming Territory.

October 15 • With financial banking from banker J.P. Morgan, Thomas A. Edison establishes the Edison Electric Light Company. In 1892, the company will merge with the Thomas-Houston Electric Company and become the General Electric Company.

November • In the midterm elections, control of both houses of Congress passes to the Democrats for the first

45th CONGRESS	
SENATE	.... 76 Members
R	 39
D	 36
O	 1
HOUSE	.... 293 Members
D	 153
R	 140
O	 0

ESTIMATED POPULATION 48,174,000

Rutherford B. Hayes
19th President
3rd Republican

William A. Wheeler
19th Vice President
Republican

UNITED STATES ECONOMY

GROSS NATIONAL PRODUCT	...........$ 9,180,000,000
RETAIL SALES	.... N/A
BANK RESOURCES	...................$ 3,081,000,000
EXPORTS	...........................$ 681,000,000
IMPORTS	...........................$ 437,000,000
FEDERAL GOVERNMENT EXPENDITURE	..$ 236,964,000
FEDERAL DEBT	......................$ 2,159,418,000

time since 1858. Fourteen members of the Greenback Labor party are elected to Congress.

International and Cultural Events • The Congress of Berlin forces Russia to modify the Treaty of San Stefano, which ended the Russo-Turkish War. James McNeill Whistler sues the art critic John Ruskin for disparaging remarks about his work. A yellow fever epidemic ravages the southern United States from late spring until winter, killing an estimated 14,000 people.

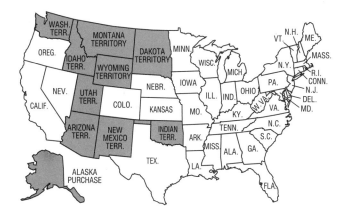

46th CONGRESS

SENATE	....	76 Members
D	....	42
R	....	33
O	....	1
HOUSE	....	293 Members
D	....	149
R	....	130
O	....	14

ESTIMATED
POPULATION
49,208,000

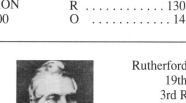

Rutherford B. Hayes
19th President
3rd Republican

William A. Wheeler
19th Vice President
Republican

UNITED STATES ECONOMY

GROSS NATIONAL PRODUCT	.... $ 9,180,000,000
RETAIL SALES	.... N/A
BANK RESOURCES	.... $ 3,313,000,000
EXPORTS	.... $ 698,000,000
IMPORTS	.... $ 446,000,000
FEDERAL GOVERNMENT EXPENDITURE	.. $ 266,948,000
FEDERAL DEBT	.... $ 2,298,913,000

Events

January 1 • As authorized by Congress in 1875, the United States government resumes making payments in specie.

February 15 • Congress grants women the right to practice law before the United States Supreme Court.

March 1 • President Hayes vetoes a bill that would limit the immigration of Chinese in contravention of the Burlingame Treaty of 1868.

March 3 • An act of Congress establishes the United States Geological Survey, of which Clarence King is the first director.

April 29 • President Hayes vetoes an appropriation bill to which Congress has added a rider preventing the president from employing troops in elections, as provided in Reconstruction Force Acts. This and other similar vetoes are sustained with Republican votes.

May 7 • California, where opposition to Chinese immigration has been particularly strong, adopts a new constitution that includes a provision forbidding employers to hire Chinese workers.

June 28 • The Mississippi River Commission is created by Congress to improve navigability.

September–October • Ute Indians living on the White River in Colorado rebel against a dictatorial agent. They ambush a military force and attack the agency, but hostilities soon end.

October 21 • Thomas A. Edison tests his perfected incandescent lamp; it burns for 24 hours. On December 31, he demonstrates the lamp, for which he receives a patent on January 27, 1880.

International and Cultural Events • The French Panama Canal Company is organized by Ferdinand de Lesseps. British troops are massacred by Zulus at Isandhlwana. Henrik Ibsen's *A Doll's House* is staged. Henry George publishes *Progress and Poverty*.

President Rutherford B. Hayes meets with Indian chiefs in the White House.

United States of America 1880

Events

February 12 • President Hayes issues a proclamation warning settlers not to trespass on Indian land.

March • English members of the Salvation Army organize an American branch in Philadelphia.

March 1 • In *Strauder v. West Virginia*, the U.S. Supreme Court rules that it is unconstitutional to exclude black men from state jury panels but not women, whose place the Court will say until the mid-1970s is in the home.

June 2 • The Republican party convenes in Chicago. Divided between so-called Stalwart and Half-Breed factions, it finally nominates a compromise candidate, James A. Garfield (Ohio), for president and a Stalwart, Chester A. Arthur (New York), for vice president. The party favors a protective tariff.

June 9 • The Greenback Labor party convenes in Chicago and nominates James B. Weaver for president.

June 17 • The Prohibition party convenes in Cleveland and nominates Neal Dow for president.

June 22 • The Democratic party convenes in Cincinnati. It nominates Winfield S. Hancock (Pennsylvania) for president and William H. English (Indiana) for vice president. The party platform opposes a protective tariff.

November 2 • In the presidential election, Garfield is elected president, receiving 214 electoral votes to 155 for Hancock, his Democratic opponent. Arthur is elected

46th CONGRESS

ESTIMATED POPULATION 50,262,000

SENATE .... 76 Members
D 42
R 33
O 1

HOUSE .... 293 Members
D 149
R 130
O 14

Rutherford B. Hayes
19th President
3rd Republican

William A. Wheeler
19th Vice President
Republican

UNITED STATES ECONOMY

GROSS NATIONAL PRODUCT ....$ 9,180,000,000
RETAIL SALES .... N/A
BANK RESOURCES ....$ 3,399,000,000
EXPORTS ....$ 824,000,000
IMPORTS ....$ 668,000,000
FEDERAL GOVERNMENT EXPENDITURE . .$ 267,643,000
FEDERAL DEBT ....$ 2,090,909,000

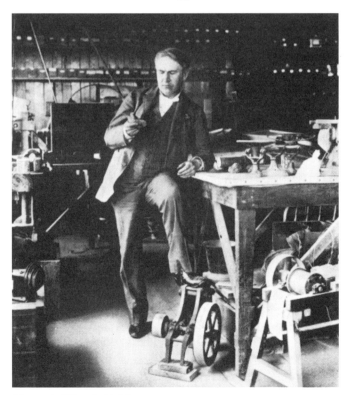

Thomas A. Edison in his laboratory.

vice president.

November 17 • The United States and China sign a treaty that permits the United States to restrict the immigration of Chinese laborers.

International and Cultural Events • The Irish Land League forbids anyone to supply the wants of British land agent Captain Charles Boycott, and a word is born.

107

1881 Garfield/Arthur

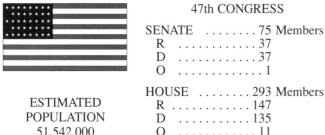

47th CONGRESS		
SENATE	....	75 Members
R	....	37
D	....	37
O	....	1
HOUSE	....	293 Members
R	....	147
D	....	135
O	....	11

ESTIMATED
POPULATION
51,542,000

James A. Garfield
20th President
4th Republican

Chester A. Arthur
20th Vice President
Republican

UNITED STATES ECONOMY

GROSS NATIONAL PRODUCT	...........$ 9,180,000,000
RETAIL SALES	.... N/A
BANK RESOURCES	...................$ 3,809,000,000
EXPORTS	.............................$ 884,000,000
IMPORTS	...........................$ 643,000,000
FEDERAL GOVERNMENT EXPENDITURE	..$ 260,713,000
FEDERAL DEBT	.....................$ 2,019,286,000

Events

January 24 • In *Springer v. United States*, the Supreme Court rules that the income tax laws enacted during the Civil War are constitutional, since they do not provide for the type of direct tax that is barred by Article I, Section 8, of the Constitution.

February 19 • To comply with a recently enacted constitutional amendment, Kansas passes a law prohibiting the sale of alcohol, except for medicinal, mechanical and scientific purposes. It is the first state to enact such a law.

March 4 • Garfield is inaugurated president.

March 5 • James G. Blaine is named secretary of state. His appointment and that of a collector of the port of New York are resented by the Stalwart faction, but its opposition proves ineffective.

April • Widespread frauds, involving contracts on the mail roads known as "Star Routes," are discovered in the Post Office Department. No convictions are obtained in trials held in 1882 and 1883.

June 24 • Secretary Blaine warns European countries against extending a joint guarantee to the canal Ferdinand de Lesseps has begun to construct across the isthmus of Panama.

July 3 • President Garfield is wounded by a shot fired by Charles J. Guiteau, an unsuccessful office seeker. The president dies on September 19, and he is succeeded in office by Vice President Arthur.

November 14–January 1882 • Guiteau is tried and convicted for President Garfield's murder. He is executed on June 30, 1882

November 22 • Secretary Blaine invites the nations of Latin America to a conference to be held a year hence in Washington. Meanwhile, Blaine's resignation, offered to President Arthur following the death of Garfield, is accepted, effective December 19. The new secretary of state, Frederick T. Frelinghuysen, withdraws the invitations to the conference.

International and Cultural Events • Czar Alexander II is assassinated and is succeeded by Alexander III. Clara Barton organizes the American Red Cross. Henry James publishes *The Portrait of a Lady*. The United States Lawn Tennis Association is formed.

James A. Garfield	
Birth	.... Cuyahoga County, OH, Nov. 19, 1831
Parents	.... Abram and Eliza Ballou Garfield
Married	.... Lucretia Rudolph
Home	.... Mentor, OH
Presidency	 1881
Death	.... Elberon, NJ, Sept. 19, 1881

Chester A. Arthur	
Birth	.... Fairfield, VT, Oct. 5, 1830
Parents	.... William and Malvina Stone Arthur
Married	.... Ellen Lewis Herndon
Home	.... New York, NY
Presidency	.... 1881 – 1885
Death	.... New York, NY, Nov. 18, 1886

United States of America 1882

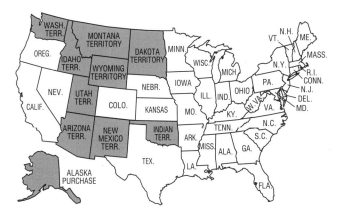

Events

January 2 • John D. Rockefeller and his associates in the Standard Oil Company of Ohio establish the Standard Oil Trust, an agreement replacing a less formal arrangement in effect since 1879. This is the first of the industrial monopolies known as trusts to be organized in the United States.

February 2 • The Knights of Columbus, a Roman Catholic fraternal order, is organized in New Haven, Connecticut.

March 16 • The Senate ratifies the Geneva Convention on the care of wounded soldiers. The convention is proclaimed on July 26.

March 22 • President Arthur signs the Edmunds Act, an anti-Mormon measure that prohibits polygamists from voting and holding public office and establishes various penalties for polygamy.

May 6 • The Chinese Exclusion Act is adopted over the April 4 veto of President Arthur. Under its provisions, no Chinese laborers are to be admitted to the United States for 10 years.

May 15 • An act of Congress empowers the president to establish a tariff commission consisting of nine members.

May 22 • The United States and Korea sign a treaty of friendship and commerce. The United States also recognizes Korean independence. The treaty is ratified by the Senate on February 13, 1883.

April 3 • A member of the James gang, Robert Ford, shoots Jesse James (alias Thomas Howard) in the back of the head at the outlaw's home in St. Joseph, Missouri.

August 3 • Congress adopts a bill barring the immigration of undesirables: convicts, paupers and the insane. A 50-cent tax is levied on immigrants.

September 4 • The Edison Electric Illuminating Company, founded by Thomas A. Edison, begins operating a steam-powered central station on Pearl Street, New York City.

September 5 • As suggested by Peter J. McGuire, the Central Labor Union of New York City institutes the observance of Labor Day. Beginning with Oregon in 1887, 32 states make the first Monday in September a legal holiday by 1894, when Labor Day becomes a national holiday by an act of Congress.

November 7 • Grover Cleveland, the Democratic candidate, is elected governor of New York by a landslide vote. In the national elections, the Democrats regain control of the House of Representatives by a substantial margin, while the Republicans gain slightly in the Senate.

December 4 • The members of the tariff commission

47th CONGRESS

SENATE . . . . 75 Members
R 37
D 37
O 1

HOUSE . . . . 293 Members
R 147
D 135
O 11

ESTIMATED POPULATION
52,821,000

Chester A. Arthur
21st President
5th Republican

Vice President
None

UNITED STATES ECONOMY

GROSS NATIONAL PRODUCT $11,300,000,000
RETAIL SALES . . . . N/A
BANK RESOURCES . . . .$ 4,031,000,000
EXPORTS . . . .$ 733,000,000
IMPORTS . . . .$ 725,000,000
FEDERAL GOVERNMENT EXPENDITURE .$ 257,981,000
FEDERAL DEBT . . . .$ 1,856,916,000

appointed by President Arthur present their report. They urge that rates be lowered.

International and Cultural Events • Disorder follows the land eviction of thousands of Irish families. Two British officials are murdered in Phoenix Park, Dublin; Charles Parnell is accused of complicity but disavows the terrorists. Popular literary works this year are Joel Chandler Harris' *Uncle Remus* and Lew Wallace's *Ben-Hur.*

48th CONGRESS

SENATE .... 76 Members
  R 38
  D 36
  O 2

ESTIMATED
POPULATION
54,100,000

HOUSE .... 325 Members
  D 197
  R 118
  O 10

Chester A. Arthur
21st President
5th Republican

Vice President
None

UNITED STATES ECONOMY

GROSS NATIONAL PRODUCT $11,300,000,000
RETAIL SALES .... N/A
BANK RESOURCES .... $ 4,208,000,000
EXPORTS ....$ 804,000,000
IMPORTS ....$ 723,000,000
FEDERAL GOVERNMENT EXPENDITURE .$ 265,408,000
FEDERAL DEBT ....$ 1,721,959,000

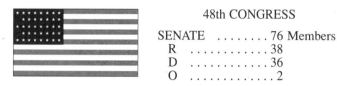

Events

January 16 • The Pendleton Civil Service Act is adopted. Drawn up by the reformer Dorman B. Eaton and sponsored by Senator George H. Pendleton, it initiates a merit system for the federal government. The act creates a Civil Service Commission, of which Eaton becomes the first head. It also provides for competitive examinations for applicants for civil service posts, and it prohibits the assessment of federal officials for political contributions.

March 3 • An act of Congress provides for the construction of three steel cruisers. Completed in 1887, they initiate the U.S. Navy's modernization.

March 3 • The Tariff Act of 1883 is adopted. It provides for a five percent reduction in rates.

May 24 • The Brooklyn Bridge, a suspension bridge designed by John A. Roebling, is opened between Manhattan and Brooklyn.

October 15 • In the Civil Rights cases, the Supreme Court rules that the Civil Rights Act of 1875 is unconstitutional insofar as protecting blacks from infringement of their civil rights by private persons is concerned. The 14th Amendment, it is held, applies only to state action.

November 18 • Multiple and conflicting time systems are eliminated when Canadian and American railroads set standard time zones 15 degrees wide.

International and Cultural Events • Karl Marx dies, and Benito Mussolini is born. Work begins on Chicago's Home Insurance Building, the first to use the steel skeletal construction of skyscrapers. The Metropolitan Opera House opens in New York City.

A steel mill in Pittsburgh.

United States of America 1884

Events

May 14 • A convention in Chicago forms the Anti-Monopoly party. The new party nominates Benjamin F. Butler for president.

May 17 • An act of Congress extends the laws of the state of Oregon to Alaska.

May 28 • The Greenback Labor party convenes in Indianapolis. It nominates Benjamin F. Butler for president and Alanson M. West for vice president.

June 3 • The Republican party convenes in Chicago. It nominates James G. Blaine (Maine) for president and John A. Logan (Illinois) for vice president.

June 16 • Independent Republicans, called Mugwumps by other Republicans, convene in New York. Unable to support Blaine, they vote to support a reform candidate chosen by the Democratic party.

June 27 • Congress creates the Bureau of Labor in the Department of the Interior.

July 8 • The Democratic party convenes in Chicago. It nominates Governor Grover Cleveland of New York for president and Thomas A. Hendricks (Indiana) for vice president.

July 23 • The Prohibition party convenes in Pittsburgh. It nominates John P. St. John for president and Williams Daniel for vice president.

August • The so-called Mulligan Letters, written by James G. Blaine to a businessman in Boston while Blaine was speaker of the House of Representatives, are printed in *Harper's Weekly*. They show that Blaine used his position to his financial advantage.

August 5 • The cornerstone of the pedestal of the Statue of Liberty is laid at Bedloe's Island (present-day Liberty Island).

August 26 • Ottmar Mergenthaler obtains a patent for the Linotype machine to set type.

October • The United States hosts the International Prime Meridian Conference. Meeting in Washington, D.C., delegates designate Greenwich, England, as the prime meridian for the world.

October 6 • The United States Naval War College is founded in Newport, Rhode Island.

October 29 • A remark by a Blaine supporter characterizing the Democratic party as the party of "rum, Romanism, and rebellion" loses the Republicans Roman Catholic votes in New York state.

November 4 • In the presidential election, Cleveland is elected president, receiving 219 electoral votes to 182 for Blaine, his Republican opponent. Hendricks is elected vice president. The Democrats retain their majority in the House of Representatives.

December 16 • The World's Industrial and Cotton Cen-

48th CONGRESS	
SENATE	.... 76 Members
R	 38
D	 36
O	 2
HOUSE	.... 325 Members
D	 197
R	 118
O	 10

ESTIMATED
POPULATION
55,379,000

Chester A. Arthur
21st President
5th Republican

Vice President
None

UNITED STATES ECONOMY

GROSS NATIONAL PRODUCT	..........$11,300,000,000
RETAIL SALES	.... N/A
BANK RESOURCES	..................$ 4,221,000,000
EXPORTS	.............................$ 725,000,000
IMPORTS	.............................$ 668,000,000
FEDERAL GOVERNMENT EXPENDITURE	.$ 244,126,000
FEDERAL DEBT	......................$ 1,625,307,000

tennial Exposition of 1884-1885 opens in New Orleans.

International and Cultural Events • The Fabian Society, organized by British socialists, attracts G.B. Shaw, H.G. Wells, Sidney and Beatrice Webb, and Annie Besant. Mark Twain publishes *The Adventures of Huckleberry Finn*. Work begins on the first "skyscrapper" in the world, the 10-story Home Life Insurance Building in Chicago. The Maxim machine gun, widely used in World War I, goes into production.

111

1885 Grover Cleveland

49th CONGRESS

SENATE .... 77 Members
R 43
D 34
O 0

HOUSE .... 325 Members
D 183
R 140
O 2

ESTIMATED
POPULATION
56,658,000

Grover Cleveland
22nd President
7th Democrat

Thomas A. Hendricks
21st Vice President
Democrat

UNITED STATES ECONOMY

GROSS NATIONAL PRODUCT $11,300,000,000
RETAIL SALES .... N/A
BANK RESOURCES .... $ 4,427,000,000
EXPORTS .... $ 727,000,000
IMPORTS .... $ 578,000,000
FEDERAL GOVERNMENT EXPENDITURE . $ 260,227,000
FEDERAL DEBT .... $ 1,578,551,000

Grover Cleveland

Birth .... Caldwell, NJ, Mar. 18, 1837
Parents .... Richard F. and Ann Neal Cleveland
Married .... Frances Folsom
Home .... Buffalo, NY
Presidency .... 1885 – 1889; 1893 – 1897
Death .... Princeton, NJ, June 24, 1908

Events

January 29 • The Senate refuses to ratify a treaty for the construction of a canal across Nicaragua that was signed in 1881.

February 21 • The Washington Monument is dedicated in Washington.

February 25 • A bill barring the enclosure of public land without permission is adopted. On August 17, the president orders illegal fences removed.

February 26 • The Contract Labor Act is adopted. With some exceptions, it bars immigrant laborers who have contracted to work for an employer who pays for their passage.

March 4 • Cleveland is inaugurated president.

March 13 • President Cleveland warns prospective settlers (who are known as Boomers) to stay out of unassigned Indian lands in the Indian Territory.

July 1 • In accordance with a joint resolution of Congress of 1883, the United States abrogates the fishery article of the Treaty of Washington of 1871.

November 25 • Vice President Thomas A. Hendricks dies in Indianapolis.

International and Cultural Events • Charles (Chinese) Gordon is killed by the Mahdi at the siege of Khartoum. The German East Africa protectorate, which includes Tanganyika, Rwanda and Burundi, is established. The Canadian Pacific Railway is completed five years ahead of schedule.

The Washington Monument, Washington, D.C.

United States of America 1886

Events

January 19 • The Presidential Succession Act is adopted. It stipulates that if both the president and the vice president die, resign or otherwise are unable to function, the presidential succession shall pass to the members of the cabinet in the order in which their offices were established.

February 7-8 • Anti-Chinese sentiment in Seattle, Washington, results in local residents rounding-up Chinese immigrants living in the city in preparation for a forced departure aboard the *Queen of the Pacific*. After a judge temporarily stops the proceeding to determine if the Chinese truly want to leave, the Chinese are permitted to depart. Local residents will collect the money to pay for their fare.

March 1 • President Cleveland informs the Senate that despite the Tenure of Office Act, the president is authorized by the Constitution to suspend or remove officers without the consent of the Senate.

March 1–May 3 • Railroad workers belonging to the Knights of Labor wage an unsuccessful general strike against the railroad system controlled by Jay Gould.

April 8 • A bill calling for the free coinage of silver, sponsored by Representative Richard P. Bland, is narrowly defeated in the House of Representatives.

May 4 • At a mass meeting in Haymarket Square, Chicago, called to protest the shooting of striking workers on May 3, a bomb is thrown, killing seven policemen and injuring many others.

May 10 • In *Santa Clara County v. Southern Pacific Railroad*, the Supreme Court rules that the due process clause of the 14th Amendment protects the rights of corporations as legal "persons."

June 19–August 20 • Eight alleged anarchists accused of conspiracy in the Haymarket bombing are convicted in a trial in Chicago. Seven of them are sentenced to death and one to prison. Two of the death sentences are commuted to life imprisonment, and one man commits suicide; the other four men are hanged on November 11, 1887. The three survivors are pardoned in 1893 by Governor John Peter Altgeld, who severely criticizes the trial.

August 3 • An act of Congress authorizes the construction of additional ships for the United States Navy, which is brought up to date by Secretary of the Navy William C. Whitney.

September 4 • The Apache chief Geronimo and his band are captured by General Nelson A. Miles, ending a struggle in Arizona, New Mexico and Mexico that has lasted since 1876.

October 28 • The Statue of Liberty, given to the United States by the people of France, is dedicated by President

49th CONGRESS	
SENATE .... 77 Members	
R 43	
D 34	
O 0	
HOUSE .... 325 Members	
D 183	
R 140	
O 2	

ESTIMATED POPULATION 57,938,000

Grover Cleveland
22nd President
7th Democrat

Vice President
None

UNITED STATES ECONOMY

GROSS NATIONAL PRODUCT	$11,300,000,000
RETAIL SALES	N/A
BANK RESOURCES	$ 4,542,000,000
EXPORTS	$ 666,000,000
IMPORTS	$ 635,000,000
FEDERAL GOVERNMENT EXPENDITURE .	$ 242,483,000
FEDERAL DEBT	$ 1,555,660,000

Cleveland on Bedloe's (Liberty) Island, New York Harbor.

December 8 • The American Federation of Labor evolves from the annual convention of the Federation of Organized Trades and Labor Unions. Samuel Gompers is its first president.

International and Cultural Events • The Liberal government of William Gladstone falls after he endorses Irish home rule. The social event of the Washington season is the president's marriage to Miss Frances Folsom in a White House ceremony.

1887 United States of America

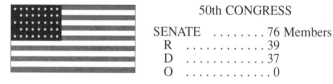

50th CONGRESS

SENATE .... 76 Members
R 39
D 37
O 0

HOUSE .... 325 Members
D 169
R 152
O 4

ESTIMATED
POPULATION
59,217,000

Grover Cleveland
22nd President
7th Democrat

Vice President
None

UNITED STATES ECONOMY

GROSS NATIONAL PRODUCT $12,300,000,000
RETAIL SALES .... N/A
BANK RESOURCES .... $ 5,193,000,000
EXPORTS .... $ 703,000,000
IMPORTS .... $ 692,000,000
FEDERAL GOVERNMENT EXPENDITURE .$ 267,932,000
FEDERAL DEBT .... $ 1,465,485,000

Events

January • Congress adopts the Dependent Pension bill, which would furnish pensions for all veterans, honorably discharged after serving a minimum of 90 days, who engage in manual labor but cannot earn enough money to support themselves. On February 11, the bill is vetoed by President Cleveland, who believes it would facilitate fraudulent claims. The president has also vetoed a number of private pension bills after investigation.

January 20 • The Senate ratifies a renewal of the 1875 commercial treaty with Hawaii that gives the United States alone the right to construct a naval base at Pearl Harbor, Oahu.

February 3 • The Electoral Count Act is adopted. To eliminate disputes in national elections, Congress is required to accept as valid returns made under state electoral laws unless wrongdoing is evident.

February 4 • The Interstate Commerce Act is adopted to fill the need for regulation of the railroads after the Supreme Court had found state regulation unconstitutional (*Wabash, St. Louis and Pacific Railroad Company v. Illinois*, 1886). It establishes the Interstate Commerce Commission as a regulatory body. The act specifies that railroad rates should be reasonable and nondiscriminatory.

February 8 • The Dawes Severalty Act is adopted. Under its provisions, most Indian tribes, except for the Five Civilized Tribes, are no longer to be considered distinct entities. Tribal lands are to be allotted to families and individuals, who may not sell their allotments for 25 years.

March 2 • The Hatch Act is adopted. It provides for federal aid to agricultural experiment stations in the various states.

March 2 • In reaction to Canadian interference with American fishermen after the abrogation in 1885 of the fishery article of the Treaty of Washington, Congress empowers the president to adopt various measures in retaliation.

March 5 • Congress repeals the Tenure of Office Act.

June 7 • President Cleveland angers Union veterans when he approves the return of captured Confederate battle flags to the South. He will reverse himself on June 15, and the battle flags will not be returned until 1905.

November 22 • A six-member Anglo-American commission begins meeting in Washington to resolve the dispute over the Canadian fisheries.

December 5 • In *Mugler v. Kansas*, the U.S. Supreme Court, in an eight-to-one decision, rules that a state has the constitutional right to prohibit the manufacture and sale of intoxicating beverages. The Court pronounced such laws a proper use of a state's policing power.

December 6 • In his annual message to Congress, President Cleveland, who has become increasingly concerned about the effect of high tariff rates on the economy, urges that the rates be lowered, arousing opposition in both parties.

International and Cultural Events • Queen Victoria celebrates her Golden Jubilee. Paris crowds cheer General Georges Boulanger, "the man on horseback." France unites Vietnam and Cambodia as Indochina. Laos is added to the union in 1893.

United States of America 1888

Events

February 15 • The Bayard-Chamberlain Treaty, drafted by the Anglo-American commission on the Canadian fisheries, is signed in Washington. Although the Senate, on August 21, refuses to ratify the treaty, an annual arrangement for American use of the fisheries is continued until 1923.

February 22 • The Industrial Reform party convenes in Washington, D.C. It nominates Albert E. Redstone of California for president and John Colvin of Kansas for vice president.

February • The secret ballot is introduced into the United States in a municipal election in Louisville, Kentucky.

March 11 • The Northeast is struck by a memorable blizzard. New York City is without transportation, communications and food supplies, and many lives are lost. Damage is estimated at $25 million.

May 16 • The Union Labor party convenes in Cincinnati. It nominates A.J. Sweeter of Illinois for president and Charles E. Cunningham of Arkansas for vice president.

May 17 • The United Labor party convenes in Cincinnati. It nominates Robert H. Cowdrey of Illinois for president and W.H.T. Wakefield of Kansas for vice president.

May 30 • The Prohibition party convenes in Indianapolis. It nominated Clinton B. Fisk for president.

June 5 • The Democratic party convenes in St. Louis. It nominates President Cleveland for re-election and Allen G. Thurman (Ohio) for vice president.

June 13 • An act of Congress creates a separate Department of Labor not headed by a cabinet member.

June 19 • The Republican party convenes in Chicago. It nominates Benjamin Harrison (Indiana) for president and Levi P. Morton (New York) for vice president. It adopts a platform favoring high duties to protect American manufacturers, a position that attracts wide support.

July 13 • With the approval of Congress, Secretary of State Thomas F. Bayard invites the nations of Latin America to an inter-American conference to be held in Washington in 1889.

October 1 • The return to the United States of Chinese laborers who have left the country is forbidden by act of Congress.

October 21 • Republicans publish a letter written by Lord Sackville-West, British minister in Washington, in response to a letter from a supposed naturalized citizen of British birth (actually a Republican from California), advising him to vote for Cleveland. The hoax gains the Republicans a number of votes. On October 24, Sackville-West is sent home.

November 6 • In the presidential election, Harrison is elected president, receiving 233 electoral votes to 168 for

50th CONGRESS

SENATE	....	76 Members
R	....	39
D	....	37
O	....	0
HOUSE	....	325 Members
D	....	169
R	....	152
O	....	4

ESTIMATED
POPULATION
60,496,000

Grover Cleveland
22nd President
7th Democrat

Vice President
None

UNITED STATES ECONOMY

GROSS NATIONAL PRODUCT	..........$12,300,000,000
RETAIL SALES	.... N/A
BANK RESOURCES	..................$ 5,471,000,000
EXPORTS	..........................$ 684,000,000
IMPORTS	..........................$ 724,000,000
FEDERAL GOVERNMENT EXPENDITURE	.$ 267,922,000
FEDERAL DEBT	.....................$ 1,384,632,000

Cleveland, who receives a majority of the popular vote. Morton is elected vice president, and the Republicans gain a majority in the House of Representatives.

International and Cultural Events • William II becomes the emperor of Germany. The Convention of Constantinople guarantees Suez Canal passage to all powers in both peace and war. Edward Bellamy's utopian novel *Looking Backward, 2000–1887* lays the foundations for the Nationalist party.

1889 Benjamin Harrison

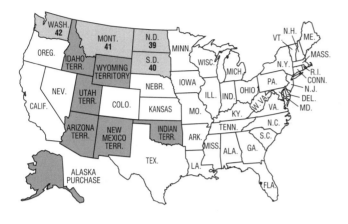

ESTIMATED POPULATION 61,775,000

51st CONGRESS

SENATE .... 76 Members
R 39
D 37
O 0

HOUSE .... 325 Members
R 166
D 159
O 0

Benjamin Harrison
23rd President
6th Republican

Levi P. Morton
22nd Vice President
Republican

UNITED STATES ECONOMY

GROSS NATIONAL PRODUCT $12,300,000,000
RETAIL SALES .... N/A
BANK RESOURCES .... $ 5,945,000,000
EXPORTS .... $ 730,000,000
IMPORTS .... $ 745,000,000
FEDERAL GOVERNMENT EXPENDITURE .$ 299,289,000
FEDERAL DEBT .... $ 1,249,471,000

Benjamin Harrison

Birth .... North Bend, OH, Aug. 20, 1833
Parents .... John Scott and Elizabeth Irwin Harrison
Married ...... Lavinia Scott; Mary Scott Lord Dimmick
Home .... Indianapolis, IN
Presidency .... 1889 – 1893
Death .... Indianapolis, IN Mar. 13, 1901

Events

March 4 • Harrison is inaugurated president.

April 22 • Former unassigned Indian lands in the Indian Territory are opened to settlement at noon. In less than one day, Guthrie and Oklahoma City are established and 1.9 million acres are claimed.

May 31 • Thousands of lives are lost in Johnstown, Pennsylvania, when the Conemaugh Dam breaks.

June 14 • The United States, Great Britain and Germany sign a treaty in Berlin whereby they guarantee the independence of Samoa under their joint protection. The treaty is ratified in 1890.

August 3 • The Sioux Indians cede 11 million acres of land in Dakota Territory to the United States.

October 2 • The First International Conference of American States opens in Washington. It founds the International Bureau of American Republics (later Pan American Union) and adjourns on April 19, 1890.

November 2 • North Dakota is admitted to the Union as the 39th state and South Dakota as the 40th state. Montana is admitted as the 41st state on November 8, and, on November 11, Washington becomes the 42nd state.

International and Cultural Events • The Eiffel Tower is erected for the Paris Exposition. Archduke Rudolf of Austria commits suicide at Mayerling. General Boulanger flees France to escape prosecution for treason. Elizabeth Cochrane Seaman, known to New York *World* readers as Nellie Bly, sets off to circle the globe in imitation of Jules Verne's *Around the World in Eighty Days*. She trims the fictional record by almost eight days.

A painting of a Sioux Indian chief by Frederic Remington.

United States of America 1890

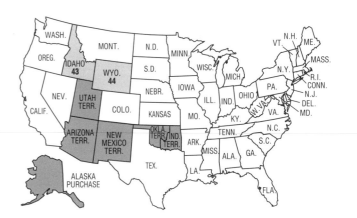

Events

January 25 • Miners belonging to the American Federation of Labor and their counterparts in the Knights of Labor join together to establish the United Mine Workers.

February 10 • Land ceded by the Sioux Indians in South Dakota in 1889 is opened for settlement.

March 3 • In *Louisville, New Orleans and Texas Railway Company v. Mississippi*, the U.S. Supreme Court, in a seven-to-two decision, rules that a state can require railroads to provide separate accommodations for its black and white customers. After accepting the state court's conclusion that such requirements affect only intrastate railroad operations, the Court pronounces the requirements no burden on interstate commerce.

March 24 • In *Chicago, Milwaukee & St. Paul Railroad Company v. Minnesota*, the Supreme Court rules that a state law authorizing a commission to set rates not subject to judicial review is unconstitutional.

May 2 • Oklahoma Territory is created by an act of Congress from part of the Indian Territory.

June 27 • An act of Congress authorizes the payment of service pensions to disabled veterans and their dependents.

July 2 • The Sherman Antitrust Act is adopted. It makes trusts and other combinations in restraint of trade illegal, and it provides for their dissolution by federal action.

July 3 • Idaho is admitted to the Union as the 43rd state. On July 10, Wyoming is admitted to the Union as the 44th state.

July 14 • The Sherman Silver Purchase Act is adopted. The result of a political compromise, it stipulates that the Treasury buy 4.5 million ounces of silver a month and issue Treasury notes redeemable in silver or gold to pay for the full amount.

October 1 • The McKinley Tariff Act is adopted. It increases average rates to almost 50 percent and permits

51st CONGRESS

SENATE .... 76 Members	
R 39	
D 37	
O 0	

ESTIMATED POPULATION 63,056,000

HOUSE .... 325 Members	
R 166	
D 159	
O 0	

Benjamin Harrison
23rd President
6th Republican

Levi P. Morton
22nd Vice President
Republican

UNITED STATES ECONOMY

GROSS NATIONAL PRODUCT	$12,300,000,000
RETAIL SALES	N/A
BANK RESOURCES	$ 6,358,000,000
EXPORTS	$ 845,000,000
IMPORTS	$ 789,000,000
FEDERAL GOVERNMENT EXPENDITURE	$ 318,041,000
FEDERAL DEBT	$ 1,122,397,000

reciprocal agreements by the president.

December 15 • Sitting Bull is killed during a Sioux uprising. On December 29, troops of the Seventh Cavalry massacre a band of Sioux at Wounded Knee Creek.

International and Cultural Events • Bismarck is dismissed as German chancellor. Irish nationalists split as Parnell resigns following a divorce scandal. William James's *The Principles of Psychology* founds the modern empirical science.

A political cartoon of the influence of the trusts on the Senate.

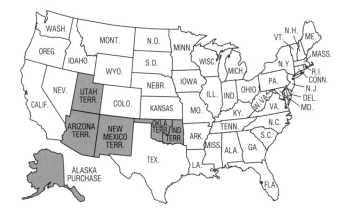

52nd CONGRESS

SENATE .... 88 Members
R 47
D 39
O 2

HOUSE .... 332 Members
D 235
R 88
O 9

ESTIMATED
POPULATION
64,361,000

Benjamin Harrison
23rd President
6th Republican

Levi P. Morton
22nd Vice President
Republican

UNITED STATES ECONOMY

GROSS NATIONAL PRODUCT	$12,300,000,000
RETAIL SALES	N/A
BANK RESOURCES	$ 6,562,000,000
EXPORTS	$ 872,000,000
IMPORTS	$ 845,774,000
FEDERAL GOVERNMENT EXPENDITURE	$ 365,774,000
FEDERAL DEBT	$ 1,002,807,000

Events

March 3 • The Timber Culture Act of 1873 is repealed by an act of Congress.

March 3 • The Forest Reserve Act is adopted. Under its provisions, the president may reserve forest lands in the public domain for use as national parks. By 1897, Presidents Harrison and Cleveland set aside 34 million acres as forest reserves.

March 3 • An act of Congress transfers the appellate jurisdiction of the federal circuit courts to new circuit courts of appeal.

March 4 • The International Copyright Act is adopted. Beginning on July 1, works by writers from Belgium, France, Great Britain and Switzerland are to be protected in the United States. Later, writers of other nations are also given protection.

March 14 • A mob in New Orleans, enraged by the acquittal of Italians accused of murdering the chief of police, lynches 11 Italian-born prisoners, of whom three are citizens of Italy. Protests by the Italian government lead to the offer and acceptance of an indemnity in April 1892.

May 19 • Farmer and labor groups, meeting in a convention in Cincinnati, propose the formation of a new party. The Populist (People's) party is founded in St. Louis on February 22, 1892.

September 22 • President Harrison opens for settlement 900,000 acres of former Sauk, Fox and Potawatomi land in the Indian Territory.

October 16 • A mob in Valparaiso, provoked by the seizure by the United States of arms for use in the Chilean civil war, attacks sailors from the USS *Baltimore*, killing two of them. Chile, at first adamant, apologizes and pays an indemnity in 1892.

International and Cultural Events • Work on the Trans-Siberian Railway begins; it is completed in 1904. A five-day music festival opens New York's Carnegie Hall. Edison patents his Kinetoscope. The zipper is patented by Whitcomb L. Judson.

Mulberry Street on New York's east side.

United States of America 1892

Events

January 1 • Having assumed from the states responsibility for immigration the previous year, the U.S. government opens an immigrant station on Ellis Island. Between 1892 and 1954, when the station is closed, approximately 12 million immigrants (seven million physically) will be processed for entry into the United States at the facilities on Ellis Island.

February 29 • The United States and Great Britain agree to refer the dispute over sealing rights in the Bering Sea to international arbitration. The arbitration tribunal decides on August 15, 1893, that the United States cannot bar sealers of other countries from the Bering Sea and awards Great Britain damages. However, it forbids all sealing in a specified area for certain months of the year.

March • The Standard Oil Trust is dissolved by court order in Ohio.

April 19 • President Harrison opens three million acres of Cheyenne and Arapaho lands in the Indian Territory to settlement.

Mary 5 • The exclusion of Chinese laborers is extended for 10 years by the Geary Chinese Exclusion Act. Those residents in the United States must register; any not given permission to remain may be deported.

June 7 • The Republican party convenes in Minneapolis. It nominates President Harrison for re-election and Whitelaw Reid (New York) for vice president. Its platform again supports protective tariffs.

June 21 • The Democratic party convenes in Chicago. It nominates former president Cleveland for president and Adlai E. Stevenson (Illinois) for vice president. The platform endorses a tariff solely for revenue purposes.

June 29 • The Prohibition party convenes in Cincinnati. It nominates John Bidwell for president.

July 2 • The Populist party convenes in Omaha. It nominates James B. Weaver (Iowa) for president.

July 6 • Striking steel workers battle Pinkerton guards brought to Homestead, Pennsylvania, to protect strikebreakers; 10 men are killed. The militia is brought in, and the strike ends on November 20 with the union's defeat.

July 11 • Striking union silver miners in Coeur d'Alene, Idaho, fight with nonunion miners. On July 14, the federal government sends troops to the area. Martial law is proclaimed.

August 28 • The Socialist Labor party convenes in New York. It nominates Simon Wing for president and Charles H. Matchett for vice president.

October 15 • President Harrison opens the Crow reservation in Montana to white settlement.

November 8 • In the presidential election, Cleveland is elected president, receiving 277 electoral votes to 145 for Harrison and 22 for Weaver.

International and Cultural Events • Ferdinand de Lesseps is charged with fund misuse after his Panama company goes bankrupt. Rudolf Diesel patents his internal combustion engine. Stephen Crane's novel *Maggie: A Girl of the Streets* realistically reflects the slum life earlier reported on by Jacob Riis in *How the Other Half Lives* (1890).

52nd CONGRESS

SENATE	.... 88 Members
R	 47
D	 39
O	 2
HOUSE	.... 332 Members
D	 235
R	 88
O	 9

ESTIMATED POPULATION 65,666,000

Benjamin Harrison
23rd President
6th Republican

Levi P. Morton
22nd Vice President
Republican

UNITED STATES ECONOMY

GROSS NATIONAL PRODUCT	.$13,100,000,000
RETAIL SALES	N/A
BANK RESOURCES	.$ 7,245,000,000
EXPORTS	.$ 1,106,000,000
IMPORTS	.$ 827,000,000
FEDERAL GOVERNMENT EXPENDITURE	.$ 345,023,000
FEDERAL DEBT	.$ 968,219,000

1893 Grover Cleveland

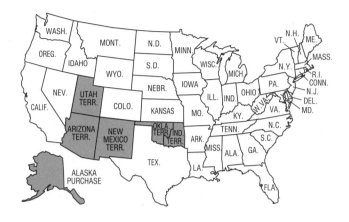

53rd CONGRESS

SENATE .... 85 Members
  D 44
  R 38
  O 3

HOUSE .... 356 Members
  D 218
  R 127
  O 11

ESTIMATED
POPULATION
66,970,000

Grover Cleveland
24th President
8th Democrat

Adlai E. Stevenson
23rd Vice President
Democrat

UNITED STATES ECONOMY

GROSS NATIONAL PRODUCT $13,100,000,000
RETAIL SALES .... N/A
BANK RESOURCES ....$ 7,192,000,000
EXPORTS ....$ 831,000,000
IMPORTS ....$ 866,000,000
FEDERAL GOVERNMENT EXPENDITURE .$ 383,478,000
FEDERAL DEBT ....$ 961,432,000

Events

January 4 • Amnesty is offered to polygamists who in the future obey the statutes against polygamy.

January 16–17 • John L. Stevens, United States minister to Hawaii, helps sugar planters overthrow the government of Queen Liliuokalani. The provisional government negotiates a treaty of annexation to the United States, which is submitted to the Senate on February 15. It is withdrawn by President Cleveland on March 9.

March 4 • Cleveland is inaugurated president.

April–June • The Panic of 1893 results from a decline in gold reserves and a sharp drop in stock prices. On June 30, as a remedial measure, President Cleveland calls a special session of Congress to repeal the Sherman Silver Purchase Act.

May–October 30 • The World's Columbian Exposition is held in Chicago. Louis Sullivan's Transportation Building dominates the exhibits.

September • Charles and Frank Duryea operate a gasoline-powered automobile after an unsuccessful trial in 1892.

September 16 • More than 100,000 settlers participate in a run into the Cherokee Strip (Cherokee Outlet), the six million acres purchased from the Cherokee Indians in 1891 for $8.5 million. The area is made part of Oklahoma Territory.

October 30 • After lengthy debate, Congress votes to repeal the Sherman Silver Purchase Act; the president signs the measure on November 1.

December 18 • An investigation having shown that the provisional Hawaiian government came to power irregularly, the president tells Congress that he will not resubmit the annexation treaty.

International and Cultural Events • A second home rule bill for Ireland is defeated in the House of Lords. Frederick Jackson Turner lectures on "The Significance of the Frontier in American History." Women's suffrage is adopted in Colorado.

Cartoon depicting mutinous sailors trying to force gold-standard-supporter Cleveland to walk the "Free Silver" plank of the ship *Democracy*.

United States of America 1894

Events

January 17 • Because the gold reserve has continued to decline despite the repeal of the Sherman Silver Purchase Act, the Treasury offers a $50 million bond issue. The bonds are purchased by banks when the public fails to subscribe.

February 8 • Congress returns control of elections to the states when it repeals the Enforcement Act of 1871.

March 17 • The United States and China sign a new treaty in which China accepts continued exclusion of its laborers from the United States.

April 30 • A group of several hundred unemployed men led by Jacob S. Coxey of Ohio, known as Coxey's Army, arrive in Washington to demand a large-scale program of public construction that would furnish them with jobs. The next day, Coxey and two other men are arrested as trespassers at the Capitol, and their followers leave Washington.

May 11 • Employees of the Pullman Palace Car Company, whose wages have been cut, strike at the company shops outside Chicago. They are members of the American Railway Union, which is led by Eugene V. Debs, and on June 26, he calls a general strike of rail workers in their support.

June 21 • A convention of pro-silver Democrats, meeting in Omaha, urges the unlimited coinage of silver at a ratio to gold of 16 to 1, as advocated by William Jennings Bryan.

July 2 • A federal injunction fails to halt the railway strike, and on July 3, President Cleveland orders troops to Chicago. There are outbreaks of violence in Chicago and elsewhere, but train service is soon restored, and the strike is broken. On July 17, Debs is arrested for violating the injunction; on December 14, he receives a six-month prison term.

July 4 • The provisional government of Hawaii proclaims the establishment of a republic, which is recognized by President Cleveland on August 7.

August 18 • The Carey Act is adopted. Under its provisions, states containing public land may receive as much as one million acres for reclamation and settlement.

August 28 • The Wilson-Gorman Tariff Act is adopted without the signature of President Cleveland, who objects to many protectionist amendments. Rates are reduced to an average of 40 percent. The law also includes a provision for a federal income tax.

November • In the midterm elections, the Republicans gain control of both houses of Congress.

November 13 • The Treasury offers its second $50 million bond issue of the year, as the gold reserve continues to decline.

53rd CONGRESS

SENATE .... 85 Members
  D 44
  R 38
  O 3

HOUSE .... 356 Members
  D 218
  R 127
  O 11

ESTIMATED POPULATION 68,275,000

Grover Cleveland
24th President
8th Democrat

Adlai E. Stevenson
23rd Vice President
Democrat

UNITED STATES ECONOMY

GROSS NATIONAL PRODUCT	$13,100,000,000
RETAIL SALES	N/A
BANK RESOURCES	$ 7,291,000,000
EXPORTS	$ 869,000,000
IMPORTS	$ 655,000,000
FEDERAL GOVERNMENT EXPENDITURE	$ 367,525,000
FEDERAL DEBT	$ 1,016,898,000

November 22 • The United States and Japan sign a commercial treaty.

International and Cultural Events • A French military court sentences Captain Alfred Dreyfus to Devil's Island for treason. The music of the American Charles Ives, a student of Horatio Parker, anticipates European experiments in polytonality. William Hope Harvey publishes *Coin's Financial School*, a highly popular booklet on the value of a free silver policy.

121

1895 United States of America

54th CONGRESS

SENATE .... 88 Members
R 43
D 39
O 6

HOUSE .... 356 Members
R 244
D 105
O 7

ESTIMATED
POPULATION
69,580,000

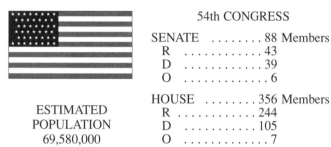

Grover Cleveland
24th President
8th Democrat

Adlai E. Stevenson
23rd Vice President
Democrat

UNITED STATES ECONOMY

GROSS NATIONAL PRODUCT $13,100,000,000
RETAIL SALES .... N/A
BANK RESOURCES .... $ 7,610,000,000
EXPORTS .... $ 793,000,000
IMPORTS .... $ 732,000,000
FEDERAL GOVERNMENT EXPENDITURE .$ 356,195,000
FEDERAL DEBT .... $ 1,096,913,000

Events

January • In *United States v. E.C. Knight Company*, the Supreme Court rules that the Sherman Antitrust Act bars combinations in restraint of commerce, not manufacturing monopolies within a single state.

January 22 • The National Association of Manufacturers is organized at a meeting held in Cincinnati.

February 8 • The Treasury arranges to sell bonds to a syndicate of bankers led by August Belmont and J.P. Morgan in exchange for $62 million in gold.

February 20 • A proposal by President Cleveland, in December 1894, that he arrange arbitration of the dispute between British Guiana and Venezuela regarding common boundary is endorsed by Congress.

February 24 • Cubans begin a rebellion against Spanish rule that draws the sympathy of many Americans, some of whom attempt to give active aid. On June 12, President Cleveland calls on Americans to observe neutrality in the struggle.

March 5 • A group of Democrats in the House of Representatives issue an appeal for the free coinage of silver that has been drafted by William Jennings Bryan and Richard P. Bland.

May 20 • In *Pollock v. Farmers' Loan and Trust Company*, the Supreme Court rules that income tax provisions of the Wilson-Gorman Tariff Act of 1894 are unconstitutional. It decides that a tax on personal property is a direct tax and, as such, is prohibited under Article I, Section 8, of the Constitution.

May 27 • In *In re Debs*, the Supreme Court denies a writ of habeas corpus to Eugene V. Debs, sentenced to prison in 1894 for disobeying an injunction in the railway strike. The government had obtained the injunction under the Sherman Antitrust Act, but the Court bases its ruling on the government's responsibility for interstate commerce and the mails.

July 20 • Secretary of State Richard Olney sends a strongly worded note to Great Britain in which he invokes the Monroe Doctrine and advises the settlement of the Venezuela boundary dispute by arbitration. Replying on November 26, Lord Salisbury, prime minister and foreign secretary of Britain, refuses to consider arbitration.

September 18 • Atlanta, Georgia, hosts the Cotton States and International Exposition. Among the speakers at the exposition is Booker T. Washington, who delivers a speech proposing a program of accommodation between the races. This proposal will become known as the Atlanta Compromise. Washington contends that blacks in the south only want economic equality, not social equality.

December 17 • The president asks Congress to authorize a commission whose findings in the Venezuelan boundary dispute would, if necessary, be enforced by the United States.

International and Cultural Events • Ideas basic to psychoanalytic theory are outlined in *Studies in Hysteria* by Josef Breuer and Sigmund Freud. Louis and Auguste Lumière patent their cinematograph. Guglielmo Marconi experiments with sending wireless telegraph signals. In Chicago, a Duryea car wins the first United States automobile race.

United States of America 1896

Events

January 1 • A commission is appointed in the Venezuela boundary dispute with the acquiescence of Lord Salisbury, who fears war in South Africa.

January 4 • Utah is admitted to the Union as the 45th state. Its constitution includes women's suffrage and prohibits polygamy.

January 6 • The Treasury offers a $100 million bond issue to the public. Its subscription helps alleviate the reserve situation temporarily.

April 6 • Congress adopts a resolution to recognize the rebels in Cuba as belligerents and to have the president serve as arbiter. On May 22, Spain refuses to accept arbitration.

May 18 • In *Plessy v. Ferguson*, the Supreme Court rules that segregated facilities are not illegal under the Fourteenth Amendment, provided those available for both races are of equal quality—that is, "separate but equal."

June 16 • The Republican party convenes in St. Louis. It nominates William McKinley (Ohio) for president and Garret A. Hobart (New Jersey) for vice president. The platform endorses a high tariff and the gold standard.

July 4 • The Socialist Labor party convenes in New York and names C. H. Matchett for president.

July 7 • The Democratic party convenes in Chicago. It nominates William Jennings Bryan (Nebraska) for president and Arthur Sewall (Maine) for vice president. The platform endorses the free coinage of silver as advocated by Bryan in his "Cross of Gold" speech on July 8.

July 22 • The National Silver Republican party, formed by westerners who have left the Republican party on the gold issue, convenes in St. Louis. It endorses the Democratic candidates. Bryan gets the Populist party nomination the same day.

August 16 • Gold is discovered in the Klondike, near the Alaskan border in the Yukon District of Canada.

September 2 • The National Democratic party, composed of supporters of the gold standard who left the Democratic Convention, convenes in Indianapolis. It nominates John M. Palmer for president and Simon B. Buckner for vice president.

October 1 • The Post Office inaugurates its rural free delivery (R.F.D.) service.

November 3 • In the presidential election, McKinley is elected president, receiving 271 electoral votes to 176 for Bryan, his Democratic opponent. Control of Congress remains in Republican hands.

International and Cultural Events • A telegram sent by William II congratulating Transvaal president Kruger on

54th CONGRESS

SENATE	. . . . 88 Members
R	 43
D	 39
O	 6
HOUSE	. . . . 356 Members
R	 244
D	 105
O	 7

ESTIMATED
POPULATION
70,885,000

Grover Cleveland
24th President
8th Democrat

Adlai E. Stevenson
23rd Vice President
Democrat

UNITED STATES ECONOMY

GROSS NATIONAL PRODUCT	. . . .$13,100,000,000
RETAIL SALES	. . . . N/A
BANK RESOURCES	. . . .$ 7,554,000,000
EXPORTS	. . . .$ 863,000,000
IMPORTS	. . . .$ 780,000,000
FEDERAL GOVERNMENT EXPENDITURE	.$ 352,179,000
FEDERAL DEBT	. . . .$ 1,222,729,000

suppressing a British raid provokes an Anglo-German crisis. Alfred Nobel's will establishes prizes for peace, science and literature. The American physicist Samuel P. Langley experiments with steam-propelled model aircraft. The "Butcher," a name that U.S. journalists have attached to General Valeriano Weyler, arrives in Cuba to suppress the rebellion. Athens, Greece, hosts the games of the first modern Olympiad. Athletes from 13 nations, including the United States, participate.

1897 William A. McKinley

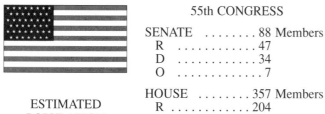

ESTIMATED
POPULATION
72,189,000

55th CONGRESS

SENATE .... 88 Members
R 47
D 34
O 7

HOUSE .... 357 Members
R 204
D 113
O 40

William A. McKinley
25th President
7th Republican

Garret A. Hobart
24th Vice President
Republican

UNITED STATES ECONOMY

GROSS NATIONAL PRODUCT	$16,800,000,000
RETAIL SALES	N/A
BANK RESOURCES	$ 8,432,000,000
EXPORTS	$ 1,032,000,000
IMPORTS	$ 765,000,000
FEDERAL GOVERNMENT EXPENDITURE	$ 365,774,000
FEDERAL DEBT	$ 1,226,794,000

William A. McKinley

Birth	Niles, OH, Jan. 29, 1843
Parents	William and Nancy Allison McKinley
Married	Ida Saxton
Home	Canton, OH
Presidency	1897 – 1901
Death	Buffalo, NY, Sept. 14, 1901

Events

January 11 • President Cleveland submits to the Senate the Olney-Pauncefote Treaty, providing for the settlement by arbitration of disputes between the United States and Great Britain. Although it is favored also by the new administration, the Senate withholds ratification.

March 1 • In *Allgeyer v. Louisiana*, the United States Supreme Court, in a unanimous decision, declares that the 14th Amendment protects the freedom to make contracts. It is the first use of the "freedom of contract" doctrine.

March 2 • President Cleveland vetoes a bill that, in a new departure, would make literacy tests mandatory for prospective immigrants.

March 4 • William A. McKinley is inaugurated president.

April • A commission is appointed by President McKinley to go to Europe to get overseas opinion on international bimetallism.

June • News of the gold discoveries in the Klondike is published, and a rush to the Yukon begins. On July 14, the *Excelsior* arrives in San Francisco with gold worth $750,000. Many gold seekers will die after ignoring warnings of snowed-in passes and inadequate food supplies.

June 19 • Japan protests the signature of a treaty whereby Hawaii is annexed by the United States (June 16). The Senate fails to ratify the treaty. Queen Liliuokalani protests its ratification by the Republic of Hawaii (September 14).

June 27 • General Valeriano Weyler's cruel actions in Cuba are protested by Secretary of State John Sherman. Weyler will soon be recalled to Spain by a more conciliatory Spanish government.

July 7 • Congress approves the Dingley tariff bill, which restores duties on wool and hides and raises the average rate of all tariffs to a record-breaking 57 percent.

July 24 • The president appoints a commission to study possible routes for the construction of a canal across Nicaragua.

November 25 • The new Spanish government of Premier Práxedes Sagasta grants Cuba a greater degree of self-government. These concessions are considered insufficient by the rebels.

December 6 • President McKinley, in his annual message to Congress, voices optimism on the Cuban problem.

International and Cultural Events • Turkey and Greece wage war over Crete. Theodor Herzl calls a World Zionist Congress in Basel, Switzerland. Queen Victoria celebrates the Diamond Jubilee of her reign. John Philip Sousa writes "The Stars and Stripes Forever." The first Boston Marathon is run from Hopkinton to the Back Bay.

United States of America 1898

Events

January 1 • Brooklyn, Queens and Staten Island are consolidated with New York (including the Bronx) to form the City of New York.

February 9 • The pro-intervention New York *Journal* publishes an intercepted letter of Dupuy de Lôme, Spanish minister to the United States, criticizing President McKinley. The minister resigns.

February 15 • A submarine mine causes the explosion of the battleship *Maine*, which is in Havana harbor to protect American lives and property. Responsibility for the disaster, in which 260 are killed, has never been established.

March • Cries of "Remember the Maine" incite war fever. Congress authorizes $50 million for defense, and Navy ships are sent to the Cuban area.

March 28 • In *United States v. Wong Kim Ark*, the U.S. Supreme Court rules that children born in the United States, even if they are children of unwanted aliens, are citizens of the United States.

April 11 • President McKinley, abandoning his anti-war stand, asks Congress to authorize the use of naval and military force in Cuba. Resolutions adopted by Congress on April 19 declare the independence of Cuba and give the president the authorization he requested.

April 24 • Spain declares war on the United States. On April 25, Congress formally declares that the country has been at war with Spain since April 21.

May 1 • The battle of Manila Bay is won in seven hours by Commodore George Dewey. His force, the Asiatic Squadron, puts all the ships of the Spanish squadron out of action.

June 1 • The Erdman Act for the mediation of railroad disputes is adopted.

July 1 • United States forces in Cuba capture El Caney and San Juan Hill.

July 3 • The Spanish fleet is destroyed off Santiago. On July 17, the city surrenders.

July 4 • The United States acquires Wake Island.

July 7 • A bill for the annexation of Hawaii is signed by the president.

July 25 • United States forces land in Puerto Rico.

August 24 • United States forces in Cuba, which have been stricken with yellow fever and food poisoning, are ordered home.

August 12 • A protocol provides for the cessation of hostilities and the holding of a peace conference.

August 14 • Manila surrenders to United States forces.

October 1 • The United States begins peace negotiations with Spain in Paris.

December 10 • The Treaty of Paris concludes the Spanish-American War. The United States is given Guam and Puerto Rico and agrees to pay Spain $20 million for

55th CONGRESS

SENATE	.... 88 Members
R	 47
D	 34
O	 7

ESTIMATED POPULATION 73,494,000

HOUSE	.... 357 Members
R	 204
D	 113
O	 40

William A. McKinley
25th President
7th Republican

Garret A. Hobart
24th Vice President
Republican

UNITED STATES ECONOMY

GROSS NATIONAL PRODUCT	$16,800,000,000
RETAIL SALES	N/A
BANK RESOURCES	$ 9,218,000,000
EXPORTS	$ 1,210,000,000
IMPORTS	$ 616,000,000
FEDERAL GOVERNMENT EXPENDITURE	$ 443,369,000
FEDERAL DEBT	$ 1,232,743,000

the Philippines. Cuba, to which Spain renounces its claims, becomes independent.

International and Cultural Events • The anti-foreign Boxers organize in China. Emile Zol's "J'accuse" defends Captain Dreyfus. E.N. Westcott's best-selling *David Harum* creates an American folk hero. The Kellogg brothers discover a way to make good tasting cornflakes by adding malt flavoring to the mixture and by using the heart of the corn.

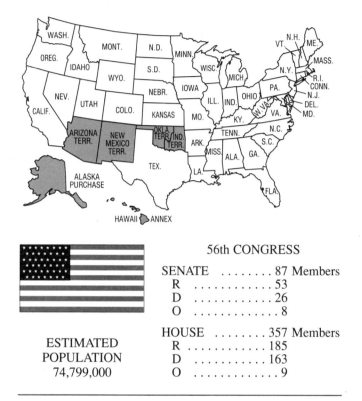

56th CONGRESS

SENATE . . . . 87 Members
R 53
D 26
O 8

HOUSE . . . . 357 Members
R 185
D 163
O 9

ESTIMATED
POPULATION
74,799,000

William A. McKinley
25th President
7th Republican

Garret A. Hobart
24th Vice President
Republican

UNITED STATES ECONOMY

GROSS NATIONAL PRODUCT $16,800,000,000
RETAIL SALES . . . . N/A
BANK RESOURCES $16,679,000,000
EXPORTS . . . .$ 1,204,000,000
IMPORTS . . . .$ 697,000,000
FEDERAL GOVERNMENT EXPENDITURE .$ 605,072,000
FEDERAL DEBT . . . .$ 1,436,701,000

Events

January 20 • President McKinley appoints a Philippine Commission, headed by Jacob G. Schurman, to determine what the United States should do with the islands. The commission will suggest that the United States retain the Philippines until a time in the future when the people of the islands are ready for self-government.

February 4 • Filipinos who want immediate independence rebel under the leadership of Emilio Aguinaldo, who attempts to take Manila. Aguinaldo is captured on March 23, 1901, and the last Filipino resistance ends a year later.

February 6 • After lengthy debate, the Senate ratifies the Treaty of Paris despite objections from anti-imperialists. President McKinley signs the instrument of ratification on February 10.

March 2 • Congress authorizes a call for 35,000 volunteers to aid the enlarged regular U.S. Army in putting down the revolt in the Philippines.

April 11 • The Treaty of Paris is proclaimed.

May 18 • The First Hague Conference opens with the United States in attendance. Representatives of 26 nations discuss disarmament and related topics and reach agreement on the creation of the Permanent Court of Arbitration, a tribunal for the peaceful adjustment of international differences. The conference formally adjourns on July 29.

July 19 • Secretary of War Russell A. Alger resigns because of widespread criticism of his administration of the War Department during the Spanish-American War. Supplies, training, and leadership have been deficient.

September 6 • Secretary of State John Hay sends a circular letter to United States embassies in countries with interests in China, asking them to secure the agreement of the respective governments to an open-door policy in their spheres. Under this policy, the commerce of all nations would receive equal treatment. On March 20, 1900, Hay states that France, Germany, Great Britain, Italy, Japan and Russia have all agreed to support the open-door policy.

October 4 • After talks with Admiral George Dewey, President McKinley orders more warships and troops to the Philippines.

October 14 • President McKinley becomes the first U.S. president to ride in an automobile when he takes a ride in a Stanley Steamer.

November 21 • Vice President Garret A. Hobart dies in Paterson, New Jersey.

December 2 • Germany, Great Britain and the United States sign a treaty on Samoa in Washington. The islands are divided between Germany and the United States, Great Britain having withdrawn its claims to the islands. The Senate ratifies the treaty on January 16, 1990.

December 5 • Trusts and monopolies are attacked by President McKinley in his annual message to Congress.

International and Cultural Events • The Boer War begins in South Africa. W.E.B. DuBois' *The Philadelphia Negro* is a sociological landmark. Rudyard Kipling publishes the poem, "The White Man's Burden," which helps bolster the cause of expansionists in the United States.

United States of America 1900

Events

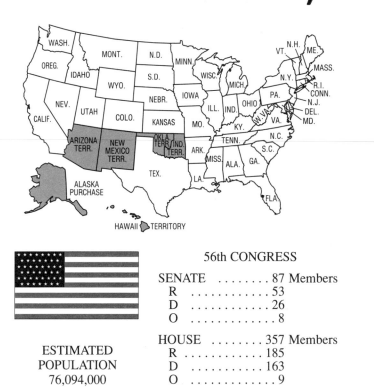

February 5 • The United States and Great Britain sign the first Hay-Pauncefote Treaty, giving the United States the sole right to construct an isthmian canal. In ratifying the treaty on December 20, the Senate adds an amendment that would allow the canal to be fortified.

March 6 • The Social Democratic party convenes in Indianapolis. It nominates Eugene V. Debs for president and Job Harriman for vice president.

March 14 • The Currency Act, which makes the gold dollar of 25.8 grains, nine-tenths fine, the standard of value, is adopted by Congress. A gold reserve of $150 million is established.

April 12 • The Foraker Act, which establishes Puerto Rico as an unorganized territory, is adopted by Congress.

April 29 • On the evening of April 29, railroad engineer Casey Jones, driving the "Cannonball," roars into a freight train blocking the tracks. Casey manages to save the lives of his passengers, but not his own. His heroic act will be retold in ballads and folktales for years to come.

May 14 • In *Knowlton v. Moore*, the U.S. Supreme Court rules that the inheritance tax is constitutional.

June 2 • The Socialist Labor party convenes in New York. It nominates Joseph P. Maloney for president and Valentine Remmel for vice president.

June 14 • Under an act of Congress adopted on April 30, Hawaii becomes an organized territory.

June 19 • The Republican party convenes in Philadelphia. It nominates President McKinley for re-election and Theodore Roosevelt (New York) for vice president and endorses the Currency Act and the administration's policy in foreign affairs.

July 4 • The Democratic party convenes in Kansas City. It nominates William Jennings Bryan (Nebraska) for president and adopts a platform favoring the free coinage of silver and opposing imperialism. The candidates are endorsed also by the Fusion Populist party.

August 14 • United States troops join other western forces in the relief of the legations in Peking following the Boxer Rebellion.

September 8 • Galveston, Texas, is devastated by a hurricane. Water from the Gulf of Mexico floods the city and drowns about 6,000 persons. Influenced by the disaster, Galveston adopts a commission form of government, the first city in the United States to do so.

September 18 • Minnesota holds the country's first direct primary.

November 6 • In the presidential election, McKinley is re-elected, receiving 292 electoral votes to 155 for Bryan, his Democratic opponent. Theodore Roosevelt is elected vice president.

56th CONGRESS

SENATE	.... 87 Members
R	 53
D	 26
O	 8

HOUSE	.... 357 Members
R	 185
D	 163
O	 9

ESTIMATED POPULATION
76,094,000

William A. McKinley
25th President
7th Republican

Vice President
None

UNITED STATES ECONOMY

GROSS NATIONAL PRODUCT	$16,800,000,000
RETAIL SALES	N/A
BANK RESOURCES	$11,388,000,000
EXPORTS	$ 1,371,000,000
IMPORTS	$ 850,000,000
FEDERAL GOVERNMENT EXPENDITURE	$ 520,861,000
FEDERAL DEBT	$ 1,263,417,000

December 16 • Mark Hanna and Samuel Gompers are chosen president and vice president, respectively, of the National Civic Federation, formed to promote the arbitration of labor disputes.

International and Cultural Events • Count Ferdinand von Zeppelin builds the first rigid airship. The German physicist Max Planck evolves his quantum theory. Gregor Mendel's heredity experiments (1866) are rediscovered by scientists. Theodore Dreiser's *Sister Carrie* is attacked as obscene.

1901 McKinley/Roosevelt

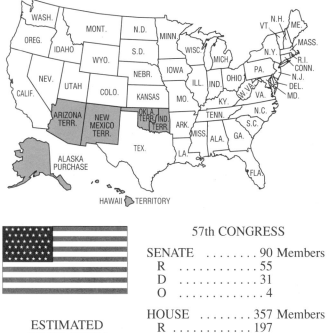

57th CONGRESS

SENATE .... 90 Members
R 55
D 31
O 4

HOUSE .... 357 Members
R 197
D 151
O 9

ESTIMATED
POPULATION
77,585,000

William A. McKinley
25th President
7th Republican

Theodore Roosevelt
25th Vice President
Republican

UNITED STATES ECONOMY

GROSS NATIONAL PRODUCT $16,800,000,000
RETAIL SALES .... N/A
BANK RESOURCES $13,037,000,000
EXPORTS .... $ 1,460,000,000
IMPORTS .... $ 823,000,000
FEDERAL GOVERNMENT EXPENDITURE . $ 524,617,000
FEDERAL DEBT .... $ 1,221,572,000

Theodore Roosevelt

Birth .... New York, NY, Oct. 27, 1858
Parents .... Theodore and Martha Bulloch Roosevelt
Married ..... Alice Hathaway Lee; Edith Kermit Carow
Home .... Oyster Bay, NY
Presidency .... 1901 – 1909
Death .... Oyster Bay, NY, Jan. 6, 1919

Events

February 21 • The first billion-dollar corporation, the United States Steel Corporation, is established under the leadership of John Pierpont Morgan and Elbert H. Gary.

March 2 • The Platt Amendment to the Army Appropriations Act sets conditions under which the United States can intervene in Cuba and provides for United States naval bases on the island. On June 12, it is reluctantly added to the Cuban Constitution.

March 4 • McKinley begins his second term as president.

May 27 • In the *Insular Cases*, the U.S. Supreme Court rules that Puerto Rico, as a result of annexation, is no longer a foreign country but neither is it a part of the United States that is protected by the Constitution, which only applies to states and incorporated territories.

September 2 • At the Minnesota State Fair, Vice President Roosevelt advises the nation to "speak softly and carry a big stick."

September 6 • Visiting the Pan-American Exposition in Buffalo, President McKinley is shot by an anarchist, Leon Czolgosz.

September 14 • McKinley dies in Buffalo. Theodore Roosevelt is sworn in as his successor.

October 16 • President Roosevelt entertains Booker T. Washington at a luncheon in the White House. He is sharply criticized in the South.

November 18 • The United States and Great Britain sign a second Hay-Pauncefote Treaty, since the British had refused to ratify the first one after it had been amended by Congress. Superseding the Clayton-Bulwer Treaty of 1850, the new treaty authorizes the United States to construct and operate an isthmian canal open to all nations. The British also agree that the canal may be fortified.

December 3 • President Roosevelt sends his first annual message to Congress. He urges that large-scale combinations be regulated by law.

International and Cultural Events • Queen Victoria dies; Edward VII ascends the throne. George Barr McCutcheon's romantic *Graustark* is a best seller.

The *Empire State Express*, considered the fastest train in the world in the early 1900s.

United States of America 1902

Events

January 6• In *Capital City Dairy Company v. Ohio*, the U.S. Supreme Court rules that states can enact laws prohibiting the sale of items made in the "immitation of yellow butter" (oleomargarine), so long as they do not interfere with the interstate transportation of the product. Approximately 30 states have laws protecting butter.

January 18 • A federal commission recommends that an isthmian canal be constructed through Panama and not through Nicaragua.

January 24 • Representatives of the United States and Denmark sign a treaty for the purchase by the United States of the Danish West Indies (Virgin Islands), but it is not ratified by the Danish Parliament.

March 10 • Attorney General Philander C. Knox files an antitrust suit against the Northern Securities Company, a railroad holding company.

April 29 • The Chinese Exclusion Act is broadened to apply to Chinese from island territories of the United States.

May 12 • Anthracite coal miners, members of the United Mine Workers of America, strike when operators will not agree to the arbitration of demands for higher wages and an eight-hour day.

May 20 • The United States relinquishes its rule of Cuba, and the Cubans install their first president.

June 17 • Congress adopts the Newlands Act, which provides for the use of funds from public land sales in 16 southwestern and western states for irrigation projects.

June 28 • Congress adopts the Spooner Act, setting up the Isthmian Canal Commission. A canal is to be built through Panama if the interests of France's New Panama Canal Company can be acquired and control of the necessary land secured from Colombia. Otherwise a Nicaraguan canal is authorized.

July 1 • Congress adopts the Philippine Government Act, which provides for the civil government of the islands. As an unorganized territory, the Philippines are to be governed by the Taft Commission, appointed by President McKinley in 1900.

August 11 • Oliver Wendell Holmes, Jr., is appointed to the Supreme Court.

September 15 • The United States submits a dispute with Mexico over arrears of interest on the Pious Fund of the California to the Hague Court of Arbitration. It is the first country to use the court.

October 16 • President Roosevelt appoints a commission headed by George Gray to investigate and mediate the anthracite coal strike.

October 21 • The coal miners return to work.

December 12 • At the request of Venezuela, President

57th CONGRESS

SENATE	.... 90 Members
R	 55
D	 31
O	 4

HOUSE	.... 357 Members
R	 197
D	 151
O	 9

ESTIMATED
POPULATION
79,160,000

Theodore Roosevelt
26th President
8th Republican

Vice President
None

UNITED STATES ECONOMY

GROSS NATIONAL PRODUCT	...........$23,500,000,000
RETAIL SALES	.... N/A
BANK RESOURCES	...................$14,026,000,000
EXPORTS	............................$ 1,355,000,000
IMPORTS	............................$ 903,000,000
FEDERAL GOVERNMENT EXPENDITURE	.$ 483,234,000
FEDERAL DEBT	......................$ 1,178,031,000

Roosevelt proposes arbitration of a dispute over unpaid debts that has led Great Britain, Germany and Italy to attack Venezuelan warhsips and bombard and blockade Venezuelan ports. The European powers agree on December 19.

International and Cultural Events • Great Britain wins the Boer War, but almost 22,000 of its soldiers are dead of wounds or disease. With E.S. Porter's *The Great Train Robbery*, movies begin to tell a story.

1903 United States of America

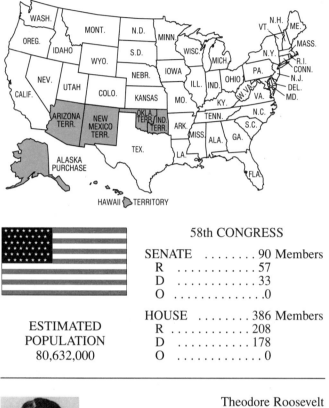

ESTIMATED
POPULATION
80,632,000

58th CONGRESS

SENATE	....	90 Members
R	....	57
D	....	33
O	....	0
HOUSE	....	386 Members
R	....	208
D	....	178
O	....	0

Theodore Roosevelt
26th President
8th Republican

Vice President
None

UNITED STATES ECONOMY

GROSS NATIONAL PRODUCT	.... $23,500,000,000
RETAIL SALES	.... N/A
BANK RESOURCES	.... $14,901,000,000
EXPORTS	.... $ 1,392,000,000
IMPORTS	.... $ 1,026,000,000
FEDERAL GOVERNMENT EXPENDITURE	.$ 517,006,000
FEDERAL DEBT	.... $ 1,159,406,000

Events

January 22 • The United States and Colombia sign the Hay-Herrán Treaty, providing for the lease of a six-mile strip across the Isthmus of Panama. The United States is to pay Colombia $10 million plus a yearly rental of $250,000. The treaty is ratified by the United States on March 17, but the Colombian Senate refuses to ratify it (August 12).

January 24 • The United States and Great Britain sign an agreement to establish a commission to settle a dispute over the boundary between the Alaska Panhandle and Canada.

February 11 • Congress adopts the Expedition Act, empowering the attorney general to ask for and receive precedence in United States circuit courts in antitrust suits.

February 14 • The president signs into law an act creating the Department of Commerce and Labor.

February 14 • The Army General Staff Corps is created to centralize military planning.

February 19 • Congress adopts the Elkins Act, which defines discrimination between shippers engaged in interstate commerce. The act is designed to eliminate the practice of giving rebates.

February 23 • In *Champion v. Ames*, the Supreme Court rules that the police power of the federal government overrides that of the states, thus upholding the federal ban on the interstate mailing of lottery tickets.

March 22 • The Gray Commission awards shorter hours and a 10 percent wage increase to the anthracite coal miners who struck in May 1902.

May 23 • The first direct primary for party elections is adopted by Wisconsin.

October 20 • The joint commission investigating the Alaska boundary dispute rules in favor of the United States.

November 3 • The Panamanians declare their independence from Colombia after President Roosevelt orders United States naval vessels to the isthmus. The new republic receives United States recognition on November 6.

November 18 • The United States and Panama sign the Hay-Bunau-Varilla Treaty, whereby the United States receives a permanent lease on a strip of land 10 miles wide in exchange for $10 million and a yearly rental of $150,000 beginning in nine years. The independence of Panama is guaranteed.

December 17 • Orville Wright makes the first flight in a powered heavier-than-air machine, an airplane he designed with his brother, Wilbur.

December 30 • At the Iroquois Theater in Chicago, a fire erupts at a matinee performance at which many children are in attendance. As the panic-stricken crowd rushes for the exits, many of which are locked, the fire engulfs the theater, killing approximately 596 people as they clustered at the exits.

International and Cultural Events • British suffragist Emmeline Pankhurst forms the Women's Social and Political Union. G.B. Shaw publishes *Man and Superman*. Boston (American League) and Pittsburgh (National League) play the first World Series. A Packard becomes the first automobile to complete a coast-to-coast trip.

United States of America 1904

Events

January 4 • President Roosevelt presents in a message to Congress a defense of his actions at the time of the Panama revolt.

February 23 • The Senate ratifies the Hay-Bunau-Varilla Treaty. On February 29, a presidential commission is formed to build the Panama Canal.

March 14 • The Supreme Court rules that, under the terms of the Sherman Antitrust Act, the Northern Securities Company must be dissolved.

April 23 • The American Academy of Arts and Letters is established in New York.

April 30 • The Louisiana Purchase Exposition opens in St. Louis. The official song of the exposition is "Meet Me In St. Louis, Louis," by Andrew B. Sterling.

May 1 • The Socialist party convenes in Chicago. It nominates Eugene V. Debs for president and Benjamin Hanford for vice president.

May 4 • The United States takes control of the Panama Canal Zone.

June 21 • The Republican party convenes in Chicago. It nominates President Roosevelt for re-election and Charles W. Fairbanks (Indiana) for vice president and adopts a conservative platform.

June 29 • The Prohibition party nominates Silas C. Swallow for president. On July 2, the Socialist Labor party gives its nomination to Charles H. Corregan, and two days later the People's (Populist) party nominates Thomas E. Watson.

July 6 • The Democratic party convenes in St. Louis. It nominates Alton B. Parker (New York) for president and Henry G. Davis (West Virginia) for vice president and adopts a platform opposing the trusts.

October 27 • The first part of the New York City subway system is opened in Manhattan.

November 8 • In the presidential election, Roosevelt is re-elected, receiving 236 electoral votes to 140 for Parker, his Democratic opponent. Charles W. Fairbanks is elected as vice president.

December 6 • In his annual message to Congress, President Roosevelt extends the Monroe Doctrine with a corollary that comes to bear his name. There has been a possibility of intervention in the Dominican Republic by European creditor nations anxious to collect unpaid debts. Now, Roosevelt states, the United States may use "an international police power" and intervene itself in the Western Hemisphere.

International and Cultural Events • Competition for Korea and Manchuria leads to the Russo-Japanese War when, without a declaration of war, Japan attacks the Russian fleet at Port Arthur. Britain and France sign an

Entente Cordiale in which they agree to recognize their respective interests in Egypt and Morocco. Ida Minerva Tarbell's *McClure's* exposés are collected and published as *History of the Standard Oil Company*. New York becomes the first state to impose speed limits on automobiles. Limits range from 10 miles per hour in the cities to 20 miles per hour in the country. St. Louis hosts the summer games of the Third Olympiad.

58th CONGRESS

SENATE	.... 90 Members
R	 57
D	 33
O	 0

ESTIMATED POPULATION 82,165,000

HOUSE	.... 386 Members
R	 208
D	 178
O	 0

Theodore Roosevelt
26th President
8th Republican

Vice President
None

UNITED STATES ECONOMY

GROSS NATIONAL PRODUCT	..........$23,500,000,000
RETAIL SALES	...............................N/A
BANK RESOURCES	.................$15,848,000,000
EXPORTS	..........................$ 1,435,000,000
IMPORTS	...........................$ 991,000,000
FEDERAL GOVERNMENT EXPENDITURE	.$ 583,660,000
FEDERAL DEBT	.....................$ 1,136,259,000

1905 United States of America

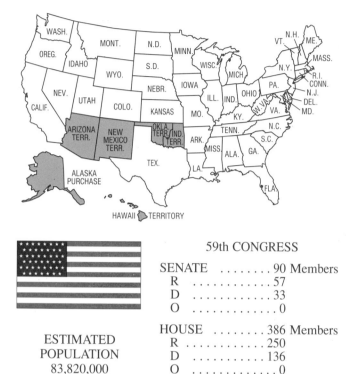

59th CONGRESS

SENATE .... 90 Members
R 57
D 33
O 0

HOUSE .... 386 Members
R 250
D 136
O 0

ESTIMATED
POPULATION
83,820,000

Theodore Roosevelt
26th President
8th Republican

Charles W. Fairbanks
26th Vice President
Republican

UNITED STATES ECONOMY

GROSS NATIONAL PRODUCT $23,500,000,000
RETAIL SALES .... N/A
BANK RESOURCES $17,511,000,000
EXPORTS .... $ 1,492,000,000
IMPORTS .... $ 1,118,000,000
FEDERAL GOVERNMENT EXPENDITURE .$ 567,279,000
FEDERAL DEBT .... $ 1,132,357,000

Events

January 13 • Alarmed by the effect on the open-door policy of the Russo-Japanese War, which has been underway since February 8, 1904, Secretary of State Hay says it is the intention of the United States "to maintain the integrity of China and the Open Door in the Orient."

January 20 • The Roosevelt corollary is put to use with the signing of an agreement with the Dominican

Republic for the payment of its debt to creditors through customs supervision by the United States. Roosevelt reaches an arrangement with the Dominican Republic for its acceptance of a customs receiver named by him (March 31).

January 30 • In *Swift & Company v. United States*, the Supreme Court rules in favor of the federal government in its antitrust suit against the meat-packing industry. However, the government fails to obtain an injunction against the meat company, and the packing monopoly continues.

February 20 • In *Jacobson v. Massachusetts*, the U.S. Supreme Court rules that state compulsory vaccination laws are constitutional. Seventh-day Adventists had objected to the smallpox vaccination requirement on religious grounds.

March 4 • Theodore Roosevelt begins his first full term as president.

April 17 • In *Lochner v. New York*, the Supreme Court finds a state limitation of daily working hours to 10 in New York bakeries unconstitutional, because it impairs the right of free contract.

June 8 • At Japan's request (May 31), the president asks Japan and Russia to negotiate a peace.

June 27–July 8 • At a convention held in Chicago under the leadership of William D. Haywood, the Industrial Workers of the World (IWW) is organized as a proponent of industrial unionism, in opposition to the craft

President Theodore Roosevelt with Japanese and Russian envoys at Portsmouth, New Hampshire, in 1905. This mediation ended the Russo-Japanese War and won President Roosevelt the Nobel Peace Prize.

unionism of the American Federation of Labor.

July • Dissatisfied with the leadership of Booker T. Washington, W.E.B. DuBois calls 29 black leaders to a meeting in the vicinity of Niagara Falls. The Niagara Movement, as the meeting comes to be known, issues a "Declaration of Principles," calling for equal rights and opportunities for all Americans and promising to pursue their goal with "persistent, manly agitation."

July 21 • China begins a boycott of United States goods due to new restrictions that bar educated Chinese from entering the United States.

July 29 • Secretary of War William H. Taft agrees secretly with Japanese Prime Minister Taro Katsura that, if Japan relinquishes all rights that it may have in the Philippines, it will not encounter United States opposition in Korea.

August 9 • A peace conference opens in Portsmouth, New Hampshire, with President Roosevelt mediating between the Japanese and the Russians.

September 5 • The Treaty of Portsmouth is signed. Japan obtains the South Manchurian Railway and the Russian lease of the southern Liaotung Peninsula as well as Russian recognition of its claims in Korea, but because of Roosevelt's influence, it takes only half of Sakhalin Island and does not receive an indemnity from Russia. Korea is placed under Japanese protection on December 21.

International and Cultural Events • A St. Petersburg massacre of workers petitioning the czar brings on the Revolution of 1905, which results in limited democratic concessions. The *Sinn Fein* movement is organized politically in Dublin. A New Orleans yellow fever epidemic kills 400. Alfred Stieglitz establishes his influential 291 Gallery for photography in New York. The cross-country trip of two Oldsmobiles to the Lewis and Clark Exposition in Portland, Oregon, inspires Tin Pan Alley lyricist Vincent Bryan, in collaborate with Gus Edwards, to write the song, "In My Merry Oldsmobile." The Staten Island ferry opens in New York. New York launches an investigation of life insurance companies; future Supreme Court justice and Republican presidential nominee Charles Evans Hughes will gain a national reputation as a result.

The main building for processing immigrants on Ellis Island in 1905.

1906 United States of America

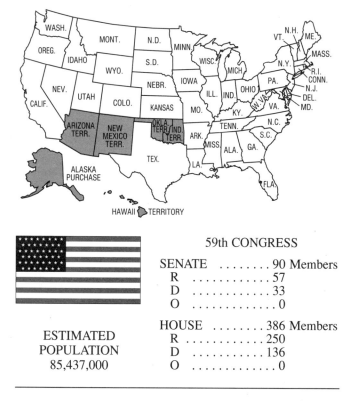

ESTIMATED
POPULATION
85,437,000

59th CONGRESS

SENATE	.... 90 Members
R	 57
D	 33
O	 0

HOUSE	.... 386 Members
R	 250
D	 136
O	 0

Theodore Roosevelt
26th President
8th Republican

Charles W. Fairbanks
26th Vice President
Republican

UNITED STATES ECONOMY

GROSS NATIONAL PRODUCT	.... $23,500,000,000
RETAIL SALES	.... N/A
BANK RESOURCES	.... $18,704,000,000
EXPORTS	.... $ 1,718,000,000
IMPORTS	.... $ 1,227,000,000
FEDERAL GOVERNMENT EXPENDITURE	.$ 570,202,000
FEDERAL DEBT	.... $ 1,142,523,000

Events

January 16–April 7 • With the aid of President Roosevelt's good offices, a conference is held in Algeciras, Spain, to settle an international crisis over Morocco. The resulting Act of Algeciras, a compromise between the positions of France and Germany, is ratified by the Senate in December.

March 17 • President Roosevelt delivers a speech titled "The Man with the Muckrake," condemning the extremism of some writers in exposing abuses. The writers are hereafter known as muckrakers.

April 18 • An earthquake occurs in San Francisco. Followed by a fire that lasts three days, it destroys much of the city and claims 500 lives.

May 21 • The United States and Mexico sign a treaty providing for equal distribution of Rio Grande water for irrigation purposes.

June 29 • Congress adopts the Hepburn Act, which enlarges the powers of the Interstate Commerce Commission to regulate railroads and other interstate carriers, particularly in the establishment of maximum rates. In addition, the number of members of the commission is increased from five to seven.

June 29 • An executive order requires all coal lands to be withdrawn from entry for appraisal. Later, the lands will be offered for sale.

June 30 • Congress adopts the Pure Food and Drug Act. Influenced by the exposes of the muckrakers, it bans from interstate commerce foods and drugs that are adulterated or mislabeled.

June 30 • Congress adopts the Meat Inspection Act, which provides that meat sold in interstate commerce must be inspected by the federal government.

July 27 • Secretary of State Elihu Root addresses the Third International Conference of American States, meeting in Rio de Janeiro, in a speech foreshadowing the "Good Neighbor" policy.

August 23 • Unable to subdue a rebellion, Cuban president Tomás Estrada Palma asks President Roosevelt for assistance. Roosevelt establishes a provisional government with William H. Taft (September 29) and then Charles E. Magoon (October 3) as governor. After new presidential elections in Cuba, United States forces leave the island on February 1, 1909.

October 11 • By order of the San Francisco Board of Education, children of Japanese, Korean and Chinese origin are to attend an Oriental school. On March 13, 1907, the order is rescinded at President Roosevelt's request in exchange for promised restrictions on Japanese labor immigration.

November 9 • Traveling by battleship, President Roosevelt takes a trip in which he visits the Panama Canal Zone. This is the first time an incumbent president has traveled outside the United States.

December 10 • The Nobel Peace Prize is awarded by Roosevelt for his Russo-Japanese War mediation.

International and Cultural Events • Captain Dreyfus is exonerated in France. Upton Sinclair's *The Jungle* indicts conditions in Chicago's stockyards. The face of breakfast is changed with the introduction of Kelloggs' Toasted Corn Flakes.

United States of America 1907

Events

January 26 • An act of Congress forbids corporations from contributing to election campaigns for national office.

February 8 • The United States and the Dominican Republic sign a treaty incorporating the arrangement of 1905 for United States handling of the Dominican customs. It is ratified by the United States Senate on February 25.

February 20 • Congress creates an immigration commission and revises immigration regulations.

March 5 • The first broadcast of a musical composition occurs when Lee De Forest transmits the "Overture" to Rossini's *William Tell* by wireless from the Telharmonic Hall, in New York, to the Brooklyn Navy Yard.

March 14 • President Roosevelt appoints the Inland Waterways Commission to examine congestion problems.

March 14 • President Roosevelt prohibits the entry of Japanese workers into the United States.

April 1 • President Roosevelt revamps the Panama Canal Commission, placing construction of the canal under the control of Secretary of War Taft.

June 15 • The Second Hague Conference is held with 46 nations in attendance. Proposed by President Roosevelt in 1904, the conference has been delayed by the Russo-Japanese War. Ten conventions on the rules of war and related topics are adopted, and the conference forbids creditor nations from employing armed force to obtain repayment of debts by nations of the Western Hemisphere.

July 30 • Members of the Philippine Assembly are chosen in the first national election in the territory.

September • The United States government institutes a suit against the Standard Oil Company of New Jersey, seeking to dissolve it as an illegal trust.

October 18 • Transatlantic wireless service begins between Ireland and Nova Scotia.

October 21–22 • A run on the Knickerbocker Trust Company exhausts its reserves and causes a panic. Many other banks fail, and security prices decline sharply. The panic is brought to an end in December after the federal government and J.P. Morgan and Company intervene.

November 16 • Oklahoma, formed from Oklahoma and Indian Territories, is admitted to the Union as the 46th state.

December 6 • In Monongah, West Virginia, 361 coal-miners are killed during a mine explosion. It is one of the worst coal-mining accidents in U.S. history.

December 16 • The Great White Fleet of 16 United States battleships leaves on a cruise around the world. It

	60th CONGRESS	
	SENATE	.... 92 Members
	R	 61
	D	 31
	O	 0
ESTIMATED	HOUSE	.... 386 Members
POPULATION	R	 222
87,000,000	D	 164
	O	 0

Theodore Roosevelt
26th President
8th Republican

Charles W. Fairbanks
26th Vice President
Republican

UNITED STATES ECONOMY

GROSS NATIONAL PRODUCT $30,400,000,000
RETAIL SALES ....N/A
BANK RESOURCES $20,114,000,000
EXPORTS ....$ 1,854,000,000
IMPORTS ....$ 1,434,000,000
FEDERAL GOVERNMENT EXPENDITURE .$ 579,129,000
FEDERAL DEBT ....$ 1,147,178,000

returns home on February 22, 1909, having displayed the power of the United States Navy.

International and Cultural Events • Mohandas K. Gandhi initiates civil disobedience in South Africa. Vladimir I. Lenin flees Russia as Premier Pyotr A. Stolypin steps up antirevolutionary efforts. *The Education of Henry Adams* appears in a private edition. The world's first gasoline station opens in Seattle, Washington.

135

1908 United States of America

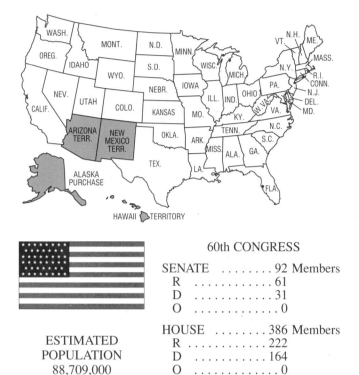

60th CONGRESS

SENATE .... 92 Members
R 61
D 31
O 0

HOUSE .... 386 Members
R 222
D 164
O 0

ESTIMATED
POPULATION
88,709,000

Theodore Roosevelt
26th President
8th Republican

Charles W. Fairbanks
26th Vice President
Republican

UNITED STATES ECONOMY

GROSS NATIONAL PRODUCT $30,400,000,000
RETAIL SALES .... N/A
BANK RESOURCES $19,946,000,000
EXPORTS ....$ 1,835,000,000
IMPORTS ....$ 1,194,000,000
FEDERAL GOVERNMENT EXPENDITURE .$ 659,196,000
FEDERAL DEBT ....$ 1,177,690,000

Events

February 3 • The Supreme Court decides in *Loewe v. Lawlor* (Danbury Hatters' case) that a secondary union boycott restrains interstate trade and thus violates the Sherman Antitrust Act.

February 18 • The "gentlemen's agreement" of 1907 between the United States and Japan is confirmed in a note to the United States ambassador in Tokyo. Japan will not issue passports to laborers who wish to go to the United States, and it accepts President Roosevelt's order barring Japanese laborers with passports permitting them to go to Mexico, Canada and Hawaii from entering the United States.

April 2 • The People's (Populist) party nominates Thomas E. Watson for president.

May 1 • Daniel B. Turney receives the United Christian party's nomination for president.

May 10 • Socialists, at their national nominating convention in Chicago, choose Eugene V. Debs as their candidate for president and Benjamin Hanford as their candidate for vice president.

May 13 • A White House conservation conference meets at the request of President Roosevelt to discuss the report by the Inland Waterways Commission on natural resources. On June 8, the president appoints Gifford Pinchot to head a National Conservation Commission.

May 28 • An act of Congress regulates the employment of child labor in the District of Columbia.

May 30 • Congress adopts the Aldrich-Vreeland Act, which empowers national banks to issue notes backed by commercial paper and bonds of state and local governments. The act also establishes the National Monetary Commission.

June 16 • The Republican party convenes in Chicago. It nominates William H. Taft (Ohio) for president and James S. Sherman (New York) for vice president and adopts a platform favoring conservation of natural resources and opposing trusts.

July 2 • The Socialist Labor party convenes in New York. It nominates Martin R. Preston for president and Donald L. Munro for vice president. Preston is ineligible for the office, and the party nominates August Gillhaus in his stead on July 24.

July 7 • The Democratic party convenes in Denver. It nominates William Jennings Bryan (Nebraska) for president and John W. Kern (Indiana) for vice president and adopts a platform favoring the imposition of an income tax and lower tariff taxes.

July 15 • The Prohibition party nominates Eugene W. Chafin for president.

July 27 • Thomas L. Hisgen receives the Independence party nomination for president.

August 14 • Race riots rage in Springfield, Illinois. Several blacks are hanged. Governor Charles S. Deneen declares martial law, but rioters defy the militia.

September 12 • Testing his airplane for the U.S. Army at Fort Myer, Virginia, Orville Wright breaks his record by flying one hour, 14 minutes, and 20 seconds. During a test flight on September 17, the airplane falls and is destroyed; a passenger is killed and Wright is hurt. On September 21, Wilbur Wright breaks the world's record

United States of America 1908

in Le Mans, France, with a flight of 92 minutes.

September 16 • William Durant incorporates the General Motors Company in New Jersey. A holding company, General Motors is permitted under New Jersey law to own stock in other companies. In October, the Buick Motor Company will become General Motors' first acquisition. During its first year of operation, General Motors sells 25,000 cars and trucks, or 19 percent of the automobiles sold in the United States. Net sales for the first year total $29,030,000.

October 1 • Selling for $850, the Ford Motor Company introduces the first Model T, which will become one of the most popular cars ever produced. Affectionately called the "Tin Lizzie," it will later (1913) become the first automobile to be manufactured on a moving assembly line. Ford will manufacture 15,007,033 Model Ts before it ends production in May 1927.

November 3 • William H. Taft is elected president, receiving 321 electoral votes to 162 for Bryan, his Democratic opponent. James S. Sherman is elected vice president.

November 28 • Approximately 100 miners die when an explosion occurs in the Marianna Mine at Monongahela, Pennsylvania.

November 30 • Secretary of State Root and Baron Kogoro Takahira, ambassador for Japan, exchange notes reiterating support for the open-door policy and the independence of China. The agreement also states that the two countries will uphold the status quo in the Pacific area, which implies tacit American approval of the Japanese presence in Manchuria and Korea.

December 2 • The Federal Council of the Churches of Christ in America, which includes 30 Protestant denominations, is founded in Philadelphia.

International and Cultural Events • The Young Turk uprising restores the Constitution in the Ottoman Empire. The Congo Free State becomes the Belgian Congo when Leopold II cedes his holdings to the nation. The British physicist Ernest Rutherford is awarded the Nobel Prize for his work on radioactivity. Jack Johnson becomes the first black world boxing champion by defeating Tommy Burns in Australia; he reaffirms his title by defeating James J. Jeffries in 1910. America weeps over *The Trail of the Lonesome Pine* by John Fox, Jr.

Child labor: a young girl and an overseer at a bobbin-winding machine.

137

1909 William H. Taft

61st CONGRESS

ESTIMATED
POPULATION
90,492,000

SENATE .... 93 Members
R 61
D 32
O 0

HOUSE .... 391 Members
R 219
D 172
O 0

William H. Taft
27th President
9th Republican

James S. Sherman
27th Vice President
Republican

UNITED STATES ECONOMY

GROSS NATIONAL PRODUCT $30,400,000,000
RETAIL SALES .... N/A
BANK RESOURCES $21,489,000,000
EXPORTS .... $ 1,638,000,000
IMPORTS .... $ 1,312,000,000
FEDERAL GOVERNMENT EXPENDITURE .$ 693,744,000
FEDERAL DEBT .... $ 1,148,315,000

William H. Taft

Birth .... Cincinnati, OH, Sept. 15, 1857
Parents .... Alphonso and Louisa Torrey Taft
Married .... Helen Herron
Home .... Washington, D.C.
Presidency .... 1909 – 1913
Death .... Washington, D.C., Mar. 8, 1930

Events

January 11 • The United States and Great Britain sign a treaty on boundary water between the United States and Canada. The International Joint Commission is established to handle disputes.

January 22 • In a special message to Congress, President Roosevelt urges Congress to establish federal agencies to oversee the natural resources of the United States.

January 27 • The United States and Great Britain sign a treaty submitting their dispute over the North Atlantic fisheries to the Permanent Court of Arbitration at The Hague.

February 9 • Congress outlaws the importation or use of opium for other than medical purposes.

February 19 • Congress doubles the standard homestead maximum of 160 acres in grazing areas of certain western states.

March 4 • William H. Taft is inaugurated president.

April 6 • Robert E. Peary places the United States flag on the North Pole, which he has reached in the company of four Eskimos and Matthew Henson, his black assistant. Decades later, it will be determined that he did not reach the North Pole.

April 9 • The Payne-Aldrich tariff bill, a compromise but generally protectionist measure, is adopted. Duties are reduced to an average of 38 percent.

May–June • The National Association for the Advancement of Colored People is founded in New York under the leadership of W.E.B. DuBois.

June 1 • Seattle is the site for the opening of the Alaska-Yukon-Pacific Exposition.

July 12 • Congress proposes the adoption of the 16th Amendment, calling for an unapportioned income tax.

July 15 • As part of a policy known as "dollar diplomacy," President Taft asks China to assure United States inclusion in a group financing Chinese railways. An accord is signed on May 20, 1911.

September 27 • Continuing President Roosevelt's policy of conservation, President Taft withdraws three million acres of public oil lands in the West.

November 6 • A United States plan to finance the building of railroads in Manchuria is proposed. Although it is not carried out, it influences the conclusion of a Russo-Japanese treaty that violates the open-door policy.

November 13 • An explosion at the St. Paul mine in Cherry, Illinois, kills 259 miners.

November 18–December 16 • The United States supports a successful revolt against the Nicaraguan dictator José Santos Zelaya.

International and Cultural Events • Sigmund Freud and Carl Jung lecture on psychoanalytic theory at Clark University.

United States of America 1910

Events

January 7 • President Taft dismisses Gifford Pinchot, head of the Forest Service, who has severely criticized Secretary of the Interior Richard A. Ballinger. Pinchot had accused the secretary of undermining the conservation program.

March 19 • Under the leadership of Progressive Republicans, the autocratic speaker of the House of Representatives, Joseph G. Cannon, is stripped of his power to appoint members of the Rules Committee, which henceforth is elected by the full House. The speaker may not be a member.

April 18 • Suffragists storm the Capitol, bringing a petition with 500,000 names to senators and representatives. They applaud in the Senate galleries when their petition is presented.

May 11 • Congress creates Glacier National Park in Montana.

June 18 • Congress adopts the Mann-Elkins Act, which enlarges the powers of the Interstate Commerce Commission and adds cable, wireless, telephone, and telegraph companies to its responsibilities.

June 25 • Congress founds the postal savings system with authority to pay two percent interest on deposits.

June 25 • Congress adopts the Mann Act, which forbids the transportation of women from one state to another for immoral purposes.

June 25 • Congress adopts the Publicity Act, which makes it mandatory for representatives to report campaign contributions.

July 12 • The Fourth International Conference of American States opens in Buenos Aires. Conventions on copyrights and inventions are adopted.

August 31 • Former president Roosevelt, in a disagreement with the Taft administration, outlines his New Nationalism in a speech at Osawatomie, Kansas : "I stand for the square deal; property shall be the servant and not the master of the commonwealth."

September 7 • The Hague Court reaches a compromise in settling the North Atlantic fisheries case. On July 20, 1912, the United States and Great Britain sign a convention confirming the award.

October 1 • Twenty people are killed and 17 injured when the McNamara brothers blow up the building of the Los Angeles *Times*, which has favored the open shop.

November 8 • The Democrats gain a majority in the House of Representatives and elect many governors.

December 14 • The Carnegie Endowment for International Peace is established.

International and Cultural Events • The glittering Edwardian Age closes with the death of Edward VII and the accession of George V. The Boy Scouts of America and the Camp Fire Girls are formed. Halley's Comet, last visible at Mark Twain's birth, is visible again at his death. William James publishes his famous essay, *The Moral Equivalent of War*, predicting the "gradual advent of some sort of a social equilibrium." The Mexican Revolution begins under the leadership of Francisco I. Madero.

61st CONGRESS

SENATE	.... 93 Members
R	 61
D	 32
O	 0
HOUSE	.... 391 Members
R	 219
D	 172
O	 0

ESTIMATED POPULATION 92,407,000

William H. Taft
27th President
9th Republican

James S. Sherman
27th Vice President
Republican

UNITED STATES ECONOMY

GROSS NATIONAL PRODUCT	..........$30,400,000,000
RETAIL SALES	.... N/A
BANK RESOURCES	.................$22,922,000,000
EXPORTS	.........................$ 1,710,000,000
IMPORTS	.........................$ 1,557,000,000
FEDERAL GOVERNMENT EXPENDITURE	.$ 693,617,000
FEDERAL DEBT	.....................$ 1,146,940,000

1911 United States of America

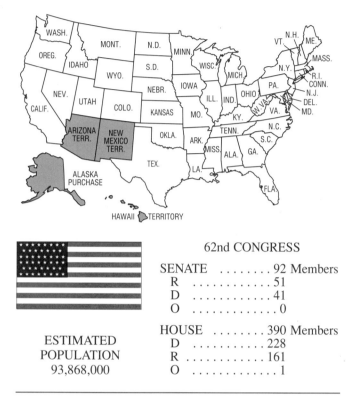

62nd CONGRESS

SENATE .... 92 Members
R 51
D 41
O 0

HOUSE .... 390 Members
D 228
R 161
O 1

ESTIMATED
POPULATION
93,868,000

William H. Taft
27th President
9th Republican

James S. Sherman
27th Vice President
Republican

UNITED STATES ECONOMY

GROSS NATIONAL PRODUCT $30,400,000,000
RETAIL SALES .... N/A
BANK RESOURCES $24,026,000,000
EXPORTS .... $ 2,014,000,000
IMPORTS .... $ 1,527,000,000
FEDERAL GOVERNMENT EXPENDITURE .$ 691,202,000
FEDERAL DEBT .... $ 1,153,985,000

Events

January 21 • Senator Robert M. La Follette of Wisconsin and other insurgent Republicans found the National Progressive Republican League to further such progressive steps as the direct election of senators and national convention delegates and direct primary elections. On October 16, La Follette is chosen as its presidential candidate.

February 21 • The United States and Japan sign a commerce and navigation treaty that includes the "gentlemen's agreement" of 1907.

March 7 • As fighting in the Mexican revolt against President Díaz intensifies, a protective United States force of 20,000 is sent to the border, where it remains until June 24.

April 14 • President Taft warns the Mexican government that fighting must not continue on the border. He demands that no more innocent Americans be killed. President Díaz rejects the American warning and disclaims responsibility. His regime is overthrown by Francisco Madero on May 25.

May 1 • In *United States v. Grimaud*, the U.S. Supreme Court upholds the constitutionality of federal laws that vest the executive branch with a certain degree of administrative discretion when it came to the disposition and administration of public lands. In its ruling, the Court distinguishes between "administrative discretion," which it holds is constitutional, and the delegation of legislative power, which it holds is unconstitutional.

May 15 • The Supreme Court, in an antitrust decision, rules that the Standard Oil Company of New Jersey be dissolved as an unreasonable combination in restraint of trade.

May 29 • In the American Tobacco Company case, the Supreme Court decides that, under the rule of reason, the so-called tobacco trust is an illegal combination in restraint of trade.

June 6 • The United States and Nicaragua sign the Knox-Castrillo Convention providing for United States customs and bank loans. It is not ratified by the Senate.

July 7 • The sealing industry in the northern Pacific is regulated by the signing of a convention by the United States, Great Britain, Russia and Japan. Pelagic sealing north of 30° is forbidden for 15 years.

August 22 • President Taft vetoes a joint resolution of Congress to admit Arizona to the Union. He objects to a provision for the recall of judges in Arizona's constitution.

October 26 • The federal government files suit against the United States Steel Corporation under the Sherman Antitrust Act. In 1915, a New Jersey district court will rule that the act has not been violated.

November 10 • The Carnegie Corporation of New York is set up with a $125 million endowment.

International and Cultural Events • The Norwegian explorer Roald Amundsen reaches the South Pole. F.W. Taylor's *The Principles of Scientific Management* outlines assembly-line methods. A fire at the Triangle Shirtwaist Company in New York kills 145 women and leads to a revised industrial code that is followed nationally. The country dances to Irving Berlins' "Alexander's Ragtime Band."

United States of America 1912

Events

January 6 • New Mexico is admitted to the Union as the 47th state.

January 9 • United States Marines arrive in Honduras to protect American property.

February 14 • After removing the constitutional clause to which President Taft objected, Arizona is admitted to the Union as the 48th state. It then restores the clause.

February 24 • Theodore Roosevelt replies to a letter written to him by seven Republican governors, saying that he will run again if drafted.

March 14 • The United States bans arms shipments to opponents of Mexican president Madero.

April 7 • The Socialist Labor party nominates Arthur E. Reimer for president. The Socialist party nominates Eugene V. Debs on May 12.

April 15 • The *Titanic*, a luxury liner on its maiden voyage from Great Britain to the United States, collides with an iceberg and sinks; 1,513 lives are lost.

May 16 • Congress proposes the adoption of the Seventeenth Amendment, calling for the direct election of United States senators.

June 18 • The Republic party convenes in Chicago. It nominates President Taft and Vice President Sherman for re-election. Sherman dies in Utica, New York, on October 30.

June 22 • Roosevelt is asked to lead a third party.

June 25 • The Democratic party convenes in Baltimore. It nominates Woodrow Wilson (New Jersey) for president and Thomas R. Marshall (Indiana) for vice president.

July 10 • The Prohibition party convenes in Atlantic City. It nominates Eugene W. Chafin for president and Aaron S. Watkins for vice president.

August 2 • The Senate approves what will become known as the Lodge Corollary to the Monroe Doctrine, a resolution that declares that it is the intention of the United States to protect the Panama Canal and any other harbor or strategic position in the American continents from any threat to the communication or safety of the United States.

August 5 • The Progressive (Bull Moose) party convenes in Chicago. Theodore Roosevelt, who has captured Progressive support from Senator La Follette, is nominated for president; Hiram W. Johnson (California) is nominated for vice president.

August 14 • United States Marines arrive in Nicaragua after a revolt has broken out. Elections are held under American control.

August 24 • Congress makes Alaska an organized territory.

October 14 • Former president Roosevelt is slightly wounded by a would-be assassin in Milwaukee.

62nd CONGRESS

SENATE . . . . 92 Members
R 51
D 41
O 0

HOUSE . . . . 390 Members
D 228
R 161
O 1

ESTIMATED
POPULATION
95,331,000

William H. Taft
27th President
9th Republican

James S. Sherman
27th Vice President
Republican

UNITED STATES ECONOMY

GROSS NATIONAL PRODUCT $38,900,000,000
RETAIL SALES . . . . N/A
BANK RESOURCES $25,372,000,000
EXPORTS . . . .$ 2,170,000,000
IMPORTS . . . .$ 1,653,000,000
FEDERAL GOVERNMENT EXPENDITURE .$ 689,881,000
FEDERAL DEBT . . . .$ 1,193,839,000

November 5 • Woodrow Wilson is elected president, receiving 435 electoral votes to 88 for Roosevelt and eight for Taft. Marshall is elected vice president.

International and Cultural Events • The First Balkan War leads to Turkish expulsion from continental Europe, except Constantinople. D. W. Griffith's *The New York Hat* makes Mary Pickford "America's sweetheart;" almost five million people go to the movies daily. The Girl Scouts of the U.S.A. is founded.

1913 Woodrow Wilson

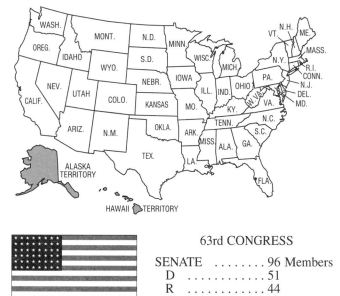

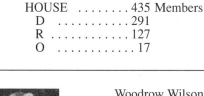

Woodrow Wilson
28th President
9th Democrat

Thomas R. Marshall
28th Vice President
Democrat

63rd CONGRESS

SENATE . . . . 96 Members
D 51
R 44
O 1

HOUSE . . . . 435 Members
D 291
R 127
O 17

ESTIMATED
POPULATION
97,227,000

UNITED STATES ECONOMY

GROSS NATIONAL PRODUCT $38,900,000,000
RETAIL SALES . . . . N/A
BANK RESOURCES $26,103,000,000
EXPORTS . . . .$ 2,429,000,000
IMPORTS . . . .$ 1,813,000,000
FEDERAL GOVERNMENT EXPENDITURE .$ 724,512,000
FEDERAL DEBT . . . .$ 1,193,048,000

Woodrow Wilson	
Birth . . . . Staunton, VA, Dec. 28, 1856	
Parents . . . . Joseph and Janet Woodrow Wilson	
Married . . . . Ellen Axson; Edith Bolling Galt	
Home . . . . Washington, D.C.	
Presidency . . . . 1913 – 1921	
Death . . . . Washington, D.C., Feb. 3, 1924	

Events

January • Garment workers strike in New York and, the following month, in Boston, demanding higher wages, shorter hours, and recognition of their union. These demands are met when the strike is settled in March (New York) and April (Boston).

January 11 • President-elect Woodrow Wilson, in a speech in Chicago, says, "The business of the United States must be set absolutely free of every feature of monopoly."

February 14 • President Taft vetoes a bill that would require a literacy test of would-be immigrants.

February 25 • The 16th Amendment to the United States Constitution is adopted. It gives Congress power to lay taxes on incomes without apportionment among the states.

February 28 • A congressional subcommittee headed by Representative Arsène Pujo of Louisiana reports that a "growing concentration of control of money and credit" exists in a few hands.

March 1 • Congress passes the Physical Valuation Act, which gives the Interstate Commerce Commission the power to determine the physical value of railroad property in order to establish rates and profits.

March 1 • Congress adopts the Webb-Kenyon Interstate Liquor Act over the veto of President Taft. The act makes it illegal to ship liquor into states where the sale of liquor is prohibited.

March 4 • Congress creates two separate cabinet-rank departments from the Department of Commerce and Labor.

March 4 • Wilson is inaugurated president. In his inaugural address, he calls for reforms in keeping with his philosophy of the New Freedom.

March 11 • President Wilson indicates his opposition to the government in Mexico of Victoriano Huerta, who in February overthrew President Madero. He ends the policy of dollar diplomacy.

April 8 • President Wilson appears before a special session of Congress to deliver a message on the need for new tariff legislation. This is the first time since 1800 that a president has appeared before Congress.

May 14 • The Rockefeller Foundation, chartered by the state of New York, receives $100 million from John D. Rockefeller.

May 31 • The 17th Amendment to the Constitution is adopted. It replaces the system of having the state legislatures choose United States senators with popular election in each state.

June 19 • The Supreme Court decides that, in the Minnesota rate cases, a state may establish railroad rates

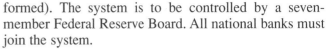

within its own borders if no conflict with federal laws on interstate commerce exists.

June 23 • Congress is urged by President Wilson to legislate banking and currency reforms.

August 16 • With opposition increasing to his rule, Mexican president Huerta rejects President Wilson's plan for an armistice and elections to resolve the dispute. On August 27, Wilson adopts a "watchful waiting" policy toward Mexico.

September • A coal miners' strike begins in Colorado. It is called off three months later by the United Mine Workers after much violence and federal intervention.

October 3 • Congress adopts the Underwood Tariff Act, which reduces rates to an average of 26 percent and greatly expands the list of free goods.

October 27 • Resisting demands for intervention in Mexico, President Wilson states that it is not the policy of the United States to gain any more territory by conquest.

November 1 • President Wilson sends a note asking President Huerta to resign. Huerta refuse to do so, and on November 24, a second note states that the United States will aid his opponents.

December 23 • The Federal Reserve System is created by the Owens-Glass Act, which authorizes the division of the country into between eight and 12 districts with a Federal Reserve bank in each (12 such districts are formed). The system is to be controlled by a seven-member Federal Reserve Board. All national banks must join the system.

International and Cultural Events • The Second Balkan War concludes with Bulgaria's defeat. Marcel Proust begins publication of *Remembrance of Things Past*. The Fabians Beatrice and Sidney Webb found *The New Statesman*. The Danish physicist Niels Bohr presents his theory of atomic structure. Charles A. Beard publishes *An Economic Interpretation of the Constitution of the United States*. Marcel Duchamp's *Nude Descending a Staircase* is the sensation of the New York Armory Show of modern European art.

ARTICLE XVI

Income Tax

The Congress shall have power to lay and collect taxes on incomes, from whatever source derived, without apportionment among the several States, and without regard to any census or enumeration.

(Adopted in 1913)

ARTICLE XVII

Election of Senators

The Senate of the United States shall be composed of two Senators from each State, elected by the people thereof, for six years; and each Senator shall have one vote. The electors in each State shall have the qualifications requisite for electors of the most numerous branch of the State legislatures.

When the vacancies happen in the representation of any State in the Senate, the executive authority of such State shall issue writs of election to fill such vacancies: Provided, That the legislature of any State may empower the executive thereof to make temporary appointments until the people fill the vacancies by election as the legislature may direct.

This amendment shall not be so construed as to affect the election or term of any Senator chosen before it becomes valid as part of the Constitution.

(Adopted in 1913)

President William Howard Taft greets his successor, Woodrow Wilson, before Wilson's inauguration on March 4, 1913.

63rd CONGRESS

SENATE .... 96 Members
D 51
R 44
O 1

HOUSE .... 435 Members
D 291
R 127
O 17

ESTIMATED
POPULATION
99,118,000

Woodrow Wilson
28th President
9th Democrat

Thomas R. Marshall
28th Vice President
Democrat

UNITED STATES ECONOMY

GROSS NATIONAL PRODUCT $38,900,000,000
RETAIL SALES .... N/A
BANK RESOURCES $27,349,000,000
EXPORTS .... $ 2,330,000,000
IMPORTS .... $ 1,894,000,000
FEDERAL GOVERNMENT EXPENDITURE .$ 735,081,000
FEDERAL DEBT .... $ 1,188,235,000

Events

January 20 • President Wilson, in an address to Congress, calls for the strengthening of antitrust laws.

April 9 • United States Marines land at Tampico, Mexico, for supplies and are arrested by President Huerta's government. Although the Mexicans release them and apologize, Admiral Henry Thomas Mayo demands, among other things, a 21-gun salute to the U.S. flag.

April 20 • President Wilson asks Congress for authorization to employ force, if necessary, to make certain that the rights of the United States are respected. Congress grants such authorization on April 22.

April 21 • Veracruz is seized by United States Marines, who remain until November 23. (On July 15, Huerta is forced to resign as president by Venustiano Carranza.)

May 7 • Congress passes a bill designating the second Sunday in May as "Mother's Day."

May 8 • The Smith-Lever Act is adopted. It provides for grants for agricultural extension work to be developed by the land-grant colleges and the Department of Agriculture.

August 15 • The official opening of the Panama Canal takes place.

August 20 • Great Britain issues an order-in-council on wartime trade, the first of a series that make it increasingly difficult for goods of any sort to reach Germany. These draw protests from the United States as interference with the rights of neutrals.

September 5 • President Wilson orders the Department of the Navy to provide wireless stations for transatlantic communication. As a courtesy, Wilson will permit German diplomats to use the system. The Germans will use it to transmit coded messages, one of which will gain notoriety as the Zimmerman Telegram.

September 26 • The Federal Trade Commission Act is adopted. It is designed primarily to bar unfair competition in interstate trade.

October 15 • The Clayton Antitrust Act is adopted. It is intended to eliminate monopolistic practices that had developed since the passage of the Sherman Antitrust Act. Both companies and individual corporate officers may be subject to prosecution. The act also states that labor and agricultural organizations are not illegal combinations under the antitrust laws. Boycotts, strikes, and peaceful picketing are not to be subject to injunction.

International and Cultural Events • World War I begins when, following the assassination of Archduke Francis Ferdinand and his wife at Sarajevo, Austria declares war on Serbia. The United States proclaims its neutrality as the conflict spreads. In August, Japan joins the Allies, and early in November the Ottoman empire (Turkey) is drawn in on the side of the Central Powers. Responding to the latter events, Great Britain declares Egypt a protectorate. Americans are reading Edgar Rice Burrough's *Tarzan of the Apes*, listening to W.C. Handy's "St. Louis Blues," and attending showings of the Italian movie epic *Cabiria*. Commenting on Balkan War movies, *The New York Times* notes that the camera can be both a spur to courage and "an element capable of adding much to the shame of defeat."

United States of America 1915

Events

January 28 • Congress passes a bill establishing the United States Coast Guard.

February 10 • The United States protests Germany's declaration of a war zone around the British Isles. Germany is to be held accountable for the loss of any American lives.

March 30 • The United States protests the British blockade of German ports by an order-in-council of March 11, saying that it interferes with legitimate neutral trade.

May 1 • A statement issued by the German embassy in Washington puts Americans on notice that traveling in the war zone is a risky endeavor.

May 7 • The *Lusitania*, a British steamship, is sunk by a German submarine; 1,198 lives are lost, including 128 Americans. On May 13, the United States dispatches the first *Lusitania* note. The German reply of May 28 is deemed unsatisfactory.

June 7 • Secretary of State William Jennings Bryan resigns because of his unwillingness to sign the second *Lusitania* note, which he thinks may draw the United States into war.

June 9 • The second *Lusitania* note, signed by the new secretary of state, Robert Lansing, demands German disavowal of the sinking, indemnification for the victims, and an end to attacks on passenger vessels.

July 8 • Germany replies to the second *Lusitania* note, promising safe passage for Americans in neutral ships, but it does not offer definite pledges.

July 15 • A Secret Service agent discovers the blueprints for a German espionage ring in the United States that includes German consuls, embassy staff, German-Americans and officials of the Hamburg-American Steamship Line. The release of this information inflames public opinion against Germany.

July 21 • The United States sends the third and sharpest *Lusitania* note to Germany.

July 24 • A briefcase of the German propaganda director in the United States, containing plans for German sabotage in the United States, comes into the hands of the Secret Service.

July 29 • United States Marines land in Haiti to quell disorders. American protection is regularized by a treaty signed on September 16, and the Marines remain until 1936.

September 1 • German ambassador Johann-Heinrich von Bernstorff pledges that German submarines will not sink passenger ships without warning and without providing for the safety of the passengers if the ships do not attempt to escape.

October 15 • A $500 million loan is made by American

banks to France and Great Britain.

December 7 • President Wilson offers a national defense program to Congress.

International and Cultural Events • Italy joins the Allies. German Zeppelins attack London, which sings "Pack Up Your Troubles in Your Old Kit Bag." Henry Ford sends a peace ship to Europe. D.W. Griffith's epic movie *Birth of a Nation* is attacked by civil rights leaders. Telephone service between San Francisco and New York is inaugurated; America sings "Hello Frisco."

64th CONGRESS

SENATE . . . . 96 Members
D 56
R 40
O 0

HOUSE . . . . 435 Members
D 230
R 196
O 9

ESTIMATED
POPULATION
100,549,000

Woodrow Wilson
28th President
9th Democrat

Thomas R. Marshall
28th Vice President
Democrat

UNITED STATES ECONOMY

GROSS NATIONAL PRODUCT $38,900,000,000
RETAIL SALES . . . . .N/A
BANK RESOURCES $28,363,000,000
EXPORTS . . . .$ 2,716,000,000
IMPORTS . . . .$ 1,674,000,000
FEDERAL GOVERNMENT EXPENDITURE .$ 760,587,000
FEDERAL DEBT . . . .$ 1,191,264,000

1916 United States of America

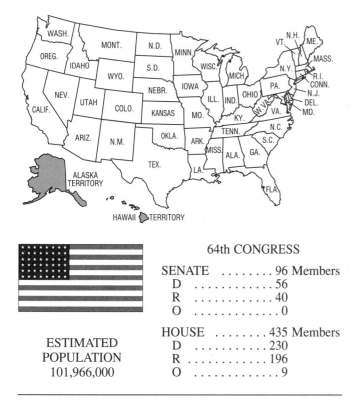

64th CONGRESS

SENATE . . . . 96 Members
D 56
R 40
O 0

HOUSE . . . . 435 Members
D 230
R 196
O 9

ESTIMATED
POPULATION
101,966,000

Woodrow Wilson
28th President
9th Democrat

Thomas R. Marshall
28th Vice President
Democrat

UNITED STATES ECONOMY

GROSS NATIONAL PRODUCT $38,900,000,000
RETAIL SALES . . . . N/A
BANK RESOURCES $32,697,000,000
EXPORTS . . . .$ 5,423,000,000
IMPORTS . . . .$ 2,392,000,000
FEDERAL GOVERNMENT EXPENDITURE .$ 734,056,000
FEDERAL DEBT . . . .$ 1,225,146,000

Events

January 27 • President Wilson begins a speaking tour emphasizing preparedness.

January 28 • President Wilson appoints Louis D. Brandeis to the Supreme Court.

February 10 • Secretary of War Lindley M. Garrison resigns because he opposes reliance on an expanded national guard, which the president and Congress favor.

The President appoints a pacifist, Newton D. Baker, to succeed him (March 9).

March 15 • A United States punitive expedition, under the command of General John J. Pershing, enters Mexico in pursuit of the revolutionary leader Pancho Villa, who, on January 10, executed 18 American mining engineers in Santa Ysabel, Sonora, and, on March 9 raided Columbus, New Mexico, causing 17 deaths. The search fails to find the elusive Villa, and the expedition is withdrawn (February 5, 1917).

March 24 • An unarmed passenger ship, the *Sussex*, is torpedoed without warning in the English Channel with the loss of American lives. A United States note of April 18 warns Germany that diplomatic relations will be broken if it does not stop sinking ships without provision for the passengers' safety.

April 23 • At their national nominating convention in New York, members of the Socialist Labor party choose Arthur E. Reimer as their party's presidential candidate and Caleb Harrison as their party's vice presidential candidate.

May • In the wake of disorders, United States forces are landed in the Dominican Republic, where they remain until 1924.

May 8 • Secretary of State Lansing accepts German assurances given in reply to the *Sussex* note that merchantmen will not be sunk without warning unless they try to escape. However, he rejects German demands that the United States be responsible for making Great Britain observe international law regarding blockades.

June 3 • Congress adopts the National Defense Act, which increases the size of the U.S. Army to 175,000 and that of the U.S. National Guard to 2,450,000. In addition, a Reserve Officers Training Corps program is authorized.

June 7 • The Republican party convenes in Chicago. It nominates Charles Evans Hughes (New York) for president and Charles W. Fairbanks (Indiana) for vice president.

June 7 • The Progressive party convenes in Chicago. It nominates Theodore Roosevelt for president and John M. Parker for vice president. Roosevelt declines the nomination in favor of Charles Evans Hughes. The question of endorsing Hughes splits the party.

June 14 • The Democratic party convenes in St. Louis. It nominates President Wilson and Vice President Marshall for re-election. "He kept us out of war" becomes Wilson's campaign slogan.

July 17 • Congress adopts the Federal Farm Loan Act, which sets up 12 Farm Loan Banks to extend long-term loans to farmers.

July 21 • At their national nominating convention in St. Paul, Minnesota, members of the Prohibition party choose Frank Hanly as their party's presidential candidate and Ira D. Landrith as their party's vice presidential candidate.

July 22 • Ten people are killed and scores wounded when a bomb is thrown during the Preparedness Day parade in San Francisco. Thomas Mooney and others involved in the labor movement are arrested. Mooney is sentenced to life imprisonment after a controversial trial. He is pardoned in 1939.

July 30 • A munitions dump on Black Tom Island, New Jersey, is blown up by German saboteurs. Damage is estimated at $22 million.

August 4 • A treaty is signed for the sale of the Danish West Indies (Virgin Islands) the United States for $25 million.

August 11 • Congress adopts the Warehouse Act, which is designed to enable farmers to secure loans on the basis of warehouse receipts.

August 29 • Congress adopts the Army Appropriations Act, which creates the Council of National Defense.

August 29 • Congress adopts the Jones Act, which provides a representative form of government for the Philippines. Eventually the islands are to be granted independence.

September 1 • The Keaty-Owen Child Labor bill is signed into law, barring from interstate commerce any item made by a child. On June 3, 1918, the U.S. Supreme Court, in *Hammer v. Dagenhart*, will declare the act unconstitutional. The five-member majority will hold that the act is an infringement on the local regulation of labor conditions.

September 3 • The Adamson bill is signed into law, establishing an eight-hour workday for railroad employees.

September 7 • President Wilson signs the Shipping Board Act, which provides for a five-member board to acquire ships through the Emergency Fleet Corporation.

November 7 • Wilson is re-elected president, receiving 277 electoral votes to 254 for Hughes, his Republican opponent. Elected in Montana, Jeannette Rankin becomes the first congresswoman.

December 18 • The president asks all the belligerents to apprise him in confidence of their terms for peace. The Central Powers refuse; the Allies, on January 10, 1917, list terms that will be rejected by the Central Powers.

December 29 • An act of Congress increases the size of a homestead composed of grazing land to 640 acres.

International and Cultural Events • Dublin is shaken by the Easter Rebellion. The Irish patriot Roger Casement is hanged for treason. James Joyce's *A Portrait of the Artist as a Young Man* is brought out in book form by an American publisher.

Women campaign for Wilson in New York.

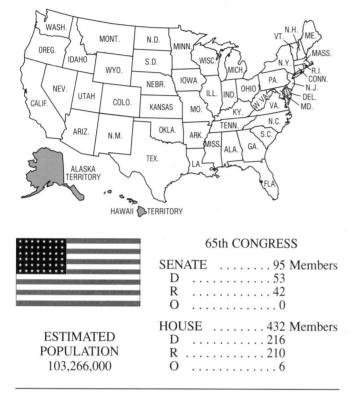

ALASKA TERRITORY

HAWAII TERRITORY

65th CONGRESS

SENATE	....	95 Members
D	....	53
R	....	42
O	....	0
HOUSE	....	432 Members
D	....	216
R	....	210
O	....	6

ESTIMATED
POPULATION
103,266,000

Woodrow Wilson
28th President
9th Democrat

Thomas R. Marshall
28th Vice President
Democrat

UNITED STATES ECONOMY

GROSS NATIONAL PRODUCT	.........$71,600,000,000
RETAIL SALES	..............................N/A
BANK RESOURCES	.................$37,540,000,000
EXPORTS	.........................$ 6,170,000,000
IMPORTS	.........................$ 2,952,000,000
FEDERAL GOVERNMENT EXPENDITURE	.$ 1,977,682,000
FEDERAL DEBT	....................$ 2,975,619,000

Events

January 17 • The United States and Denmark exchange ratifications of a treaty transferring the Virgin Islands to the United States. On March 31, the transfer takes effect.

January 22 • Hoping to avoid United States involvement in the war, President Wilson makes a speech before the Senate in which he calls for "peace without victory" and suggests the creation of an international federation to maintain peace in the future.

January 29 • President Wilson vetoes a bill requiring immigrants to pass a literacy test. Congress votes to override the veto on February 5.

February 3 • President Wilson informs Congress that he has broken diplomatic relations with Germany after being informed (January 31) that unrestricted submarine warfare is to recommence. The Senate approves his action on February 7.

February 23 • Federal aid is provided for vocational education under the Smith-Hughes Act.

March 1 • An intercepted note from German foreign secretary Arthur Zimmermann to the German ambassador to Mexico is made public. In the event of war between Germany and the United States, the foreign secretary asks the ambassador to try to induce Mexico to join Germany in an anti-United States alliance in return for its lost, and U.S. annexed, territory.

March 2 • Congress adopts the Jones Act, which provides for the organization of Puerto Rico as a United States territory. Its inhabitants are to be American citizens.

March 5 • Wilson begins his second term as president.

March 8 • After a filibuster has prevented passage of a bill to arm merchant ships in the regular congressional session, the Senate approves a cloture rule in a special session. Learning that congressional approval is not required, Wilson arranges to have merchant ships armed in the war zones.

March 31 • The Council of National Defense establishes the General Munitions Board.

April 2 • Wilson asks Congress to declare war against Germany. Congress does so on April 6.

April 14 • President Wilson forms the Committee on Public Information, often known as the Creel Committee for its chairman, journalist George Creel.

April 24 • The Liberty Loan Act is adopted. It provides for the public sale of bonds and the extension of loans to the Allied Powers. The first subscription drive, in June, will raise approximately $2 billion. The second drive, in November, will raise $3.8 billion. The third drive, in May 1918, will raise $4.2 billion. The fourth drive, in October 1918, will raise $6 billion. The fifth drive, the so-called Victory Loan, in April 1919, will raise $4.5 billion.

May 18 • Congress adopts the Selective Service Act, which provides for the registration of men between the ages of 21 and 31.

June 14 • General John J. Pershing, commander of the American Expeditionary Force (AEF), arrives in Paris. The first American combat troops land on June 25.

June 15 • The Espionage Act is adopted. It is directed against people who assist the enemy or interfere in various ways with the conduct of the war. In addition, the postmaster general is authorized to prevent the

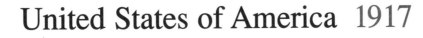

circulation by mail of seditious material.

July 4 • Rantoul, Illinois, becomes the site of the first training school for military aviators. At this time, the U.S. Army has about 4,500 aviators and only 55 planes.

July 28 • The General Munitions Board is succeeded by the War Industries Board, which, after its powers are increased in March 1918, effectively mobilizes industry under the leadership of Bernard Baruch.

August 10 • The Lever Food and Fuel Control Act is adopted to increase the production of food and fuel and to provide for their effective distribution. The act also includes a provision that makes it illegal to use foodstuffs in the manufacturing of distilled spirits and to import alcoholic beverages. The food program, which is administered by Herbert Hoover, is particularly effective.

September 21 • Major General Tasker Bliss is appointed chief of staff of the United States Army with the rank of general.

October 3 • The War Revenue Act is adopted. It provides for graduated personal income and excess profits taxes, increased corporation and excise taxes and higher postal rates.

October 6 • The Trading with the Enemy Act is adopted. It establishes the Office of Alien Property Custodian to handle enemy property in the United States (much of this property is subsequently sold). Trading with the enemy is prohibited, and all imports are placed under the control of the War Trade Board.

October 21 • The first American troops are assigned to the front, in the Toul sector.

November 2 • Viscount Kikujiro Ishii, special envoy for Japan, and Secretary of State Lansing, sign an agreement whereby the United States recognizes the fact that Japan has special interests in its near neighbor, China. Although Japan reiterates its adherence to the open-door policy, it considers that it enjoys political power in China.

December 7 • The United States declares war on Austria-Hungary.

December 18 • Congress proposes the adoption of the 18th Amendment, which prohibits the manufacture, sale or transportation of intoxicating liquors.

December 26 • The United States Railroad Administration, under the direction of William Gibbs McAdoo, takes charge of the railroads, which remain under government control until 1920.

International and Cultural Events • British merchant shipping losses exceed four million tons. Czar Nicholas II abdicates, and Aleksandr Kerenski forms a liberal government that is overthrown by the Bolsheviks in November. They conclude an armistice with Germany at Brest-Litovsk. The Italian army makes a tragic retreat from Caporetto. Jazz and bobbed hair sweep the United States, where Beethoven vanishes from concert programs and sauerkraut is renamed liberty cabbage. Charlie Chaplin and other movie stars go on Liberty Bond tours. The Columbia School of Journalism awards the first Pulitzer prizes.

The United States at war.

1918 United States of America

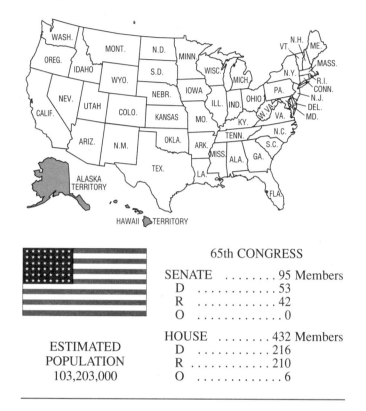

65th CONGRESS

SENATE .... 95 Members
D 53
R 42
O 0

HOUSE .... 432 Members
D 216
R 210
O 6

ESTIMATED
POPULATION
103,203,000

Woodrow Wilson
28th President
9th Democrat

Thomas R. Marshall
28th Vice President
Democrat

UNITED STATES ECONOMY

GROSS NATIONAL PRODUCT $71,600,000,000
RETAIL SALES .... N/A
BANK RESOURCES $41,097,000,000
EXPORTS .... $ 6,048,000,000
IMPORTS .... $ 3,031,000,000
FEDERAL GOVERNMENT EXPENDITURE ..$12,696,702,000
FEDERAL DEBT $12,455,225,000

Events

January 7 • The U.S. Supreme Court, in *Arver v. United States*, upholds the constitutionality of the recently enacted conscription law. The Court rules that Congress, due to its constitutionally derived power "to declare war...to raise and support armies," has the right to draft men into the military.

January 8 • President Wilson, speaking before Congress, presents 14 Points for peace: (1) "open covenants of peace, openly arrived at...;" (2) "absolute freedom of navigation upon the seas,...in peace and war...;" (3) "the removal, so far as possible, of all economic barriers and the establishment of an equality of trade conditions ...;" (4) "adequate guarantees...that national armaments will be reduced to the lowest point consistent with domestic safety;" (5) "a free, open-minded, and...impartial adjustment of all colonial claims...;" (6) "the evacuation of all Russian territory and...an unhampered and unembarrassed opportunity for [Russia to obtain] the independent determination of her own political development and national policy...;" (7) the evacuation and restoration of Belgium; (8) the evacuation and restoration of French territory and the return of Alsace Lorraine to France; (9) "a readjustment of the frontiers of Italy...along clearly recognizable lines of nationality;" (10) "...the freest opportunity of autonomous development" for the peoples of Austria-Hungary; (11) the evacuation of Serbia, Montenegro, and Romania, the restoration of occupied territories, and "free and secure access to the sea" for Serbia; (12) secure sovereignty for the Turkish portions of the Ottoman empire, an opportunity of autonomous development for the other nationalities under Turkish rule, and the opening of the Dardanelles as a free passage to the ships of all nations; (13) the erection of an independent Polish state with access to the sea; and (14) the formation of "a general association of nations... under specific covenants for the purpose of affording mutual guarantees of political independence and territorial integrity to great and small states alike."

February 18 • President Wilson approves the Muscle Shoals project.

March 21 • The Germans begin the first of five drives that cut deeply into the Allied lines. The fifth drive, known as the Second Battle of the Marne, is halted by the French on July 17.

March 21 • The Railroad Control Act is adopted. It provides for the operation of the railroads on a regional basis and the determination of the compensation due the railroads while the lines are under federal control.

April 5 • The War Finance Corporation is established to help banks finance the operation of war industries. The National War Labor Board is established on April 8 to settle labor disputes and avoid the interruption of war production.

April 10 • The Webb-Pomerene Act is adopted. Under its provisions, exporters may combine in export trade associations and not be prosecuted under the antitrust laws.

May 16 • The Sedition Act is adopted to supplement the Espionage Act of 1917. It is directed against people responsible for seditious statements about the country, its institutions, and its war effort. Eugene V. Debs is among those imprisoned, his 10-year sentence (September 14) being commuted in 1921.

May 20 • The Overman Act is adopted. It empowers the president to reorganize government agencies in the interest of efficiency.

May 28 • The First Division wins the battle of Cantigny, the first independent American action in the war.

June 4 • The Battle of Belleau Wood begins. By July 1, the Marine Brigade of the United States Second Division, at the cost of heavy casualties, will have captured Bouresches and Belleau Wood, and the Third Infantry Brigade will have taken Vaux.

July 16 • The federal government takes control of the telephone and telegraph systems.

July 18–August 6 • Eight United States divisions participate in the Aisne-Marne offensive, in which the Allies take the initiative.

August 10 • General Pershing takes command of the United States First Army in addition to his duties as AEF commander.

September • A world influenza epidemic reaches the United States from Europe. It continues into 1919, causing approximately 500,000 deaths.

September 12–16 • The First Army, led by General Pershing, reduces the Saint-Mihiel salient.

September 26–November 11 • A total of 1.2 million American soldiers participate in the Meuse-Argonne offensive, the southern pincer of the final Allied offensive. They sustain 120,000 casualties.

October 4 • The governments of Germany and Austria-Hungary send notes to President Wilson asking that peace be negotiated on the basis of the 14 Points. Replying on October 8, Wilson asks the new German chancellor, Prince Max of Baden, whether he represents merely the authorities that have conducted the war. In a note of October 12, the German Foreign Office states that the chancellor speaks for both the government and the people. When Wilson lists four conditions for an armistice, the Germans, on October 20, offer new concessions. On October 23, Wilson agrees to present the armistice question to the Allies, who are at first unwilling to agree to an armistice based on the 14 Points. On November 5, Wilson tells the Germans that the Allies are ready to receive delegates, and on November 9, the Germans accept the Allies' terms.

November 3 • Delegates of Austria-Hungary sign an armistice on Allied terms at Villa Giusti, near Padua.

November 5 • Although President Wilson has asked the electorate to show its support by maintaining Democratic majorities in Congress, control of both houses passes to the Republicans in the midterm elections.

November 11 • The Germans sign an armistice at Compiègne, and the war ends at 11 a.m. Of the 120,144 American soldiers who died, 50,604 were killed in action or died of combat wounds; 62,668 died of disease.

November 18 • President Wilson announces that he will attend the peace conference, scheduled to open in January 1919 in Paris, France. He will anger Senate Republicans by his failure to include them in the official delegation. Wilson will leave for Paris on December 4 aboard the *George Washington*.

International and Cultural Events • Allied forces, including Americans, land in the Arkhangelsk area of Russia to protect supplies and aid anti-Bolsheviks. The emperors of Germany and Austria abdicate. The German philosopher Oswald Spengler begins publication of *The Decline of the West*.

Lieutenant Eddie V. Rickenbacker, American ace, and his Spad plane near Rembercourt, France.

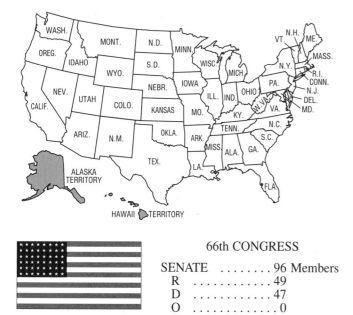

66th CONGRESS

SENATE .... 96 Members
R 49
D 47
O 0

HOUSE .... 433 Members
R 240
D 190
O 3

ESTIMATED
POPULATION
104,512,000

Woodrow Wilson
28th President
9th Democrat

Thomas R. Marshall
28th Vice President
Democrat

UNITED STATES ECONOMY

GROSS NATIONAL PRODUCT $71,600,000,000
RETAIL SALES .... N/A
BANK RESOURCES $47,603,000,000
EXPORTS .... $ 7,750,000,000
IMPORTS .... $ 3,904,000,000
FEDERAL GOVERNMENT EXPENDITURE .$18,514,880,000
FEDERAL DEBT $25,484,506,000

Events

January 18 • The formal opening of the peace conference is held in Paris. Of the principal Allies, Great Britain is represented by David Lloyd George; France, by Georges Clemenceau; Italy, by Vittorio Orlando; and the United States, by Wilson.
January 29 • The 18th Amendment to the United States Constitution is ratified.

February 14 • The draft Covenant of the League of Nations, to be included in the peace treaty, is presented by President Wilson to the peace conference. As amended, it is voted into the treaty on April 28.
March 2 • Thirty-nine senators and senators-elect sign a round robin petition, declaring that the League of Nations should not be discussed as part of the peace treaty.
May 7 • The peace treaty, completed at the cost of many compromises with the 14 Points, is presented to the German delegates.
June 4 • Congress proposes the 19th Amendment, which provides for woman suffrage.
July 10 • The Treaty of Versailles, signed by the Allies and Germany on June 28, is presented to the Senate by President Wilson.
September 25 • On a tour seeking approval of the League of Nations, President Wilson collapses in Pueblo, Colorado. On October 2, after returning to Washington, he suffers a severe stroke.
October 28 • The Volstead Act is adopted to enforce the 18th Amendment.
November 19 • The Senate rejects a resolution, submitted by Henry Cabot Lodge, that would ratify the Treaty of Versailles on condition that 14 attached reservations, which limited United States participation in the League, are also accepted.
International and Cultural Events • Benito Mussolini founds the Italian Fascist party. The Boston police strike focuses attention on Governor Calvin Coolidge. The "Black Socks" World Series scandal shocks the nation. Fannie Brice sings "My Man."

ARTICLE XVIII

Prohibition

Section 1. After one year from the ratification of this article the manufacture, sale, or transportation of intoxicating liquors within, the importation thereof into, or the exportation thereof from the United States and all territory subject to the jurisdiction thereof for beverage purposes is hereby prohibited.

Section 2. The Congress and the several States shall have concurrent power to enforce this article by appropriate legislation.

Section 3. This article shall be inoperative unless it shall have been ratified as an amendment to the Constitution by the Legislatures of the several States, as provided in the Constitution, within seven years from the date of the submission hereof to the States by the Congress.

(Adopted in 1919)

United States of America 1920

Events

January–May • The Department of Justice, in a "Red hunt," arrests thousands of radicals. The aliens among them are deported.

January 16 • The 18th Amendment goes into effect.

February 28 • The Esch-Cummins Act ends government control of the railroads and gives the Interstate Commerce Commission power to fix railroad rates and to regulate financing. It also establishes the Railroad Labor Board.

March 19 • The Senate fails in its last attempt to ratify the Treaty of Versailles.

May 8 • The Socialist party convenes in New York. It nominates Eugene V. Debs (now in prison) for president and Seymour Stedman for vice president. Other minor parties offering candidates include the Socialist Labor, Farmer-Labor, Single Tax, and Prohibition parties.

May 10 • At their national nominating convention, members of the Socialist Labor party choose W.W. Cox as their party's candidate for president and August Gilhaus as their party's candidate for vice president.

May 20 • Congress adopts a joint resolution declaring that the United States is no longer at war. The resolution is vetoed by President Wilson.

June 8 • The Republican party convenes in Chicago. It nominates Warren G. Harding (Ohio) for president and Calvin Coolidge (Massachusetts) for vice president. In the campaign, Harding urges a "return to normalcy."

June 10 • The Water Power Act is adopted. It creates the Federal Power Commission.

June 28 • The Democratic party convenes in San Francisco. It nominates James M. Cox (Ohio) for president and Franklin D. Roosevelt (New York) for vice president. In the campaign, President Wilson and the candidates urge support of the League of Nations.

August 26 • The 19th Amendment is ratified. It provides for woman suffrage.

November 2 • In the presidential election, Warren G. Harding is elected president, receiving 404 electoral votes to 127 for Cox, his Democratic opponent. Calvin Coolidge is elected vice president.

December 10 • The Nobel Peace Prize is awarded to President Wilson.

International and Cultural Events • The League of Nations comes into force without American participation. Paul Whiteman's band spreads the jazz craze on a triumphant European tour. Prohibition begins in the United States. Commercial radio broadcasting begins, and as women vote for the first time, election results go out over the airwaves. Sinclair Lewis satirizes small towns in *Main Street*.

66th CONGRESS

SENATE .... 96 Members
- R 49
- D 47
- O 0

HOUSE .... 433 Members
- R 240
- D 190
- O 3

ESTIMATED POPULATION
106,466,000

Woodrow Wilson
28th President
9th Democrat

Thomas R. Marshall
28th Vice President
Democrat

UNITED STATES ECONOMY

GROSS NATIONAL PRODUCT	$71,600,000,000
RETAIL SALES	N/A
BANK RESOURCES	$53,094,000,000
EXPORTS	$ 8,080,000,000
IMPORTS	$ 5,278,000,000
FEDERAL GOVERNMENT EXPENDITURE	$ 6,403,344,000
FEDERAL DEBT	$24,299,321,000

ARTICLE XIX

Woman Suffrage

The right of citizens of the United States to vote shall not be denied or abridged by the United States or by any State on account of sex.

Congress shall have power to enforce this article by appropriate legislation.

(Adopted in 1920)

1921 Warren G. Harding

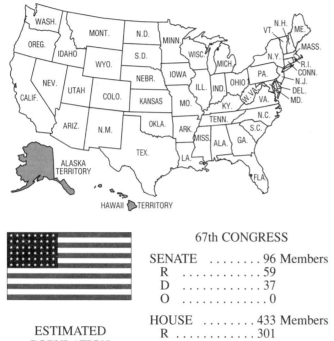

67th CONGRESS		
SENATE	....	96 Members
R	....	59
D	....	37
O	....	0
HOUSE	....	433 Members
R	....	301
D	....	131
O	....	1

ESTIMATED
POPULATION
108,541,000

Warren G. Harding
29th President
10th Republican

Calvin Coolidge
29th Vice President
Republican

UNITED STATES ECONOMY

GROSS NATIONAL PRODUCT	.........$71,600,000,000
RETAIL SALES	.... N/A
BANK RESOURCES	.................$49,633,000,000
EXPORTS	...........................$ 4,379,000,000
IMPORTS	...........................$ 2,509,000,000
FEDERAL GOVERNMENT EXPENDITURE	.$ 5,115,928,000
FEDERAL DEBT	....................$23,977,451,000

Warren G. Harding

Birth	... Caledonia (Blooming Grove), OH, Nov. 2, 1865
Parents	.... George and Phoebe Dickerson Harding
Married	.... Florence Kling De Wolfe
Home	.... Marion, OH
Presidency	.... 1921 – 1923
Death	.... San Francisco, CA, Aug. 2, 1923

Events

January 4 • The War Finance Corporation is reactivated to assist farm areas, which are seriously affected by a recession.

March 4 • Harding is inaugurated president.

May 19 • Congress adopts the Emergency Quota Act, which restricts annual immigration to three percent of the people of each nationality living in the United States in 1910. The annual total is limited to 357,000.

May 27 • The Emergency Tariff Act is adopted. Rates are increased on farm products.

June 10 • Congress adopts the Budget and Accounting Act, which establishes the General Accounting Office and the Bureau of the Budget.

June 30 • President Harding appoints former president William Howard Taft chief justice of the United States Supreme Court. Taft, who will occupy the position until his death in 1930, is the only person to have served as chief justice and president.

July 2 • A joint resolution of Congress ends the war with Austria, Germany and Hungary.

July 14 • Two Italian-born workingmen, Nicola Sacco and Bartolomeo Vanzetti, are convicted of murder in an armed robbery that took place on April 15, 1921. Widespread criticism of the trial is prevelent, many believing that the men are not guilty and have been convicted due to their anarchist opinions. After having their case reviewed, the men are executed on August 23, 1927.

August 9 • The Veterans Bureau is created.

August 11 • President Harding invites major powers to a conference on the limitation of naval armaments and problems affecting the Pacific and Far East. The conference is held from November 12, 1921, to February 6, 1922. Of the nine treaties signed during the conference, the most important are a five-power treaty limiting naval tonnage and setting tonnage ratios of capital ships at five each for the United States and Great Britain, three for Japan, and 1.67 each for France and Italy; a nine-power treaty binding its signatories to respect the territorial integrity of China and the open-door policy; and a treaty of consultation between the United States, Great Britain, Japan and France.

August • The United States signs separate peace treaties with Austria, Germany and Hungary.

September 26–30 • A conference on unemployment, which now exceeds five million, is held in Washington under the chairmanship of Herbert Hoover. It urges lower prices and the creation of jobs.

International and Cultural Events • France occupies the Ruhr to force German reparations. Lenin initiates the New Economic Policy. Speakeasies defy prohibition. Charlie Chaplin stars in *The Kid*.

United States of America 1922

Events

February 9 • Congress creates the World War Foreign Debt Commission to reach agreements with the various debtor nations that owe the United States more than $10 billion for loans extended during the war and after the war for relief purposes. The United States refuses to consider canceling the debts and makes agreements for the payment of principal and interest. By 1926, however, the United States has recognized the inability of the debtors to pay the full amounts and has agreed to cancel substantial parts of the debts and to reduce interest rates on the balance. Nonetheless, Europeans resent having to make even partial payments.

February 18 • The Capper-Volstead Act is adopted. It permits farmers to sell their products and buy equipment cooperatively without violating antitrust laws.

April 7 • Secretary of the Interior Albert B. Fall secretly leases a United States naval oil reserve at Teapot Dome, Wyoming, to Harry Sinclair's Mammoth Oil Company. Subsequently, he leases a second naval oil reserve, in Elk Hills, California, to Edward L. Doheny. In 1924, in the wake of a congressional investigation, Fall, Sinclair and Doheny and his son are charged with bribery and conspiracy. In 1931, Fall is sentenced to a year in prison.

May 26 • A bill establishing the Narcotics Control Board is signed by President Harding.

June 3 • Congress amends the Federal Reserve Act to provide for agricultural representation on the Federal Reserve Board.

September 21 • Congress adopts the Fordney-McCumber Tariff Act, which increases rates substantially on both manufactures and agricultural products. In addition, the president is authorized to change rates to cover differences in production costs between foreign and domestic goods.

September 22 • The Cable Act is adopted. Under its provisions, marriage does not affect a woman's citizenship. An American woman remains an American citizen if she marries an alien; conversely, a foreign woman who marries an American citizen does not thereby become an American citizen herself.

October 3 • Rebecca L. Felton, the first female senator, is appointed by the governor of Georgia.

December 4 • At the invitation of the United States, the Second Central American Conference meets in Washington to resolve differences between Honduras and Nicaragua. Before adjourning on February 7, 1923, it drafts a neutrality treaty and revives the Central American Court of Justice.

December 11 • In *United States v. Lanza*, a unanimous U.S. Supreme Court declares that it does not constitute

Warren G. Harding
29th President
10th Republican

Calvin Coolidge
29th Vice President
Republican

UNITED STATES ECONOMY

GROSS NATIONAL PRODUCT	...........$84,800,000,000
RETAIL SALES	.... N/A
BANK RESOURCES	...................$50,368,000,000
EXPORTS	...........................$ 3,765,000,000
IMPORTS	...........................$ 3,113,000,000
FEDERAL GOVERNMENT EXPENDITURE	.$ 3,372,608,000
FEDERAL DEBT	......................$22,693,382,000

double jeopardy for the federal government and a state government to make the same act a crime.

International and Cultural Events • The World Court holds its first session at The Hague. Mussolini's Black Shirts march on Rome. The Irish Free State is established. The Lincoln Memorial is dedicated in Washington. Emily Post publishes *Etiquette: The Blue Book of Social Usage*. The movie industry establishes the Hays Office.

1923 Harding/Coolidge

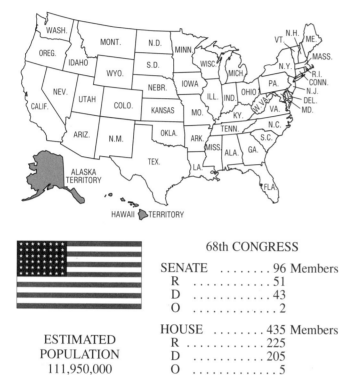

68th CONGRESS

SENATE .... 96 Members
R 51
D 43
O 2

HOUSE .... 435 Members
R 225
D 205
O 5

ESTIMATED
POPULATION
111,950,000

Warren G. Harding
29th President
10th Republican

Calvin Coolidge
29th Vice President
Republican

UNITED STATES ECONOMY

GROSS NATIONAL PRODUCT $84,800,000,000
RETAIL SALES .... N/A
BANK RESOURCES $54,144,000,000
EXPORTS .... $ 4,091,000,000
IMPORTS .... $ 3,792,000,000
FEDERAL GOVERNMENT EXPENDITURE .$ 3,294,628,000
FEDERAL DEBT $22,349,707,000

Calvin Coolidge	
Birth	Plymouth, VT, July 4, 1872
Parents	John and Victoria Moor Coolidge
Married	Grace Goodhue
Home	Northampton, MA
Presidency	1923 – 1929
Death	Northampton, MA, Jan. 5, 1933

Events

January • Florence E. Allen becomes the first woman in the United States to sit on the bench of a state supreme court. She will serve the state of Ohio until December 1928.

March 4 • The Intermediate Credit Act is adopted. It authorizes the creation of an intermediate credit bank in each of the Federal Reserve districts to make funds available to agricultural cooperatives.

April 9 • The Supreme Court rules in *Adkins v. Children's Hospital* that a minimum wage law for women in the District of Columbia is unconstitutional. The Supreme Court states that the law violated the freedom of contract clause contained in Article I, Section 10.

June 4 • The Supreme Court rules that a Nebraska law forbidding the teaching of foreign languages in public schools is unconstitutional.

June 20 • President Harding leaves for a tour of the West and Alaska.

August 2 • President Harding dies of an embolism in San Francisco. He had taken ill on July 31.

August 3 • Calvin Coolidge takes the oath as president in Plymouth, Vermont.

September 10 • The United States and Mexico sign a claims convention dealing with damages resulting from the Mexican revolution.

September 15 • Governor J.C. Walton is forced to declare Oklahoma under martial law because of outrages perpetrated by the Ku Klux Klan. New York and Baltimore newspapers have disclosed crimes attributed to Klan members in other states.

October 13 • The Coolidge administration declares its intention to enforce prohibition through the Volstead Act.

December 6 • President Coolidge delivers his first annual message to Congress. He states that his administration will favor the reduction of both taxes and governmental expenditures and the encouragement of business.

December 15 • President Coolidge appoints Charles G. Dawes to head a committee charged with formulating a plan to put Germany on a firm financial footing, thus allowing it to make reparations payments to the Allies. German passive resistance to French and Belgian occupation of the Ruhr had led to the destruction of the value of the old mark, and a new one was adopted in November.

International and Cultural Events • Great Russia, the Ukraine, White Russia and Transcaucasia are confederated into the Union of Soviet Socialist Republics. Mustafa Kemal (Atatürk) is elected president of Turkey, the sultanate having been abolished in 1922. In Germany, Adolf Hitler's National Socialist party attempts a *putsch* in Munich. Mussolini dissolves the political opposition in Italy. Henry Luce founds *Time* magazine.

United States of America 1924

Events

February 3 • Former president Woodrow Wilson dies in Washington.

March • President Coolidge requests the resignation of Attorney General Harry M. Daugherty, who has been accused of accepting bribes. In 1927, Daugherty is acquitted on charges of conspiracy.

April 9 • The Dawes Plan provides for a loan to Germany of 800 million gold marks and increasing yearly reparations payments. It is approved at an international conference in London on August 16.

April 23 • Congress adopts a bill that provides bonuses in the form of 20-year certificates to World War I veterans below the rank of major. Vetoed by President Coolidge on May 15, the bill is passed over his veto on May 19.

May 26 • Congress adopts a bill that halves the immigration quota and bases national allocations on two percent of the population of a given nationality resident in the United States at the 1890 census. Beginning in 1929, the annual quota, set at 150,000, is divided according to the proportions of inhabitants of various national origins in 1920. All Japanese are barred.

June 2 • A law is enacted extending U.S. citizenship to all Indians born in the United States.

June 2 • Congress sends a child labor amendment to the states for ratification. Only 26 states, 10 less than the required 36, will ever ratify it. The amendment would have extended to Congress control over workers younger than 18 years of age.

June 10 • The Republican party convenes in Cleveland. It nominates President Coolidge for re-election and Charles G. Dawes (Illinois) for vice president.

June 24 • The Democratic party convenes in New York. On July 9, after a prolonged struggle between adherents of Alfred E. Smith and William G. McAdoo, it nominates John W. Davis (West Virginia) for president and Charles W. Bryan (Nebraska) for vice president. Candidates are also put forward by the Commonwealth Land (Single Tax), Socialist Labor, American and Prohibition parties.

July 4 • The Conference for Progressive Political Action, meeting in Cleveland, forms the new Progressive party, which nominates Robert M. La Follette for president and Burton K. Wheeler for vice president.

July 11 • The Workers' (Communist) party convenes in Chicago. It nominates William Z. Foster for president and Benjamin Gitlow for vice president.

November 4 • In the presidential election, Coolidge is re-elected, receiving 382 electoral votes to 136 for Davis and 13 for La Follette. Charles G. Dawes is elected vice president.

68th CONGRESS

SENATE . . . . 96 Members
R 51
D 43
O 2

ESTIMATED
POPULATION
114,113,000

HOUSE . . . . 435 Members
R 225
D 205
O 5

Calvin Coolidge
30th President
11th Republican

Vice President
None

UNITED STATES ECONOMY

GROSS NATIONAL PRODUCT $84,800,000,000
RETAIL SALES . . . . N/A
BANK RESOURCES $57,420,000,000
EXPORTS . . . .$ 4,498,000,000
IMPORTS . . . .$ 3,610,000,000
FEDERAL GOVERNMENT EXPENDITURE .$ 3,048,678,000
FEDERAL DEBT $21,250,813,000

International and Cultural Events • The anti-Facist leader Giacømo Matteotti is murdered in Italy. Great Britain's first Labor government is formed by Ramsay MacDonald. In America, "symphonic jazz" becomes popular when critics and the public acclaim George Gershwin's *Rhapsody in Blue*. Red Grange, All-American halfback, scores four touchdowns for Illinois in 12 minutes. Buster Keaton in *The Navigator* and Douglas Fairbanks in *The Thief of Bagdad* delight movie audiences.

1925 United States of America

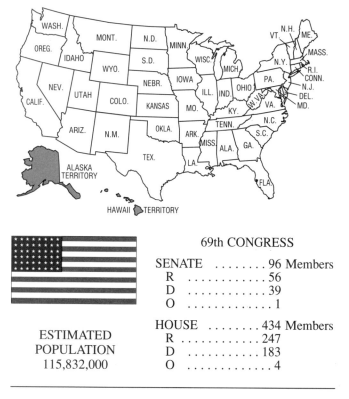

	69th CONGRESS
	SENATE .... 96 Members
	R 56
	D 39
	O 1
ESTIMATED	HOUSE .... 434 Members
POPULATION	R 247
115,832,000	D 183
	O 4

Calvin Coolidge
30th President
11th Republican

Charles G. Dawes
30th Vice President
Republican

UNITED STATES ECONOMY

GROSS NATIONAL PRODUCT $84,800,000,000
RETAIL SALES .... N/A
BANK RESOURCES $62,232,000,000
EXPORTS ....$ 4,819,000,000
IMPORTS ....$ 4,227,000,000
FEDERAL GOVERNMENT EXPENDITURE .$ 3,063,105,000
FEDERAL DEBT $20,516,194,000

Events

January 5 • Nellie Tayloe Ross, widow of Governor William B. Ross, takes the oath of office, becoming the first woman governor in the country.
February 2 • Gunnar Kasson delivers by dog sled a much needed antidiphtheria serum to Nome, Alaska.
February 4 • Charles R. Forbes, head of the Veterans Bureau in the Harding administration, is sentenced to

two years in prison for fraud, conspiracy, and bribery.
February 24 • Agricultural experiment stations are authorized funds for economic research by the Purnell Act.
March 4 • President Coolidge is inaugurated.
May • The federal government makes use of the U.S. Coast Guard to wage an all-out war on rumrunners, who are increasing the scope of their operations. The rumrunners retaliate by sabotaging U.S. Coast Guard vessels.
June 6 • Walter P. Chrysler reorganizes the Maxwell Motor Corporation into the Chrysler Corporation.
June 8 • In *Gitlow v. New York*, the U.S. Supreme Court rules that First Amendment protections apply to actions of state governments. The Court bases its decision on its interpretation of the 14th Amendment. This decision is the first of many decisions in which the nation's highest court will apply the Bill of Rights to states.
June 12 • Secretary of State Frank B. Kellogg protests the danger to American citizens in Mexico.
July 10 • The so-called monkey trial, a case involving an educator, John T. Scopes, who is accused of teaching evolution in a public school, begins in Dayton, Tennessee. It pits agnostic Clarence Darrow for the defense against fundamentalist William Jennings Bryan for the prosecution. Scopes is convicted and fined (July 21), but the sentence is set aside. Bryan dies on July 26.
August 3 • The last of an occupation force of United States Marines leave Nicaragua after 13 years. It will return in 1926.
September 3 • The United States Navy dirigible *Shenandoah* is destroyed in a storm over Ohio.
October 5–16 • Treaties guaranteeing the Franco-German and Belgo-German frontiers and providing for arbitration between Germany and its neighbors are drawn up in Locarno. They are signed in London on December 1.
October 28–December 17 • The court-martial of Colonel William (Billy) Mitchell of the U.S. Army Air Service is held. An ardent advocate of air power and an outspoken critic of the military and naval establishment, he is found guilty of insubordination and suspended from the air service for five years. In January 1926, he resigns.
November 21 • David C. Stephenson, grand dragon of the Ku Klux Klan in Indiana, is convicted of second-degree murder. The trial breaks Klan power in the midwest and exposes local corruption.
December 6 • The United States is awarded $2.5 million by a joint American-German claims commission for losses suffered in the sinking of the passenger liner *Lusitania* by a German submarine in 1915.
International and Cultural Events • Adolf Hitler publishes the first part of *Mein Kampf*, written during nine months in prison. In the United States, Theodore Dreiser publishes *An American Tragedy*, and F. Scott Fitzgerald publishes *The Great Gatsby*.

United States of America 1926

Events

January 27 • By a vote of 76 to 17, the Senate approves United States membership in the Permanent Court of Arbitration, but with several reservations. Since one of these reservations is not accepted by the court, the United States does not become a member.

February 26 • President Coolidge signs the Revenue Act. Income and inheritance taxes are lowered, and some taxes are removed.

March 7 • A radiotelephone conversation takes place between London and New York.

April 29 • The United States and France sign a debt-funding agreement, allowing France to repay $4.025 billion over a period of 62 years at 1.6 percent interest.

May 9 • Richard E. Byrd and Floyd Bennett fly over the North Pole.

May 10 • United States Marines are dispatched to Nicaragua during a revolt. They remain in the country until January 1933.

May 18–26 • The United States is represented at the initial meeting of the Preparatory Commission for a disarmament conference, which is held in Geneva.

May 20 • The Railway Labor Act is adopted. It substitutes a mediation board for the Railroad Labor Board.

May 20 • Under the Air Commerce Act, Congress makes the Department of Commerce responsible for the licensing of aircraft and pilots.

June 20 • A million pilgrims are drawn to Chicago for the opening of the Eucharistic Congress of the Roman Catholic Church, the first such gathering to be held in the United States.

July 2 • Congress authorizes the U.S. Army Air Corps.

September 29 • The eight-hour day and the five-day week are introduced by Henry Ford at the Ford Motor Company as a means of coping with declining sales.

October 10 • Lightning strikes a naval ammunition depot at Lake Denmark, New Jersey, killing 31 people and causing $93 million in damages.

October 25 • In a six to three decision, the U.S. Supreme Court rules that the president of the United States has the sole power to remove executive branch officers. The case, *Myers v. United States*, stemmed from President Wilson's dismissal of his postmaster general.

November 2 • In the midterm elections, Republicans suffer losses in both houses of Congress.

November 11 • President Coolidge declares that, "unless the requirements of the Senate are met by the other nations, I can see no prospect of this country adhering to the [World] Court."

December 4 • According to a report made by Colonel Carmi Thompson on his return from a fact-finding

mission to the Philippines, the islands are not ready for independence.

International and Cultural Events • A general strike hits Great Britain. Leon Trotsky is expelled from the Communist Politburo. Józef Pilsudski stages a coup d'état in Warsaw. Walter Gropius completes the Bauhaus building in Dessau. Gertrude Ederle of New York becomes the first woman to swim the English Channel.

69th CONGRESS		
SENATE	....	96 Members
R	....	56
D	....	39
O	....	1
HOUSE	....	434 Members
R	....	247
D	....	183
O	....	4

ESTIMATED POPULATION 117,399,000

Calvin Coolidge
30th President
11th Republican

Charles G. Dawes
30th Vice President
Republican

UNITED STATES ECONOMY

GROSS NATIONAL PRODUCT	$84,800,000,000
RETAIL SALES	N/A
BANK RESOURCES	$65,079,000,000
EXPORTS	$ 4,712,000,000
IMPORTS	$ 4,431,000,000
FEDERAL GOVERNMENT EXPENDITURE	$ 3,097,612,000
FEDERAL DEBT	$19,643,216,000

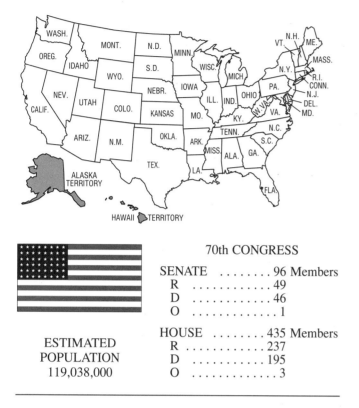

70th CONGRESS

SENATE .... 96 Members
R 49
D 46
O 1

HOUSE .... 435 Members
R 237
D 195
O 3

ESTIMATED
POPULATION
119,038,000

Calvin Coolidge
30th President
11th Republican

Charles G. Dawes
30th Vice President
Republican

UNITED STATES ECONOMY

GROSS NATIONAL PRODUCT $89,900,000,000
RETAIL SALES .... N/A
BANK RESOURCES $67,893,000,000
EXPORTS .... $ 4,759,000,000
IMPORTS .... $ 4,185,000,000
FEDERAL GOVERNMENT EXPENDITURE .$ 2,974,030,000
FEDERAL DEBT $18,511,907,000

Events

January 7 • Radiotelephone service is begun between London and New York.

January 27 • As new Mexican laws placing limits on petroleum concessions and on the ownership of land by non-Mexicans go into effect, the United States Senate adopts a unanimous resolution asking that differences on these issues be arbitrated. In September, newly appointed ambassador Dwight W. Morrow induces the Mexican government to eliminate some of the new law's objectionable features.

February 10 • President Coolidge requests that Great Britain, France, Italy and Japan attend a conference limiting the construction of destroyers, submarines and cruisers. The conference, which is held in Geneva from June 20 to August 4, is unproductive. Italy and France do not attend, and Great Britain and the United States cannot reach an agreement.

February 11 • The Senate passes the McNary-Haugen bill, first introduced in Congress in 1924. Under its provisions, agricultural surpluses could be purchased by the federal government and sold at the world price. If this price happened to be lower than the domestic price for a particular commodity, producers of that commodity would pay the government an equalization fee. The House passes the bill on February 17, but President Coolidge vetoes it on February 25, mainly because of its price-fixing feature.

March 3 • The Prohibition Reorganization Act is adopted. It creates the Prohibition Bureau in the Treasury Department.

March 7 • In *Tumey v. Ohio*, the U.S. Supreme Court rules that states must comply with the due process requirements contained in the Constitution. The ruling marks the first time that a state conviction is overturned for this reason.

April 6 • Aristide Briand, foreign minister for France, suggests that the United States and France sign an agreement outlawing war. Secretary of State Kellogg is receptive, and on December 28, he suggests that such a document be signed by all nations. A draft outlawing war as an instrument of national policy is ready by January 11, 1928, and on August 27, the Pact opf Paris is signed by 15 nations. Eventually 62 countries will sign it.

April • The Mississippi Valley suffers widespread damage from floods.

May 20–21 • Flying alone, Charles A. Lindbergh pilots the monoplane *Spirit of St. Louis* in the first successful nonstop flight from New York to Paris.

August 2 • President Coolidge announces that he will not run for re-election.

November 12 • The double vehicular Holland Tunnel, connecting Jersey City and New York under the Hudson River, is the first such American tunnel.

International and Cultural Events • Civil war begins between the Kuomintang and the Communists. United States Army Air Corps pilots fly between San Francisco and Honolulu. Babe Ruth hits 60 home runs in a 154-game season. Movie actress Clara Bow is dubbed the "It" girl by novelist Elinor Glyn. The first "talkie," *The Jazz Singer*, starring Al Jolson, begins showing in movie theaters across the country.

United States of America 1928

Events

January 16 • President Coolidge opens the sixth International Conference of American States in Havana. A resolution against the right to intervene in the internal affairs of other nations fails of adoption due to United States opposition.

April 13 • The Socialist party convenes in New York. It nominates Norman Thomas for president and James H. Maurer for vice president.

May 3 • Congress once more passes the McNary-Haugen farm bill. It is again vetoed by President Coolidge, who views Senate Bill 3555 as unconstitutional.

May 15 • The Flood Control Act is adopted. It provides for a 10-year levee improvement program in the Mississippi Valley.

June 12 • The Republican party convenes in Kansas City, Missouri. It nominates Herbert C. Hoover (California) for president and Charles Curtis (Kansas) for vice president. A popular campaign slogan during the election is "A Chicken in Every Pot, a Car in Every Garage."

June 26 • The Democratic party convenes in Houston. It nominates Alfred E. Smith (New York) for president and Joseph T. Robinson (Arkansas) for vice president.

July 11 • The Farmer-Labor party convenes in Chicago. It nominates George W. Norris for president and Will Vereen for vice president. When Norris declines the nomination, it selects Frank E. Webb for president. Candidates are also put up by the Workers', Socialist Labor, and Prohibition parties.

August 25 • Richard E. Byrd leaves New York in the ice ship *The City of New York* on an expedition to the Antarctic. He returns to the United States in 1930.

September 8 • The League of Nations unanimously elects Charles Evans Hughes to the Permanent Court of Arbitration.

November 6 • Herbert C. Hoover is elected president, receiving 444 electoral votes to 87 for Smith, his Democratic opponent. Charles Curtis is elected vice president.

November 19 • President-elect Hoover leaves on a tour of Latin America. He returns to the United States on January 6, 1929.

December 12 • The federal government participates in the production of hydroelectric power with the passage of the Boulder Dam Project Act.

December 17 • Undersecretary of State J. Reuben Clark draws up a memorandum on the Monroe Doctrine that states in part: "The Doctrine does not concern itself with purely inter-American relations." The Roosevelt Corollary is not considered part of the doctrine. The Clark Memorandum is published in 1930.

Calvin Coolidge
30th President
11th Republican

Charles G. Dawes
30th Vice President
Republican

70th CONGRESS

SENATE	96 Members
R	49
D	46
O	1
HOUSE	435 Members
R	237
D	195
O	3

ESTIMATED POPULATION
120,501,000

UNITED STATES ECONOMY

GROSS NATIONAL PRODUCT	$89,900,000,000
RETAIL SALES	N/A
BANK RESOURCES	$71,121,000,000
EXPORTS	$ 5,030,000,000
IMPORTS	$ 4,091,000,000
FEDERAL GOVERNMENT EXPENDITURE	$ 3,103,265,000
FEDERAL DEBT	$17,604,293,000

International and Cultural Events • The Soviet Union initiates the first of six five-year plans to speed industrialization. Alexander Fleming discovers penicillin. Amelia Earhart becomes the first woman passenger to fly the Atlantic; in 1932, she is the first woman to fly it solo. George Gershwin composes *An American in Paris*. Station WGY in Schenectady, New York, inaugurates the first program of scheduled television broadcasts (May 11).

1929 Herbert C. Hoover

71st CONGRESS

SENATE .... 96 Members
R 56
D 39
O 1

HOUSE .... 435 Members
R 267
D 167
O 1

ESTIMATED
POPULATION
121,770,000

Herbert C. Hoover
31st President
12th Republican

Charles Curtis
31st Vice President
Republican

UNITED STATES ECONOMY

GROSS NATIONAL PRODUCT $104,400,000,000
RETAIL SALES .... $ 48,459,000,000
BANK RESOURCES .... $ 72,315,000,000
EXPORTS .... $ 5,157,000,000
IMPORTS .... $ 4,399,000,000
FEDERAL GOVERNMENT EXPENDITURE .. $ 3,298,000,000
FEDERAL DEBT .... $ 16,931,088,000

Herbert C. Hoover	
Birth	West Branch, IA, Aug. 10, 1874
Parents	Jesse and Hulda Minthorn Hoover
Married	Lou Henry
Home	New York, NY
Presidency	1929 – 1933
Death	New York, NY, Oct. 20, 1964

Events

January 15 • The Senate ratifies the Pact of Paris.

February 11–June 7 • An international committee meeting in Paris under the chairmanship of Owen D. Young draws up a plan for the payment of German reparations to replace the Dawes Plan. A schedule of annual payments is established, and the Bank for International Settlements is created to handle the transactions.

February 13 • Congress adopts the Cruiser Act, authorizing the construction of 19 new cruisers and one aircraft carrier.

March 4 • Hoover is inaugurated president.

April 9 • The Canadian government protests the sinking of the *I'm Alone*, a suspected rumrunner of Canadian registry, by a United States Coast Guard cutter 200 miles offshore in the Gulf of Mexico.

April 15 • At President Hoover's request, a special session of Congress meets to consider agricultural problems and other matters.

May 20 • President Hoover creates the National Commission on Law Observance and Enforcement to conduct an investigation into the enforcement of prohibition and related problems. Its chairman is George W. Wickersham.

May 27 • The Supreme Court rules that the use of the pocket veto by the president is constitutional.

June 15 • Congress adopts the Agricultural Marketing Act, which sets up the Federal Farm Board to help sell surplus agricultural products at stable prices. In 1930, several stablization corporations are established by the board, which also extends loans to cooperatives. The board continues until 1933.

July 1 • The Immigration Act of 1924, which uses a quota system based on the national origins of the country's 1920 population, goes into effect.

September 24 • The first successful "blind" airplane flight (instruments only) is made by Lieutenant General James Doolittle.

October 24 • Prices on the New York stock market, which speculation had driven to record levels before a slight decline in the summer and early fall, collapse when 13 million shares are unloaded (Black Thursday). On October 29 (Black Tuesday), 16 million shares are sold in a market collapse that is the first phase of the Great Depression of the 1930s.

November 29 • Richard E. Byrd flies over the South Pole.

International and Cultural Events • The Lateran Treaty ends the Roman question. Chicago's St. Valentine's Day Massacre shocks the nation.

United States of America 1930

Events

January 2 • President Hoover discusses with leaders of Congress the desirability of an expanded public works program.

January 21–April 22 • The London Naval Conference is held to supplement the work of the Washington Conference of 1921. The United States, Great Britain and Japan reach agreement on ratios of 10:10:6 for large cruisers and 10:10:7 for other auxiliary ships and on parity for submarines. No new capital ships are to be constructed until 1936. Although France and Italy attend the conference, they do not accept its principal conclusions. The United States Senate ratifies the London Naval Treaty on July 21.

February 3 • President Hoover names Charles Evans Hughes chief justice of the United States Supreme Court.

March 31 • Congress adopts the Public Buildings Act, which appropriates $130 million for the construction of public buildings.

April 4 • Congress approves the appropriation of $300 million for the continuance of federal aid for state road building.

April 21 • A fire at the Ohio State Penitentiary kills 320 prisoners. The prison, built to hold 1,500 prisoners, has an inmate population of 4,300.

June 17 • The Smoot-Hawley Tariff Act is signed by President Hoover. Duties are raised sharply on a wide variety of raw materials and manufactured goods, provoking other countries similarly to raise their tariffs.

July 3 • The Veterans Administration is established by an act of Congress.

August 15 • President Hoover calls the governors of drought-stricken southern and midwestern states to a White House conference.

September 9 • Due to the increasing number of unemployed workers in the United States, the State Department prohibits the entry of most foreign workers into the country.

September 17 • Construction of Boulder Dam (now Hoover Dam) is begun near Las Vegas, Nevada.

October • The number of unemployed is estimated at 4.5 million, and President Hoover appoints the President's Committee for Unemployment Relief.

November 4 • In the midterm elections, the Democrats gain control of the House of Representatives. They also acquire eight additional seats in the Senate.

December 2 • President Hoover asks Congress to appropriate $100 to $150 million for public works projects. On December 20, Congress appropriates $116 million for this purpose.

December 11 • The Bank of the United States in New York, with more than 400,000 depositors, closes its

doors. By March 1933, more than 9,000 banks throughout the country fail.

December 20 • Congress authorizes the expenditure of $45 million for drought relief.

International and Cultural Events • France begins constructing the Maginot Line. Gandhi's civil disobedience campaign in India leads to his imprisonment. James Joyce's *Ulysses* is seized as obscene by the United States Customs Service. A *Literary Digest* poll reveals that most Americans favor the repeal of Prohibition.

71st CONGRESS

SENATE	.... 96 Members
R	 56
D	 39
O	 1
HOUSE	.... 435 Members
R	 267
D	 167
O	 1

ESTIMATED
POPULATION
123,188,000

Herbert C. Hoover
31st President
12th Republican

Charles Curtis
31st Vice President
Republican

UNITED STATES ECONOMY

GROSS NATIONAL PRODUCT	..........$91,100,000,000
RETAIL SALES	...............................N/A
BANK RESOURCES	...................$74,290,000,000
EXPORTS	...........................$ 3,781,000,000
IMPORTS	...........................$ 3,061,000,000
FEDERAL GOVERNMENT EXPENDITURE	.$ 5,440,269,000
FEDERAL DEBT	.....................$16,185,310,000

1931 United States of America

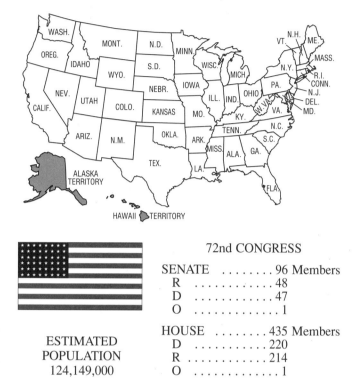

72nd CONGRESS

SENATE . . . . 96 Members
R 48
D 47
O 1

HOUSE . . . . 435 Members
D 220
R 214
O 1

ESTIMATED
POPULATION
124,149,000

Herbert C. Hoover
31st President
12th Republican

Charles Curtis
31st Vice President
Republican

UNITED STATES ECONOMY

GROSS NATIONAL PRODUCT $76,300,000,000
RETAIL SALES . . . . N/A
BANK RESOURCES $70,070,000,000
EXPORTS . . . .$ 2,378,000,000
IMPORTS . . . .$ 2,091,000,000
FEDERAL GOVERNMENT EXPENDITURE .$ 3,577,434,000
FEDERAL DEBT $16,801,281,000

Events

January 20 • President Hoover submits to Congress the report of the Wickersham Commission on the ineffectiveness of efforts to enforce the 18th Amendment. The report suggests revising rather than repealing the amendment.
February 27 • Congress passes over the president's veto a bill providing for loans amounting to one-half the value of veterans' bonus certificates.
February • Civil government is instituted in the Virgin Islands.
March 3 • President Hoover vetoes the Muscle Shoals bill, which proposed government operation of facilities constructed at the Muscle Shoals of the Tennessee River in Alabama during World War I.
May 1 • The world's tallest building at the time, the Empire State Building is dedicated in New York.
June 20 • President Hoover proposes a one-year moratorium on intergovernmental debts and reparation payments in order to alleviate an international financial crisis caused by the failure of the Austrian Credit-Anstalt in May. By July 6, all the major creditor nations accept his proposal.
October 16 • The Council of the League of Nations asks the United States to send a representative to deliberations on the crisis caused by the Japanese occupation of Mukden and other Manchurian cities in September. On January 7, 1932, Secretary of State Henry L. Stimson states that the United States will not recognize any situation or agreement produced in violation of the Pact of Paris. Specifically, the doctrine of nonrecognition extends to the maintenance of the territorial integrity of China and of the open-door policy.
December 8 • President Hoover suggests to Congress that it establish a federal lending agency to extend loans to banks, insurance companies, and other organs. To finance these loans, the agency would be empowered to issue bonds.
International and Cultural Events • A revolution establishes the Republic of Spain. The Scottsboro case rallies civil rights proponents. Boris Karloff stars in *Frankenstein*.

Cartoon depicting economic problems that beset the Hoover administration.

164

United States of America 1932

Events

January 7 • Responding to Japanese seizures of Manchurian cities, Secretary of State Henry L. Stimson declares that the United States will not "recognize any treaty or agreement...which may impair...the sovereignty, the independence, or the territorial and administrative integrity of the Republic of China." This response to Japanese aggression becomes known as the Stimson Doctrine.

January 15 • As requested by President Hoover on December 8, 1931, Congress adopts an act creating the Reconstruction Finance Corporation (RFC), which is to lend funds to revitalize the economy. The RFC begins operations on February 2.

March 3 • Congress proposes the adoption of the 20th Amendment, which eliminates "lame duck" congressional sessions by providing that Congress assemble each year on January 3. Terms of the president and vice president are to begin on January 20.

March 23 • Congress adopts the Norris–La Guardia Act, which bars using injunctions to curb unions.

May 21 • The Socialist party again nominates Norman Thomas for president, and this time he polls more than 800,000 votes. Candidates are also put forward by the Socialist Labor, Communist, Prohibition, Farmer-Labor and Liberty parties.

May 29 • Veterans anxious to obtain cash for the full value of their bonus certificates begin arriving in Washington, where many camp out. The majority leave after a bill for payment is rejected in the Senate on June 17; the rest are removed on July 28–29 by the U.S. Army under the command of Chief of Staff Douglas MacArthur. His aide at the time is Major Dwight D. Eisenhower.

June 14 • The Republican party convenes in Chicago. It nominates President Hoover and Vice President Curtis for re-election.

June 27 • The Democratic party convenes in Chicago. It nominates Franklin D. Roosevelt (New York) for president and John Nance Garner (Texas) for vice president. In an unprecedented appearance before the convention, Roosevelt calls for a new deal and promises to help the forgotten man.

July 21 • President Hoover signs the Relief and Construction Act, which enhances the ability of the RFC to aid industry and agriculture and to finance public works.

July 22 • Congress adopts the Federal Home Loan Bank Act, which authorizes the creation of regional banks to help financial institutions lend money to homeowners.

November 8 • Franklin D. Roosevelt is elected president, receiving 472 electoral votes to 59 for President Hoover. John Nance Garner is elected vice president.

72nd CONGRESS

SENATE	96 Members
R	48
D	47
O	1
HOUSE	435 Members
D	220
R	214
O	1

ESTIMATED POPULATION
124,949,000

Herbert C. Hoover
31st President
12th Republican

Charles Curtis
31st Vice President
Republican

UNITED STATES ECONOMY

GROSS NATIONAL PRODUCT	$58,500,000,000
RETAIL SALES	N/A
BANK RESOURCES	$57,295,000,000
EXPORTS	$ 1,576,000,000
IMPORTS	$ 1,323,000,000
FEDERAL GOVERNMENT EXPENDITURE	$ 4,659,203,000
FEDERAL DEBT	$19,487,002,000

International and Cultural Events • The nations of the world are represented at the Geneva Disarmament conference. The infant son of Charles A. Lindbergh is kidnapped and murdered in New Jersey. Vermont's Bennington College for women revolutionizes education by eliminating compulsory courses and competitive grades. The Olympic Games are held in Los Angeles. Mayor James J. Walker of New York resigns after disclosures of corruption. *Scarface* depicts gangland warfare.

1933 Franklin D. Roosevelt

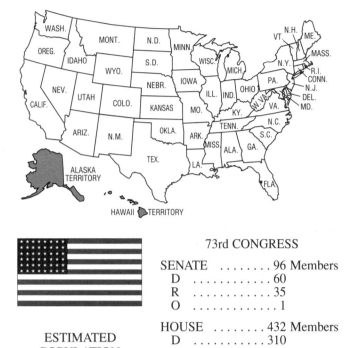

73rd CONGRESS

SENATE .... 96 Members
D 60
R 35
O 1

HOUSE .... 432 Members
D 310
R 117
O 5

ESTIMATED
POPULATION
125,690,000

Franklin D. Roosevelt
32nd President
10th Democrat

John Nance Garner
32nd Vice President
Democrat

UNITED STATES ECONOMY

GROSS NATIONAL PRODUCT $56,000,000,000
RETAIL SALES $24,517,000,000
BANK RESOURCES $51,359,000,000
EXPORTS ....$ 1,647,000,000
IMPORTS ....$ 1,450,000,000
FEDERAL GOVERNMENT EXPENDITURE .$ 4,622,865,000
FEDERAL DEBT $22,538,673,000

Franklin D. Roosevelt	
Birth	Hyde Park, NY, Jan. 30, 1882
Parents	James and Sara Delano Roosevelt
Married	Eleanor Roosevelt
Home	Hyde Park, NY
Presidency	1933 – 1945
Death	Warm Springs, GA, Apr. 12, 1945

Events

February 6 • The 20th Amendment ("lame duck") to the Constitution is adopted.

February 15 • Giuseppe Zangara attempts to assassinate President-elect Roosevelt in Miami. Mayor Anton Cermak of Chicago, who is with Roosevelt, is wounded and dies on March 6. Zangara is executed on March 20.

February 20 • Congress proposes the adoption of the 21st Amendment, calling for the repeal of the 18th Amendment (Prohibition).

March 4 • Roosevelt is inaugurated president. He tells the nation that "the only thing we have to fear is fear itself" and the world that the United States wants to be a good neighbor.

March 5 • President Roosevelt calls a special session of Congress and proclaims a four-day national bank holiday beginning March 6.

March 9 • Congress convenes and adopts the Emergency Banking Relief Act.

March 12 • The president speaks by radio to the nation in the first of his "fireside chats."

March 20 • The president signs the Economy Act, which reduces salaries of employees of the federal government.

March 22 • The Beer-Wine Revenue Act is signed. It permits the sale of wine and beer of low alcoholic content.

March 31 • Congress adopts the Reforestation Relief Act, which creates the Civilian Conservation Corps (CCC) to provide jobs for young men.

April 19 • The United States ceases to base its currency on the gold standard.

May 12 • Congress adopts the Federal Emergency Act, which grants funds to the states for relief purposes. Unemployment reaches 14 million.

May 12 • President Roosevelt signs the Agricultural Adjustment Act, which subsidizes farmers who decrease the number of acres devoted to surplus crops and establishes parity prices for certain farm products.

May 18 • The Tennessee Valley Authority (TVA) is established by an act of Congress to carry out a vast development program.

May 27 • Congress adopts the Federal Securities Act, which requires the publication of full information on new securities.

June 6 • Congress adopts the National Employment System Act, creating the United States Employment Service.

June 12–July 27 • The London Economic Conference is held. The United States is concerned with tariff negotiation, but countries on the gold standard emphasize stabilization of currency. Because of these divergent priorities the conference accomplishes nothing.

United States of America 1933

June 13 • The Home Owners Refinancing Act is adopted. It establishes the Home Owners Loan Corporation to give mortgage and other assistance to owners of homes.

June 16 • Congress adopts the Glass-Steagall Act, which creates the Federal Deposit Insurance Corporation to protect individual bank deposits of $5,000 or less.

June 16 • Congress adopts the Farm Credit Act, which is designed to help farmers obtain mortgage and other financing.

June 16 • President Roosevelt signs the National Industrial Recovery Act (NIRA), which establishes two new agencies, the Public Works Administration (PWA) and the National Recovery Administration (NRA).

June 16 • The Emergency Railroad Transportation Act provides for railroad reorganization under a federal coordinator.

June 16 • A special session of the 73rd Congress adjourns. Known as the "Hundred Days," it has followed President Roosevelt's lead in enacting significant New Deal legislation that makes fundamental changes in the outlook and direction of the country.

August 5 • President Roosevelt sets up the National Labor Board, as authorized by the NIRA, to protect labor's right to engage in collective bargaining.

October 18 • The Commodity Credit Corporation is established for the purpose of making crop loans to farmers.

November 8 • The Civil Works Administration (CWA) is founded to provide emergency employment.

November 16 • On President Roosevelt's initiative, the United States and the Soviet Union enter into diplomatic relations.

December 5 • The 21st Amendment to the Constitution is adopted: repeal of Prohibition.

International and Cultural Events • Adolf Hitler is appointed chancellor of Germany. Reacting to a report critical of its Manchuria actions, Japan serves notice it will quit the League of Nations in two years' time. Roosevelt's informal advisers are dubbed the "Brain Trust." Secretary of Labor Frances Perkins becomes the first female cabinet member.

ARTICLE XX

Terms of President and Vice President and Congress

Section 1. The terms of the President and Vice President shall end at noon on the 20th day of January, and the terms of Senators and Representatives at noon on the 3rd day of January, of the years in which such terms would have ended if this article had not been ratified; and the terms of their successors shall then begin.

Assembling of Congress

Section 2. The Congress shall assemble at least once in every year, and such meeting shall begin at noon on the 3rd day of January, unless they shall by law appoint a different day.

Emergency Election of President

Section 3. If, at the time fixed for the beginning of the term of the President, the President elect shall have died, the Vice President elect shall become President. If a President shall not have been chosen before the time fixed for the beginning of his term, or if the President elect shall have failed to qualify, then the Vice President elect shall act as President until a President shall have qualified; and the Congress may by law provide for the case wherein neither a President elect nor a Vice President elect shall have qualified, declaring who shall then act as President, or the manner in which one who is to act shall be selected, and such person shall act accordingly until a President or Vice President shall have qualified.

Choice of President by House and of Vice President by Senate

Section 4. The Congress may by law provide for the case of the death of any of the persons from whom the House of Representatives may choose a President whenever the right of choice shall have devolved upon them, and for the case of the death of any of the persons from whom the Senate may choose a Vice President whenever the right of choice shall have devolved upon them.

Section 5. Sections 1 and 2 shall take effect on the 15th day of October following the ratification of this article.

(Adopted in 1933)

ARTICLE XXI

Repeal of Prohibition

Section 1. The eighteenth article of amendment to the Constitution of the United States is hereby repealed.

Section 2. The transportation or importation into any State, Territory, or possession of the United States for delivery or use therein of intoxicating liquors, in violation of the laws thereof, is hereby prohibited.

(Adopted in 1933)

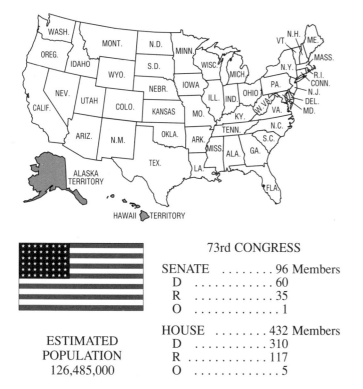

73rd CONGRESS

SENATE .... 96 Members
D 60
R 35
O 1

HOUSE .... 432 Members
D 310
R 117
O 5

ESTIMATED POPULATION
126,485,000

Franklin D. Roosevelt
32nd President
10th Democrat

John Nance Garner
32nd Vice President
Democrat

UNITED STATES ECONOMY

GROSS NATIONAL PRODUCT $65,000,000,000
RETAIL SALES .... N/A
BANK RESOURCES $55,915,000,000
EXPORTS ....$ 2,100,000,000
IMPORTS ....$ 1,636,000,000
FEDERAL GOVERNMENT EXPENDITURE .$ 6,693,900,000
FEDERAL DEBT $27,053,141,000

Events

January 1 • Francis E. Townsend, a retired California physician, announces his Old Age Revolving Pension Plan, popularly known as the Townsend Plan. Unhappy with President Roosevelt's New Deal proposals, Townsend proposes that the federal government grant each person 60 years of age or older a monthly pension of $200 per month. Money not spent at the end of the month would be returned to the government.

January 8 • In *Home Building & Loan Association v. Blaisdell*, the U.S. Supreme Court rules that a Minnesota emergency mortgage moratorium law does not impair the obligation of contracts. In his opinion for the five-member majority, Chief Justice Charles Evans Hughes states that the prohibition against a state passing a law impairing the obligations of contracts "is not an absolute one and is not to be read with literal exactions like a mathematical formula."

January 30 • The Gold Reserve Act is adopted. Under its provisions, the president is authorized to set the value of the dollar in terms of gold at 50 to 60 cents. The gold of the Federal Reserve banks is to be transferred to the Treasury, and the government is to benefit from any increase in its value.

January 31 • President Roosevelt issues a proclamation establishing the value of the dollar at 59.06 cents and the price of gold at $35 an ounce.

January 31 • The Farm Mortgage Refinancing Act creates the Federal Farm Mortgage Corporation.

February 2 • The First Export-Import Bank of Washington is established by executive order of the president to encourage trade with the Soviet Union. In March, the Second Export-Import Bank is set up to facilitate purchases by Cuba. The two banks are merged in 1936. Over the years, the Export-Import Bank comes to focus its attention on trade and aid for the nations of Latin America.

February 15 • The Civil Works Emergency Relief Act is adopted. Under its provisions, funds are authorized for the Federal Emergency Relief Administration. On April 1, the Civil Works Administration is phased out.

February 23 • The Crop Loan Act is adopted to continue the loan program of the Farm Credit Administration in 1934.

March 24 • The Tydings-McDuffie Act is adopted. Under its provisions, the Philippines is to become independent 10 years after the terms of the act have been fulfilled, with sovereignty to be transferred the following July 4. The 10-year period, during which the Philippines constitutes a commonwealth, begins with the approval of a new Philippine constitution in 1935.

March 27 • The Vinson Naval Parity Act is signed into law. It authorizes the construction of 100 warships and more than 1,000 airplanes over a five-year period. Congress, however, does not begin providing the necessary funding until 1938.

March 28 • Overriding a veto by President Roosevelt, Congress adopts the Independent Offices Appropriations Act, which raises veterans' allowances and the salaries of federal employees.

April 7 • The Jones-Connally Farm Relief Act is adopted.

It places several additional commodities under the jurisdiction of the Agricultural Adjustment Administration.

April 12 • The Senate authorizes the establishment of an investigating committee to determine the influence of munitions profits on United States policy in World War I. The committee, which meets under the chairmanship of Senator Gerald P. Nye until 1936, reinforces a trend toward neutrality.

April 13 • An act of Congress forbids the extension of loans to any government in default on payments due on debts to the United States. By mid-1934, all countries that owe payments on war debts, except Finland, are in default.

April 18 • The legislature of Puerto Rico asks for statehood in a resolution.

April 21 • Congress passes the Bankhead Act, designed to control the production of cotton on a mandatory, rather than voluntary, basis.

May 9 • The Jones-Costigan Act is adopted. It authorizes crop controls for cane and beet sugar and sugar import quotas.

May 18 • In the wake of rising crime statistics, six new crime laws are enacted. They include authorizing the death penalty for kidnappers who take their victims across state lines.

May 29 • The United States and Cuba sign a treaty abolishing the Platt Amendment.

June 6 • President Roosevelt signs the Securities Exchange Act, which creates the Securities and Exchange Commission (SEC) and empowers it to regulate exchanges and transactions in securities.

June 7 • The Corporate Bankruptcy Act is adopted. Under its provisions, a corporation may be reorganized if two-thirds of its creditors agree.

June 12 • Congress adopts the Farm Mortgage Foreclosure Act to permit the president to negotiate reciprocal trade agreements changing duties by a maximum of 50 percent. The most-favored-nation rule is applicable to the new duties.

June 15 • By an act of Congress, the national guard is incorporated into the U.S. Army in times of war or during a congressionally declared national emergency.

June 19 • Congress passes the Communications Act, which replaces the Federal Radio Commission with the Federal Communications Commission (FCC) and transfers to the FCC some functions of the Interstate Commerce Commission.

June 19 • By an act of Congress, the National Labor Relations Board (NLRB) is established, replacing the National Labor Board.

June 28 • Congress creates the Federal Housing Administration (FHA) to insure private loans for homes.

June 28 • Congress adopts the Taylor Grazing Act, which designates eight million (later 142 million) acres of public land for grazing.

June 28 • The Tobacco Control Act is adopted. It provides for mandatory crop quotas.

June 28 • Congress places a moratorium on the foreclosing of farm mortgages by lending institutions. In 1935, the U.S. Supreme Court, in *Louisville Joint Stock Land Bank v. Radford*, will declare the Federal Farm Bankruptcy Act unconstitutional.

August 6 • The last of the United States Marines occupying Haiti are withdrawn.

November 6 • Nebraska becomes the first state to adopt a unicameral state legislature when an amendment to the state constitution, written by George W. Norris, is ratified.

International and Cultural Events • A popular plebiscite approves Hitler's investment as *Der Führer*. Japan denounces the naval treaties of 1922 and 1930. The Dionne quintuplets are born in Canada. John Dillinger, America's "Public Enemy Number One," is shot down by FBI agents.

Eleanor Roosevelt.

1935 United States of America

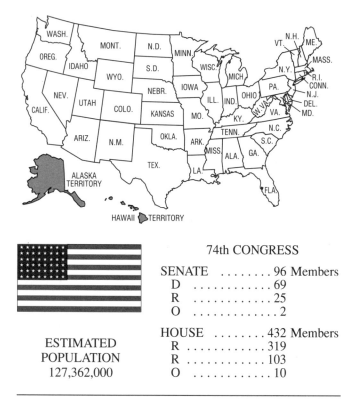

74th CONGRESS

SENATE	.... 96 Members
D	 69
R	 25
O	 2

HOUSE	.... 432 Members
R	 319
R	 103
O	 10

ESTIMATED
POPULATION
127,362,000

Franklin D. Roosevelt
32nd President
10th Democrat

John Nance Garner
32nd Vice President
Democrat

UNITED STATES ECONOMY

GROSS NATIONAL PRODUCT	$72,500,000,000
RETAIL SALES	$32,791,000,000
BANK RESOURCES	$59,951,000,000
EXPORTS	$ 2,243,000,000
IMPORTS	$ 2,039,000,000
FEDERAL GOVERNMENT EXPENDITURE ..	$ 6,520,966,000
FEDERAL DEBT	$28,700,893,000

Events

January 4 • President Roosevelt asks Congress to enact legislation to help the needy and the unemployed. Initiating the second phase of the New Deal, he calls for measures to assure social security, better housing, equitable taxation, and farm assistance.

January 7 • In its first ruling on a New Deal measure, the U.S. Supreme Court, by a vote of eight to one, hands President Roosevelt his first setback. The Court rules in *Panama Refining Company v. Ryan* that part of the NIRA is unconstitutional, because it delegates power to the executive without providing any specific limits on its use.

January 29 • By a vote of 52 to 36, the U.S. Senate rejects United States membership in the World Court.

April 8 • The Emergency Relief Appropriation Act is adopted. Under its provisions the Works Progress Administration (WPA) is set up on May 6 with Harry L. Hopkins as administrator. Renamed the Works Projects Administration in 1939, the WPA continues to sponsor employment projects until 1943.

April 27 • The Soil Conservation Service is created by an act of Congress. It is designed to prevent such conditions as the dust storms that have afflicted Oklahoma and other western states.

May 1 • Acting under the Emergency Relief Appropriation Act, the president sets up the Resettlement Administration to help poor farming families move to better land and urban workers to so-called greenbelt towns.

May 11 • Acting under the Emergency Relief Appropriation Act, the president creates the Rural Electrification Administration (REA) to lend funds for the provision of electricity in areas to which private utility companies have not extended service.

May 22 • President Roosevelt vetoes a bill calling for cash redemption of veterans' bonus certificates. The veto is promptly overridden by the House of Representatives but is sustained by the Senate on May 23.

May 27 • In *Schechter Poultry Corporation v. United States*, the Supreme Court rules unanimously that the National Industrial Recovery Act is unconstitutional, holding that Congress lacks the power to legislate in this manner.

June 26 • Acting under the Emergency Relief Appropriation Act, the president sets up the National Youth Administration to provide jobs for students and others aged 16 to 25.

July 5 • President Roosevelt signs the Wagner-Connery Act, which sets up the new National Labor Relations Board. The board is to protect the right of employees to engage in collective bargaining.

August 9 • The Motor Carrier Act is adopted. It gives the Interstate Commerce Commission regulatory power over interstate trucks and buses.

August 14 • President Roosevelt signs the Social Security Act, which provides for a system of old age pensions; grants to assist the states in financing aid to dependent children, the blind and the aged; and unemployment insurance in cooperation with the states.

August 23 • The Banking Act of 1935, revising the Federal Reserve System, is adopted.

August 28 • The Wheeler-Rayburn Act is adopted. It provides that a public utility holding company may operate only in a particular area.

August 30 • The Guffey-Snyder Bituminous Coal Stabilization Act is adopted. It reapplies NRA regulations to the bituminous coal industry.

August 30 • The Revenue Act of 1935 is adopted. Under its provisions estate and gift taxes are increased, income taxes for small corporations are lowered slightly, and taxes on large individual incomes are raised sharply.

August 31 • President Roosevelt signs the Neutrality Act of 1935, which forbids the shipment of arms to belligerents after the president has proclaimed that a state of war exists.

September 8 • Huey P. Long, a demagogic senator with presidential aspirations, is fatally wounded by an assassin in Baton Rouge, Louisiana. He dies on September 10.

September 17 • Manuel Quezon is elected as the first president of the Philippines.

October 5 • The president proclaims United States neutrality in the war initiated by Italy's invasion of Ethiopia (October 3). Arms shipments to belligerents are prohibited. On October 11, the League of Nations brands Italy the aggressor.

November 9 • John L. Lewis forms the Committee for Industrial Organization within the American Federation of labor. In 1938, the CIO becomes the independent Congress of Industrial Organizations.

December 9 • The Second London Naval Conference opens.

International and Cultural Events • The Saar is restored to Germany; the Nazi Nuremberg Laws deprive Jews of citizenship. China's Red Army completes its Long March to the north. Benny Goodman, Gene Krupa, and Teddy Wilson form a swing trio, which Lionel Hampton makes a quartet in 1936. George Gershwin's *Porgy and Bess* opens on Broadway for a 16-week engagement.

The town square in Camden, Tennessee, in 1935.

1936 United States of America

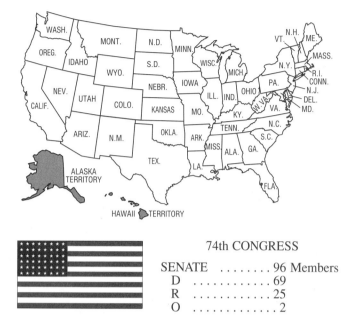

74th CONGRESS

SENATE .... 96 Members
D 69
R 25
O 2

HOUSE .... 432 Members
R 319
R 103
O 10

ESTIMATED
POPULATION
128,181,000

Franklin D. Roosevelt
32nd President
10th Democrat

John Nance Garner
32nd Vice President
Democrat

UNITED STATES ECONOMY

GROSS NATIONAL PRODUCT $82,700,000,000
RETAIL SALES $38,339,000,000
BANK RESOURCES $66,854,000,000
EXPORTS ....$ 2,419,000,000
IMPORTS ....$ 2,424,000,000
FEDERAL GOVERNMENT EXPENDITURE .$ 8,493,486,000
FEDERAL DEBT $33,778,543,000

Events

January 6 • In *United States v. Butler*, the Supreme Court holds the Agricultural Adjustment Act of 1933 unconstitutional.

January 22 • Congress passes the Adjusted Compensation Act, which authorizes the cash redemption of veterans' bonus certificates. Vetoed by President Roosevelt on February 24, the act is adopted over his veto that same day.

February 17 • In *Brown v. Mississippi*, a unanimous U.S. Supreme Court declares that coerced confessions are inadmissible in court. Writing for the Court, Chief Justice Hughes calls such involuntary statements a clear violation of the due process clause.

February 29 • The Neutrality Act of 1936, extending the act of 1935 to May 1, 1937, is adopted. It bars loans to belligerents.

February 29 • Congress passes the Soil Conservation and Domestic Allotment Act as a substitute for the Agricultural Adjustment Act. Farmers are to be paid for withdrawing acreage from crops that deplete the soil.

March 2 • The United States and Panama sign a treaty improving the latter's position in the Panama Canal Zone. The United States Senate will not ratify the treaty until July 25, 1939.

March 25 • The United States joins Great Britain and France in a treaty that ends the London Naval Conference after Japan's withdrawal.

May 18 • In *Carter v. Carter Coal Company et al.*, the Supreme Court rules that the Guffey-Snyder Bituminous Coal Stabilization Act of 1935 is unconstitutional.

May 23 • The Socialist party nominates Norman Thomas for president. A split within the movement results in fewer votes than in 1932.

June 9 • The Republican party convenes in Cleveland. It nominates Alfred M. Landon (Kansas) for president and Frank Knox (Illinois) for vice president. The convention approves an anti-New Deal platform.

June 20 • The Robinson-Patman Act is adopted. It forbids the use of excessively low prices and discriminatory practices that are designed to eliminate competition.

June 22 • The Revenue Act of 1936, taxing the undistributed profits of corporations, is adopted.

June 22 • An act of Congress authorizes a territorial legislature for the Virgin Islands.

June 23 • The Democratic party convenes in Philadelphia. It nominates President Roosevelt and Vice President Garner for re-election. The convention approves a platform endorsing New Deal policies.

June 24 • The Communist party nominates Earl Browder for president. Candidates are also named by the Socialist Labor and Prohibition parties.

June 26 • The Merchant Marine Act is adopted. It creates the United States Maritime Commission to replace the United States Shipping Board.

June 30 • The Walsh-Healey Act is adopted. It sets a minimum wage scale and maximum hours for employees of contractors doing business with the federal government.

November 3 • In the presidential election Roosevelt is re-elected, receiving 523 electoral votes to eight (Maine and Vermont) for Landon, his Republican opponent.

United States of America 1936

December 1–23 • The Inter-American Conference for the Maintenance of Peace is held in Buenos Aires. It opens with an address by President Roosevelt and closes with an agreement on consultation in the face of aggression.

December 21 • In *United States v. Curtiss-Wright Export Corporation*, the U.S. Supreme Court declares that the president is supreme in the area of foreign affairs. Writing for the seven-member majority, Justice George Sutherland states that "the President alone has the power to speak as a representative of a nation. He makes treaties with the advice and consent of the Sentae; but he alone negotiates. Into the field of negotiation the Senate cannot intrude; and Congress is powerless to invade it."

December 30 • The second shift of General Motor's Fisher Body Plant No. 1 in Flint, Michigan, stages a sit-down strike in support of a similar strike at the Fisher Body plant in Cleveland, Ohio. Strikers will disobey an injunction odering them to leave the plants.

International and Cultural Events • Germany demilitarizes the Rhineland. The Italo-Ethiopian War ends in an Italian victory. The Spanish Civil War begins and quickly becomes a testing ground for weapons of the Rome-Berlin Axis, which supports the anti-republican insurgents. Jesse Owen, black United States track star, scores a triumph at the Berlin Olympics. Edward VIII renounces the British throne for a divorcée, Wallis Simpson. Margaret Mitchell's *Gone with the Wind* is a national best seller.

When Roosevelt spoke in Charlotte, North Carolina, on September 10, 1936, it rained even though it was a drought year.

A dust storm in Cimarron County, Oklahoma, in 1936.

1937 United States of America

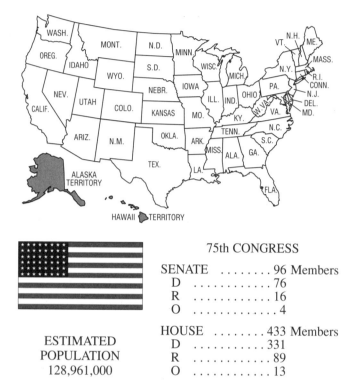

Franklin D. Roosevelt
32nd President
10th Democrat

John Nance Garner
32nd Vice President
Democrat

UNITED STATES ECONOMY

GROSS NATIONAL PRODUCT $90,800,000,000
RETAIL SALES $42,150,000,000
BANK RESOURCES $68,402,000,000
EXPORTS .... $ 3,299,000,000
IMPORTS .... $ 3,010,000,000
FEDERAL GOVERNMENT EXPENDITURE .$ 7,756,021,000
FEDERAL DEBT $36,424,614,000

Events

January 6 • A joint resolution that prohibits shipping munitions to either side in the Spanish Civil War is adopted by Congress.

January 20 • President Roosevelt is inaugurated for his second term. In his address, he emphasizes the needs of the third of the nation that ekes out an existence below minimum living standards.

February • Sitdown strikes end with agreements between the United Automobile Workers and the management of General Motors and Chrysler.

February 5 • Frustrated by judicial rulings declaring New Deal legislation unconstitutional, President Roosevelt asks Congress to add six justices to the Supreme Court and make other changes in the federal court system. Opposition to this plan mounts, and a bill incorporating its provisions is returned to the Judiciary Committee on July 22. However, new rulings approving New Deal legislation and the opportunity afforded by resignations to appoint liberal justices change the political climate.

March 1 • The United States Steel Corporation accepts a contract with the United Steel Workers. Except for Inland Steel, which follows suit in July, the Little Steel companies do not agree to bargain with the union until 1941.

March 1 • The Supreme Court Retirement Act, allowing justices to retire at 70, is adopted.

April 12 • The Supreme Court rules that the Wagner-Connery Act is constitutional.

April 26 • The Guffey-Vinson Bituminous Coal Act, replacing in part the Guffey-Snyder Act of 1935 (the little NRA), is adopted.

May 1 • President Roosevelt signs the Neutrality Act of 1937, which places the sale of certain commodities (not including munitions) to belligerents on a cash-and-carry basis and prohibits American citizens from traveling on belligerent ships.

May 24 • The Supreme Court rules that the Social Security Act of 1935 is constitutional.

A political cartoon depicting President Roosevelt's attempt to change the makeup of the Supreme Court in order to secure a more favorable climate for his New Deal legislation.

July 2 • Amelia Earhart, on a round-the-world flight, disappears when radio contact with her plane is lost over the Pacific Ocean.

July 22 • The Bankhead-Jones Farm Tenant Act is adopted. It supersedes the Resettlement Administration with the Farm Security Administration and establishes a loan program to enable tenants and others to acquire farms.

August 18 • The Miller-Tydings Enabling Act is adopted. It attempts to establish fair-trade prices for brand-name goods in interstate commerce by exempting from antitrust laws contracts for resale at fixed prices.

August 26 • The president signs the Judicial Procedure Reform Act, which affects the lower courts. On the same day, the Revenue Act of 1937 makes income tax evasion more difficult.

September 1 • Congress passes the Wagner-Steagall Act (National Housing Act), which creates the United States Housing Authority (USHA). The USHA is empowered to lend funds for the construction of low-rent public housing.

September 14 • An executive order bars government ships from carrying munitions to China and Japan.

October 5 • President Roosevelt delivers a major address on foreign policy in Chicago, proposing that aggressor nations be quarantined.

November 15–December 21 • A special session of Congress, called by President Roosevelt to deal with conservation, agriculture, labor standards and other matters, does not adopt any of his recommendations.

December 12 • The United States gunboat *Panay* is sunk by Japanese planes in the Yangtze River. On December 14, the Japanese government offers its apologies, promises to pay an indemnity, and gives assurances against such incidents in the future.

International and Cultural Events • Japan invades China after an incident on the Marco Polo Bridge near Peiping. Hundreds are purged as "spies" in the Soviet Union. Pablo Picasso's *Guernica* mural memorializes the destruction of the Spanish town by German planes. Joe Louis, the Brown Bomber, wins the world's heavyweight boxing championship.

President Roosevelt delivers a fireside chat.

1938 United States of America

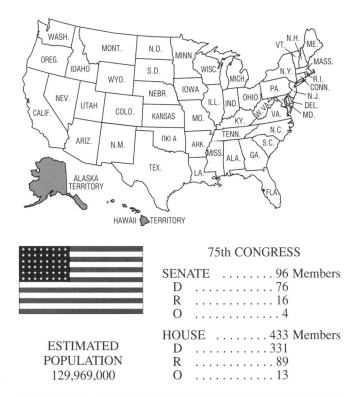

75th CONGRESS

SENATE .... 96 Members
D 76
R 16
O 4

HOUSE .... 433 Members
D 331
R 89
O 13

ESTIMATED
POPULATION
129,969,000

Franklin D. Roosevelt
32nd President
10th Democrat

John Nance Garner
32nd Vice President
Democrat

UNITED STATES ECONOMY

GROSS NATIONAL PRODUCT $85,200,000,000
RETAIL SALES $38,053,000,000
BANK RESOURCES $67,730,000,000
EXPORTS ....$ 3,057,000,000
IMPORTS ....$ 1,950,000,000
FEDERAL GOVERNMENT EXPENDITURE .$ 6,791,838,000
FEDERAL DEBT $37,164,740,000

Events

January 6 • The president states his opposition to the Ludlow resolution, which calls for a popular referendum on a declaration of war unless the United States is invaded. The resolution is returned to committee by a bare majority (January 10).

January 28 • The president asks Congress to authorize the construction of new warships and various other types of armaments.

February 16 • President Roosevelt signs the Agricultural Adjustment Act of 1938, which provides for restrictions on acreage, quotas for crops, storage of surpluses and payments to assure parity.

March 18 • American and British oil properties are nationalized by the Mexican government.

April 1 • The United States, which has been paying a price higher than the world price for Mexican silver, ceases to do so. However, the issues in dispute between the two countries are resolved between 1939 and 1942, and in 1941, the United States again purchases Mexican silver at a special price.

April 25 • In *United States v. Carolene Products Company*, the U.S. Supreme Court, by a vote of eight to one, ruled that a federal law barring the transportation of certain milk products was constitutional. Signaling a shift from matters of property rights to personal rights, Justice Harlan Fiske Stone, in what will become known as the "famous footnote 4," implicitly states that the Court will now begin to hold legislation to a double standard. If a law is challenged on the basis that it violates a personal liberty, the Court, the justice writes, will not be inclined to assume the law's validity. He warns, however, that if the law is economic in nature and is challenged on the basis that it is a violation of states' rights or the free flow of commerce, the Court will be inclined to presume that it is constitutional.

May 11 • Congress adopts the Revenue Act of 1938, which provides for an effective reduction in corporate income taxes as a means of aiding the economy. President Roosevelt does not sign the measure, which becomes law without his signature on May 27.

May 17 • The Vinson Naval Act, providing for a 10-year program of naval expansion, is adopted.

May 26 • The House of Representatives forms a committee to investigate un-American activities. Its chairman is Martin Dies.

June 21 • President Roosevelt signs the Emergency Relief Appropriation Act, which includes a variety of measures designed to deal with a persistent economic recession.

June 23 • The Civil Aeronautics Authority is established by an act of Congress as a regulatory body.

June 24 • Congress adopts the Food, Drug and Cosmetic Act, which provides for the disclosure of the ingredients of cosmetics, drugs and food on labels, with penalties for misbranding as well as for false advertising.

June 25 • President Roosevelt signs the Fair Labor Standards Act, which stipulates minimum wages and maximum workweeks for businesses engaged in interstate commerce, to take effect over eight years.

September 21 • A severe hurricane causes widespread

damage in the northeast, particularly in the coastal areas of New England; more than 450 people die.

September 27 • President Roosevelt urges a peaceful solution to the crisis brought on by German instigation of demands by German-speaking inhabitants of Czechoslovakia for the autonomy of the Sudetenland. On September 29, at the Munich Conference, British prime minister Neville Chamberlain and French prime minister Édouard Daladier agree to German acquisition of the Sudetenland. On his return home, Chamberlain announces "peace in our time."

November 8 • In the midterm elections, the Republicans make their first gains in 10 years, adding seven seats in the Senate and almost doubling their representation in the House.

December 12 • The U.S. Supreme Court renders the first in a series of decisions that will eventually overturn the "separate but equal" doctrine of *Plessy v. Ferguson*. In *Missouri ex rel. Gaines v. Canada*, the Court, by a vote of seven to two, rules that a state cannot prohibit an African American student from attending its all-white law school, even if the state offers to pay the tuition for the student to attend a school in a neighboring state.

December 24 • The Eighth International Conference of American States approves the Declaration of Lima, whereby the American republics affirm their resistance to threats against their security and integrity and their readiness to consult with each other if such threats eventuate.

International and Cultural Events • Austrian chancellor Kurt von Schuschnigg is forced from office, and German troops cross the border "to preserve order"; on March 13, Hitler achieves his goal of *anschluss* by annexing Austria. American pilot Douglas (Wrong-Way) Corrigan illegally solos across the Atlantic and says that he thought he was headed for California. Helen Wills wins the women's singles tennis championship for the eighth time at Wimbledon. Orson Welles broadcasts a radio play that leads many listeners to believe that an actual invasion from Mars has occurred.

A sharecropper's cabin in Louisiana.

1939 United States of America

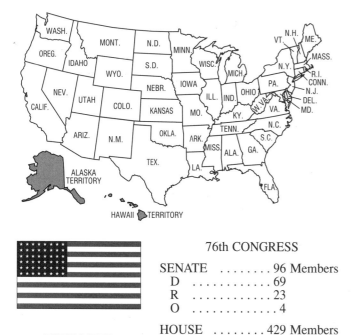

76th CONGRESS

SENATE	....	96 Members
D	....	69
R	....	23
O	....	4
HOUSE	....	429 Members
D	....	261
R	....	164
O	....	4

ESTIMATED
POPULATION
121,028,000

Franklin D. Roosevelt
32nd President
10th Democrat

John Nance Garner
32nd Vice President
Democrat

UNITED STATES ECONOMY

GROSS NATIONAL PRODUCT	$91,000,000,000
RETAIL SALES	$42,042,000,000
BANK RESOURCES	$73,193,000,000
EXPORTS	$ 3,123,000,000
IMPORTS	$ 2,276,000,000
FEDERAL GOVERNMENT EXPENDITURE	$ 8,858,458,000
FEDERAL DEBT	$40,439,532,000

Events

January 4–5 • After calling the attention of Congress to the gravity of the international situation in his annual message, President Roosevelt submits a budget that allocates $1.319 billion for defense.

February 27 • The Supreme Court rules that sitdown strikes are unconstitutional.

March 9 • The United States agrees to extend aid for the development of Brazil.

April 3 • President Roosevelt signs the Administrative Reorganization Act of 1939. Under its authorization, he submits five plans for reorganizing federal agencies, which, not being disapproved by Congress, go into effect in 1939 and 1940.

April 15 • In a letter to Hitler and Mussolini, President Roosevelt asks the two leaders to refrain from attacking any European or Middle Eastern country for 10 years in return for United States cooperation in trade and armament issues. Hitler's response, which will contain a denial of any warlike intentions, is filled with grievances against the United States.

May 10 • The Methodist Episcopal Church, the Methodist Episcopal Church, South, and the Methodist Protestant Church reunite to form the Methodist Church.

May 16 • A food stamp plan is inaugurated in Rochester, New York, to aid the poor.

June 7–12 • King George VI and Queen Elizabeth visit the United States on a goodwill trip.

June 28 • Regular transatlantic air service begins.

June 30 • An act of Congress curtails the scope of the WPA program for 1939–1940. Meanwhile, lack of funds has forced the dismissal of some WPA workers.

July 13 • Congress approves liberalizing amendments to the Social Security Act of 1935.

August 2 • Albert Einstein writes the president about the feasibility of an atomic bomb.

August 2 • The Hatch Act, restricting the participation in politics of the majority of federal employees, is signed by the president.

September 5 • The president proclaims United States neutrality as war spreads in Europe. A limited national emergency is declared (September 8).

November 4 • President Roosevelt signs the Neutrality Act of 1939, which enables belligerents to buy arms by paying for them in full before transporting them; American ships may not be used.

International and Cultural Events • In March, Germany takes over the rest of Czechoslovakia. Great Britain and France pledge their support to the Polish government as Hitler denounces his 1934 nonaggression pact with Poland and demands a change in the status of the free city of Danzig (Gdańsk). General Franco's antirepublican insurgents have won in Spain. In April, Spain joins Germany, Italy and Japan in the Anti-Comintern Pact, as Italian forces invade Albania. On August 23, a Soviet-German nonaggression pact is concluded in Moscow. German forces invade Poland on September 1, and on September 3, France and Great Britain declare war on Germany. On September 17, Poland is invaded by the U.S.S.R., which on September 28, divides the country with Germany. On November 30, Soviet forces invade Finland.

178

United States of America 1940

Events

January 26 • Japan is advised that the expiring trade treaty of 1911 with the United States will not be renewed.

April 7 • The Socialist party nominates Norman Thomas for president. Candidates are also named by the Socialist Labor, Prohibition and Communist parties.

June 10 • In a widely approved speech, President Roosevelt notes that United States policy is changing from neutrality to "nonbelligerency."

June 20 • President Roosevelt appoints two Republicans, Henry L. Stimson and Frank Knox, secretary of war and secretary of the navy, respectively.

June 24 • The Republican party convenes in Philadelphia. It nominates Wendell L. Willkie (New York) for president and Charles L. McNary (Oregon) for vice president.

June 28 • The Alien Registration Act (Smith Act) is adopted. In addition to providing for the registration of aliens, the act makes it illegal to belong to an organization that favors forcibly overthrowing any government in the United States.

July 15 • The Democratic party convenes in Chicago. It nominates President Roosevelt for re-election and Henry A. Wallace (Iowa) for vice president.

July 30 • Meeting in Havana, members of the Pan American Union take steps to prevent the transfer of European colonies in the Western Hemisphere.

September 3 • The United States trades 50 destroyers for leases on bases in British possessions in the Western Hemisphere.

September 16 • The president signs the Selective Training and Service Act, which requires men from 21 to 35 to register for military training.

September 26 • An embargo is placed on scrap steel and iron shipments outside the Western Hemisphere (Great Britain excepted).

November 5 • In the presidential election, Roosevelt is elected to an unprecedented third term, receiving 449 electoral votes to 82 for Willkie.

December 20 • President Roosevelt establishes the Office of Production Management and appoints William S. Knudsen to direct it. The new agency is to expedite the defense program and help the United States serve as the "arsenal of democracy," as the president states in a radio address on December 29.

International and Cultural Events • The German *blitzkrieg* continues with the invasion of Denmark, Norway, The Netherlands, Luxembourg, and Belgium. The British Expeditionary Force is evacuated from Dunkirk. Winston Churchill becomes prime minister.

	76th CONGRESS
	SENATE .... 96 Members
	D 69
	R 23
	O 4
ESTIMATED	HOUSE .... 429 Members
POPULATION	D 261
132,122,000	R 164
	O 4

Franklin D. Roosevelt
32nd President
10th Democrat

John Nance Garner
32nd Vice President
Democrat

UNITED STATES ECONOMY

GROSS NATIONAL PRODUCT	$100,600,000,000
RETAIL SALES	$ 46,375,000,000
BANK RESOURCES	$ 79,729,000,000
EXPORTS	$ 3,934,000,000
IMPORTS	$ 2,541,000,000
FEDERAL GOVERNMENT EXPENDITURE .	$ 9,062,032,000
FEDERAL DEBT	$ 42,967,531,000

Italy enters the war in June. On June 22, France capitulates before the force of the German army. The *Luftwaffe* bombs Great Britain unmercifully, but it is defeated by the Royal Air Force, and Hitler abandons his plan to invade the island. Finland capitulates, and the U.S.S.R. seizes Estonia, Latvia, and Lithuania. In September, Japan joins the Rome-Berlin Axis. Italian forces invade Greece.

1941 United States of America

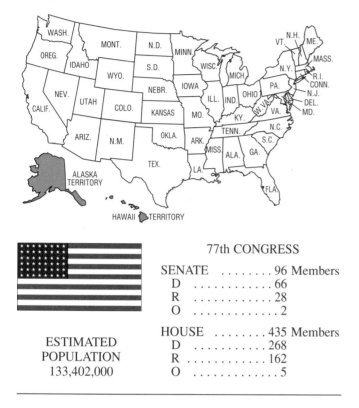

77th CONGRESS

SENATE .... 96 Members
D 66
R 28
O 2

HOUSE .... 435 Members
D 268
R 162
O 5

ESTIMATED
POPULATION
133,402,000

Franklin D. Roosevelt
32nd President
10th Democrat

Henry A. Wallace
33rd Vice President
Democrat

UNITED STATES ECONOMY

GROSS NATIONAL PRODUCT $126,417,000,000
RETAIL SALES ....$ 55,490,000,000
BANK RESOURCES ....$ 87,324,000,000
EXPORTS ....$ 5,020,000,000
IMPORTS ....$ 3,222,000,000
FEDERAL GOVERNMENT EXPENDITURE .$ 13,262,204,000
FEDERAL DEBT ....$ 48,961,444,000

Events

January 6 • Addressing Congress, President Roosevelt looks to a world that would be "founded upon four essential freedoms:" freedom of speech and of worship and freedom from want and from fear.

February 3 • In *United States v. Darby Lumber Company*, the Supreme Court holds that the Fair Labor Standards Act of 1938 is constitutional.

February 4 • Six national organizations form the United Service Organizations (USO) to meet the welfare, religious, educational, and social needs of servicemen and defense workers.

March 5 • The United States receives permission to install air defenses in Panama outside the Canal Zone for use until the end of the war.

March 11 • President Roosevelt signs the Lend-Lease Act, which provides for lending arms and other goods to countries whose defense is judged by the president to be important to the United States.

March 19 • The National Defense Mediation Board is formed to deal with labor disputes.

April 9 • The United States agrees with Denmark to defend Greenland.

April 11 • The Office of Price Administration [and Civilian Supply] (OPA) is set up to control prices.

April 11 • To help counter the increasing effectiveness of German submarine warfare, the security zone covered by United States patrols is extended eastward to 26°W. On May 21, a submarine sinks an American ship, the *Robin Moor,* in the southern Atlantic.

May 27 • The president issues a proclamation declaring a state of unlimited national emergency.

June 14 • The assets of Germany and Italy in the United States are frozen. On June 16, the president sets July 10 as the deadline for closing German and Italian consulates in the United States.

June 15 • A presidential order creates the Fair Employment Practices Committee to prevent racial discrimination in defense work.

June 24 • American aid is promised the U.S.S.R., which was invaded by Germany on June 22.

July 7 • United States troops arrive in Iceland with the approval of its government.

July 25 • Japan's credits in the United States are frozen after Japanese forces occupy southern French Indochina.

August 14 • After meeting on shipboard off Newfoundland from August 9 to 12, President Roosevelt and Prime Minister Winston Churchill issue the Atlantic Charter, in which they state eight goals, including the right of people to choose their form of government, access to trade and raw materials, freedom from fear and want, freedom to traverse the seas, and the disarming of aggressors.

August 18 • Military service under the Selective Service and Training Act is extended for 18 months.

September 4 • While patrolling near Iceland, a United States destroyer, the *Greer*, is attacked by a German submarine. On September 11, the president orders U.S. Navy planes and ships to shoot on sight Axis ships in United States defensive waters.

October 17 • The United States destroyer *Kearny* is attacked by a submarine off Iceland. On October 30, the destroyer *Reuben James* is sunk off Iceland.

November 6 • Lend-lease aid is extended to the U.S.S.R.

November 17 • President Roosevelt signs a bill amending the Neutrality Act of 1939 to permit American merchant ships to be armed and to call at belligerent ports.

November 20 • Japanese envoys propose to Secretary Hull that the United States remove restrictions on trade with Japan, refrain from interfering with its actions in China, and half any expansion of United States forces in the southern Pacific. Rejecting these proposals on November 26, Hull urges that Japan withdraw all forces from both China and Indochina, after which trade restrictions would be removed. The counterproposals are rejected by Japan on December 1 (formally on December 7).

December 7 • Planes launched from a Japanese naval task force attack the naval base at Pearl Harbor and other United States installations on Oahu, sinking or severely damaging 19 warships and destroying planes on the ground; 2,403 people are killed.

December 8 • Congress declares war on Japan.

Congresswoman Jeanette Rankin casts an antiwar vote, as she did in 1917.

December 10 • Japanese forces invade the Philippines.

December 11 • Germany and Italy declare war on the United States, and Congress declares that a state of war exists with them.

December 13 • Japanese forces seize Guam.

December 19 • An act of Congress makes men aged 20 to 44 subject to military service.

December 23 • Japan seizes Wake Island.

International and Cultural Events • In April, Japan and the U.S.S.R. conclude a neutrality pact. Axis forces complete the conquest of Yugoslavia. Germany completes the conquest of Greece. The groundwork is laid for the Manhattan Project, which eventually develops the atomic bomb with the help of British and Canadian scientists; it is established in 1942 under the Army Corps of Engineers. Orson Welles films *Citizen Kane*. W. J. Cash's *The Mind of the South*, a now-classic study of regional analysis, explodes many social myths.

The Japanese launch a surprise attack on Pearl Harbor on December 7, 1941.

1942 United States of America

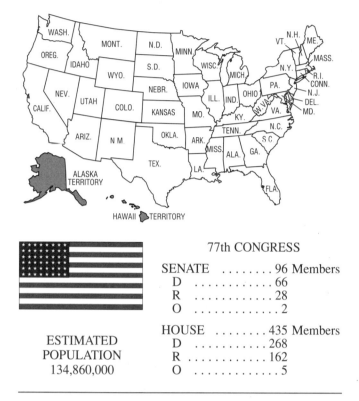

77th CONGRESS

SENATE .... 96 Members
D 66
R 28
O 2

HOUSE .... 435 Members
D 268
R 162
O 5

ESTIMATED
POPULATION
134,860,000

Franklin D. Roosevelt
32nd President
10th Democrat

Henry A. Wallace
33rd Vice President
Democrat

UNITED STATES ECONOMY

GROSS NATIONAL PRODUCT $159,100,000,000
RETAIL SALES ....$ 57,212,000,000
BANK RESOURCES ....$ 91,930,000,000
EXPORTS ....$ 8,003,000,000
IMPORTS ....$ 2,780,000,000
FEDERAL GOVERNMENT EXPENDITURE .$ 34,045,679,000
FEDERAL DEBT ....$ 72,422,455,000

Events

January 1 • Representatives of 26 countries sign the Declaration of the United Nations in Washington.

January 2 • Manila is abandoned to the Japanese as United States forces withdraw to the Bataan Peninsula, where they hold out until April 9. On May 6, the fortress on Corregidor falls to the Japanese.

January 12 • The National Defense Mediation Board is superseded by the National War Labor Board.

January 12 • The United States and Mexican governments set up a joint defense commission.

January 14 • A presidential proclamation orders all aliens in the United States to register with the government.

January 15–28 • The foreign ministers of the American republics meet in Rio de Janeiro and agree to recommend that those nations that have not already severed relations with the Axis Powers do so promptly. Chile waits until 1943; and Argentina until 1944.

January 16 • The War Production Board is created; it supersedes the Office of Production Management.

January 26 • United States troops arrive in Northern Ireland, the first U.S. troops in Europe since World War I.

January 28 • The Office of Civilian Defense is created. On January 30, President Roosevelt signs the Emergency Price Control Act.

January 31 • British forces are withdrawn from Malaya to Singapore, which falls to the Japanese on February 15.

February 7 • The War Shipping Administration is created by executive order, as are the National Housing Agency (February 24), the War Manpower Commission (April 18), and the Office of War Information (June 13).

February 27–March 1 • Allied naval forces sustain heavy losses in the battle of the Java Sea.

March • Japanese and persons of Japanese ancestry are moved from the Pacific Coast states and Arizona to relocation camps farther inland.

Aircraft plant production line manufacturing B-17 bombers.

United States of America   1942

A ship launching off the shipways into the harbor at Baltimore, Maryland.

March 7–8 • Japanese forces land on the north coast of New Guinea. On March 9, they complete the conquest of the Netherlands East Indies.

April 18 • Tokyo is raided by United States B-25 bombers led by Major General James H. Doolittle.

May 7–8 • In the battle of the Coral Sea, the Japanese are deflected from landing at Port Moresby.

May 15 • An act of Congress authorizes the Women's Auxiliary Army Corps, later the Women's Army Corps (WAC). On July 30, Congress authorizes a women's Naval Reserve branch, the WAVES.

May 20 • Japan completes the conquest of Burma.

June 3–6 • United States naval forces defeat the Japanese in the battle of Midway, turning the direction of the war in the Pacific.

June 6–7 • Japanese forces invade Attu and Kiska in the Aleutian Islands.

August 7 • United States Marines land on Guadalcanal, launching an offensive against the Japanese in the Solomon Islands. Several naval battles ensue.

August 12–15 • A British-Soviet-American conference on the war is held in Moscow.

August 13 • Brigadier General Leslie R. Groves is awarded command of the Manhattan Engineer District, which will develop the atomic bomb. In September, construction begins on the district's three main installations, which are located at: Los Alamos, New Mexico (the bomb development laboratory), Oak Ridge, Tennessee (the U-235 separation plant), and Hanford, Washington (the plutonium production works).

September 29 • Japan is turned back in New Guinea.

November 8 • United States and British forces under Lieutenant General Dwight D. Eisenhower land in North Africa.

November 18 • The age at which men become subject to military service is changed to 18.

International and Cultural Events • The Germans execute the adult male population of Lidice, Czechoslovakia, as a reprisal measure. The Beveridge Report proposes "cradle to the grave" social security for Britons. The 1,523-mile Alaska Highway opens. The Italian-born physicist Enrico Fermi, working in Chicago, achieves a self-sustaining nuclear chain reaction.

1943 United States of America

78th CONGRESS

SENATE .... 96 Members
D 58
R 37
O 1

ESTIMATED
POPULATION
136,739,000

HOUSE .... 430 Members
D 218
R 208
O 4

Franklin D. Roosevelt
32nd President
10th Democrat

Henry A. Wallace
33rd Vice President
Democrat

UNITED STATES ECONOMY

GROSS NATIONAL PRODUCT	$192,500,000,000
RETAIL SALES	$ 63,235,000,000
BANK RESOURCES	$116,729,000,000
EXPORTS	$ 12,842,000,000
IMPORTS	$ 3,390,000,000
FEDERAL GOVERNMENT EXPENDITURE	$ 79,407,030,000
FEDERAL DEBT	$136,696,090,000

Events

January 14–24 • A British–United Sates conference, attended by Prime Minister Churchill and President Roosevelt, is held in Casablanca, Morocco. Sicily is to be the next Allied target, but no decision is made on the main second front in Western Europe. The war must end with the unconditional surrender of the Axis Powers.

January 27 • For the first time in the war, an all-U.S.

bombing raid is conducted on Germany. The daylight attack is on Wilhelmshaven.

February 7 • As a wartime measure, the government orders the rationing of shoes. Each person is limited to three pairs of new shoes annually.

February 9 • United States Marines take Guadalcanal.

February 14–23 • Reinforced German forces in Tunisia drive United States troops back, breaking through the Kasserine Pass before they are halted.

March 2–4 • United States planes sink 21 Japanese ships carrying 15,000 troops in the battle of the Bismarck Sea.

April 1 • The government orders the rationing of meat, fats and cheese.

April 8 • The president issues an executive order freezing prices, salaries, and wages.

May 1–2 • Federal seizure of the eastern coal mines ends a strike called by John L. Lewis to protest the wage freeze.

May 11–30 • United States forces retake Attu.

May 12–25 • The Trident conference is held in Washington; British and American leaders agree on May 1, 1944, for the launching of a cross-Channel invasion.

May 13 • The German forces in Tunisia surrender, freeing North Africa from Axis control.

May 27 • The Office of War Mobilization is created by executive order.

May 27 • The president issues an order that all contracts

The Baltimore shipyards.

Stalin, Roosevelt and Churchill at the Teheran Conference.

with war industries forbid racial discrimination. Detroit is the scene of race riots in June.

June • The Current Tax Payment Act goes into effect. Derided as the "Pay-As-You-Go-Act," it introduces to American workers concept of the federal withholding tax.

June 25 • The War Labor Disputes Act (Smith-Connally Act) is adopted by Congress over the veto of the president. It requires a union to give notice 30 days before calling a strike in a war plant and outlaws strikes in government-operated plants.

July 10–August 17 • Sicily is taken by United States and British troops.

July 16 • President Roosevelt and Prime Minister Churchill ask the Italian people to surrender.

August 14–24 • The Quadrant Conference is held in Quebec. Roosevelt, Churchill, and the Combined Chiefs of Staff discuss plans for the invasion of France in 1944.

September 3 • British and Canadian troops cross the Strait of Messina to the Italian mainland. The Italian government of Marshal Pietro Badoglio, formed when

Mussolini was compelled to resign (July 25), signs a secret armistice effective September 8. On October 13, Italy declares war on Germany.

September 9 • United States troops land at Salerno.

October 19–30 • The foreign ministers of the United States, Great Britain, and the U.S.S.R. meet in Moscow and agree on the need for an international organization designed to preserve peace.

November 21–24 • United States Marines take Tarawa.

November 22–26 • Chiang Kai-shek meets President Roosevelt and Prime Minister Churchill in Cairo to plan strategy against Japan.

November 28–December 1 • President Roosevelt, Prime Minister Churchill, and Premier Stalin meet in Teheran to discuss plans to invade France.

International and Cultural Events • Twenty-two Nazi divisions surrender at Stalingrad. The Germans level the Warsaw ghetto after an uprising by its Jewish inhabitants. Wendell L. Willkie reports in *One World* on his trip to Allied fronts.

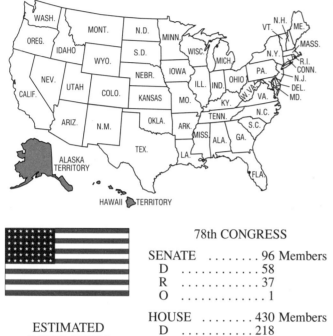

ALASKA TERRITORY

HAWAII TERRITORY

78th CONGRESS		
SENATE	....	96 Members
D	....	58
R	....	37
O	....	1
HOUSE	....	430 Members
D	....	218
R	....	208
O	....	4

ESTIMATED
POPULATION
138,397,000

Franklin D. Roosevelt
32nd President
10th Democrat

Henry A. Wallace
33rd Vice President
Democrat

UNITED STATES ECONOMY

GROSS NATIONAL PRODUCT	.........$211,400,000,000
RETAIL SALES	......................$ 70,208,000,000
BANK RESOURCES	..................$138,842,000,000
EXPORTS	..........................$ 14,162,000,000
IMPORTS	..........................$ 3,887,000,000
FEDERAL GOVERNMENT EXPENDITURE	.$ 95,058,708,000
FEDERAL DEBT	....................$201,003,387,000

Events

January 16 • General Eisenhower takes up his post in Great Britain as supreme commander, Allied Expeditionary Force, to prepare for the invasion of the European Continent.

January 23 • Allied forces land at Anzio, Italy.

February 1–23 • United States troops seize Kwajalein, in the western Mariana Islands, and then move on to Eniwetok. Saipan is secured on July 9, and on August 1, Tinian is taken.

February 3 • For the first time in the war, U.S. war ships shell Japanese soil, attacking the Kurile Islands.

February 29–March 25 • United States forces seize the Admiralty Islands. On April 22, Allied forces land at Hollandia, in Dutch New Guinea.

March 6 • The United States Army Air Corps conducts its first raid on Berlin using 660 bombers.

April 3 • In *Smith v. Allwright*, the U.S. Supreme Court strikes down a Texas law prohibiting African Americans from voting in primary elections.

May 18 • In the last of four attacks, the Allies capture Cassino, a strongpoint in the Gustav Line, the German's defensive line across the Italian peninsula.

June 4 • The Germans are driven from Rome.

June 6 • The Allied cross-channel invasion of the European continent begins with amphibious landings in Normandy (D-Day).

June 16 • U.S. "Superfortresses" (B-29s) conduct the first aerial attack on the main island of Japan, bombing Yawata.

June 19–20 • Carrier-based United States aircraft sink three Japanese carriers and destroy hundreds of planes in the battle of the Philippine Sea.

June 22 • The Servicemen's Readjustment Act is signed by the president. Known as the GI Bill of Rights, it offers veterans grants for education and other assistance.

June 26 • The Republican party convenes in Chicago. It nominates Thomas E. Dewey (New York) for president and John W. Bicker (Ohio) for vice president.

July 1–22 • Delegates of 44 nations attend the United Nations Monetary and Financial Conference at Bretton Woods, New Hampshire, which creates the International Monetary Fund and the International Bank for Reconstruction and Development (World Bank).

July 6 • A circus tent belonging to Ringling Brothers and Barnum and Bailey catches fire in Hartford, Connecticut. The fire kills 168 people.

July 19 • The Democratic party convenes in Chicago. It nominates President Roosevelt for re-election and Senator Harry S Truman (Missouri) for vice president.

July 21–August 10 • The United States regains Guam.

August 15 • The Allies invade southern France.

August 21–October 7 • The Dumbarton Oaks Conference is held in Washington, D.C. Representatives of the United States, Great Britain, China, and the U.S.S.R. discuss the structure of the future United Nations.

August 25 • Allied forces liberate Paris.

September 12 • The U.S. Army, advancing only a few miles beyond the Belgian border near Aachen, enter Germany for the first time.

September 12–16 • The Octagon Conference is held in Quebec. Churchill and Roosevelt take up a variety of

topics, including the postwar status of Germany.

September 15–October 21 • United States forces secure the Palau Islands.

October 20 • General MacArthur leads United States forces in the invasion of the Philippines, landing on Leyte Island. The Japanese Navy is overwhelmingly defeated in the battle of Leyte Gulf (October 23–26).

November 7 • In the presidential election, Roosevelt is re-elected, receiving 432 electoral votes to 99 votes for Dewey, his Republican opponent.

December 16–26 • A major German counteroffensive launched in the Ardennese is halted (Battle of the Bulge).

December 18 • In *Korematsu v. United States*, the U.S. Supreme Court rules that the relocation of U.S. citizens of Japanese ancestry from the West Coast to inland relocation camps is a valid wartime measure. The Court, however, warns that "all legal restrictions that curtail the civil rights of a single racial group are suspect...[and that] the courts must subject them to the most rigid scrutiny."

International and Cultural Events • General Hideki Tojo resigns as Japanese prime minister. Dissident officers of the German Army carry out an unsuccessful bomb plot against Hitler. General Charles de Gaulle forms a provisional French government. The Swedish sociologist Gunnar Myrdal publishes *An American Dilemma*, a study of race relations in the United States.

General Dwight D. Eisenhower giving orders to paratroopers before they leave for Normandy.

1945 Roosevelt/Truman

79th CONGRESS

SENATE . . . . 95 Members
D 56
R 38
O 1

HOUSE . . . . 434 Members
D 242
R 190
O 2

ESTIMATED
POPULATION
139,928,000

Franklin D. Roosevelt
32nd President
10th Democrat

Harry S Truman
34th Vice President
Democrat

UNITED STATES ECONOMY

GROSS NATIONAL PRODUCT $213,600,000,000
RETAIL SALES . . . .$ 78,034,000,000
BANK RESOURCES $162,169,000,000
EXPORTS . . . .$ 9,585,000,000
IMPORTS . . . .$ 4,098,000,000
FEDERAL GOVERNMENT EXPENDITURE .$ 98,416,220,000
FEDERAL DEBT $258,682,187,000

Harry S Truman	
Birth . . . . Lamar, MO, May 8, 1884	
Parents . . . . John and Martha Young Truman	
Married . . . . Bess Wallace	
Home . . . . Independence, MO	
Presidency . . . . 1945 – 1953	
Death . . . . Kansas City, MO, Dec. 26, 1972	

Events

February 4–11 • At a conference held in Yalta, President Roosevelt, Prime Minister Churchill, and Premier Stalin discuss German reparations, voting at the United Nations, the orders of Poland, and territory to be ceded to the U.S.S.R. in return for its joining the conflict with Japan.

February 19 • United States Marines land on Iwo Jima, which is secured on March 16. Manila is liberated on February 23, and Okinawa is taken by United States troops (April 1–June 21).

March 7 • United States troops cross the Rhine River over a bridge seized intact at Remagen.

April 12 • President Roosevelt dies at Warm Springs, Georgia. Vice President Harry S Truman succeeds to the presidency.

April 25–June 26 • Representatives of 50 nations convene in San Francisco and draw up the Charter of the United Nations.

April 29 • German forces in Italy sign an instrument of surrender, effective May 2.

May 1 • Hitler's death is announced. On May 2, Soviet troops take Berlin.

May 7 • Germany surrenders unconditionally at Reims. May 8 is designated V-E Day.

June 5 • Germany is divided into British, French, Soviet, and United States occupation zones. Berlin is under four-power control.

July 16 • An atomic bomb is exploded successfully on a test site at Alamogordo, New Mexico.

July 17–August 2 • President Truman, Premier Stalin, and Prime Minister Churchill (succeeded by Clement R. Attlee) meet in Potsdam and discuss peace treaties with the minor Axis nations and German problems. The Potsdam Declaration of July 26 demands Japan's unconditional surrender.

July 28 • By a vote of 89 to two, the U.S. Senate approves the United Nations Charter.

August 6 • An atomic bomb is dropped on Hiroshima. On August 8, the U.S.S.R. declares war on Japan, which surrenders on August 14. August 15 is designated V-J Day.

August 9 • The Allies drop a second atomic bomb on the Japanese city of Nagasaki.

September 11–October 2 • The Council of Foreign Ministers meets in London without results. A second meeting, held in Moscow on December 16–26, discusses Korea, Japan, and the peace treaties.

International and Cultural Events • After a Labor landslide in British elections, Attlee forms a government. Mussolini is executed by partisans, and his body is exhibited in Milan.

United States of America 1946

Events

January 10 • The General Assembly of the United Nations convenes in London for its first session. On January 24, it establishes the United Nations Atomic Energy Commission.

January 19 • The International Military Tribunal for the Far East is set up to try Japanese leaders charged with war crimes. In 1948, it sentences seven men to death and 16 to life imprisonment.

February 21 • President Truman re-establishes the Office of Economic Stabilization.

March 5 • At Westminster College in Fulton, Missouri, former British prime minister Winston Churchill declares that "an iron curtain has descended across the [European] Continent allowing 'police governments' to rule Eastern Europe."

April–May • Strikes by coal miners and railroad workers end when the mines and railroads are seized by the federal government.

April 25 • The foreign ministers of Great Britain, France, the United States, and the Soviet Union, meeting at the Paris Peace Conference and in New York, draw up peace treaties with Italy, Bulgaria, Romania, Hungary, and Finland. These are signed in Paris on February 10, 1947.

June 14 • Bernard M. Baruch offers the United Nations Atomic Energy Commission a United States plan for atomic control, which is approved by the General Assembly in 1948, but Soviet opposition prevents it from being put into effect.

July 1 • The United States conducts the first of several atomic tests on the Pacific island of Bikini in the Marshall Islands.

July 4 • President Truman proclaims the independence of the Philippines.

August 1 • President Truman signs the McMahon Act, which creates the United States Atomic Energy Commission.

August 1 • President Truman signs the Fulbright Act, which authorizes the utilization of foreign currencies obtained from the sale of surplus property for an educational exchange program.

September 20 • The president obtains the resignation of Secretary of Commerce Henry A. Wallace, who, on September 12, made a speech criticizing the administration's dealings with the U.S.S.R.

October 1 • The International Military Tribunal in Nuremberg sentences 12 Nazi leaders to death.

October 23–December 15 • The second part of the first session of the General Assembly is held in New York. On December 14, it votes to accept a gift of $8.5 million from John D. Rockefeller, Jr., to acquire a site on the East River in New York for the United Nations headquarters.

79th CONGRESS

SENATE	. . . .	95 Members
D	. . . .	56
R	. . . .	38
O	. . . .	1
HOUSE	. . . .	434 Members
D	. . . .	242
R	. . . .	190
O	. . . .	2

ESTIMATED
POPULATION
141,389,000

Harry S Truman
33rd President
11th Democrat

Vice President
None

UNITED STATES ECONOMY

GROSS NATIONAL PRODUCT	. . . .$210,700,000,000
RETAIL SALES	. . . .$102,488,000,000
BANK RESOURCES	. . . .$171,529,000,000
EXPORTS	. . . .$ 9,500,000,000
IMPORTS	. . . .$ 4,825,000,000
FEDERAL GOVERNMENT EXPENDITURE	.$ 60,447,574,000
FEDERAL DEBT	. . . .$269,422,099,000

November 5 • In the mid-term elections, the Republicans regain control of both houses of Congress.

November 9 • Price controls are abolished, with the exception of those on rents, rice, and sugar.

International and Cultural Events • Civil war erupts in Greece. Frances Xavier Cabrini becomes the first American saint. Dr. Benjamin Spock publishes *The Common Sense Book of Baby and Child Care.*

1947 United States of America

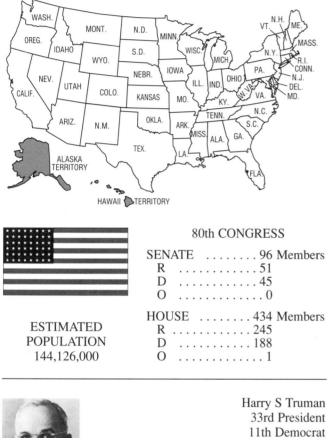

80th CONGRESS

SENATE .... 96 Members
R 51
D 45
O 0

HOUSE .... 434 Members
R 245
D 188
O 1

ESTIMATED
POPULATION
144,126,000

Harry S Truman
33rd President
11th Democrat

Vice President
None

UNITED STATES ECONOMY

GROSS NATIONAL PRODUCT $234,300,000,000
RETAIL SALES $119,604,000,000
BANK RESOURCES $166,336,000,000
EXPORTS ....$ 14,252,000,000
IMPORTS ....$ 5,666,000,000
FEDERAL GOVERNMENT EXPENDITURE .$ 39,032,393,000
FEDERAL DEBT $258,286,383,000

Events

January 21 • General of the Army George C. Marshall takes the oath of office as secretary of state.

March 6 • The Supreme Court upholds a fine against John L. Lewis, head of the United Mine Workers, for a strike called in November 1946 in defiance of an injunction.

March 10–April 24 • The Council of Foreign Ministers

meets in Moscow to discuss treaties with Austria and Germany and problems relating to reparations and the governmental structure of Germany. Soviet differences with the British and Americans, who, on December 2, 1946, had combined the economies of their occupation zones, prevent the achievement of any substantial agreement. Another meeting of the council, held in London from November 25 to December 15, fails to reach any agreement.

March 12 • President Truman, speaking before a joint session of Congress, outlines a doctrine of containing Soviet communism. He requests Congress to appropriate $400 million for aid for the defense of Greece and Turkey.

March 24 • Congress proposes the 22nd Amendment, which would limit presidents to two terms in office.

April 2 • United States trusteeship of the former mandated Japanese islands in the Pacific is approved by the United Nations Security Council.

April 16 • A chance explosion in the cargo hold of the French SS *Grandchamp*, which had been in the process of loading ammonium nitrate (a key component of fertilizer), erupts with such velocity that it destroys a large portion of Texas City, Texas. The ensuing fire destroys the docks, nearby oil storage tanks and businesses and homes. The death toll will reach 512.

May 31 • The president signs a bill appropriating $350 million for foreign relief. A bill appropriating $540 million for Austria, China, France, and Italy is adopted on December 19.

June 5 • Secretary Marshall presents a plan for the economic recovery of Europe. A conference held on July 12–15 is attended by 16 nations (the U.S.S.R. and its satellites refuse to participate). It appoints a committee that estimates four-year aid requirements at $22.4 billion.

June 23 • Congress adopts the Taft-Hartley Act over the president's veto. The new law prohibits the closed shop and restricts union activities.

July 18 • President Truman signs the Presidential Succession Act, which designates the speaker of the House and the president pro tempore of the Senate as next in succession after the vice president.

July 26 • The president signs the National Security Act, which creates the National Military Establishment, uniting the Army, Navy, and Air Force. On September 17, James V. Forrestal is sworn in as the first secretary of defense.

December 8 • The Senate ratifies the Inter-American Treaty of Reciprocal Assistance.

International and Cultural Events • Andrei A. Zhdanov sets up the Cominform to direct European Communist parties. Princess Elizabeth, heir to the British throne, marries Philip Mountbatten. Jackie Robinson joins the Brooklyn Dodgers and is the first black player on a major league team.

United States of America 1948

Events

March 8 • In *Illinois ex rel. McCollum v. Board of Education*, the Supreme Court rules that religious instruction in public school buildings is unconstitutional.

April 3 • President Truman signs a bill authorizing $6.098 billion in foreign aid, including $5.3 billion for the European Recovery Program.

April 30 • The Ninth International Conference of American States, meeting in Bogotá, establishes the Organization of American States.

April–May • The United States tests three atomic weapons at Eniwetok in the Marshall Islands.

May 14 • The United States is the first country to recognize the state of Israel.

June 11 • The Senate adopts a resolution, introduced by Arthur H. Vandenberg, approving the extension of aid to defensive alliances.

June 21 • The Republican party convenes in Philadelphia. It nominates Thomas E. Dewey (New York) for president and Earl Warren (California) for vice president.

June 24 • President Truman signs the Selective Service Act, which requires men between 18 and 25 to register for military service.

June 24 • Currency reform in West Berlin is the pretext for a Soviet blockade of all land routes between the city and West Germany. To supply the beleaguered city, the Western Allies mount an airlift until the blockade is lifted on May 12, 1949.

June 25 • President Truman signs a bill authorizing the immigration to the United States of 205,000 displaced people.

July 12 • The Democratic party convenes in Philadelphia. It nominates President Truman for re-election and Alben W. Barkley (Kentucky) for vice president.

July 17 • "Dixiecrats" opposed to the president's strong civil rights stand form the States Rights party and nominate J. Strom Thurmond for president. On July 23, the Progressive party further weakens the Democratic ticket by nominating Henry A. Wallace.

July 26 • President Truman, by executive order, declares that "there shall be equality of treatment and opportunity for all persons in the armed services without regard to race, color, religion, or national origin." The president also establishes a committee to investigate racial discrimination in the armed forces and to recommend a solution for ending the practice.

August 16 • The president signs a limited anti-inflation bill provided by Congress.

November 2 • In the presidential election, Truman is re-elected, receiving 303 electoral votes to 189 for Dewey

80th CONGRESS

SENATE	....	96 Members
R	....	51
D	....	45
O	....	0
HOUSE	....	434 Members
R	....	245
D	....	188
O	....	1

ESTIMATED POPULATION
146,631,000

Harry S Truman
33rd President
11th Democrat

Vice President
None

UNITED STATES ECONOMY

GROSS NATIONAL PRODUCT	$259,400,000,000
RETAIL SALES	$130,721,000,000
BANK RESOURCES	$170,052,000,000
EXPORTS	$ 12,532,000,000
IMPORTS	$ 7,092,000,000
FEDERAL GOVERNMENT EXPENDITURE	$ 33,068,709,000
FEDERAL DEBT	$252,292,247,000

and 39 for Thurmond. The Democrats gain control of both houses of Congress.

International and Cultural Events • Arab forces invade Israel. Communists take power in Czechoslovakia and Hungary. Mohandas Gandhi is assassinated. A.C. Kinsey and his researchers published *Sexual Behavior in the Human Male*. Bell Telephone Laboratories perfect the transistor. Columbia Records introduces the LP.

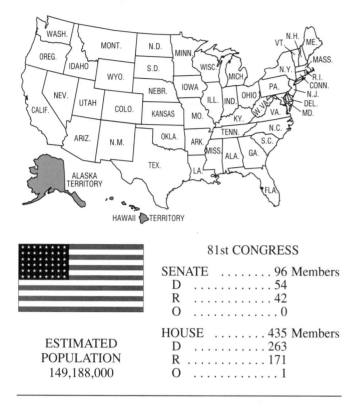

81st CONGRESS

SENATE .... 96 Members
D 54
R 42
O 0

HOUSE .... 435 Members
D 263
R 171
O 1

ESTIMATED
POPULATION
149,188,000

Harry S Truman
33rd President
11th Democrat

Alben W. Barkley
35th Vice President
Democrat

UNITED STATES ECONOMY

GROSS NATIONAL PRODUCT $258,100,000,000
RETAIL SALES $130,521,000,000
BANK RESOURCES $170,810,000,000
EXPORTS .... $ 11,936,000,000
IMPORTS .... $ 6,592,000,000
FEDERAL GOVERNMENT EXPENDITURE .$ 39,506,989,000
FEDERAL DEBT $252,770,360,000

Events

January 7 • Secretary of State Marshall resigns effective January 20. On January 21, Dean Acheson is sworn in as his successor.

January 20 • President Truman is inaugurated. In his inaugural address, he lists four basic points of United States foreign policy, the fourth of which is the need to help underdeveloped areas with technical assistance and investment.

April 4 • Representatives of the United States, Canada, and 10 western European nations sign the North Atlantic Treaty, a mutual defense pact. The treaty is ratified by the United States Senate on July 21. The North Atlantic Treaty Organization (NATO) comes into being with the establishment of the North Atlantic Council on September 17.

April 8 • The United States, France, and Great Britain agree on an occupation statute merging their zones in West Germany, effective with the establishment of a federal government. The Federal Republic of Germany is established under the Basic Law of May 8, and Allied military government ends on September 21 with the inauguration of the Allied High Commission.

May 23–June 30 • The Council of Foreign Ministers meets in Paris. It makes no progress on German problems but reaches agreement on some points for an Austrian treaty.

June 20 • President Truman signs the Reorganization Act, which allows the president to issue orders reorganizing the executive branch of the federal government. The orders become effective if not vetoed by Congress within 60 days.

July 15 • The president signs the Housing Act of 1949, which authorizes expanded federal aid for public housing.

August 10 • The president signs the National Security Act, which transforms the National Military Establishment into the Department of Defense. On August 11, General Omar N. Bradley is appointed the first chairman of the Joint Chiefs of Staff.

September–November • Major strikes occur in the coal and steel industries.

September 23 • Following the Soviets' successful testing of an atomic device, President Truman informs the American public that the Soviet Union has nuclear weapons capability.

October 6 • President Truman signs a bill appropriating $5.81 billion for foreign economic aid.

October 21 • Eleven United States Communist leaders, found guilty of conspiracy under the Smith Act, are sentenced to prison.

October 26 • The president signs a bill amending the Fair Labor Standards Act and increasing the minimum hourly wage to 75 cents.

International and Cultural Events • The Soviet Union explodes an atomic bomb. The People's Republic of China is proclaimed under Chairman Mao Tse-tung. The Republic of Ireland is born. Arthur Miller's *Death of a Salesman* is staged on Broadway.

United States of America 1950

Events

January 21 • Alger Hiss, a former official with the State Department, is convicted of perjury for his denial of charges of espionage.

January 31 • President Truman announces that he has ordered the Atomic Energy Commission to work on a hydrogen bomb.

February 20 • Senator Joseph R. McCarthy, a Republican from Wisconsin, says that the State Department employs 81 people whose loyalty is suspect. On July 17, a Senate subcommittee reports that the charges are unfounded.

April 10 • The Supreme Court upholds the conviction of two Hollywood writers for contempt of Congress for refusing to affirm or deny membership in the Communist party.

June 27 • President Truman orders naval and air forces to aid South Korea, which was invaded by North Korea on June 25. The Security Council requests United Nations member nations to aid South Korea. Seoul falls on June 28. On June 30, Truman commits United States ground forces. Seoul is recaptured on September 26.

July 8 • General of the Army Douglas MacArthur is appointed commander of United Nations forces in Korea.

September 23 • Congress overrides President Truman's veto of the Internal Security Act of 1950. The new law sets up the Subversive Activities Control Board to handle the registration of Communist and Communist-front organizations.

October 7 • The United Nations General Assembly implicitly approves the crossing of the 38th-parallel boundary of North Korea by United Nations forces. On October 20, United States and South Korean troops take P'yŏngyang.

October 15 • General MacArthur and President Truman confer on Wake Island.

November 1 • Puerto Rican nationalists fail in an attempt to assassinate President Truman.

November • Chinese Communist forces intervene in large numbers in the Korean conflict. On November 26, they launch a major attack, driving the United Nations forces back toward the 38th parallel.

November 28 • The Atomic Energy Commission announces plans to build the Savannah River Site in South Carolina. When constructed, the plants will produce hydrogen bomb explosives.

December 16 • President Truman declares a state of national emergency.

December 19 • General of the Army Eisenhower is named commander of NATO forces.

International and Cultural Events • Commonwealth

81st CONGRESS	
SENATE . . . . 96 Members	
D 54	
R 42	
O 0	
HOUSE . . . . 435 Members	
D 263	
R 171	
O 1	

ESTIMATED
POPULATION
151,683,000

Harry S Truman
33rd President
11th Democrat

Alben W. Barkley
35th Vice President
Democrat

UNITED STATES ECONOMY

GROSS NATIONAL PRODUCT $284,600,000,000
RETAIL SALES $143,689,000,000
BANK RESOURCES $179,165,000,000
EXPORTS . . . .$ 10,142,000,000
IMPORTS . . . .$ 8,743,000,000
FEDERAL GOVERNMENT EXPENDITURE .$ 39,617,003,000
FEDERAL DEBT $257,357,352,000

ministers meeting in Colombo, Ceylon, evolve a plan to aid in the development of South and Southeast Asia. William Faulkner wins the Nobel Prize for literature. Televised sessions of Estes Kefauver's Senate Committee on Crime win a national audience. Althea Gibson is the first African American to compete in the United States women's championship tennis singles.

1951 United States of America

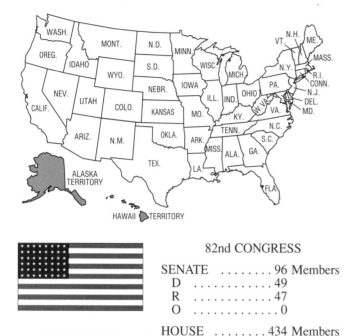

82nd CONGRESS

SENATE .... 96 Members
D 49
R 47
O 0

HOUSE .... 434 Members
D 234
R 199
O 1

ESTIMATED
POPULATION
154,360,000

Harry S Truman
33rd President
11th Democrat

Alben W. Barkley
35th Vice President
Democrat

UNITED STATES ECONOMY

GROSS NATIONAL PRODUCT $329,000,000,000
RETAIL SALES $156,548,000,000
BANK RESOURCES $188,338,000,000
EXPORTS .... $ 14,879,000,000
IMPORTS .... $ 10,817,000,000
FEDERAL GOVERNMENT EXPENDITURE .$ 44,057,831,000
FEDERAL DEBT $255,221,977,000

Events

January 26 • Most prices and wages are frozen by order of the Economic Stablization Agency.

February 1 • The United Nations General Assembly finds Communist China responsible for aggression in Korea.

February 26 • The 22nd Amendment to the United States Constitution is adopted.

March 14 • United Nations forces recapture Seoul, which had fallen again on January 4. Crossing the 38th parallel on March 27, they continue their advance until April 23, when the Communists launch the first of two offensives.

March 29 • Julius and Ethel Rosenberg are convicted of atomic espionage; on April 5, they are sentenced to death. They are executed on June 19, 1953.

April 11 • General MacArthur is relieved of his commands in Korea and Japan due to his differences with the administration. (He is succeeded by General Matthew B. Ridgway.) Addressing Congress on April 19, he attempts to gather support for direct action against Communist China.

June 4 • The Supreme Court upholds the conviction in 1949 of 11 Communist leaders under the Smith Act (*Dennis et al v. United States*).

July 8 • Korean truce negotiations begin at Kaesŏng. Broken off on August 23, they are resumed at Panmunjom on October 25.

September 8 • Forty-eight nations sign a peace treaty with Japan in San Francisco.

October 24 • President Truman proclaims the formal end of the war between the United States and Germany.

International and Cultral Events • Winston Churchill forms a new Conservative government; diplomats Guy Burgess and Donald Maclean are unmasked as Soviet spies. *South Pacific* is a Broadway hit. James Jones's *From Here to Eternity* and Herman Wouk's *The Caine Mutiny* are best sellers.

ARTICLE XXII

Limiting Presidential Tenure to Two Terms

No person shall be elected to the office of the President more than twice, and no person who has held the office of President, or acted as President, for more than two years of a term to which some other person was elected President shall be elected to the office of the President more than once. But this Article shall not apply to any person holding the office of President when this Article was proposed by the Congress, and shall not prevent any person who may be holding the office of President, or acting as President, during the term within which this Article becomes operative from holding the office of President or acting as President during the remainder of such term.

(Adopted in 1951)

United States of America 1952

Events

March 20 • The Senate ratifies the Japanese Peace Treaty and security treaties with Japan, the Philippines, Australia and New Zealand.

March 29 • President Truman states that he will not run for re-election. Senator Estes Kefauver, who announced his candidacy on January 23, is considered a leading contender for the nomination.

April 3 • Newbold Morris, appointed by the president to investigate corruption in the federal government, is removed by Attorney General J. Howard McGrath. Truman obtains McGrath's resignation and names James P. McGranery to succeed him.

April 8 • President Truman orders the seizure of most of the steel mills as their workers are about to strike. After the steel companies, on April 29, obtain an injunction against the seizure, a strike is called, but it is ended on May 2 at the president's request. On June 2, however, the Supreme Court rules that the president lacks the power to seize the mills, and a new strike is called. Workers and management settle their dispute on July 26.

April 9 • President Truman declares the war with Japan over.

May 23 • Almost two years after the U.S. Army assumed control of the railroads in the country, railroad owners regain control of their companies. On August 27, 1950, President Truman had ordered the U.S. Army to operate the railroads in order to avert a threatened strike by railway workers.

June 27 • The Immigration and Nationality Act of 1952 (McCarran-Walter Act) is adopted despite its veto by President Truman, who considers its national origins provisions illiberal.

July 7 • The Republican party convenes in Chicago. It nominates Dwight D. Eisenhower (New York) for president and Richard M. Nixon (California) for vice president.

July 21 • The Democratic party convenes in Chicago. It nominates Adlai E. Stevenson (Illinois) for president and John J. Sparkman (Alabama) for vice president.

July 25 • The Commonwealth of Puerto Rico is established under United States jurisdiction. The United States had acquired the Caribbean island under terms of the Treaty of Paris of 1898.

October 3 • The Soviet Union demands the recall of Ambassador George F. Kennan due to statements that it considers slanderous.

November 1 • The United States explodes the first hydrogen bomb at Eniwetok in the Marshall Islands.

November 4 • In the presidential election, Eisenhower is victorious, receiving 442 electoral votes to 89 for

Harry S Truman
33rd President
11th Democrat

Alben W. Barkley
35th Vice President
Democrat

82nd CONGRESS

SENATE	96 Members
D	49
R	47
O	0
HOUSE	434 Members
D	234
R	199
O	1

ESTIMATED POPULATION 157,028,000

UNITED STATES ECONOMY

GROSS NATIONAL PRODUCT	$347,000,000,000
RETAIL SALES	$162,353,000,000
BANK RESOURCES	$201,795,000,000
EXPORTS	$ 15,049,000,000
IMPORTS	$ 10,747,000,000
FEDERAL GOVERNMENT EXPENDITURE	$ 65,407,585,000
FEDERAL DEBT	$259,105,179,000

Stevenson, his Democratic opponent. The Republicans also gain control of both houses of Congress.

December 2–5 • Eisenhower visits Korea to carry out a campaign pledge to see what can be done to bring peace.

International and Cultural Events • Colonel Gamal Abdel Nasser is a leader of any army coup that overthrows King Karouk of Egypt. Elizabeth II ascends the British throne on the death of George VI. Fulgencio Batista seizes power in Cuba. Cinerama is first projected.

1953 Dwight D. Eisenhower

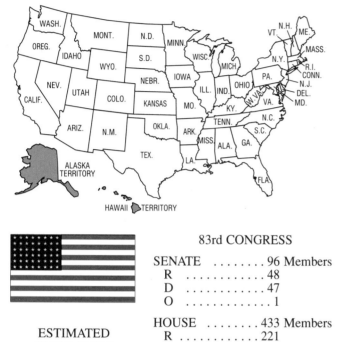

83rd CONGRESS

SENATE .... 96 Members
R 48
D 47
O 1

ESTIMATED POPULATION 159,636,000

HOUSE .... 433 Members
R 221
D 211
O 1

Dwight D. Eisenhower
34th President
13th Republican

Richard M. Nixon
36th Vice President
Republican

UNITED STATES ECONOMY

GROSS NATIONAL PRODUCT	.$365,400,000,000
RETAIL SALES	.$169,094,000,000
BANK RESOURCES	.$207,760,000,000
EXPORTS	.$ 15,652,000,000
IMPORTS	.$ 10,779,000,000
FEDERAL GOVERNMENT EXPENDITURE	.$ 74,274,257,000
FEDERAL DEBT	.$266,071,062,000

Dwight D. Eisenhower

Birth	Denison, TX, Oct. 14, 1890
Parents	David and Ida Stover Eisenhower
Married	Mamie Doud
Home	Gettysburg, PA
Presidency	1953 – 1961
Death	Washington, D.C., Mar. 28, 1969

Events

January 7 • Senator John W. Bricker of Ohio proposes a constitutional amendment that would limit the power of the president to make treaties and agreements. Opposed by the administration, it is defeated in the Senate on February 25, 1954.

January 20 • Eisenhower is inaugurated president.

February 2 • In his State of the Union message, President Eisenhower announces that the Seventh Fleet will no longer be used to shield communist China from attacks from Taiwan.

February 6 • All wage controls are suspended by executive order of the president.

March 17 • The Office of Price Stabilization removes the last price controls.

March 26 • President Eisenhower promises French premier René Mayer that the United States will help France economically in its war in Indo-China. On May 23, the president will inform the Senate Foreign Relations Committee that he has provided France with a $60 million aid grant.

March 30 • A joint resolution of Congress approves the establishment of the Department of Health, Education and Welfare. It is signed by President Eisenhower on April 1. On April 11, Oveta Culp Hobby is named its first secretary.

May 22 • The president signs the Submerged Lands Act, giving coastal states the rights to submerged and reclaimed lands within their historic boundaries.

July 27 • The two sides in the Korean conflict sign an armistice at Panmunjom.

August 7 • President Eisenhower signs the Refugee Relief Act, which allows 214,000 aliens to be admitted to the United States outside the regular quotas.

September 30 • Earl Warren is appointed chief justice of the United States Supreme Court.

October–December • A subcommittee headed by Senator Joseph R. McCarthy begins investigating the U.S. Army Signal Corps at Fort Monmouth, New Jersey.

November 13 • Citing executive prerogative, Truman rejects a congressional subpoena to testify in the investigation of Harry Dexter White.

November 27 • Recognizing that Puerto Rico has been a self-governing commonwealth since July 25, 1952, the United Nations General Assembly decides that the United States no longer needs to report on it.

December 8 • President Eisenhower presents to the United Nations his Atoms for Peace program, the sharing of fissionable materials through an international agency.

International and Cultural Events • Joseph Stalin dies; the Soviet Union explodes a hydrogen bomb. Edmund Hillary and Tenzing Norkey climb Mount Everest. General George C. Marshall is awarded the Nobel Peace Prize.

United States of America 1954

Events

January 1 • The *Nautilus*, the first attack-class nuclear-powered submarine, is commissioned. The submarine was constructed at the Electric Boat yard in Groton, Connecticut, by the Electric Boat Division, General Dynamics Corporation.

January 12 • Secretary of State Dulles advocates a policy of "massive retaliation" to deter aggression.

January 26 • The Senate ratifies a mutual defense treaty with South Korea.

March 1 • Puerto Rican nationalists shoot from the visitors' gallery of the House of Representatives, wounding five congressmen.

March 8 • A Japanese–United States mutual defense agreement is signed in Tokyo.

April 1 • President Eisenhower signs into law a bill establishing the Air Force Academy. The academy will move from its temporary location in Denver, Colorado, to its permanent location near Colorado Springs in 1958.

April 22–June 17 • Senate hearings are held in the dispute between Senator McCarthy and the Department of the Army over his methods in the investigation of alleged subversion at Fort Monmouth. They lead to McCarthy's censure by the Senate on December 2 for conduct unbecoming a senator.

May 13 • The president signs the St. Lawrence Seaway bill, which provides for a United States–Canadian project designed to integrate the St. Lawrence estuary with ports on the Great Lakes.

May 17 • The Supreme Court, in the historic case of *Brown v. Board of Education of Topeka, Kansas*, rules that segregation in education is unconstitutional.

June 1 • The atomic physicist J. Robert Oppenheimer, suspended as a consultant to the Atomic Energy Commission for security reasons in 1953, is denied reinstatement, although his loyalty is affirmed.

August 2 • President Eisenhower signs the Housing Act of 1954, which provides for assistance for urban renewal, 35,000 public housing units and liberalized mortgage requirements. The act is expanded in 1955.

August 24 • The president signs the Communist Control Act, which effectively outlaws the Communist party.

August 28 • The Agricultural Act of 1954, providing for flexible price supports, is signed into law.

August 30 • The president signs the Atomic Energy Act of 1954, which authorizes private nuclear development and the extension of information to friendly countries.

September 8 • A treaty creating the Southeast Asia Treaty Organization is signed in Manila by the United States and seven other countries.

November 2 • Democratic control of Congress is restored

83rd CONGRESS

SENATE .... 96 Members
R 48
D 47
O 1

HOUSE .... 433 Members
R 221
D 211
O 1

ESTIMATED
POPULATION
162,417,000

Dwight D. Eisenhower
34th President
13th Republican

Richard M. Nixon
36th Vice President
Republican

UNITED STATES ECONOMY

GROSS NATIONAL PRODUCT $363,100,000,000
RETAIL SALES $169,135,000,000
BANK RESOURCES $218,896,000,000
EXPORTS .... $ 14,981,000,000
IMPORTS .... $ 10,240,000,000
FEDERAL GOVERNMENT EXPENDITURE .$ 67,772,353,000
FEDERAL DEBT $271,259,599,000

in midterm elections.

December 2 • Nationalist China and the United States sign a mutual defense treaty that excludes Quemoy and other islands just off the mainland.

International and Cultural Events • The pro-Communist Arbenz government is overthrown in Guatemala. After the French defeat at Dienbienphu, an armistice divides Vietnam at 17°N. An antipolio vaccine developed by Dr. Jonas E. Salk is tested.

1955 United States of America

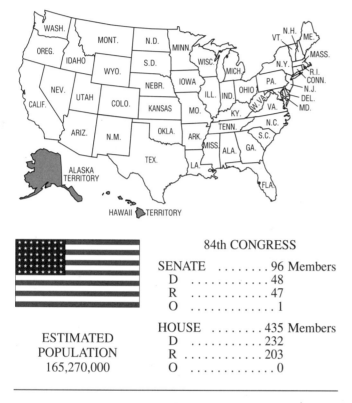

84th CONGRESS

SENATE	....	96 Members
D	....	48
R	....	47
O	....	1

ESTIMATED
POPULATION
165,270,000

HOUSE	....	435 Members
D	....	232
R	....	203
O	....	0

Dwight D. Eisenhower
34th President
13th Republican

Richard M. Nixon
36th Vice President
Republican

UNITED STATES ECONOMY

GROSS NATIONAL PRODUCT	.........$397,500,000,000
RETAIL SALES	.....................$183,851,000,000
BANK RESOURCES	...................$229,626,000,000
EXPORTS	.........................$ 15,419,000,000
IMPORTS	.........................$ 11,337,000,000
FEDERAL GOVERNMENT EXPENDITURE	.$ 64,569,973,000
FEDERAL DEBT	....................$274,374,223,000

Events

January 1 • The U.S. Foreign Operations Administration begins directing money to Cambodia, Laos and South Vietnam. By the end of the year, these three Southeast Asian countries will have received $216 million from the United States.

January 19 • The first televised presidential press conference takes place.

January 28 • At President Eisenhower's request, Congress adopts a resolution empowering him to defend Taiwan and the Pescadores with armed force.

February 1 • The Senate ratifies the Southeast Asia Collective Defense Treaty. The first meeting of the SEATO Council is held in Bangkok on February 23–25.

April 1 • The Senate ratifies agreements concluded in Paris on October 1954 that confer sovereignty on the Federal Republic of Germany (West Germany). On May 9, West Germany joins NATO.

May 10 • Looking toward a summit conference, President Eisenhower states that he is willing to meet with "anyone, anywhere" in the interest of world peace.

May 15 • The foreign ministers of Austria, France, Great Britain, the Soviet Union, and the United States sign the Austrian State Treaty, which reestablishes Austria as a sovereign state with boundaries as of January 1, 1938. The U.S. Senate, by a vote of 63 to three, will approve the treaty on June 17.

May 31 • The Supreme Court relegates school desegregation to the federal district courts and does not stipulate a time limit.

July 11 • President Eisenhower cancels the Dixon-Yates contract for a plant to supply power to Memphis through the TVA, negotiated in 1954 by the Atomic Energy Commission. Opposed by supporters of public power, the proposed plant becomes unnecessary when Memphis decides on a municipal plant.

July 18–23 • The heads of government of France, Great Britain, the Soviet Union and the United States attend a summit conference in Geneva. They discuss various disarmament proposals but reach no agreement. Neither do their four foreign ministers, who meet in Geneva from October 27 to November 16.

August 8–20 • The International Conference on the Peaceful Uses of Atomic Energy convenes in Geneva.

August 12 • The president signs a bill amending the Fair Labor Standards Act to raise the minimum wage to $1 per hour on March 1, 1956.

September 24 • President Eisenhower suffers a heart attack. He remains in a hospital in Denver until November 11.

November 25 • The Interstate Commerce Commission orders all buses and trains that cross state lines to end their segregation practices.

December • Dr. Martin Luther King, Jr., leads a black boycott of the Montgomery, Alabama, bus system.

December 5 • The American Federation of labor and the Congress of Industrial Organizations merge.

International and Cultural Events • Leaders of 29 African and Asian nations meet in Bandung, Indonesia, to discuss mutual problems. The Argentine dictator Juan Perón is deposed by a military coup. Vladimir Nabokov's *Lolita* is published in Paris.

United States of America 1956

Events

February 17 • Objecting to lobbying pressures, President Eisenhower vetoes a bill that would exempt producers of natural gas from federal price regulation.

April 11 • President Eisenhower signs a bill providing for an irrigation and power project on the upper Colorado River.

May 28 • The Agricultural Act of 1956 sets up a soil bank to reduce farm surpluses.

June 9 • Following an attack of ileitis, President Eisenhower undergoes an operation.

July 17 • Egypt accepts a U.S. offer of $56 million to help offset the cost of constructing the Aswan High Dam on the Nile River. Two days later, the United States withdraws its offer, citing Egypt's cozy relationship with the Soviet Union.

July 26 • Egypt, upset at the loss of funding for the Aswan High Dam, nationalizes the Suez Canal Company, precipitating a crisis in the Middle East. On October 29, Israeli forces invade the Sinai Peninsula, and on October 31, Great Britain and France open hostilities to gain control of the canal. The influence of the United States helps produce a cease-fire on November 5, and troop withdrawal.

August 1 • President Eisenhower signs a bill extending and liberalizing Social Security coverage.

August 7 • The president signs a bill authorizing 70,000 public housing units and liberalizing mortgage requirements.

August 13 • The Democratic party convenes in Chicago. It nominates Adlai E. Stevenson (Illinois) for president and Estes Kefauver (Tennessee) for vice president.

August 20 • The Republican party convenes in San Francisco. It nominates President Eisenhower and Vice President Nixon for re-election.

September 14 • The States Rights party nominates T. Coleman Andrews for president. The Socialist and Socialist Labor parties also name candidates.

October 26 • The Statute of the International Atomic Energy Agency is signed in New York by representatives of 70 nations.

November 6 • In the presidential election, President Eisenhower is re-elected, receiving 457 electoral votes to 74 for Stevenson, his Democratic opponent (Stevenson's total is reduced to 73 when an Alabama elector does not cast his ballot for him).

November 8 • A presidential order provides for the admission to the United States of 5,000 refugees after Soviet troops crush a revolt in Hungary. On December 1, the total is increased to 21,500.

November 13 • The Supreme Court rules that an

84th CONGRESS

SENATE .... 96 Members
D 48
R 47
O 1

HOUSE .... 435 Members
D 232
R 203
O 0

ESTIMATED
POPULATION
168,174,000

Dwight D. Eisenhower
34th President
13th Republican

Richard M. Nixon
36th Vice President
Republican

UNITED STATES ECONOMY

GROSS NATIONAL PRODUCT $419,200,000,000
RETAIL SALES $189,729,000,000
BANK RESOURCES $238,128,000,000
EXPORTS ....$ 18,940,000,000
IMPORTS ....$ 12,516,000,000
FEDERAL GOVERNMENT EXPENDITURE .$ 66,539,776,000
FEDERAL DEBT $272,750,814,000

Alabama law and a Montgomery, Alabama, ordinance requiring racial segregation in intrastate buses is invalid.
International and Cultural Events • Nikita S. Khrushchev denounces Stalin's personality cult. Life in the American corporation and the small town are focused on in W.H. Whyte's *The Organization Man* and Grace Metalious's *Peyton Place*. American actress Grace Kelly marries Prince Rainer III of Monaco.

1957 United States of America

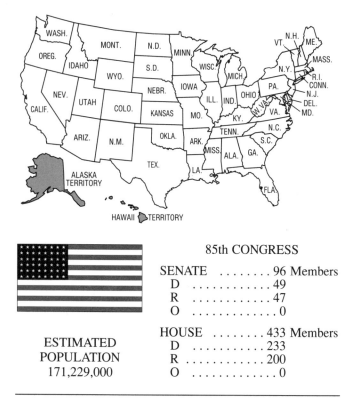

Dwight D. Eisenhower
34th President
13th Republican

Richard M. Nixon
36th Vice President
Republican

85th CONGRESS

SENATE . . . . 96 Members
D 49
R 47
O 0

HOUSE . . . . 433 Members
D 233
R 200
O 0

ESTIMATED
POPULATION
171,229,000

UNITED STATES ECONOMY

GROSS NATIONAL PRODUCT $440,300,000,000
RETAIL SALES $200,002,000,000
BANK RESOURCES $242,629,000,000
EXPORTS . . . .$ 20,630,000,000
IMPORTS . . . .$ 12,921,000,000
FEDERAL GOVERNMENT EXPENDITURE .$ 69,433,078,000
FEDERAL DEBT $270,527,172,000

Events

January 5 • In a message to Congress, the president presents a proposal that comes to be known as the Eisenhower doctrine. It states that the United States will use armed force to aid any nation in the Middle East that requests assistance against communist aggression. Congressional approval is obtained in a joint resolution on March 7.

January 20 • President Eisenhower is inaugurated in private; then, on January 21, in a public ceremony.

February 8 • President Eisenhower and King Saud of Saudi Arabia agree to renew for five years the United States lease of the Dhahran airfield in exchange for United States military aid.

March 21–24 • President Eisenhower and Prime Minister Harold Macmillan renew Anglo-American ties at a conference in Bermuda.

April 25 • The United States orders the Sixth Fleet to the eastern Mediterranean to support King Hussein against an uprising in Jordan.

May 11 • A communiqué issued in Washington after talks between President Eisenhower and Ngo Dinh Diem, president of South Vietnam, emphasizes cooperation against communism.

June 3 • The Supreme Court rules that violations of the antitrust laws have been produced by the control E.I. du Pont de Memours & Co. exercises over the General Motors Corporation through its ownership of 23 percent of the latter's stock.

June 24 • In its first ruling on the subject, the U.S. Supreme Court declares that obscene materials are not protected by the free speech provisions of the First Amendment. The Court decides *Roth v. United States* and *Alberts v. California* by votes of seven-to-one and six-to-three, respectively.

July 12 • President Eisenhower signs the Housing Act of 1957, which is designed to improve housing programs, particularly for the elderly, and to liberalize mortgage requirements.

August 29 • Congress adopts the Civil Rights Act of 1957, which provides penalties for the violation of voting rights and creates the Civil Rights Commission.

September 2–4 • Governor Orval Faubus employs units of the Arkansas National Guard to prevent the integration of Central High School in Little Rock. On September 25, a federalized Arkansas National Guard and United States Army units sent by the president escort nine black students to school.

November 25 • President Eisenhower suffers a mild stroke. Recovering his health, he attends a North Atlantic Council meeting in Paris in December.

December 6 • The AFL-CIO expels the Teamsters Union, which is charged with corruption.

International and Cultural Events • The International Geophysical Year spurs environmental studies by scientists all over the world. The Soviet Union launches *Sputnik 1*, the first artificial earth satellite. The Beat Generation sits for its portrait in Jack Kerouac's novel *On the Road*. Senator John F. Kennedy wins a Pulitzer Prize for his *Profiles in Courage*. A California company introduces to the American public the Frisbee.

United States of America 1958

Events

February 26 • President Eisenhower states that he and Vice President Nixon agree on the steps to be taken if illness incapacitates the president. As disclosed on March 3, the agreement provides that the vice president would be charged with the duties of the president.

April 1 • The president signs the Emergency Housing Act, which is designed to provide jobs by stimulating housing construction and thus help combat the recession currently affecting the national economy.

April 27–May 15 • Vice President Nixon makes a goodwill tour of South America and encounters many hostile demonstrators.

May 9 • A rebellion begins against the pro-Western government of Lebanon. On July 14, President Camille Chamoun requests international assistance, and the next day, United States Marines begin landing at Beirut. The United States forces do not take part in the fighting, and with the restoration of order, they are withdrawn by October 25.

July 29 • The president signs a bill creating the National Aeronautics and Space Administration (NASA).

August 6 • The Defense Reorganization Act of 1958 increases the effectiveness of unified commands.

September 2 • The president signs the National Defense Education Act, which includes provisions for student loans and fellowships and for the stimulation of education in science and foreign languages.

September 22 • Presidential assistant Sherman Adams resigns after accepting compromising gifts.

November 4 • In the midterm elections, the Democrats increase their majorities in Congress.

December 31 • The United States, Great Britain and

Eisenhower returning as a war hero in a ticker tape parade in lower Brooklyn.

85th CONGRESS	
SENATE	96 Members
D	49
R	47
O	0
HOUSE	433 Members
D	233
R	200
O	0

ESTIMATED POPULATION
174,882,000

Dwight D. Eisenhower
34th President
13th Republican

Richard M. Nixon
36th Vice President
Republican

UNITED STATES ECONOMY

GROSS NATIONAL PRODUCT $444,500,000,000
RETAIL SALES $200,353,000,000
BANK RESOURCES $264,505,000,000
EXPORTS . . . .$ 17,945,000,000
IMPORTS . . . .$ 13,215,000,000
FEDERAL GOVERNMENT EXPENDITURE .$ 71,936,171,000
FEDERAL DEBT $276,343,000,000

France reject a Soviet proposal of November 27 that West Berlin be made a free city, believing that it would leave it at the mercy of East Germany.

International and Cultural Events • The Algerian crisis returns De Gaulle to power in France. *Explorer 1*, the first United States satellite, is launched, and the atomically powered *Nautilus* goes under the ice cap to the North Pole. Van Cliburn wins Moscow's Tchaikovsky piano competition.

1959 United States of America

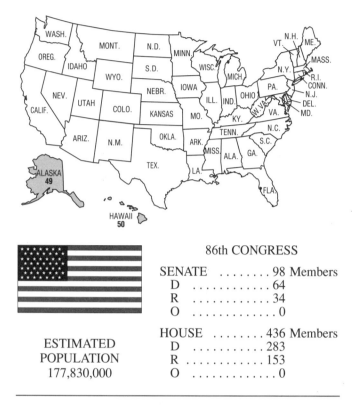

86th CONGRESS

SENATE .... 98 Members
D 64
R 34
O 0

HOUSE .... 436 Members
D 283
R 153
O 0

ESTIMATED
POPULATION
177,830,000

Dwight D. Eisenhower
34th President
13th Republican

Richard M. Nixon
36th Vice President
Republican

UNITED STATES ECONOMY

GROSS NATIONAL PRODUCT $482,700,000,000
RETAIL SALES $215,413,000,000
BANK RESOURCES $272,642,000,000
EXPORTS .... $ 19,212,000,000
IMPORTS .... $ 13,570,000,000
FEDERAL GOVERNMENT EXPENDITURE .$ 80,697,239,000
FEDERAL DEBT $284,706,000,000

Events

January 3 • Alaska is admitted to the Union as the 49th state.

April 15 • John Foster Dulles resigns as secretary of state. On April 18, Christian A. Herter is named to succeed him. Dulles dies on May 24.

June 26 • President Eisenhower and Queen Elizabeth preside at the official opening of the St. Lawrence Seaway (actual use began on April 25).

July 15 • An industrywide steel strike begins. On October 9, the president invokes the Taft-Hartley Act. An eight-day injunction, granted on October 21, is upheld on November 7, and the strikers return to their jobs.

August 21 • Hawaii becomes the 50th state.

August 26–September 7 • President Eisenhower visits Europe to confer with the leaders of West Germany, Great Britain, and France.

September 14 • President Eisenhower signs the Labor-management Reporting and Disclosure Act, which seeks to safeguard the rights of union members vis-à-vis their unions.

September 15–27 • Soviet premier Nikita Khrushchev visits the United States.

September 23 • Having vetoed two housing bills, President Eisenhower signs a third, the Housing Act of 1959, which authorizes $650 million for urban renewal and provides for 37,000 units of public housing.

October 1 • Longshoremen strike on the east and gulf coasts. After the president invokes the Taft-Hartley Act, they return to work on October 9.

December 1 • A treaty barring warlike development in Antarctica is signed in Washington by the representatives of 12 countries.

December 3–22 • President Eisenhower makes a goodwill tour of 11 countries in Asia, North Africa, and Europe.

International and Cultural Events • Fidel Castro comes to power in Cuba. Archbishop Makarios becomes president of an independent Cyprus. Pope John XXIII calls a Vatican Council. Frank Lloyd Wright's Guggenheim Museum is completed. Rigged quiz shows and "payola" scandals shock the nation.

President and Mrs. Eisenhower.

United States of America 1960

Events

January 19 • The United States and Japan sign a mutual defense treaty in Washington. Ratified by the governments of both countries, it goes into effect on June 23. Meanwhile, demonstrations against the United States in Tokyo result in the cancellation of a visit to Japan by President Eisenhower.

February 1 • African Americans begin a series of sit-in demonstrations to desegregate lunch counters and similar facilities in the South.

March 15–June 27 • A 10-nation East-West disarmament conference in Geneva fails to agree.

May 5 • Premier Khrushchev announces that a United States U-2 plane used for photographic reconnaissance was shot down over Soviet territory on May 1. Initially, the United States declares that the purpose of the flight was weather observation, but the announcement on May 7 of the capture of the pilot leads to an acknowledgment that the objective was intelligence. On May 11, Eisenhower acknowledges similar flights during the past four years.

May 6 • President Eisenhower signs the Civil Rights Act of 1960, which provides for the use of federal referees to register black voters.

May 16 • The Big Four heads of government meet in Paris for a summit conference. At the outset, Premier Khrushchev states that he will not participate in the meeting unless he receives a United States apology for the U-2 flight. The conference disbands.

June 12–20 • President Eisenhower visits Alaska, the Philippines, Taiwan, and South Korea.

June 16 • Congress proposes the adoption of the 23rd Amendment to the Constitution, calling for District of Columbia voting rights.

July 6 • President Eisenhower cuts the quota of Cuba's sugar exports to the United States by 95 percent due to Premier Castro's hostile attitude.

July 11 • The Democratic party convenes in Los Angeles. It nominates John F. Kennedy (Massachusetts) for president and Lyndon B. Johnson (Texas) for vice president.

July 27 • The Republican party convenes in Chicago. It nominates Richard M. Nixon (California) for president and Henry Cabot Lodge (Massachusetts) for vice president.

August 10 • The U.S. Senate ratifies a treaty declaring Antarctica to be a "peaceful scientific preserve." Belgium, Japan, Norway, South Africa and the United Kingdom are also signatories of the treaty. The treaty will enter into force on June 23, 1961.

September 13 • President Eisenhower signs a bill providing federal grants for medical aid to the aged.

86th CONGRESS

SENATE .... 98 Members
D 64
R 34
O 0

HOUSE .... 436 Members
D 283
R 153
O 0

ESTIMATED
POPULATION
180,684,000

Dwight D. Eisenhower
34th President
13th Republican

Richard M. Nixon
36th Vice President
Republican

UNITED STATES ECONOMY

GROSS NATIONAL PRODUCT $503,700,000,000
RETAIL SALES $219,529,000,000
BANK RESOURCES $258,359,000,000
EXPORTS ....$ 20,575,000,000
IMPORTS ....$ 14,650,000,000
FEDERAL GOVERNMENT EXPENDITURE .$ 92,268,000,000
FEDERAL DEBT $286,331,000,000

November 8 • In the presidential election, Kennedy is elected, receiving 303 electoral votes to 219 for Nixon. Harry F. Byrd receives 15 electoral votes when the Electoral College casts its ballots on December 19.

International and Cultural Events • The Nazi war criminal Adolf Eichmann is abducted to Israel; he is tried (1961) and executed (1962). Civil war grips the newly independent Belgian Congo. Federico Fellini's *La Dolce Vita* is the film of the year.

1961 John F. Kennedy

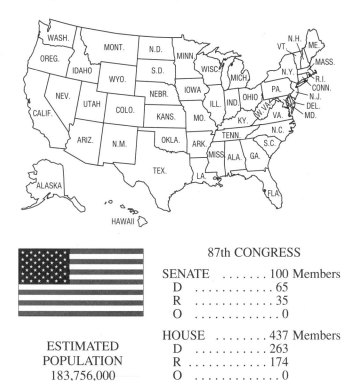

87th CONGRESS

SENATE .... 100 Members
D 65
R 35
O 0

HOUSE .... 437 Members
D 263
R 174
O 0

ESTIMATED
POPULATION
183,756,000

John F. Kennedy
35th President
12th Democrat

Lyndon B. Johnson
37th Vice President
Democrat

UNITED STATES ECONOMY

GROSS NATIONAL PRODUCT $518,200,000,000
RETAIL SALES $218,992,000,000
BANK RESOURCES $295,646,000,000
EXPORTS ....$ 24,002,000,000
IMPORTS ....$ 17,557,000,000
FEDERAL GOVERNMENT EXPENDITURE .$ 82,169,120,000
FEDERAL DEBT $288,971,000,000

John F. Kennedy	
Birth	Brookline, MA, May 29, 1917
Parents	Joseph and Rose Fitzgerald Kennedy
Married	Jacqueline Bouvier
Home	Hyannis, MA
Presidency	1961 – 1963
Death	Dallas, TX, Nov. 22, 1963

Events

January 3 • The United States breaks off diplomatic relations with Cuba.

January 17 • President Eisenhower, addressing the nation in a farewell speech on television, voices his fears of the influence of the military-industrial complex.

January 20 • Kennedy is inaugurated president. In his inaugural address, he calls for a new quest for peace. Although the United States is ready to answer any challenge to liberty, it should not be afraid to negotiate.

January 21 • President Kennedy becomes the first president to appoint a brother to the cabinet when he selects Robert Francis Kennedy to be attorney general.

February 2 • President Kennedy presents to Congress an economic program that includes increases in Social Security benefits and the minimum wage, an extension of unemployment insurance and acceleration of federal procurement and construction programs in order to stimulate the economy.

February 3 • President Kennedy orders the implementation of a $4 million program to aid Cuban refugees in the United States.

March 1 • The Peace Corps is created by executive order of the president. It is given permanent status by an act of Congress signed by the president on September 22.

March 13 • President Kennedy asks the Latin American countries to participate in the Alliance for Progress, a projected 10-year development program.

March 29 • The 23rd Amendment to the Constitution is adopted. It provides for voting by District of Columbia citizens in presidential elections.

April 17 • A small invasion force of Cuban refugees, trained and equipped by the United States Central Intelligence Agency, lands at the Bay of Pigs in the Cuban province of Las Villas. Scheduled air support is canceled, and by April 19, the force is overcome by Cuban government troops. Attempts to ransom the imprisoned survivors for tractors fail in June, but 1,173 prisoners are returned to the United States in 1962 in exchange for $55.5 million worth of food and medicine.

May • Biracial groups known as freedom riders begin to travel through the South to integrate facilities. In Alabama and other states, some groups are attacked by mobs. Other groups are arrested.

May 1 • President Kennedy signs the Area Redevelopment Act, which provides funds for areas affected by substantial unemployment.

May 5 • The United States puts its first man into space. Commander Alan B. Shepard, Jr., makes a suborbital flight in a Mercury capsule. On April 12, the Soviet cosmonaut Major Yuri A. Gagarin had orbited the earth and returned safely.

May 5 • President Kennedy signs a bill raising the minimum wage under the Fair Labor Standards Act to $1.15 in September 1961 and $1.25 in September 1963.

May 25 • President Kennedy states that the United States space program has as its objective the landing of a man on the moon during the decade.

May 31–June 5 • President and Mrs. Kennedy visit Paris, Vienna and London. In Vienna, the President has frank talks with Premier Khrushchev.

June 19 • In *Mapp v. Ohio*, the Supreme Court rules that evidence that has been seized illegally may not be used to prosecute a case in a state court.

June 30 • President Kennedy signs the Housing Act of 1961, which includes provisions for public housing, loans for college housing and housing for the elderly, mortgage assistance, urban renewal and aid to localities to buy land for open space.

June 30 • President Kennedy signs a bill liberalizing the Social Security program and increasing federal grants to the states for assistance programs.

August 15–17 • The Inter-American Social and Economic Conference is held in Punta del Este, Uruguay. With a promise of $1 billion in United States aid for the first year, the delegates draw up and sign the Charter of the Alliance for Progress.

August 20 • The United States increases the size of its garrison in West Berlin as war fears follow the construction by East Germany of the Berlin Wall, designed to cut off the increasing flow of East Germans fleeing to the West.

August 31 • After a three-year period in which the United States, Great Britain and the Soviet Union have observed an informal moratorium on nuclear testing, the Soviet Union announces that it will resume atmospheric testing. The first of several Soviet tests occurs on September 1. The United States begins underground testing on September 15.

September 5 • The United States enacts legislation making the hijacking of an aircraft a federal offense.

October 18–25 • General Maxwell D. Taylor, President Kennedy's military adviser, visits South Vietnam to determine the most effective way to help its government defend itself against attacks by communist Vietcong guerrillas. After he reports to the president, the United States sends additional advisers and training personnel to South Vietnam.

December 16–17 • President and Mrs. Kennedy visit Venezuela and Colombia in the interest of the Alliance for Progress.

December 21–22 • President Kennedy and Prime Minister Macmillan meet in Hamilton, Bermuda. They decide to prepare for atmospheric nuclear testing.

President Kennedy and Soviet premier Nikita S. Khrushchev confer at Vienna in 1961.

International and Cultural Events • A political struggle in the Republic of the Congo results in the imprisonment and eventual murder of Premier Patrice Lumumba. United Nations secretary general Dag Hammarskjöld is killed in an air crash while on a mission to the Congo's Katanga secessionists; he is posthumously awarded the Nobel Peace Prize. Wilt Chamberlain sets the National Basketball Association season record score of 4,029 points.

ARTICLE XXIII

Voting Rights for District of Columbia Citizens

Section 1. The District constituting the seat of Government of the United States shall appoint in such manner as the Congress may direct:

A number of electors of President and Vice President equal to the whole number of Senators and Representatives in Congress to which the District would be entitled if it were a State, but in no event more than the least populous State; they shall be in addition to those appointed by the States, but they shall be considered, for the purposes of the election of President and Vice President, to be electors appointed by a State; and they shall meet in the District and perform such duties as provided by the twelfth article of amendment.

Section 2. The Congress shall have power to enforce this article by appropriate legislation.

(Adopted in 1961)

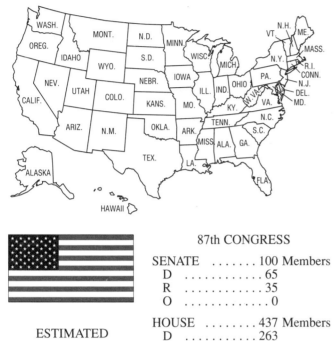

87th CONGRESS

SENATE .... 100 Members
D 65
R 35
O 0

HOUSE .... 437 Members
D 263
R 174
O 0

ESTIMATED
POPULATION
186,656,000

John F. Kennedy
35th President
12th Democrat

Lyndon B. Johnson
37th Vice President
Democrat

UNITED STATES ECONOMY

GROSS NATIONAL PRODUCT $554,900,000,000
RETAIL SALES $235,351,000,000
BANK RESOURCES $320,612,000,000
EXPORTS ....$ 24,002,000,000
IMPORTS ....$ 17,557,000,000
FEDERAL GOVERNMENT EXPENDITURE .$ 88,419,423,000
FEDERAL DEBT $298,201,000,000

Events

February 3 • The president bans all trade with Cuba except for certain medicines and foods, effective February 7.

February 8 • The United States establishes a military assistance command in Saigon.

February 20 • Lieutenant Colonel John H. Glenn, Jr., orbits the earth three times in a Mercury capsule, becoming the first American to achieve orbital flight.

February 21 • The House of Representatives defeats a bill to create a Department of Urban Affairs and Housing, which was proposed by President Kennedy.

March 2 • President Kennedy states that the United States will resume testing nuclear weapons in the atmosphere in April unless the Soviet Union signs a treaty banning all tests of nuclear weapons. Testing is resumed on April 25.

March 26 • In *Baker v. Carr*, the Supreme Court rules that federal courts have the power to order the seats in a state legislature to be reapportioned. The decision overturned a long-held view that such questions were political in nature and outside the competence of the courts.

April 11 • President Kennedy raises strong objections to a rise in steel prices, and by April 14, the raises are rescinded.

May 12 • President Kennedy dispatches naval and ground forces to Laos. He will later defend his action by calling it a "diplomatic solution."

June 25 • In *Engel v. Vitale*, the Supreme Court holds that the reading in New York public schools of a prayer composed by the New York Board of Regents is unconstitutional.

June 28 • President Kennedy signs a bill to admit certain refugees outside quota limits.

July 10 • *Telstar*, a communications satellite relaying television broadcasts between the United States and Europe, is placed in orbit.

July 17 • The Senate defeats a bill for medical care for the aged, which was proposed by President Kennedy.

August 17 • Dr. Frances O. Kelsey is honored for keeping thalidomide, a tranquilizer found to cause birth defects, off the United States market. On October 4, Congress adopts new drug controls.

August 27 • Congress proposes the adoption of the 24th Amendment, prohibiting poll tax requirements in federal elections.

October 11 • President Kennedy signs the Trade Expansion Act, permitting tariff reductions.

October 22 • President Kennedy announces a naval quarantine of Cuba in response to the installation of Soviet missile sites on the island. He calls on the Soviet Union to dismantle the sites and remove the missiles. Premier Khrushchev agrees to do so on October 28, and the quarantine is ended on November 20.

International and Cultural Events • Protestant and Orthodox observers attend Vatican II. Eero Saarinen's TWI Terminal at Idlewild (Kennedy) International Airport is inaugurated. James Meredith becomes the first black to attend the University of Mississippi. Rachel Carson publishes *Silent Spring*.

Kennedy/Johnson 1963

Events

February 28 • President Kennedy asks Congress to enact a program of civil rights legislation. On June 19, he requests antisegregation measures.

March 18 • In *Gideon v. Wainwright*, the Supreme Court rules that indigent defendants in criminal cases have a right to free counsel.

March 19 • The United States and six Latin American countries agree to resist Soviet aggression in the Western Hemisphere.

March–September • Civil rights demonstrations take place in many localities. In Mississippi, Medgar W. Evers is killed on June 12. In Alabama Dr. Martin Luther King, Jr., is arrested (April 12), black properties are bombed, and four black girls are killed when a church is bombed (September 15).

May 15–16 • Major L. Gordon Cooper, Jr., makes a space flight of 22 orbits.

June 10 • The president signs a bill forbidding sex discrimination in payment for equal work.

June 11 • Although having vowed to prevent black enrollment in the University of Alabama, Governor George Wallace relents after a symbolic show of defiance.

June 20 • The United States and the Soviet Union sign an agreement to establish a direct telegraphic link (the "hot line"). The line is put in operation on August 30.

June 23–July 3 • President Kennedy visits Germany, Ireland, England and Italy.

August 5 • Representatives of the United States, Great Britain and the Soviet Union sign a treaty in which the three powers agree to ban nuclear tests under water, in outer space and in the atmosphere. The treaty is ratified by the United States Senate on September 24 and takes effect on October 10.

August 28 • About 200,000 people converge on Washington, D.C., to demonstrate peacefully for civil rights. Dr. Martin Luther King, Jr., speaks to them of his dreams for the future.

November 22 • While visiting Dallas, President Kennedy is assassinated by Lee Harvey Oswald. Vice President Johnson is sworn in as his successor. On November 24, Oswald, then in police custody, is killed by Jack Ruby.

November 25 • A state funeral is held for Kennedy in Washington. On November 27, President Johnson promises to continue Kennedy's policies.

International and Cultural Events • The British government is rocked by a scandal involving John Profumo, secretary of state for war. John XXIII dies, and Paul VI is elected pope. Sir Winston Churchill is made an honorary United States citizen. The motion picture *Cleopatra,* starring Elizabeth Taylor and Richard Burton, opens.

88th CONGRESS

SENATE	....	100 Members
D	....	67
R	....	33
O	....	0
HOUSE	....	435 Members
D	....	258
R	....	177
O	....	0

ESTIMATED POPULATION
189,417,000

John F. Kennedy
35th President
12th Democrat

Lyndon B. Johnson
37th Vice President
Democrat

UNITED STATES ECONOMY

GROSS NATIONAL PRODUCT	.........$590,500,000,000
RETAIL SALES	.....................$235,563,000,000
BANK RESOURCES	.................$363,678,000,000
EXPORTS	.........................$ 24,002,000,000
IMPORTS	.........................$ 17,557,000,000
FEDERAL GOVERNMENT EXPENDITURE	.$ 92,642,000,000
FEDERAL DEBT	....................$305,860,000,000

Lyndon B. Johnson

Birth	.... Near Stonewall, TX, Aug. 27, 1908
Parents	.... Sam and Rebekah Baines Johnson
Married	.... Claudia (Lady Bird) Taylor
Home	.... Stonewall, TX
Presidency	.... 1963 – 1969
Death	.... Stonewall, TX, Jan. 22, 1973

1964 United States of America

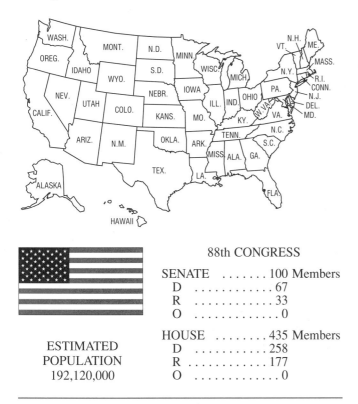

88th CONGRESS

SENATE .... 100 Members
    D 67
    R 33
    O 0

HOUSE .... 435 Members
    D 258
    R 177
    O 0

ESTIMATED
POPULATION
192,120,000

Lyndon B. Johnson
36th President
13th Democrat

Vice President
None

UNITED STATES ECONOMY

GROSS NATIONAL PRODUCT $632,400,000,000
RETAIL SALES $261,870,000,000
BANK RESOURCES $402,673,000,000
EXPORTS ....$ 24,002,000,000
IMPORTS ....$ 17,557,000,000
FEDERAL GOVERNMENT EXPENDITURE .$118,667,000,000
FEDERAL DEBT $311,713,000,000

Events

January 8 • In his State of the Union message, President Johnson asks Congress to enact legislation to abolish racial discrimination and alleviate poverty.

January 9 • American students in the Canal Zone violate an agreement by displaying only the United States flag at their school. Demonstrators from Panama enter the zone, and 25 people are killed when United States soldiers and

Panamanians exchange shots. On January 10, Panama severs diplomatic relations with the United States, but an agreement for the resumption of relations is reached on April 3.

January 11 • Surgeon General Luther L. Terry announces the finding that cigarette smoking causes lung disease. Two days later, the Federal Trade Commission will announce that it is requiring cigarette manufacturers to place labels on their products warning people of the health risks associated with cigarette smoking.

January 23 • The 24th Amendment to the Constitution, outlawing poll taxes as a requirement for voting in federal elections, is adopted.

February 6 • A dispute over the seizure of Cuban fishing boats off Florida leads Cuba to cut off the water supply of the United States naval base at Guantánamo Bay.

February 17 • In *Westberry v. Sanders*, the Supreme Court rules that congressional districts in a state should be nearly equal in population. Chief Justice Earl Warren, writing for the eight-member majority, stated that "an individual's right to vote for state legislators is unconstitutionally impaired when its weight is in substantial fashion diluted when compared with votes of citizens living in other parts of the State."

February 26 • President Johnson signs a bill reducing personal and corporate income taxes.

March 4 • James R. Hoffa, president of the Teamsters Union, is convicted of jury tampering. He is sentenced to serve an eight-year prison term on this count; on August 17, he receives a five-year term upon conviction of defrauding the union's pension fund.

March 16 • President Johnson asks Congress to help wage a war on poverty by creating a Job Corps for unemployed youths and by other measures.

April 11 • President Johnson signs a bill providing new price support programs for growers of cotton and wheat.

May 22 • In a speech delivered at the University of Michigan, President Johnson outlines his Great Society, saying, "For in your time, we have the opportunity to move not only toward the rich society and the powerful society but upward to the Great Society."

June 15 • In *Reynolds v. Sims*, the Supreme Court rules that seats in both houses of bicameral state legislatures must be apportioned so as to represent nearly equal populations.

June 21 • Three young civil rights workers engaged in a voter registration drive in Mississippi disappear. Their buried bodies, marked by bullet wounds, are found by the FBI on August 4. Other violent incidents occur in Mississippi throughout the summer.

July 2 • The president signs the Civil Rights Act of 1964, which protects voting rights, prohibits racial discrimination in employment and in public accommodations and encourages school desegregation.

July 13 • The Republican party convenes in San Francisco. It nominates Barry M. Goldwater (Arizona) for president and William E. Miller (New York) for vice president.

July–August • Rioting occurs in Harlem and in the black sections of Philadelphia and other northern cities.

August 5 • United States Navy planes bomb bases in North Vietnam in retaliation for reported attacks on United States destroyers in international waters in the Gulf of Tonkin on August 2 and August 4. On August 7, Congress adopts a joint resolution approving the bombing and authorizing the president to do what may be required to bar such attacks in the future.

August 20 • The president signs the Economic Opportunity Act, which provides for a Job Corps, a corps of volunteers (VISTA), training programs, loans and assistance to antipoverty projects.

August 24 • The Democratic party convenes in Atlantic City, New Jersey. It nominates President Johnson for re-election and Hubert H. Humphrey (Minnesota) for vice president.

September 3 • President Johnson signs a bill to establish the National Council on the Arts.

September 3 • President Johnson signs the National Wilderness Preservation Act, which inaugurates a system of preserving wilderness with the assignment of more than nine million acres in the national forests.

September 27 • Chief Justice Earl Warren, head of a commission appointed on November 29, 1963, to investigate the assassination of President Kennedy, submits a report to President Johnson. The report concludes that Lee Harvey Oswald alone was responsible for the assassination of President Kennedy. It also concludes that Jack Ruby acted alone in the slaying of Oswald.

October 14 • Dr. Martin Luther King, Jr., is awarded the Nobel Peace Prize.

November 3 • In the presidential election, Johnson is re-elected, receiving 486 electoral votes to 52 for Goldwater, his Republican opponent.

November 28 • *Mariner 4*, an unmanned spacecraft, is launched from Cape Kennedy toward Mars. As it passes the planet in July 1965, it takes 21 photographs, which it transmits to earth.

December 14 • In *Heart of Atlanta Motel v. United States*, the Supreme Court rules that the public accommodations section of the Civil Rights Act of 1964, which forbids racial discrimination in transient hotels, is constitutional.

President Johnson consults with civil-rights leader Martin Luther King in the White House.

December 18 • President Johnson states that it is the intention of the United States to negotiate a new Panama Canal treaty and to build a new sea-level canal, possibly outside Panama.

International and Cultural Events • China explodes an atomic bomb. Khrushchev falls from power in the Soviet Union and is replaced by Aleksei N. Kosygin as Premier and Leonid I. Brezhnev as Communist party chief. The British rock group The Beatles dominates the international popular music field. A World's Fair opens in New York. George Cukor's *My Fair Lady* and Stanley Kubrick's *Dr. Strangelove* are the film hits of the year.

ARTICLE XXIV

Section 1. The right of citizens of the United States to vote in any primary or other election for President or Vice President, for electors for President or Vice President, or for Senator or Representative in Congress, shall not be denied or abridged by the United States or any State by reason of failure to pay any poll tax or other tax.

Section 2. The Congress shall have power to enforce this article by appropriate legislation.

(Adopted in 1964)

1965 United States of America

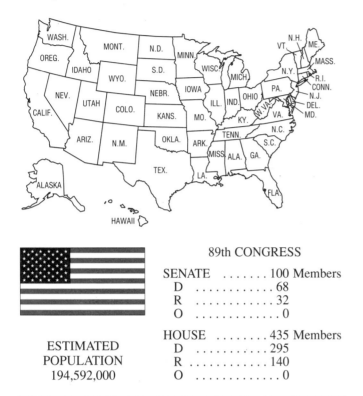

ESTIMATED
POPULATION
194,592,000

89th CONGRESS

SENATE .... 100 Members
D 68
R 32
O 0

HOUSE .... 435 Members
D 295
R 140
O 0

Lyndon B. Johnson
36th President
13th Democrat

Hubert H. Humphrey
38th Vice President
Democrat

UNITED STATES ECONOMY

GROSS NATIONAL PRODUCT	$683,900,000,000
RETAIL SALES	$284,128,000,000
BANK RESOURCES	$378,899,000,000
EXPORTS	$ 27,478,000,000
IMPORTS	$ 21,283,000,000
FEDERAL GOVERNMENT EXPENDITURE	$117,966,000,000
FEDERAL DEBT	$317,274,000,000

Events

January 4 • In his State of the Union message, President Johnson asks Congress to enact legislation to help realize a "Great Society." On January 20, he begins his first full term as president.

February 1 • Dr. Martin Luther King, Jr., and 770 other blacks are arrested in Selma, Alabama, during demonstrations against voter registration rules.

February 7 • After the Vietcong attack the United States airbase at Pleiku in South Vietnam, the United States begins air attacks on North Vietnam.

March 8 • The first combat troops arrive in South Vietnam. The United States already has about 23,000 military advisors in the country.

March 9 • President Johnson signs a bill providing for an antipoverty program in Appalachia.

March 20 • President Johnson federalizes the Alabama National Guard and mobilizes U.S. Army units to protect a freedom march from Selma to Montgomery, which takes place from March 21 to March 25. A participant in the march, Viola Liuzzo of Detroit, is killed on March 25. Trials of the man accused of her murder result, first, in a hung jury and then in an acquittal. On December 3, however, three members of the Ku Klux Klan, including the acquitted man, are convicted of a conspiracy in the murder.

March 23 • The first manned Gemini space flight takes place. Four other successful Gemini flights occur during the year.

April 11 • The president signs the Elementary and Secondary Education Act, providing funds to school districts with needy pupils.

April 28 • The United States sends troops to the Dominican Republic to help control a rebellion.

June 8 • The president commits United States ground forces in South Vietnam.

July 6 • Congress proposes the adoption of the 25th Amendment, setting forth presidential succession policies.

July 30 • President Johnson signs a bill providing medical care for elderly persons (Medicare) through Social Security.

August 6 • President Johnson signs the Voting Rights Act of 1965, ensuring black voting rights.

August 10 • The president signs a bill continuing federal housing programs for four years.

August 11–15 • Blacks riot in the Watts section of Los Angeles. Thirty-four people die.

September 9 • The president signs a bill creating the Department of Housing and Urban Development.

September 21 • The Water Quality Act addresses the quality of water as well as the quantity of water available to Americans.

October 3 • President Johnson signs a bill amending the Immigration and Nationality Act to eliminate the national origins quota system.

November 8 • The president signs the Higher Education Act of 1965, providing scholarship aid.

International and Cultural Events • Paul VI visits New York. Black leader Malcom X is killed. In November, a massive electric power failure leaves most of the northeastern United States and two Canadian provinces in the dark. The "mini-skirt" is introduced.

United States of America 1966

Events

January 12 • In his State of the Union message, President Johnson says that the United States will remain in Vietnam as long as aggression continues.

February 6–8 • President Johnson and Premier Nguyen Cao Ky of South Vietnam confer in Honolulu. They issue the Declaration of Honolulu, which states that their goals for South Vietnam are economic and social reform and a continued struggle against aggression.

March 3 • President Johnson signs the Veterans Readjustment Benefits Act of 1966, which provides educational and other aid for post-Korean War veterans.

March 16 • *Gemini 8* makes the first of the five manned United States space flights of 1966, temporarily docking with the *Agena-D* target.

May 1 • United States troops in South Vietnam begin firing into neighboring Cambodia.

May 30 • *Surveyor I* becomes the first U.S. spacecraft to make a soft landing on the moon. *Surveyor 1* will transmit 11,348 pictures back to earth.

June 13 • In *Miranda v. Arizona*, the Supreme Court rules that accused persons must be informed of their rights.

October 15 • President Johnson signs a bill creating the Department of Transportation.

October 17–November 2 • President Johnson visits Hawaii, American Samoa, New Zealand, Australia, the Philippines, South Vietnam, Thailand, Malaysia and South Korea. In Manila, he attends a conference of the countries allied in fighting in Vietnam.

November 3 • Birth of *Taylor's Encyclopedia of Government Officials, Federal and State*.

November 3 • The president signs a bill expanding the Elementary and Secondary Education Act of 1965 and authorizing new funds for two years.

November 3 • The president signs the Fair Packaging and Labeling Act.

November 3 • The Demonstration Cities and Metropolitan Development Act is signed into law.

November 3 • President Johnson signs the Clean Waters Restoration Act.

November 8 • In the midterm elections, the Republicans increase their congressional representation by three seats in the Senate and 47 seats in the House of Representatives.

November 11 • The president signs the Food for Peace Act of 1966, which expands and revises the Food for Peace program established in 1954.

December • United States forces in Vietnam total 380,000 by late December, as compared with approximately 180,000 at the beginning of 1966. Antiwar sentiment mounts in the United States.

International and Cultural Events • Indira Gandhi becomes prime minister of India. Kwame Nkrumah's pro-Communist government in Ghana is overthrown. Edward Brooke, Massachusetts Republican, is the first black senator since the Reconstruction era. Race riots and anti-war demonstrations rock many cities in the United States.

89th CONGRESS

SENATE	....	100 Members
D	....	68
R	....	32
O	....	0
HOUSE	....	435 Members
D	....	295
R	....	140
O	....	0

ESTIMATED POPULATION 196,920,000

Lyndon B. Johnson
36th President
13th Democrat

Hubert H. Humphrey
38th Vice President
Democrat

UNITED STATES ECONOMY

GROSS NATIONAL PRODUCT	.........$743,300,000,000
RETAIL SALES	......................$303,956,000,000
BANK RESOURCES	..................$406,515,000,000
EXPORTS	.........................$ 30,320,000,000
IMPORTS	..........................$ 25,360,000,000
FEDERAL GOVERNMENT EXPENDITURE	.$134,572,000,000
FEDERAL DEBT	.....................$319,907,000,000

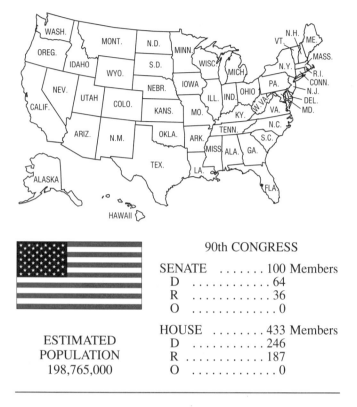

90th CONGRESS

SENATE .... 100 Members
D 64
R 36
O 0

HOUSE .... 433 Members
D 246
R 187
O 0

ESTIMATED POPULATION
198,765,000

Lyndon B. Johnson
36th President
13th Democrat

Hubert H. Humphrey
38th Vice President
Democrat

UNITED STATES ECONOMY

GROSS NATIONAL PRODUCT $785,000,000,000
RETAIL SALES $313,809,000,000
BANK RESOURCES $754,602,000,000
EXPORTS ....$ 31,534,000,000
IMPORTS ....$ 26,732,000,000
FEDERAL GOVERNMENT EXPENDITURE .$158,414,000,000
FEDERAL DEBT $326,221,000,000

Events

January 6 • In his State of the Union message, President Johnson asks Congress to levy a six percent surcharge on personal and corporate income taxes to help finance the Vietnam war and domestic reform programs.

January 27 • Three astronauts are killed when a fire breaks out on an Apollo spacecraft being tested on the launch pad at Cape Kennedy.

January 27 • An international treaty on the exploration and uses of outer space is opened for signature in Washington, London and Moscow. It prohibits the orbiting of weapons of mass destruction or their installation on celestial bodies. The treaty is ratified by the United States on April 25.

February 10 • The 25th Amendment to the Constitution is adopted. It provides for filling a vacancy in the office of vice president and for steps to be taken in the event of the inability of the president to fulfill his responsibilities.

April 12–14 • President Johnson meets with other heads of state of the Organization of American States at Punta del Este, Uruguay. With the exception of the president of Ecuador, the leaders sign a declaration to complete the formation of a Latin American common market by 1985.

May 15 • Multilateral trade negotiations, initiated under the aegis of the General Agreement on Tariffs and Trade (GATT) in 1964, are completed. Some 50 countries have engaged in this so-called Kennedy Round, which results in substantial tariff cuts.

May 15 • In *In re Gault*, the Supreme Court rules that courts must grant the same procedural safeguards in juvenile delinquency trials as in adult trials.

May 29 • In *Reitman v. Mulkey*, the Supreme Court invalidates an amendment of the California constitution that permits racial discrimination in private housing.

June 12 • In *Loving v. Virginia*, the Supreme Court rules unanimously that states cannot constitutionally bar marriages between whites and nonwhites.

June 13 • President Johnson appoints Solicitor General Thurgood Marshall, the great-grandson of slaves, to succeed Justice Tom Clark on the Supreme Court. Marshall is sworn in on October 2.

June 23 and 25 • President Johnson and Premier Aleksei N. Kosygin of the Soviet Union confer on world problems at Glassboro, New Jersey. The two leaders agree that they will let no crisis escalate into a war.

June 29 • President Johnson signs the Education Professions Development Act, which continues the Teacher Corps and authorizes an education training program.

July 12–17 • Charges of police brutality lead to widespread rioting in the black ghetto of Newark, New Jersey, in which 26 die. From July 23 to July 30, similar charges cause riots in Detroit; 43 people are killed, and order is restored only with the aid of United States troops.

July 16 • Members of the International Association of Machinists inaugurate a strike against the country's railroads. The strike, involving 600,000 railroad employees, affects approximately 95 percent of the railroad track in the country. Congress, at the urging of President Johnson, will pass an act ordering the strikers back to work and requiring the president to establish a board to settle the dispute.

July 23 • More than three-fifths of the Puerto Ricans voting in a plebiscite favor the continued association of Puerto Rico with the United States as a commonwealth.

July 27 • President Johnson appoints the Advisory Commission on Civil Disorders, headed by Governor Otto Kerner of Illinois.

August 24 • The United States and the Soviet Union submit identical treaties on the nonproliferation of nuclear weapons to the United Nations Disarmament Committee in Geneva.

October 19 • The space probe *Mariner 5*, launched on June 14, transmits data to the earth as it passes behind Venus.

October 20 • Seven men are convicted by a federal jury of conspiracy in the murder of three civil rights workers in Mississippi in 1964.

October 21–22 • Antiwar demonstrators assemble in Washington. Some of them have a violent encounter with marshals and soldiers at the Pentagon.

October 28 • The United States restores the El Chamizal area, near El Paso, to Mexico.

November 7 • Two blacks are elected mayors of major cities: Carl Stokes in Cleveland and Richard Hatcher in Gary, Indiana.

November 7 • President Johnson signs the Public Broadcasting Act of 1967, which establishes the Corporation for Public Broadcasting to allocate funds for cultural and educational broadcasts.

December 15 • Congress amends the Social Security Act to increase cash benefits, raise the amount of taxable earnings, and liberalize Medicare.

December 21–24 • President Johnson visits Australia, South Vietnam, Thailand, Pakistan and Italy.

December • United States troop strength in South Vietnam totals 486,000 by late December.

International and Cultural Events • The United Arab Republic requests the withdrawal of the United Nations troops from its common border with Israel, and on May 22, the UAR closes the Strait of Tiran to Israeli shipping. A preemptive attack by Israel on June 5 begins the Six-Day War, which ends in the decisive defeat of the UAR, Jordan and Syria. China explodes a hydrogen bomb. On a visit to Canada, President Charles de Gaulle of France calls for a "free Quebec." The revolutionary leader Che Guevara is killed in Bolivia. Dr. Christian N. Barnard performs the first successful heart transplant in Cape Town, South Africa. Svetlana Stalina, the former Soviet dictator's daughter, seeks refuge in the United States. Meeting in Geneva, Switzerland, 53 countries agree to reduce tariffs rates by 35 percent on industrial products and 50 percent on chemical products.

ARTICLE XXV

Section 1. In case of the removal of the President from office or of his death or resignation, the Vice President shall become President.

Section 2. Whenever there is a vacancy in the office of the Vice President, the President shall nominate a Vice President who shall take office upon confirmation by a majority vote of both houses of Congress.

Section 3. Whenever the President transmits to the President pro tempore of the Senate and the Speaker of the House of Representatives his written declaration that he is unable to discharge the powers and duties of his office, and until he transmits a written declaration to the contrary, such powers and duties shall be discharged by the Vice President as Acting President.

Section 4. Whenever the Vice President and a majority of the principal officers of the executive departments, or such other body as Congress may by law provide, transmit to the President pro tempore of the Senate and the Speaker of the House of Representatives their written declaration that the President is unable to discharge the powers and duties of his office, the Vice President shall immediately assume the powers and duties of the office as Acting President.

Thereafter, when the President transmits to the President pro tempore of the Senate and the Speaker of the House of Representatives his written declaration that no inability exists, he shall resume the powers and duties of his office unless the Vice President and a majority of the principal officers of the executive departments, or such other body as Congress may by law provide, transmit within four days to the President pro tempore of the Senate and the Speaker of the House of Representatives their written declaration that the President is unable to discharge the powers and duties of his office. Thereupon Congress shall decide the issue, assembling within forty-eight hours for that purpose if not in session. If the Congress, within twenty-one days after the receipt of the latter written declaration or, if Congress is not in session, within twenty-one days after Congress is required to assemble, determines by two-thirds vote of both houses that the President is unable to discharge the powers and duties of the office, the Vice President shall continue to discharge the same as Acting President; otherwise, the President shall resume the powers and duties of his office.

(Adopted in 1967)

1968 United States of America

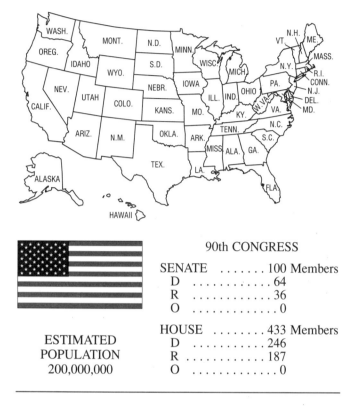

90th CONGRESS

SENATE .... 100 Members
D 64
R 36
O 0

HOUSE .... 433 Members
D 246
R 187
O 0

ESTIMATED
POPULATION
200,000,000

Lyndon B. Johnson
36th President
13th Democrat

Hubert H. Humphrey
38th Vice President
Democrat

UNITED STATES ECONOMY

GROSS NATIONAL PRODUCT $840,000,000,000
RETAIL SALES $339,324,000,000
BANK RESOURCES $542,500,000,000
EXPORTS ....$ 34,636,000,000
IMPORTS ....$ 33,226,000,000
FEDERAL GOVERNMENT EXPENDITURE .$172,400,000,000
FEDERAL DEBT $369,800,000,000

Events

January 21–April 5 • Communist forces in Vietnam mount a costly siege of United States positions at Khesanh.

January 22 • Carrying four hydrogen bombs, a U.S. B-52 crashes and explodes in North Star Bay off the coast of Newfoundland. Radioactive material is dispersed over the area.

January 23 • The *Pueblo*, an intelligence ship of the United States Navy, is captured by patrol boats off North Korea. Charging that the ship had penetrated its territorial waters, the North Korean government refuses to free the ship and its crew. The crew is freed on December 23 after the United States signs, and immediately repudiates, an admission that the ship had entered North Korean waters.

January 30 • As a truce is about to begin for Tet, the lunar New Year, the Communists attack cities in all parts of South Vietnam. Hué is occupied until February 24. The offensive is beaten back by the end of February, but the confidence of the South Vietnamese is badly shaken.

February 1 • Former vice president Richard M. Nixon formally declares himself a Republican presidential candidate. On April 30, Governor Nelson A. Rockefeller of New York also declares himself a candidate for the Republican nomination.

February 29 • The National Advisory Commission on Civil Disorders (Kerner Commission) issues a report in which it attributes black unrest to white racism and recommends measures to aid African Americans.

March 12 • In the Democratic presidential primary election in New Hampshire, Senator Eugene McCarthy, who opposes the Vietnam war, wins 42 percent of the vote (President Johnson receives 48 percent).

March 16 • Senator Robert F. Kennedy announces that he is a candidate for the Democratic presidential nomination. Vice President Humphrey announces his candidacy on April 27.

March 31 • As a step toward peace negotiations, President Johnson orders that the bombing of North Vietnam north of the 21st parallel be halted. He also states that he is not a candidate for re-election.

April 4 • Dr. Martin Luther King, Jr., is assassinated in Memphis, Tennessee. His death is followed by racial violence in 125 cities throughout the nation. Forty-six lives are lost, and widespread property damage occurs. The disorders end on April 11.

April 8 • The Bureau of Narcotics and Dangerous Drugs is established. It is the consolidation of the Federal Bureau of Narcotics and the Bureau of Drug Abuse Control. In 1973, it will be consolidated with all federal anti-drug forces into a new organization, the Drug Enforcement Administration (DEA).

April 11 • President Johnson signs the Civil Rights Act of 1968. Under its provisions, racial discrimination is forbidden in selling or renting about four-fifths of the housing in the United States.

May 3 • The United States and North Vietnam agree to hold talks in Paris to prepare for peace negotiations. The talks open on May 10 with W. Averell Harriman leading the United States delegation and Xuan Thuy the North

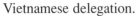

Vietnamese delegation.

May 27 • A unanimous U.S. Supreme Court, in *Green v. County School Board of New Kent, County, Virginia,* rules that freedom-of-choice plans do not foster desegregation. The school board had adopted such a rule, allowing students to choose which school they wanted to attend, in order to maintain its racially segregated schools.

June 5 • Shortly after Senator Robert F. Kennedy learns of his victory in the California Democratic presidential primary election, he is shot in Los Angeles. He dies on June 6, and the next day, Sirhan B. Sirhan, an immigrant from Jordan, is indicted for his murder.

June 8 • James Earl Ray, charged with murdering Dr. King, is arrested in London.

June 14 • Dr. Benjamin M. Spock and three others are convicted in a federal court in Boston of conspiring to abet draft evasion. Spock's conviction is reversed in 1969.

June 26 • President Johnson appoints Justice Abe Fortas to replace Chief Justice Earl Warren, who has submitted his resignation to become effective when the Senate confirms his successor. Fortas is not confirmed, and on December 4, Warren says that he will continue to serve until June 1969.

July 1 • Great Britain, the Soviet Union, the United States and 59 other nations sign a treaty for the nonproliferation of nuclear weapons. The treaty is ratified by the Senate on March 13, 1969.

July 6 • President Johnson meets in San Salvador with the presidents of the five member nations of the Central American Common Market and offers new loans for regional development.

August 1 • The president signs a bill for the construction of 1.7 million housing units within three years.

August 5 • The Republican party convenes in Miami Beach, Florida. It nominates Richard M. Nixon (New York) for president and Spiro T. Agnew (Maryland) for vice president.

August 26 • The Democratic party convenes in Chicago. It nominates Vice President Humphrey for president and Senator Edmund S. Muskie (Maine) for vice president. On the night of August 28–29, violent clashes between antiwar demonstrators and the Chicago police occur.

September 17 • The American Independent party convenes in Dallas. It nominates George C. Wallace (Alabama) for president. On October 3, Wallace chooses Curtis LeMay as his running mate.

October 11–22 • *Apollo 7*, with three United States astronauts abroad, orbits the earth 163 times.

October 31 • President Johnson announces that the United States will cease all bombing of North Vietnam on November 1, thus ending a stalemate in the Paris peace talks. Agreement is reached for the inclusion of the National Liberation Front and the government of South

Vietnam. South Vietnam, which has been reluctant to join the talks, agrees to do so on November 26.

November 5 • In the presidential election, Nixon is elected president, receiving 302 electoral votes to 191 for Humphrey and 45 for Wallace; the popular-vote margin between Nixon and Humphrey is about 250,000. Both houses of Congress remain under Democratic control.

November 5 • New York Democrat Shirley Chisholm becomes the first black congresswoman.

December 21–27 • Colonel Frank Borman, Captain James Lovell, Jr., and Major William Anders travel in *Apollo 8* to the moon, which they orbit 10 times, and return safely to the earth.

International and Cultural Events • Troops from the Soviet Union and four of its allies in the Warsaw Pact (Bulgaria, East Germany, Hungary and Poland) invade Czechoslovakia in order to reverse its trend toward liberalization. Student unrest in May leads to a national strike that completely paralyzes France. The unrest quickly spreads to the university cities of Italy. In Nigeria, the government's blockade of the secessionist state of Biafra (1967) brings starvation to millions. In New York, students ally themselves with black militants and stage a sit-in at Columbia University.

Senator Robert F. Kennedy, assassinated in June 1968.

1969 Richard M. Nixon

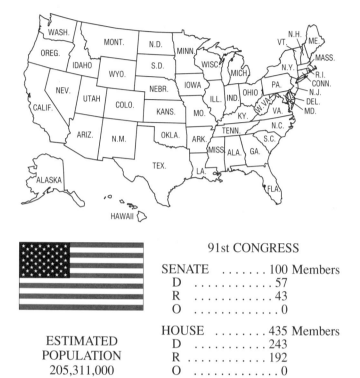

91st CONGRESS

SENATE .... 100 Members
D 57
R 43
O 0

HOUSE .... 435 Members
D 243
R 192
O 0

**ESTIMATED
POPULATION
205,311,000**

Richard M. Nixon
37th President
14th Republican

Spiro T. Agnew
39th Vice President
Republican

UNITED STATES ECONOMY

GROSS NATIONAL PRODUCT $932,000,000,000
RETAIL SALES $351,000,000,000
BANK RESOURCES $504,000,000,000
EXPORTS ....$ 55,000,000,000
IMPORTS ....$ 53,000,000,000
FEDERAL GOVERNMENT EXPENDITURE .$192,000,000,000
FEDERAL DEBT $367,000,000,000

Richard M. Nixon	
Birth	Yorba Linda, CA, Jan. 9, 1913
Parents	Francis and Hannah Milhous Nixon
Married	Patricia Ryan
Home	San Clemente, CA
Presidency	1969 – 1974
Death	New York, NY, Apr. 27, 1994

Events

January 20 • Nixon is inaugurated president.

February 23–March 2 • President Nixon visits Belgium, Great Britain, West Germany, Italy and France. He pledges continued United States support of NATO.

March 3–13 • *Apollo 9*, with three astronauts aboard, orbits the earth. On March 7, it links up with a lunar module.

March 10 • James Earl Ray is sentenced to prison after pleading guilty to Dr. King's murder. On April 17, Sirhan B. Sirhan is convicted of murdering Senator Robert F. Kennedy.

May 11–July 6 • To obtain information for the president, Governor Rockefeller makes four trips to Latin America that are accompanied by anti-American protests. He states that the protests show the need for a change in United States policy.

May 15 • Justice Fortas resigns from the Supreme Court in a conflict-of-interest scandal.

May 21 • President Nixon appoints Warren E. Burger chief justice of the United States Supreme Court.

June 8 • President Nixon announces the coming withdrawal of 25,000 American soldiers from South Vietnam. Further withdrawals of 85,000 troops are announced by October 15.

July 16–24 • The *Apollo 11* lunar mission is completed. On July 20, Neil A. Armstrong and Colonel Edwin E. Aldrin, Jr., become the first two men to step on the moon. A second moon mission is carried out by *Apollo 12* from November 14 to November 24.

July 26–August 3 • President Nixon visits eight countries on a round-the-world trip.

October 15 • The first moratorium day is observed by antiwar demonstrators throughout the nation.

October 29 • In *Alexander v. Holmes County Board of Education*, the Supreme Court rules that delay in discontinuing school segregation can no longer continue.

November 15 • Approximately 250,000 people protest the Vietnam conflict in Washington, D.C.

November 21 • The Senate refuses to confirm the appointment of Clement F. Haynsworth, Jr., to the Supreme Court.

November 25 • The president states that the United States will never use biological weapons and that its stocks of these weapons are being destroyed.

December 1 • The first lottery since World War II is held.

International and cultural Events • Mary Jo Kopechne dies when a car driven by Senator Edward M. Kennedy (Massachusetts) plunges off a bridge at Chappaquiddick Island, Massachusetts. One-half million young people attend a rock festival in Woodstock, New York.

United States of America 1970

Events

January 14 • The Supreme Court issues an order for the integration of all schools in Alabama, Florida, Georgia, Louisiana, Mississippi and Texas by February 1. Although many districts do not comply by this date, substantial progress is made by August 31.

February 25 • In *Hadley v. Junior College District*, the Supreme Court extends the "one-man, one-vote" rule to all elections of governmental officials.

March 17 • Fourteen officers are charged by the U.S. Army with concealing information about an alleged massacre of South Vietnamese civilians by American soldiers at Mylai in March 1968.

April 8 • The Senate refuses to confirm the president's nomination of G. Harrold Carswell to the Supreme Court.

April 11–17 • *Apollo 13*, with three astronauts aboard, rounds the moon and returns safely to earth after an explosion causes a severe loss of power.

April 16 • Strategic arms limitation (SALT) talks between the United States and the Soviet Union open in Vienna. Adjourning on August 14, they reopen in Helsinki (November 2–December 18).

April 22 • As national concern for the environment mounts, Earth Day is observed by millions.

April 30 • The announcement by President Nixon that United States troops are invading Cambodia, where North Vietnamese forces take sanctuary, arouses protests throughout the country. On May 4, Ohio National Guard members fire on Kent State University demonstrators, killing four students.

May 12 • The appointment of Harry A. Blackmun to the Supreme Court is confirmed by the Senate.

June 22 • President Nixon signs a bill extending the franchise to people 18 years of age. On December 21, the Supreme Court upholds its constitutionality insofar as federal elections are concerned.

June 29 • All American ground forces are reported to have been withdrawn from Cambodia.

August 12 • The president signs a bill that replaces the Post Office Department with the United States Postal Service.

September 27–October 5 • The president visits Italy, Yugoslavia, Spain, Great Britain and Ireland.

October 7 • President Nixon proposes a five-point plan for peace in Vietnam. On October 14, it is rejected by the Communist peace delegation.

October 15 • President Nixon signs the Organized Crime Control Act of 1970.

November 3 • The midterm elections leave Congress under Democratic control.

December 21 • In *Oregon v. Mitchell*, the U.S. Supreme

91st CONGRESS

SENATE . . . . 100 Members
D 57
R 43
O 0

HOUSE . . . . 435 Members
D 243
R 192
O 0

ESTIMATED
POPULATION
203,235,298

Richard M. Nixon
37th President
14th Republican

Spiro T. Agnew
39th Vice President
Republican

UNITED STATES ECONOMY

GROSS NATIONAL PRODUCT $977,100,000,000
RETAIL SALES $375,527,000,000
BANK RESOURCES $552,230,000,000
EXPORTS . . . .$ 41,963,000,000
IMPORTS . . . .$ 39,799,000,000
FEDERAL GOVERNMENT EXPENDITURE .$197,200,000,000
FEDERAL DEBT $382,603,000,000

Court rules that Congress does not have the power to lower the voting age in state elections.

International and Cultural Events • Aleksandr I. Solzhenitsyn is awarded the Nobel Prize for literature. An eight-day strike is staged by 6,000 New York postmen. Many of the major grape growers sign with the United Farm Workers after a five-year strike.

1971 United States of America

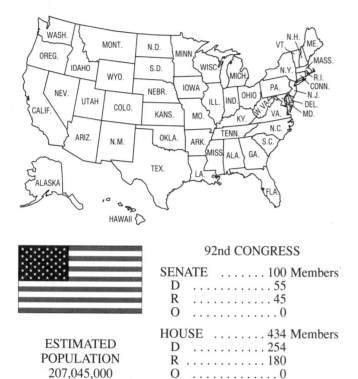

92nd CONGRESS

SENATE . . . . 100 Members
D 55
R 45
O 0

ESTIMATED
POPULATION
207,045,000

HOUSE . . . . 434 Members
D 254
R 180
O 0

Richard M. Nixon
37th President
14th Republican

Spiro T. Agnew
39th Vice President
Republican

UNITED STATES ECONOMY

GROSS NATIONAL PRODUCT . . . .$ 1,055,500,000,000
RETAIL SALES . . . .$ 408,850,000,000
EXPORTS . . . .$ 43,548,600,000
IMPORTS . . . .$ 45,562,700,000
FEDERAL GOVERNMENT
    EXPENDITURE . . . .$ 212,400,000,000
FEDERAL DEBT . . . .$ 409,468,000,000

Events

January 31–February 9 • The *Apollo 14* mission, which includes a 33-hour stay on the moon, is successfully completed. A similar mission is carried out by *Apollo 15* (July 25 to August 7).

February 11 • A treaty banning nuclear weapons from the seabed is signed in London, Moscow and Washington by 63 nations.

March 23 • Congress proposes the adoption of the 26th Amendment to the Constitution, granting 18-year-old citizens the right to vote in all elections. The adoption of the amendment, which is ratified by 38 states, is certified on July 5.

March 31 • Lieutenant William L. Calley, Jr., receives a sentence of life imprisonment for the murder of civilians in Mylai (the sentence is reduced to 20 years on August 20).

April 20 • In *Swann v. Charlotte-Mecklenburg County Board of Education*, the Supreme Court rules that busing may be used to achieve integrated education.

May 1 • Amtrak begins service.

June 13 • The *New York Times* begins publishing the Pentagon Papers, excerpts from a classified study of the Vietnam war. A government effort to halt publication by court order is overruled by the Supreme Court on June 30.

June 17 • A United States–Japanese treaty provides for the return of Okinawa to Japan in 1972.

July 15 • The president accepts an invitation to visit Communist China in 1972. On October 12, he announces that he will visit Moscow in May 1972.

August 15 • In an effort to check inflation and aid the economy, the president freezes wages and prices for 90 days. At the end of this period, on November 14, phase two of the control program begins.

November 13 • The space probe *Mariner 9*, launched on May 30, goes into orbit around Mars.

December 6 • The Senate approves the nomination of Lewis F. Powell, Jr., to the Supreme Court.

December 10 • The Senate approves the nomination of William H. Rehnquist to the Supreme Court.

December 17–18 • At a 10-nation monetary conference held in Washington, agreement is reached on the devaluation of the dollar by 8.57 percent.

International and Cultural Events • India invades Pakistan to defend Bangladesh. Communist China joins the United Nations. State troopers quash a four-day riot by inmates of the Attica State Correctional Facility, New York; 37 people are killed.

ARTICLE XXVI

Section 1. The right of citizens of the United States, who are eighteen years of age or older, to vote shall not be denied or abridged by the United States or by any State on account of age.

Section 2. The Congress shall have power to enforce this article by appropriate legislation.

(Adopted in 1971)

United States of America 1972

Events

February 28 • President Nixon makes a state visit to the People's Republic of China, inaugurating a new stage in American-Sino relations.

March 3–April 27 • The Senate Judiciary Committee holds hearings on the allegation that an antitrust suit against the International Telephone and Telegraph Corporation was settled in return for an offer to help pay for the Republican convention.

March 22 • Congress proposes a constitutional amendment on equal rights for women.

April 10 • Seventy nations sign a treaty prohibiting the stockpiling of biological weapons.

April 16–27 • The *Apollo 16* mission explores the lunar mountains. *Apollo 17* is the last mission of the series (December 7–19).

May 9 • The United States mines the harbor of Haiphong and other ports in North Vietnam.

May 15 • George C. Wallace, a candidate for the Democratic presidential nomination, is shot in an assassination attempt in Laurel, Maryland. The wound leaves him partially paralyzed.

May 22–29 • President Nixon makes a state visit to the Soviet Union, during which he signs agreements for space exploration and for the limitation of offensive and defensive weapons.

June 4 • The Environmental Protection Agency (EPA) bans the pesticide DDT, effective December 31.

June 8 • Congress adopts a higher education bill to which antibusing amendments have been added.

June 17 • Five men carrying cameras and surveillance equipment are arrested at the Democratic National Committee offices in the Watergate complex in Washington, D.C. With two men formerly employed at the White House, they are indicted on September 15.

June 29 • In *Furman v. Georgia*, the Supreme Court rules that the arbitrary manner in which the death penalty is imposed is cruel and unusual punishment, forbidden under the Eighth Amendment.

July 10 • The Democratic party convenes in Miami Beach, Florida. It nominates George McGovern (South Dakota) for president and Thomas F. Eagleton (Missouri) for vice president. Eagleton withdraws on August 1, following the disclosure that he has been treated for depression, and R. Sargent Shriver is chosen in his stead on August 8.

August 21 • The Republican party convenes in Miami Beach, Florida. It nominates President Nixon and Vice President Agnew for re-election.

October 20 • President Nixon signs a bill providing for the sharing of $30.2 billion in federal revenues over a

Richard M. Nixon
37th President
14th Republican

Spiro T. Agnew
39th Vice President
Republican

UNITED STATES ECONOMY

GROSS NATIONAL PRODUCT $1,155,200,000,000
RETAIL SALES .... $ 448,379,000,000
EXPORTS .... $ 49,218,600,000
IMPORTS .... $ 55,582,800,000
FEDERAL GOVERNMENT
   EXPENDITURE .... $ 233,100,000,000
FEDERAL DEBT .... $ 437,329,000,000

five-year period.

November 7 • President Nixon is re-elected, receiving 521 electoral votes to 17 for Senator McGovern, his Democratic opponent.

International and Cultural Events • Japanese terrorists fire into a crowd at Lod Airport in Israel. *The Godfather* receives an Academy Award. Bobby Fischer wins the world chess championship. *Life*, the pictorial magazine, ends publication.

1973 United States of America

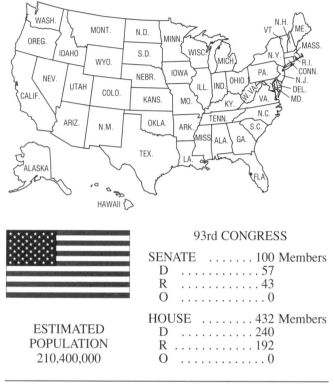

93rd CONGRESS

SENATE .... 100 Members
D 57
R 43
O 0

HOUSE .... 432 Members
D 240
R 192
O 0

ESTIMATED
POPULATION
210,400,000

Richard M. Nixon
37th President
14th Republican

Gerald R. Ford
40th Vice President
Republican

UNITED STATES ECONOMY

GROSS NATIONAL PRODUCT $1,294,900,000,000
RETAIL SALES .... $ 503,317,000,000
EXPORTS .... $ 70,823,200,000
IMPORTS .... $ 69,475,700,000
FEDERAL GOVERNMENT
  EXPENDITURE .... $ 264,200,000,000
FEDERAL DEBT .... $ 468,426,000,000

Events

January 10–30 • Appearing before Judge John J. Sirica of the United States district court in Washington, five of the seven men indicted in connection with the break-in at Democratic headquarters in the Watergate plead guilty, and two are convicted of conspiracy, burglary and other offenses.

January 11 • Phase three of the anti-inflation program begins with the abolition of many mandatory controls.

January 18 • Following a mistrial (December 1972), a new trial opens in the case of Dr. Daniel Ellsberg and Anthony J. Russo, Jr., charged on counts arising from the release of the Pentagon Papers.

January 20 • President Nixon begins his second term.

January 22 • In *Roe v. Wade*, the Supreme Court, in a seven-to-two decision, rules that a woman has a constitutional right to have an abortion during the first six months of her pregnancy (during the first three months without state regulation).

January 27 • An agreement providing for a cease-fire in Vietnam, negotiated by Henry Kissinger, adviser to President Nixon, and Le Duc Tho of North Vietnam, is signed in Paris by the United States, the governments of North and South Vietnam and the Provisional Revolutionary Government (Vietcong). The United States is to withdraw its troops and military advisers within 60 days, foreign troops are to be withdrawn from Laos and Cambodia and prisoners are to be freed. The truce is to be supervised by a four-nation commission.

January 27 • Secretary of Defense Melvin R. Laird announces that the federal government is ending the military draft.

February 7 • The Senate establishes the Select Committee on Presidential Campaign Activities (Watergate Committee). It is chaired by Samuel James Ervin, Jr., a Democrat from North Carolina.

February 12 • The U.S. dollar is devalued for a second time in 14 months.

February 22 • United States and Chinese officials agree to establish liaison offices in each other's country.

February 27 • Indian activists, members of the American Indian Movement, seize the trading post and church at Wounded Knee on the Ogala Sioux Reservation in South Dakota. Among their demands, they ask that the Senate investigate the government treatment of native Americans. They leave the site on May 8.

March 23 • Judge Sirica makes public a letter from James W. McCord, Jr., one of the people convicted in the Watergate break-in, charging that other people were guilty but lied about their involvement.

March 29 • The United States completes the withdrawal of its troops from South Vietnam, and all American prisoners of war have been returned. However, the cease-fire is widely violated, and Kissinger and Le Duc Tho meet throughout the year.

April 17 • After earlier denials of the involvement of members of the White House staff in the Watergate break-in or in efforts to cover up the affair, President Nixon says that he began a fresh investigation after receiving new information on March 21. On April 30, he accepts the resignations of H.R. Haldeman, his chief of staff, and

John D. Ehrlichman, his assistant for domestic affairs, as well as that of John W. Dean III, White House counsel, who has implicated the two others. At this time and throughout the year, the president denies any personal involvement in the Watergate affair or the cover-up.

April 20 • FBI director Patrick E. Gray resigns, having admitted that he destroyed Watergate documents on the advice of White House officials.

April 27 • It is disclosed that members of a White House group investigating security leaks (the so-called plumbers) had the office of Dr. Ellsberg's psychiatrist burglarized in 1971. On May 11, Judge William B. Byrne dismisses the charges against Ellsberg and Russo.

May 14 • *Skylab*, a space laboratory, is launched into orbit around the earth. It is manned successively by three teams of astronauts.

May 17 • The Watergate Committee opens hearings under Senator Sam J. Ervin, Jr. In succeeding weeks, aides of the Committee to Re-elect the President and White House staff members admit their involvement in the Watergate cover-up. John W. Dean III accuses the president of knowledge of the cover-up.

May 23 • The appointment of Elliot L. Richardson as attorney general is confirmed after he assures the Senate that Archibald Cox will serve as special prosecutor in the Watergate investigation.

July 1 • President Nixon signs appropriations bills to which amendments have been added to terminate United States bombing of Cambodia by August 15.

July 16 • The installation of a recording system at the White House is disclosed at the Watergate Committee hearings. A request by Cox for nine tapes is denied by the president on July 23. An order by Judge Sirica to turn over the tapes to him is sustained on appeal on October 12.

August 12 • Phase four of the control program begins.

September 21 • Henry Kissinger is the first naturalized citizen to become secretary of state.

October 10 • Vice President Agnew resigns. The same day, he pleads *nolo contendere* to income tax evasion, charges of bribery and conspiracy having been dropped. He is fined $10,000 and placed on probation for three years.

October 12 • Congress adopts a bill that would curtail the authority of the president to engage United States forces in a foreign war without its consent. Vetoed by President Nixon on October 24, the bill is repassed on November 7.

October 12 • In the first use of the 25th Amendment, President Nixon appoints Representative Gerald R. Ford of Michigan vice president. Confirmed by Congress on November 27, Ford takes the oath of office on December 6.

October 19 • The Arab oil-producing countries impose a total embargo on oil shipments to the United States to force a change in its Middle East policy. The embargo aggravates a growing energy crisis.

October 20 • Reacting to Archibald Cox's rejection of a plan to submit a summary of the tapes, President Nixon asks Attorney General Richardson to dismiss him. Richardson refuses and resigns, as does William B. Ruckelshaus, the deputy attorney general. Then Solicitor General Robert H. Bork dismisses Cox. These developments arouse widespread protests, and resolutions to impeach the president are submitted in the House of Representatives.

October 23 • President Nixon agrees to give the requested tapes to Judge Sirica. On October 31, it is disclosed that two of the tapes are not in existence, and on November 21, that part of another tape has been erased.

October 30 • The House Judiciary Committee begins deliberations on procedures for impeachment.

November 1 • William B. Saxbe is appointed attorney general; he is confirmed on December 17. Meanwhile, Leon Jaworski is named special prosecutor.

December 8 • President Nixon makes public information on his financial situation that includes controversial tax deductions.

International and Cultural Events • Egypt and Syria attack Israel on Yom Kippur (October 6). The Marxist government of President Salvador Allende in Chile is overthrown by a military junta; Allende is said to have committed suicide. In a referendum boycotted by Catholics, Ulster (Northern Ireland) votes to remain part of the United Kingdom. Billie Jean King defeats Bobby Riggs in a well-publicized tennis match. Carl Bernstein and Robert Woodward are given the George Polk Memorial Award for their coverage of the Watergate scandal in *The Washington Post*, which is itself awarded a Pulitzer prize.

President Nixon's farewell to the White House staff.

1974 Nixon/Ford

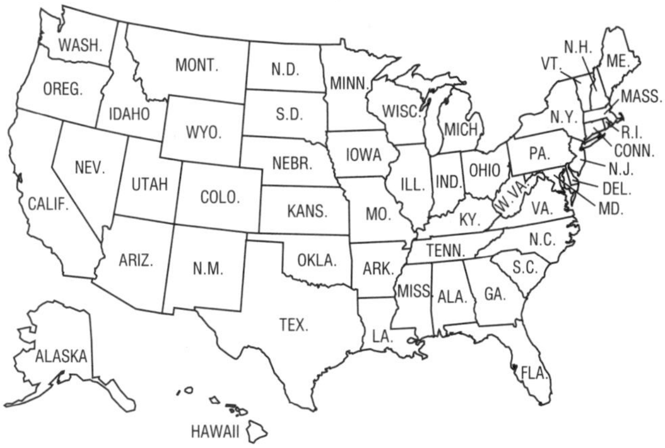

ESTIMATED POPULATION 211,910,000

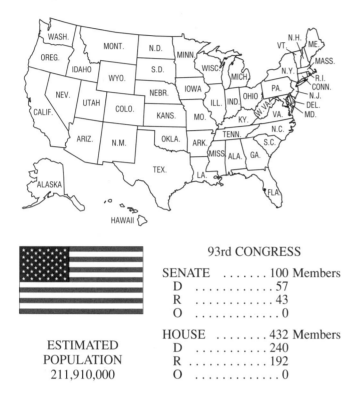

93rd CONGRESS

SENATE	100 Members
D	57
R	43
O	0
HOUSE	432 Members
D	240
R	192
O	0

Gerald R. Ford
38th President
15th Republican

Nelson A. Rockefeller
41st Vice President
Republican

UNITED STATES ECONOMY

GROSS NATIONAL PRODUCT	$1,397,400,000,000
RETAIL SALES	$ 537,782,000,000
EXPORTS	$ 97,900,000,000
IMPORTS	$ 100,970,000,000
FEDERAL GOVERNMENT EXPENDITURE (third quarter at annual rate)	$ 319,300,000,000
FEDERAL DEBT	$ 486,256,000,000

Gerald R. Ford

Birth	Omaha, NE, July 14, 1913
Parents	Gerald R. and Dorothy Gardner Ford
Married	Betty Bloomer
Home	Grand Rapids, MI
Presidency	1974 – 1977

Events

January 4 • Pleading the "confidentiality of presidential communications," President Nixon rejects Senate Watergate Committee subpoenas for approximately 500 tapes and documents.

January 30 • President Nixon outlines a 10-point program for dealing with problems of peace, inflation, energy, health, poverty, transportation and legislative reform. He reaffirms his determination not to resign.

February 6 • An overwhelming vote (410–4) gives the House Judiciary Committee broad constitutional power to pursue its presidential impeachment inquiry under the chairmanship of Peter W. Rodino, Jr., a New Jersey Democrat. Hearings begin on May 9.

February 8 • The third and last three-man team of astronauts manning *Skylab 3* returns safely to earth after a record stay in space of 84 days, 1 hour and 17 minutes.

March 1 • Former presidential aides and associates H.R. Haldeman, John D. Ehrlichman, John N. Mitchell, Charles W. Colson, Robert C. Mardian, Kenneth W. Parkinson and Gordon C. Strachan are indicted on charges of conspiring to obstruct investigation of the Watergate break-in. Colson is eventually dropped from the indictment after pleading guilty in the Ellsberg break-in. Strachan is granted a separate trial by Judge Sirica. The others are charged in a Washington court on October 1, and all except Parkinson are found guilty on January 1, 1975.

March 18 • Arab oil-producing countries agree to end their oil embargo against the United States, which they declared on October 20, 1973. The embargo has caused widespread shortages across the country.

March 29 • Eight men, one present and seven former members of the Ohio National Guard, are federally indicted for the killing of four and the wounding of nine Kent State University students (May 1970) who were protesting the United States invasion of Cambodia. On November 8, all are acquitted.

April 3 • President Nixon agrees to pay $432,787 in back taxes for the years 1969 through 1972. Controversy had emerged when it was discovered that the president had used a controversial deduction to reduce his tax liability. Congress subsequently launched an investigation, which determined that the president owed $432,787.

April 29 • In response to a House Judiciary Committee subpoena, President Nixon releases approximately 1,200 pages of edited transcripts of White House tapes. The committee votes on May 1 that the edited (and subsequently revealed as inaccurate) transcripts do not comply with its subpoena.

May 7 • The Federal Energy Administration, replacing

the Federal Energy Office, is authorized to deal with problems relating to the gasoline and energy emergency.

May 16 • Former attorney general Richard G. Kleindienst pleads guilty to misleading a congressional committee inquiring into the Nixon administration's handling of the International Telephone and Telegraph Corporation antitrust settlement. He is given a minimum fine and a suspended sentence.

June 12–18 • Increasing the tempo of his personal diplomacy campaign, President Nixon visits Saudi Arabia, Syria, Israel, Egypt and Jordan to promote Middle East peace. Between June 27 and July 3, he meets in the Soviet Union with the Communist party leader Leonid Brezhnev in an attempt to limit the proliferation of nuclear arms.

July 12 • John D. Ehrlichman and three codefendants are found guilty of conspiracy charges stemming from the Ellsberg break-in. He is given a prison sentence of 20 months to five years.

July 24 • The Supreme Court rules unanimously that President Nixon must surrender tapes and other material subpoenaed by the special Watergate prosecutor Leon Jaworski on April 18.

July 27 • The House Judiciary Committee approves (27 to 11) an article impeaching President Nixon for obstructing justice in the Watergate scandal. A second impeachment article (28 to 10) charges him with repeated failure to carry out his constitutional oath. On July 30, the committee approves (21 to 17) a third article citing the president's defiance of its subpoenas. Impeachment articles charging the president with the secret bombing of Cambodia and with filing faulty income tax returns are rejected.

August 2 • John W. Dean III, former presidential counsel, is sentenced to one to four years in prison after pleading guilty to participation in the Watergate cover-up.

August 9 • Richard M. Nixon becomes the first United States president to resign from office. His decision, announced on August 8 in a nationwide television broadcast, comes as congressional support erodes after newly released tape transcripts reveal that shortly after the Watergate break-in he had ordered a probe of the incident by the Federal Bureau of Investigation to be halted.

August 9 • Gerald R. Ford is sworn in as the 38th president of the United States. His inaugural address urges that the nation "bind up the internal wounds" of Watergate. Addressing a joint session of Congress on August 12, he calls inflation the country's major problem.

September 8 • President Ford grants former president Nixon an unconditional pardon for all federal crimes he "committed or may have committed" while in office. The pardon is widely criticized.

September 16 • A presidential plan offers amnesty to Vietnam draft evaders and deserters in exchange for a maximum of two years of public service.

September 17 • Reacting to a series of *New York Times* articles, the Senate Foreign Relations Committee orders an investigation of charges that the Central Intelligence Agency (CIA) had spent more than $8 million to promote the overthrow of Salvador Allende Gossens, Socialist president of Chile, in 1973.

October 15 • The United States enacts campaign reform legislation. It authorizes public funding for major presidential candidates and sets spending limits for presidential and congressional campaigns.

November 5 • Democratic candidates sweep the country in an anti-Watergate tide. Connecticut voters make Ella T. Grasso the first woman to be elected governor of a state without succeeding her husband.

November 18–22 • President Ford meets in Japan with Premier Kakuei Tanaka. This is the first stop on an eight-day journey that includes South Korea and Vladivostok, where, on November 23 through November 24, he and Leonid Brezhnev of the Soviet Union conclude a treaty limiting offensive nuclear arms and delivery vehicles.

November 20 • The American Telephone and Telegraph Company, Western Electric Company and Bell Laboratories are charged with violating the Sherman Antitrust Act by conspiring to monopolize telecommunications equipment.

December 19 • Nelson A. Rockefeller, nominated by President Ford on August 20, is sworn in as the 41st vice president of the United States. Congressional confirmation comes after intensive investigation and public hearings.

December 31 • CIA director William E. Colby corroborates a *New York Times* report on December 22 that the agency had maintained secret files on thousands of Americans by means of electronic eavesdropping, postal inspections, and break-ins.

December 31 • United States citizens are allowed to buy and own gold after a 41-year prohibition. Initial sales are small.

International and Cultural Events • Secretary of State Kissinger obtains the disengagement of Israeli and Egyptian forces in the Sinai. India detonates a nuclear device. Emperor Haile Selassie of Ethiopia is overthrown and arrested. Soviet author Aleksandr Solzhenitsyn is stripped of his citizenship and deported to the West. Muhammad Ali regains the world heavyweight championship. Members of the Symbionese Liberation Army (SLA) kidnap Patricia Hearst, granddaughter of newspaper mogul William Randolph Hearst.

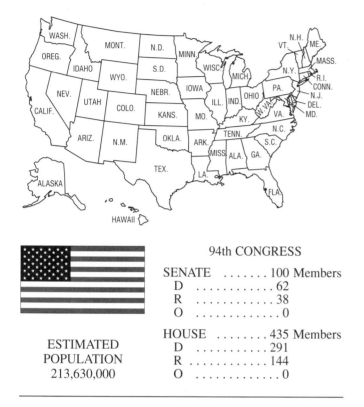

94th CONGRESS

SENATE	......	100 Members
D	....	62
R	....	38
O	....	0

HOUSE	....	435 Members
D	....	291
R	....	144
O	....	0

ESTIMATED
POPULATION
213,630,000

Gerald R. Ford
38th President
15th Republican

Nelson A. Rockefeller
41st Vice President
Republican

UNITED STATES ECONOMY

GROSS NATIONAL PRODUCT	$ 1,498,900,000,000
RETAIL SALES	$ 584,423,000,000
EXPORTS	$ 107,651,800,000
IMPORTS	$ 96,140,400,000
FEDERAL GOVERNMENT	
EXPENDITURE (third quarter at annual rate)	$ 356,900,000,000
FEDERAL DEBT	$ 544,131,000,000

Events

January 1 • John N. Mitchell, H.R. Haldeman and John D. Ehrlichman, key figures in the Watergate scandal, are found guilty on charges including conspiracy, obstruction of justice, perjury and making false declarations. They are sentenced (February 21) to two-and-a-half to eight years. Robert C. Mardian, found guilty of conspiracy only, is given 10 months. All are freed pending an appeal.

January 3 • The Trade Reform Act, reluctantly signed by President Ford bars OPEC nations from tariff advantages given other developing nations. In addition, Soviet favored-nation status is linked to freer Soviet emigration.

January 5 • Vice President Rockefeller is named to head a presidential commission investigating charges of CIA domestic spying. The final report, made public June 10, finds some unlawful activities but reports that most CIA undertakings were within its statutory authority.

January 8 • Watergate offenders John W. Dean, Herbert W. Kalmbach and Jeb Stuart Magruder are freed by Judge John Sirica, who cites their "unprecedented cooperation" and Nixon's presidential pardon.

January 15 • President Ford's State of the Union message urges a $16 billion income tax cut but calls for more taxes on oil and natural gas. He also requests a windfalls profits tax, to be implemented on April 1, when he plans to decontrol domestic crude oil.

January 21 • The FBI announces that it kept files on congressmen as "by-products" of other investigations. On February 27, the newly confirmed (February 5) attorney general, Edward H. Levi, discloses that the late J. Edgar Hoover kept files on presidents, congressmen and private individuals. FBI harassment of the late Martin Luther King, Jr., is confirmed on March 8, and illegal break-ins on July 14.

January 21 • In *Taylor v. Louisiana*, the U.S. Supreme Court rules that women cannot be excluded from the jury pool. Justice Byron R. White, writing for the eight-member majority, states that such action violates the Sixth Amendment requirement that juries reflect the ethnic and racial composition of the community from which they are drawn.

January 22 • A Democratic caucus revolt challenges the congressional seniority system by ousting the chairmen of three important House committees: Banking and Currency, Armed Services and Agriculture.

January 27 • A Senate bipartisan select committee is formed to investigate charges that the CIA and FBI spied on U.S. citizens. Senator Frank Church (Democrat, Idaho), is named chairman. The report, made public November 20 over presidential objections, indicates that government officials were involved in or privy to assassination attempts against five foreign leaders and that four actual deaths did not result directly from these plots.

January 31 • A federal court rules that tapes and documents assembled by former president Nixon during his tenure are government property.

February 3 • The president's proposed $349 billion fiscal budget predicts a $51 billion deficit for 1976. The unemployment rate is predicted to be eight percent throughout the year. By the end of March, deficit predictions top $100 billion, and in June, unemployment is reckoned at 9.2 percent.

March 12 • Former secretary of commerce Maurice Stans pleads guilty to five charges of misdemeanor relating to the 1972 Republican campaign. He is fined $5,000 on May 14.

March 17 • The Supreme Court rules that ownership of oil and natural gas resources beyond the three-mile limit on the Atlantic shelf devolves to the federal government.

April 17 • Former secretary of the treasury John Connally, Jr., is acquitted of the charge that he accepted a bribe in 1971 from interests seeking dairy price supports.

April 18 • Ceremonies at Boston's Old North Church initiate national bicentennial celebrations by commemorating Paul Revere's ride.

April 29 • The unconditional surrender of the Saigon government to the Viet Cong is followed by the evacuation of remaining Americans from the city.

May 11 • Court-ordered desegregation of Boston schools is denounced by busing foes led by city councilor Louise Day Hicks; protest demonstrations follow.

May 12 • The *Mayaguez*, a U.S. merchant ship, is seized 60 miles off the Cambodian coast by a Cambodian navy ship. In a rapid sequence of events, President Ford alerts U.S. forces in the western Pacific on May 13, and by the evening of May 14, the ship and crew are free. Three Cambodian gunboats are sunk by U.S. planes; American casualties include 15 dead, three missing, and 50 wounded.

May 20 • President Ford once again vetoes controls on strip-mining, citing energy needs.

May 28–June 3 • In a whirlwind European tour stressing U.S. commitments, President Ford attends a NATO summit in Brussels, meets with Generalissimo Franco and Prince Juan Carlos in Madrid and Egypt's president Anwar Sadat in Salzburg and visits Pope Paul VI and President Giovanni Leone in Rome.

June 9 • Daniel P. Moynihan is confirmed as U.S. ambassador to the United Nations.

June 16 • In *Goldfarb v. Virginia State Bar*, a unanimous U.S. Supreme Court rules that attorneys are not exempt from federal antitrust provisions.

June 17 • The people of the Northern Mariana Islands approve a pact making their islands a commonwealth of the United States. It is the first time since 1917 that the United States has acquired any territory. Congress will approve the *Covenant to Establish a Commonwealth of the Northern Mariana Islands in Political Union with the United States* in 1976.

July 24 • The Apollo space program concludes after 14 years with the Pacific splashdown of three astronauts who participated in the first internationally manned space flight.

July 30–August 1 • President Ford attends a three-day 35-nation Conference on Security and Cooperation in Europe, held in Helsinki. A nonbinding agreement calls for freer contacts between East and West.

August 1 • James Hoffa, ex-president of the International Brotherhood of Teamsters, is reported missing.

September 5 • Lynette Alice Fromme, a Charles Manson "Family" disciple, points a loaded piston at President Ford in Sacramento. Found guilty of attempted assassination (November 26), she receives a life sentence.

September 11 • Former UMW president W.A. Boyle is sentenced to three consecutive life terms for ordering the 1969 slaying of union rival Joseph A. Yablonski, his wife and daughter.

September 18 • Patricia Hearst, William Harris and Emily Harris are arrested in San Francisco by the FBI. Abducted by radical "Symbionese Liberation Army" in February 1974, the newspaper heiress eventually renounced her parents and, according to an October 2 indictment participated in SLA-led incidents of robbery, kidnapping and assault.

September 22 • Sara Jane Moore fires a pistol at President Ford in San Francisco. She pleads guilty to attempted assassination and is sentenced in January 1976.

September 30–October 13 • Emperor Hirohito and Empress Nagako become the first reigning Japanese monarchs to visit the United States and express regret about the "tragic interlude" of World War II.

October 17 • New York City is saved from last-minute default when the teachers union invests $150,000,000 in Municipal Assistance Corporation (Big MAC) bonds. President Ford drops opposition to federal help for the city (November 26) and, on December 9, signs a bill authorizing $2,300,000,000 in annual loans until 1978.

October 20 • The United States concludes a five-year agreement to sell the Soviet Union six to eight million tons of grain annually and to buy a maximum of 200,000 barrels daily of Soviet oil and petroleum products.

November 3 • Vice President Rockefeller announces he will not be President Ford's running mate in 1976. In a major administration shake-up, James R. Schlesinger is replaced by defense secretary Donald H. Rumsfeld; William E. Colby is ousted as CIA director in favor of George Bush; and Secretary Kissinger is removed as National Security Council director.

November 12 • William O. Douglas, 77, resigns from the Supreme Court after 36 years. President Ford replaces him with John Paul Stevens.

December 1–5 • President Ford visits the People's Republic of China, Indonesia and the Philippines. "Pacific Doctrine," announced in Honolulu (December 7), foreshadows a lower American profile in Asia.

International and Cultural Events • Civil war erupts in Lebanon and Angola. Francisco Franco dies. West Point and Annapolis decide to admit women in 1976. *Jaws* breaks box office records.

1976 United States of America

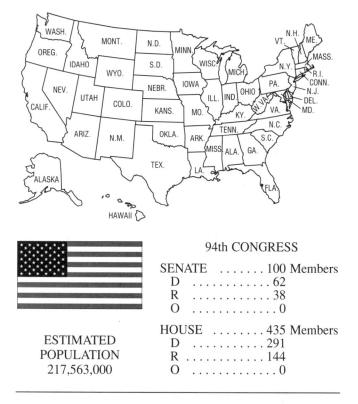

	94th CONGRESS
SENATE .... 100 Members
D 62
R 38
O 0

ESTIMATED
POPULATION
217,563,000

HOUSE .... 435 Members
D 291
R 144
O 0

Gerald R. Ford
38th President
15th Republican

Nelson A. Rockefeller
41st Vice President
Republican

UNITED STATES ECONOMY

GROSS NATIONAL PRODUCT ....$ 1,819,000,000,000
RETAIL SALES ....$ 1,353,919,000,000
EXPORTS ....$ 114,745,000,000
IMPORTS ....$ 124,228,000,000
FEDERAL GOVERNMENT
   EXPENDITURE ....$ 371,800,000,000
FEDERAL DEBT ....$ 629,000,000,000

Events

January 1 • In commemoration of the United States' bicentennial, the Liberty Bell is moved to a new glass and steel pavilion about 100 yards from its original home in Independence Hall in Philadelphia. The move will allow thousands of tourists to view the Liberty Bell during the bicentennial year.

May 24 • The supersonic Concorde jet makes its first flight to the United States, departing from Paris and arriving in Washington, DC.

May 24 • The U.S. Supreme Court strikes down a Virginia law that bans advertising of drug prices, sighting it as a violation of First Amendment rights.

May 28 • The United States and Soviet governments agree to limit underground testing of nuclear weapons and to allow inspection of nuclear test sites.

June 5 • In Newdale, Idaho, the new 30-story, earth-filled Teton Dam collapses, and the subsequent flooding forces 30,000 people to evacuate their homes.

July 2 • The U.S. Supreme Court rules that capital punishment is not unconstitutional, upholding death penalty laws in Georgia, Texas and Florida. The Court struck down death penalty laws in North Carolina and Louisiana, because they prescribed death sentences for certain crimes.

July 14 • The Democratic National Convention nominates Governor James E. (Jimmy) Carter, Jr., of Georgia as its presidential candidate. Carter chooses Walter Mondale (Minnesota) as his vice presidential running mate.

August 19 • The Republican National Convention nominates President Gerald Ford as its candidate for president. The delegates vote in favor of Ford and his running mate, Robert J. Dole (Kansas), rather than their challenger, Ronald Reagan.

September 27 • President Ford and Democratic challenger Jimmy Carter participate in the first televised presidential debate involving an incumbent president. The debate attracts about 90 million television viewers.

October 20 • A Norwegian tanker crashes into and sinks a crowded ferryboat in the Mississippi River, killing many of the 96 people aboard the ferry. At least 35 cars and trucks have to be pulled from the muddy river.

October 25 • In response to disegregation activities at two high schools in Boston, bomb materia is found and students boycott classes at South Boston High School. As buses of black students arrive, students protest.

November 2 • Jimmy Carter is elected president of the United States, defeating President Ford in the national election. In congressional elections, the Democrats retain their majority in both the House of Representatives and the Senate.

November 12 • Officials from the United States and Vietnam meet in Paris for normalization talks. On November 15, the United States vetoes the sitting of the Vietnamese ambassador to the United Nations, because the government of Vietnam still had not accounted for 800 American military servicemen listed as missing in action.

International and Cultural Events • Bicentennial celebrations are held across the nation on July fourth, including the gathering of six million people in New York City for an Independence Day extravaganza at the Statue of Liberty and the ringing of the Liberty Bell in Philadelphia.

James E. Carter, Jr. 1977

Events

January 17 • A capital punishment sentence is carried out for the first time since 1967, when a firing squad at the Utah State Prison executes Gary Gilmore.

January 20 • Jimmy Carter is inaugurated as the 39th president of the United States of America. Walter Mondale is sworn in as vice president.

January 21 • President Carter pardons those Americans who had evaded the military draft during the Vietnam War, many of whom had fled to Canada to avoid prosecution.

February 23 • The U.S. Supreme Court rules that the Environmental Protection Agency has the authority to establish waste standards for business and industry in order to control the discharge of pollutants into waterways.

March 17 • President Carter, after having cut economic aid to countries involved in major violations of human rights (Argentina, Uruguay and Ethiopia), delivers a speech on human rights to the United Nations.

April 18 • President Carter calls for a nationwide effort to conserve energy in a national address, beginning a conservation campaign by his administration.

May • Apple Computers introduces the Apple II computer, which is the first commercial personal computer. A television set is used as a monitor and an audiocassette recorder for data storage.

July 13 • A massive electrical shutdown occurs in New York City and surrounding areas after a violent electrical storm, rendering nine million people powerless for many hours. Days of chaos and looting result.

July 28 • The first barrels of oil are pumped in Valdez, Alaska, at the end of the 799-mile Trans-Alaska pipeline. Plans for the pipeline began after the 1973 oil embargo, which graphically illustrated how dependent the United States was on foreign oil imports.

August 4 • President Carter signs the order to create the Department of Energy.

September 7 • President Carter and Panamanian leader Omar Torrijos sign the Panama Canal Treaty, which would return the Panama Canal Zone to the Panamanian government by the year 2000.

December 3 • Ten thousand Vietnamese refugees are admitted into the United States by the State Department on an emergency basis after fleeing from the Communist government in their country. The refugees are referred to as "Boat People" in reference to their means of entry into the United States.

International and Cultural Events • Elvis Presley, the "King of Rock and Roll," dies at age 42 at his Memphis home, Graceland, from drug-related causes.

95th CONGRESS

SENATE	....	100 Members
D	....	61
R	....	38
O	....	1
HOUSE	....	435 Members
D	....	292
R	....	143
O	....	0

ESTIMATED
POPULATION
220,239,000

James E. Carter, Jr.
39th President
14th Democrat

Walter F. Mondale
42nd Vice President
Democrat

UNITED STATES ECONOMY

GROSS NATIONAL PRODUCT	.......$ 2,026,900,000,000
RETAIL SALES	...................$ 1,418,607,000,000
EXPORTS	........................$ 120,816,000,000
IMPORTS	........................$ 151,907,000,000
FEDERAL GOVERNMENT EXPENDITURE	...................$ 409,200,000,000
FEDERAL DEBT	...................$ 706,400,000,000

James E. Carter, Jr.

Birth	....................Plains, GA, Oct. 1, 1924
Parents	...........James E. and Lillian Gordy Carter
Married	...........................Rosalyn Smith
Home	..............................Plains, GA
Presidency	..........................1977 – 1981

1978 United States of America

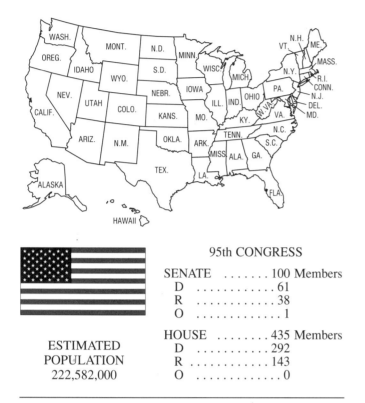

95th CONGRESS

SENATE	. . . . 100 Members
D	 61
R	 38
O	 1

HOUSE	. . . . 435 Members
D	 292
R	 143
O	 0

ESTIMATED
POPULATION
222,582,000

James E. Carter, Jr.
39th President
14th Democrat

Walter F. Mondale
42nd Vice President
Democrat

UNITED STATES ECONOMY

GROSS NATIONAL PRODUCT	$ 2,219,400,000,000
RETAIL SALES . . . . . . :	$ 1,487,879,000,000
EXPORTS	$ 142,075,000,000
IMPORTS	$ 176,002,000,000
FEDERAL GOVERNMENT	
EXPENDITURE	$ 458,700,000,000
FEDERAL DEBT	$ 776,600,000,000

Events

January 9 • A federal judge in Ohio rules that girls should not be prohibited from playing on boys' sports teams when girls' teams are not available in public high schools.

January 12 • Coal miners begin a labor strike that will become the longest coal strike in United States history. It lasts 110 days.

April 6 • President Carter signs an act raising the mandatory retirement age from 65 to 70.

April 18 • The U.S. Senate ratifies the Panama Canal Treaty after extensive deliberation and much national debate.

May 11 • The first female general in the United States Marine Corps is appointed.

June 6 • California residents vote almost two-to-one in favor of a referendum reducing local property taxes.

July 7 • A federal judge rules that past and present CIA employees may be censored in accordance with their contracts. Frank W. Snepp III, a former CIA official, had written a book in which he divulged confidential information. The judge rules that Snepp violated CIA policy and forces him to turn over any earnings from the book to the government.

September 6-17 • President Carter hosts a Middle East peace summit at Camp David, Maryland, attended by Egyptian president Anwar Sadat and Israeli prime minister Menachem Begin. The meetings will result in a "framework for peace," called the Camp David Accords, by which Egypt becomes the first Arab nation to recognize Israel's right to exist.

August 8 • President Carter authorizes a $1.6 billion loan guarantee for New York City in an attempt to bail out the city from near-bankruptcy.

October 6 • Congress extends the deadline for ratification of the Equal Rights Amendment by 38 states to June 30, 1982.

October 15 • Congress votes to deregulate the airline industry, phasing out federal control of routes and fares.

October 15 • Congress passes the National Energy Act of 1978 to set fuel efficiency standards and regulate natural gas prices. The bill becomes law when President Carter signs it on November 9, 1978.

November 7 • The Democrats retain their majority after congressional elections, although the Republicans do gain some seats.

December 15 • President Carter announces that the U.S. government will re-establish diplomatic relations with China, effective January 1, 1979.

December 30 • A report by the U.S. House Select Committee on Assassinations concludes that it was likely that a second gunman was involved in the 1963 assassination of President John F. Kennedy in Dallas. The committee also proposes that the assassinations of Kennedy and Martin Luther King, Jr., resulted from conspiracies.

International and Cultural Events • In Guyana, 914 members of the "People's Temple," a cult led by the Reverend Jim Jones, commit suicide by drinking poison. Congressman Leo Ryan, who had traveled to Guyana to investigate the cult's activities, was killed by gunmen prior to the mass suicide ordered by Jones.

United States of America 1979

Events

January 1 • Diplomatic relations between the U.S. and Chinese governments are officially reopened.

January 12 • A blizzard hits the Midwest and kills approximately 100 people.

February 8 • The U.S. government imposes sanctions against Nicaragua for human rights abuses in the country. Economic aid to the Nicaraguan government is stopped.

March 5 • The Supreme Court rules that alimony laws requiring divorced husbands, but not divorced wives, to make payments are unconstitutional.

March 26 • President Carter continues his efforts for peace in the Middle East, as Egyptian and Israeli officials meet in Washington D.C., to sign a peace agreement.

March 28 • Dangerous radioactive gases leak from a nuclear accident at the Three-Mile Island power plant near Harrisburg, Pennsylvania. Thousands of people have to evacuate the area due to the possible danger posed by the leak. Across the country, the accident prompts increased protests against nuclear power and nuclear weapons.

May 25 • An American Airlines DC-10 crashes shortly after takeoff in Chicago. Two hundred seventy-three people are killed in what is to date the worst aviation accident in U.S. history.

June 13 • In the largest Indian land claim settlement ever, the Sioux nation is granted $17.5 million for the Black Hills, South Dakota area, which were taken from them in 1877.

June 18 • In Vienna, Austria, President Carter and Soviet premier Leonid Brezhnev conclude five years of negotiations by signing the Strategic Arms Limitations Treaty (SALT II), limiting the number of nuclear missile launchers each nation can posses.

June 27 • The Supreme Court makes a ruling that supports affirmative action programs by affirming the constitutionality of promoting blacks ahead of "senior" whites as part of a program to offset racial discrimination.

September 27 • Congress approves the creation of the Department of Education as the 13th cabinet-level agency.

November 4 • Iranian revolutionaries seize the U.S. embassy in Tehran, Iran, and take about 90 people hostage. They demand that the former Shah of Iran, who is in New York for medical treatment, be returned by the U.S. government for prosecution in Iran. President Carter will deny the request, and the Iranians will keep 52 U.S. citizens hostage at the embassy.

November 12 • In response to the hostage situation in Iran, President Carter imposes an embargo on Iranian oil, and on November 14, the U.S. seizes all Iranian assets in the United States.

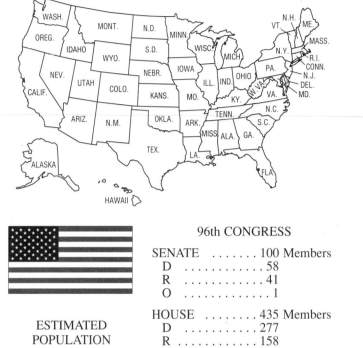

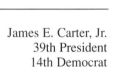

96th CONGRESS

SENATE	.... 100 Members
D	 58
R	 41
O	 1
HOUSE	.... 435 Members
D	 277
R	 158
O	 0

ESTIMATED
POPULATION
225,055,000

James E. Carter, Jr.
39th President
14th Democrat

Walter F. Mondale
42nd Vice President
Democrat

UNITED STATES ECONOMY

GROSS NATIONAL PRODUCT	........$ 2,557,500,000,000
RETAIL SALES	...................$ 1,512,980,000,000
EXPORTS	........................$ 184,439,000,000
IMPORTS	........................$ 212,007,000,000
FEDERAL GOVERNMENT EXPENDITURE	...................$ 504,000,000,000
FEDERAL DEBT	...................$ 829,500,000,000

December 27 • Soviet primier Leonid Brezhnev sends troops into Afghanistan in an attempt to counter a Muslim rebellion within the country. In response to this action, President Carter will withdraw the SALT II treaty and will stop certain exports to the Soviet Union.

International and Cultural Events • Margaret Thatcher is elected prime minister of Great Britain; she is the first woman to hold the position.

1980 United States of America

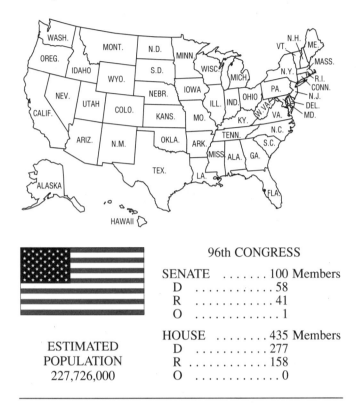

96th CONGRESS

SENATE	.... 100 Members
D	 58
R	 41
O	 1

HOUSE	.... 435 Members
D	 277
R	 158
O	 0

ESTIMATED
POPULATION
227,726,000

James E. Carter, Jr.
39th President
14th Democrat

Walter F. Mondale
42nd Vice President
Democrat

UNITED STATES ECONOMY

GROSS NATIONAL PRODUCT	$ 2,784,200,000,000
RETAIL SALES	$ 1,457,990,000,000
EXPORTS	$ 224,250,000,000
IMPORTS	$ 249,750,000,000
FEDERAL GOVERNMENT	
EXPENDITURE	$ 590,900,000,000
FEDERAL DEBT	$ 909,100,000,000

Events

February 12 • United States officials request that the International Olympics Committee move the Olympic summer games from Moscow in response to the Soviet invasion of Afghanistan. The request will be denied.

March 17 • President Carter signs the Refugee Act of 1980, increasing the maximum number of immigrants allowed to enter the United States annually. The act also broadens the term "refugee" to include people from all countries and territories.

March 18 • The U.S. government bans all sales of high-technology equipment to the Soviet Union.

April 7 • The U.S. government breaks off diplomatic relations with Iran and expels Iranian diplomats in response to the continuing hostage crisis.

April 25 • An effort by U.S. military personnel to rescue the hostages in Iran ends in disaster when a transport plane collides with a helicopter, killing eight and injuring five servicemen.

April 26 • Secretary of State Cyrus Vance resigns, citing his opposition to the botched hostage rescue attempt in Iran on the previous day.

May 17-19 • Rioting erupts in Miami, Florida, in response to the acquittal of four white policemen accused of the beating death of a black businessman. The rioting causes more than $100 million in damage and results in injuries to hundreds of people, 18 of whom die. Almost 1,000 people are arrested.

May 18 • Mount St. Helens erupts in Washington state.

June 3 • A national defense network computer system causes a false nuclear alert, sending reports that the Soviet Union has launched an attack against the United States.

June 23 - August 15 • A heat wave and drought in the southern and southwestern United States devastates crops and livestock and causes the deaths of more than 1,200 people.

July 17 • The Republican National Convention nominates Ronald W. Reagan of California as its candidate for president and George H.W. Bush as its vice presidential candidate.

August 14 • The Democratic National Convention nominates President Carter and Vice President Mondale for re-election.

October 2 • For the first time since 1861, the U.S. House of Representatives expels one of its members. Democrat Michael Joseph Myers of Pennsylvania is expelled for bribery and conspiracy activities uncovered by an FBI investigation of corruption within the federal government.

November 4 • Ronald Reagan and George Bush win the presidency and vice presidency in a landslide victory against the incumbents, Carter and Mondale. The Republicans gain a majority of seats in the Senate and 33 seats in the House of Representatives.

International and Cultural Events • The Olympic games begin on July 19 in Moscow with 45 nations boycotting events because of their opposition to the Soviet invasion of Afghanistan. John Lennon, singer and former member of the band The Beatles, is shot and killed by a crazed fan on December 8.

Ronald W. Reagan 1981

Events

January 20 • Ronald W. Reagan is inaugurated as the 40th president of the United States of America. At age 69, he is the oldest person to assume the office.

January 20 • Just minutes after President Reagan takes the oath of office, the Iranian hostage crisis ends. Fifty–two Americans, who had been taken hostage in November 1979, are released after an agreement is signed in Algiers.

February 18 • In his first State of the Union address, President Reagan calls for massive budget cuts, amounting to $41 billion, but asks for a $5 billion increase in defense spending.

March 30 • President Reagan is shot and wounded in an assassination attempt by 23-year-old John W. Hinckley, Jr., in Washington, D.C. Using a .22 caliber pistol, Hinckley wounds Reagan and three others, including Reagan's press secretary, James Brady.

April 12 • The first reusable space shuttle, *Columbia*, is launched with two astronauts on board. *Columbia* lands safely 54 hours later.

June 8 • The U.S. Supreme Court rules that women may file lawsuits seeking equal pay from their employers if they are paid less than men doing similar work. The ruling states that women do not have to do the exact same job as men in order to be eligible for equal pay.

June 16 • Secretary of State Alexander Haig announces that the Reagan Administration has decided to sell arms to the People's Republic of China.

July 17 • An overhead walkway in the new Hyatt Regency Hotel in Kansas City, Missouri, collapses, resulting in the deaths of 111 people.

August 9 • President Reagan announces that he has authorized production of a neutron bomb for use in various missiles and artillery ammunition.

August 19 • After being fired upon, U.S. Navy F–14 fighter planes shoot down two Libyan jets over Libya.

September 25 • Sandra Day O'Connor becomes the first woman to serve as justice of the United States Supreme Court.

December 1 • President Reagan and Soviet premier Leonid Brezhnev meet in Geneva, Switzerland, to begin discussions about reducing and limiting production of nuclear arms.

December 8 • The U.S. Supreme Court hands down a decision that confirms the right of religious and political groups to meet in buildings of public institutions, including schools.

International and Cultural Events • Pope John Paul II is shot and seriously wounded in St. Peter's Square at the Vatican.

97th CONGRESS

SENATE	....	100 Members
R	....	53
D	....	46
O	....	1
HOUSE	....	435 Members
D	....	242
R	....	192
O	....	1

ESTIMATED POPULATION 229,966,000

Ronald W. Reagan
40th President
16th Republican

George H.W. Bush
43rd Vice President
Republican

UNITED STATES ECONOMY

GROSS NATIONAL PRODUCT	........$3,115,900,000,000
RETAIL SALES	....................$1,463,776,000,000
EXPORTS	.........................$ 237,044,000,000
IMPORTS	.......................$ 265,067,000,000
FEDERAL GOVERNMENT EXPENDITURE	...................$ 678,200,000,000
FEDERAL DEBT	....................$ 994,800,000,000

Ronald W. Reagan

Birth	....................Tampico, IL, Feb. 6, 1911
Parents	.....................John and Nell Reagan
Married	...............................Nancy Davis
Home	....................Pacific Palisades, CA
Presidency	...........................1981 – 1989

1982 United States of America

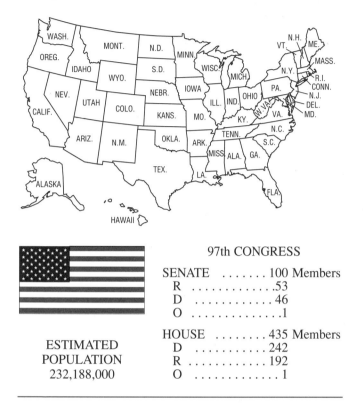

97th CONGRESS

SENATE .... 100 Members
R .... .53
D 46
O 1

HOUSE .... 435 Members
D 242
R 192
O 1

ESTIMATED
POPULATION
232,188,000

Ronald W. Reagan
40th President
16th Republican

George H.W. Bush
43rd Vice President
Republican

UNITED STATES ECONOMY

GROSS NATIONAL PRODUCT ....$ 3,242,100,000,000
RETAIL SALES ....$ 1,449,433,000,000
EXPORTS ....$ 211,157,000,000
IMPORTS ....$ 247,642,000,000
FEDERAL GOVERNMENT
   EXPENDITURE ....$ 745,800,000,000
FEDERAL DEBT ....$ 1,137,300,000,000

Events

January 7 • President Reagan announces plans to resume registration for the military draft for all young men.

January 8 • The powerful AT&T telephone company is ordered to divest its holdings in order to settle an eight-year antitrust lawsuit by the Justice Department.

January 26 • In his State of the Union address, President Reagan outlines his plan for a "New Federalism," which includes a proposal that the federal government transfer responsibility for many social programs to the states.

February 6 • President Reagan proposes a budget designed to cut domestic spending and increase defense spending by 18 percent. His budget includes a projected deficit of $91.5 billion.

March 10 • In response to ongoing disputes with Libya, President Reagan imposes economic sanctions, including an embargo on Libyan oil and a ban on the export of high-technology equipment to Libya.

May 13 • Braniff International declares bankruptcy, becoming the first major U.S. airline to do so.

June 21 • John W. Hinckley, Jr., is found not guilty by reason of insanity of the attempted murder of President Reagan.

June 24 • The U.S. Supreme Court rules that a president is not liable for damages caused by actions he has taken while in office.

June 30 • The Equal Rights Amendment fails to be ratified by a sufficient number of states to become part of the Constitution. Thirty-five of the necessary 38 states had ratified the amendment, which was introduced in 1972.

July 2 • The U.S. Supreme Court rules that the National Association for the Advancement of Colored People is not liable for damages or losses that result from the group's boycott of a business in the case *NAACP v. Clairborne Hardward Company*.

September 29–October 2 • Seven deaths in the Chicago area are attributed to cyanide poisoning. Health authorities find that capsules of Tylenol have been laced with cyanide, prompting a nationwide recall of the medicine. The killer is never found.

October 26 • President Reagan announces that the United States ended fiscal 1982 with a record deficit of $110 billion.

November 4 • In response to the September cyanide poisonings, the federal government issues requirements for tamper-resistant packaging for over-the-counter medication.

November 5 • The U.S. unemployment rate reportedly reaches 10.4 percent, the highest reported rate since 1940.

December 7 • Charles Brooks, a prisoner on death row in Texas, is the first person to die by lethal injection.

December 23 • Congress passes a bill to increase the federal fuel tax by five cents per gallon in order to repair roadways and improve mass transit systems.

International and Cultural Events • On June 7, "Graceland," the Memphis home of Elvis Presley, is opened for public viewing, attracting tourists from around the world.

United States of America 1983

Events

January 15 • The National Commission on Social Security Reform recommends changes in the Social Security system that include tax increases and the eventual raising of the retirement age.

March 23 • In a national address, President Reagan proposes the "Star Wars" system of defense, challenging scientists to develop an antiballistic missile defense system.

April 18 • In Beirut, Lebanon, a car bomb explodes, almost destroying the U.S. embassy and killing 17 U.S. citizens. Pro-Iranian terrorists are blamed, but no suspects are ever arrested.

April 26 • A federal report on the status of U.S. public education declares that a "rising tide of mediocrity" exists in public education and that it is putting the nation's future at risk.

May 24 • The U.S. Supreme Court rules that private schools practicing discrimination may be held ineligible for tax exemptions and federal funds.

June 15 • In a decision involving five different cases, the U.S. Supreme Court reaffirms the 1973 Supreme Court ruling in *Roe v. Wade*, which gave women an unrestricted right to an abortion in the first trimester of pregnancy.

June 18 • Sally Ride becomes the first American woman in space as part of the crew of the *Challenger*. She remains in space for six days.

June 23 • The U.S. Supreme Court rules in a landmark case that Congress does not have a "legislative veto" over federal regulatory agencies. The court declares that the legislative veto is an unconstitutional invasion of executive authority by the legislative branch.

July 20 • The state of Washington's public power supply system declares that it is unable to pay its debts associated with the cancellation of two nuclear power plants. It is the largest municipal default to date in U.S. history.

October 23 • In Beirut, Lebanon, 241 U.S. Marines and Navy personnel are killed by a truck bomb.

October 25 • U.S. Army Rangers, paratroopers and U.S. Marines are sent to the Caribbean island of Grenada in order to restore the civilian government that had been overthrown by military leaders and to ensure the safety of the U.S. students attending medical school on the island. Within six days, approximately 8,800 American soldiers will have pacified the Grenadian military and Cuban soldiers.

November 2 • President Reagan signs into law an act making the first Monday in January of each year a national holiday honoring Martin Luther King, Jr.

November 11 • The U.S. government expands its defense

98th CONGRESS

SENATE	....	100 Members
R	....	54
D	....	46
O	....	
HOUSE	....	435 Members
D	....	269
R	....	166
O	....	0

ESTIMATED
POPULATION
234,307,000

Ronald W. Reagan
40th President
16th Republican

George H.W. Bush
43rd Vice President
Republican

UNITED STATES ECONOMY

GROSS NATIONAL PRODUCT	........$ 3,514,500,000,000
RETAIL SALES	....................$ 1,557,518,000,000
EXPORTS	.........................$ 201,799,000,000
IMPORTS	.......................$ 268,901,000,000
FEDERAL GOVERNMENT EXPENDITURE	...................$ 808,400,000,000
FEDERAL DEBT	...................$ 1,137,300,000,000

system by stationing 160 cruise missiles in Great Britain.

December 24 • The majority of U.S. military personnel in Grenada withdraw from the island, leaving military police and civil affairs units to support the government.

International and Cultural Events • The 1963 civil rights march led by Martin Luther King, Jr., is commemorated by a 250,000-person gathering in Washington, D.C.

233

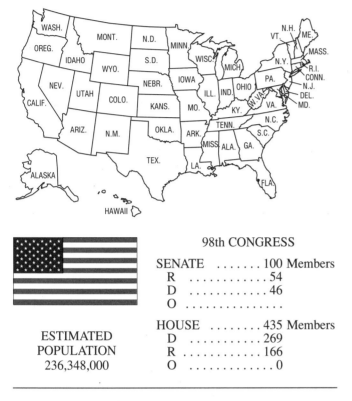

98th CONGRESS

SENATE .... 100 Members
R 54
D 46
O ....

HOUSE .... 435 Members
D 269
R 166
O 0

ESTIMATED
POPULATION
236,348,000

Ronald W. Reagan
40th President
16th Republican

George H.W. Bush
43rd Vice President
Republican

UNITED STATES ECONOMY

GROSS NATIONAL PRODUCT $3,902,400,000,000
RETAIL SALES $1,668,679,000,000
EXPORTS .... $ 219,926,000,000
IMPORTS .... $ 332,418,000,000
FEDERAL GOVERNMENT
EXPENDITURE .... $ 851,800,000,000
FEDERAL DEBT $1,564,700,000,000

Events

January 10 • The U.S. government restores diplomatic relations with the Vatican after a lapse of 117 years.
February 29 • In accordance with orders from President Reagan, 1,200 U.S. Marines complete their withdrawal from Beirut, Lebanon. Withdrawal of U.S. forces had begun on February 7.
March 5 • In a decision regarding separation of church and state, the U.S. Supreme Court rules constitutional the use of a nativity scene by a municipal government as part of its official Christmas display.
April 23 • Federal researchers announce that they have found the virus that causes Acquired Immunodeficiency Syndrome (AIDS), which has afflicted 4,000 Americans to date.
May 7 • An out-of-court settlement is reached by seven chemical companies in a lawsuit filed on behalf of hundreds of Vietnam veterans who have suffered from exposure to "Agent Orange".
June 6 • With leaders of other Allied nations, President Reagan attends ceremonies in Normandy, France, to commemorate the 40th anniversary of "Operation Overlord," the allied invasion of Nazi-occupied France.
June 12 • The U.S. Supreme Court rules that employees hired under affirmative action programs are not protected from lay-off, stating that employers may legally use a "last hired, first fired," or seniority, system.
June 26 • The Reverend Jesse Jackson negotiates with Cuban president Fidel Castro for the release of 22 Americans jailed in Cuba.
July 16 • The Democratic National Convention nominates former vice president Walter F. Mondale of Minnesota as its candidate for the presidency. Representative Geraldine Ferraro of New York will be nominated for vice president, becoming the first woman to be nominated for the office by a major political party.
August 30 • The space shuttle *Discovery* is launched on its first mission, which lasts five days.
September 20 • The U.S. Embassy in Beirut, Lebanon, is bombed again. The terrorist car-bomb attack kills 23 people, including two U.S. citizens.
October 3 • Accused of passing classified information to the Soviet Union, Richard W. Miller becomes the first FBI official to be charged with espionage.
November 6 •In a landslide victory, President Reagan and Vice President Bush are re-elected to their respective offices. In congressional elections, the Republicans gain a majority in the Senate, but Democrats retain a majority in the House of Representatives.
December 10 • U.S. astronomers announce the discovery of a planet outside our solar system, saying that they have found a gaseous object orbiting a star in the constellation Ophiuchus.
December 20 • Bell Laboratories announces the development of a megabit memory chip, which can store four times more electronic data than current computer chips. The chip, set to begin mass production, is a major step in technological advancement.
International and Cultural Events • Canada and more than 20 European nations sign an accord to reduce sulpher dioxide emissions by 30 percent by 1993.

United States of America 1985

Events

January 20 • Ronald Reagan is sworn in for his second term as president.

January 25 • Bernard Goetz, the "subway vigilante", is cleared by a New York City grand jury in charges related to the December 22, 1984, shooting of four black youths. Goetz does receive an indictment on charges of illegal possession of a handgun.

February 4 • Defaults on student loans reach $4.5 billion, leading the Department of Education to ask the Justice Department to help pursue the nearly 10 percent of student borrowers who have defaulted.

March 15 • Raymond Donovan resigns his post as secretary of labor. Donovan is the first cabinet secretary to be indicted on criminal charges while still in office.

March 18 • The U.S. Supreme Court rejects spending limits placed on political action committees.

April 12 • Senator Jake Garn of Utah serves as a member of the crew of the space shuttle *Discovery*. He becomes the first member of Congress to travel into space.

May 13 • Philadelphia police bomb *Move* headquarters; 61 homes are destroyed.

May 20 • The FBI arrests John Walker, Jr., in one of the most serious espionage cases since World War II.

June 14 • TWA flight 847 is hijacked with 153 people aboard. The hostages, including 39 Americans, are taken to Damascus, Syria, and one passenger, an American sailor, is killed. The hostages will be released on June 30.

July 18 • Worried that President Reagan will send U.S. military personnel into an armed conflict in Nicaragua, Congress bans financial aid to *contra* rebels.

August 2 • A Delta jet crashes at Dallas-Fort Worth International Airport, killing 137 people.

September 1 • United States Navy researchers, working with a French team, find the remains of the sunken *Titanic* 400 miles off the coast of Newfoundland and 12,000 feet under water.

September 6 • The U.S. unemployment rate reaches a five-year low of 6.9 percent.

September 9 • The U.S. government reverses its policy of tolerance for South Africa's policy of *apartheid* and imposes economic sanctions.

September 15 • The Commerce Department announces that the U.S. government owes more money than is owed to it for the first time since 1914.

October 7 • American Leon Klinghoffer, a passenger aboard the Italian cruise ship *Achille Lauro*, is killed by Palestinian terrorists who have hijacked the ship. Three days later, U.S. Navy jets will intercept an Egyptian plane carrying four of the hijackers, forcing it to land in Sicily.

November 19 • President Ronald Reagan and Soviet general secretary, Mikhail Gorbachev meet for the first time at summit in Geneva. The two men will meet privately for a period of about five hours.

International and Cultural Events • Mikhail Gorbachev is named first secretary of the Soviet Communist party (CPSU). Leaders of the Warsaw Pact countries meet and renew the alliance for 30 years. The Live Aid benefit concert in Philadelphia, Pennsylvania, raises $70 million for hunger relief in Africa.

99th CONGRESS

SENATE	.... 100 Members
R	 53
D	 47
O	 0
HOUSE	.... 435 Members
D	 252
R	 182
O	 1

ESTIMATED POPULATION 238,466,000

Ronald W. Reagan
40th President
16th Republican

George H.W. Bush
43rd Vice President
Republican

UNITED STATES ECONOMY

GROSS NATIONAL PRODUCT	.......$4,180,700,000,000
RETAIL SALES	....................$1,741,924,000,000
EXPORTS	.........................$ 215,915,000,000
IMPORTS	.......................$ 338,088,000,000
FEDERAL GOVERNMENT EXPENDITURE	...................$ 946,400,000,000
FEDERAL DEBT	...................$1,817,500,000,000

1986 United States of America

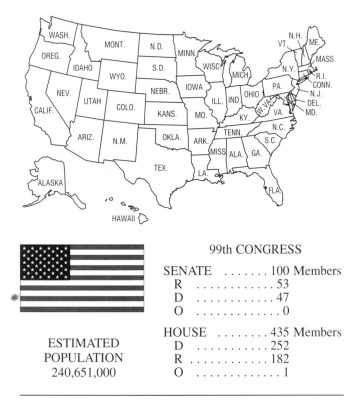

99th CONGRESS

SENATE .... 100 Members
R 53
D 47
O 0

HOUSE .... 435 Members
D 252
R 182
O 1

ESTIMATED
POPULATION
240,651,000

Ronald W. Reagan
40th President
16th Republican

George H.W. Bush
43rd Vice President
Republican

UNITED STATES ECONOMY

GROSS NATIONAL PRODUCT	$4,422,200,000,000
RETAIL SALES	$1,838,660,000,000
EXPORTS	$ 223,344,000,000
IMPORTS	$ 368,425,000,000
FEDERAL GOVERNMENT EXPENDITURE	$ 990,300,000,000
FEDERAL DEBT	$2,120,600,000,000

Events

January 3 • President Reagan imposes economic sanctions against Libya in retaliation for terrorist attacks in Rome and Vienna, Italy.

January 20 • "Martin Luther King, Jr. Day" is officially celebrated for the first time as a national holiday.

January 28 • The space shuttle *Challenger* explodes just 73 seconds after lift-off. All members of the crew are killed in the explosion, including school teacher Christa McAuliffe. NASA will be found to be at fault for relaxing safety standards.

February 27 • Filipino president Ferdinand Marcos arrives in Hawaii after resigning his office. Corazon Aquino had assumed control of the government on February 25. Marcos and his wife, Imelda, will gain attention for their extravagant expenditures while in the United States.

April 15 • From U.S. bases in Great Britain, U.S. Air Force FB-111 bombers attack ground targets in Tripoli, Libya, in retaliation for a terrorist bombing in West Berlin. A U.S. Army sergeant was killed in the terrorist attack.

May 25 • Between five and six million Americans join hands as part of "Hands Across America" to raise money for hunger relief and the homeless.

July 1-21 • Philadelphia garbage collectors go on strike; garbage will quickly pile up throughout the city.

July 26 • Father Lawrence Martin Jenco of Joliet, Illinois, who had been taken hostage by pro-Iranian terrorists in Beirut, Lebanon, is freed after 19 months in captivity.

August 31 • An Aeromexico passenger jet collides with a private plane near Los Angeles, California, killing 67 people. Fifteen others are killed on the ground by falling debris.

September 17 • William H. Rehnquist is sworn in as the 16th chief justice of the U.S. Supreme Court, and Antonin Scalia is sworn in as associate justice.

September 23 • Congress votes to designate the rose as the official flower of the United States.

October 2 • The Senate overturns a presidential veto sanctioning South Africa.

October 4-5 • Flooding occurs in 15 midwestern states.

October 10-11 • President Reagan and Premier Gorbachev meet in Iceland to discuss nuclear arms. The president will refuse to limit "Star Wars" research.

November 3 • A Lebanese magazine reports that the United States sold arms to Iran. Later, Attorney General Edwin Meese will disclose that funds from sales have been diverted to the Nicaraguan *contra* rebels. The disclosure will also result in the resignation of national security advisor Admiral John Poindexter and the dismissal of U.S. Marine lieutenant colonel Oliver North. Reagan will admit knowing about the arms sales but deny that he traded arms for hostages.

November 4 • In congressional elections, the Democrats win control of the Senate.

November 6 • President Reagan signs a bill that seeks to limit illegal migration into the United States.

International and Cultural Events • A chemical explosion and fire occurs at the Chernobyl nuclear power facility in Ukraine.

United States of America 1987

Events

January • Ronald Reagan submits the first trillion dollar budget in U.S. history. It has a projected deficit of $107.8 billion.

January 13 • The U.S. Supreme Court upholds a law requiring employers to grant as much as four months unpaid leave to pregnant women.

February 16 • John Demjanjuk, who had lived in the United States for 40 years, is brought to trial in Jerusalem, Israel, after being identified as "Ivan the Terrible", the guard accused of heinous crimes against Jews at the Nazi death camp at Treblinka, Poland.

February 27 • The Tower Commission, a federal commission investigating the Iran-*contra* affair, reports that it has found President Reagan to be confused and uninformed about arms trade dealings and out-of-touch with national security affairs.

April 27 • The U.S. Justice Department bans Austrian president Kurt Waldheim from entering the United States due to his alleged participation in Nazi activities as a member of the German army during World War II.

May 5-August 3 • Iran-*contra* hearings are held by Senate and House committees investigating the events that led to the arms trade deal. The televised hearings include 250 hours of testimony and 28 witnesses.

May 17 • An Iraqi air-launched missile hits the U.S. frigate *Stark*, killing 37 sailors.

July 1 • President Reagan nominates Robert Bork to replace retiring justice Lewis F. Powell, Jr., on the U.S. Supreme Court.

July 11 • It is announced that the population of the world has reached five billion.

July 21 • The U.S. government offers naval protection to Kuwaiti tankers in the Persian Gulf.

August 3 • The congressional hearings investigating the Iran-*contra* scandal are concluded.

August 12 • President Reagan denies that he knew that funds from arms sales to Iran were to be diverted to Nicaraguan *contra* rebels.

October 19 • After reaching a record high in August, the Dow Jones Industrial Average plunges 508 points for a record drop of 22.6 percent.

October 23 • The Senate rejects President Reagan's nomination of Robert Bork for Supreme Court associate justice by a vote of 58 to 42.

November 5 • Caspar Weinberger resigns as secretary of defense.

November 18 • In a report on the Iran-*contra* affair, a congressional joint committee blames President Reagan for abusing the law. Eight Republicans in Congress refuse to sign the report.

100th CONGRESS

SENATE	100 Members
D	55
R	45
O	0
HOUSE	435 Members
D	258
R	177
O	0

ESTIMATED POPULATION
243,419,000

Ronald W. Reagan
40th President
16th Republican

George H.W. Bush
43rd Vice President
Republican

UNITED STATES ECONOMY

GROSS NATIONAL PRODUCT	$4,692,300,000,000
RETAIL SALES	$1,890,695,000,000
EXPORTS	$ 250,208,000,000
IMPORTS	$ 409,765,000,000
FEDERAL GOVERNMENT EXPENDITURE	$1,003,900,000,000
FEDERAL DEBT	$2,346,100,000,000

December 2 • President Reagan and Canadian prime minister Brian Mulroney sign a free trade agreement.

December 7-10 • President Reagan and Soviet premier Mikahil Gorbachev meet in Washington, D.C. and agree to an Intermediate-range Nuclear Forces (INF) Treaty, vowing to dismantle intermediate-range weapons.

International and Cultural Events • Political parties are legalized in Chile. Klaus Barbie, wartime Gestapo chief, is convicted of crimes against humanity in France.

1988 United States of America

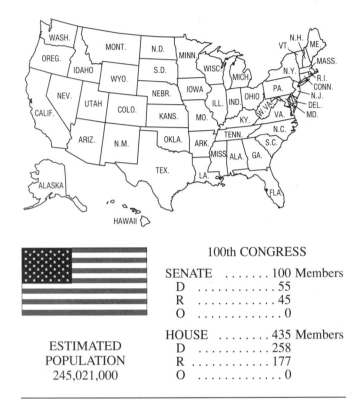

100th CONGRESS

SENATE .... 100 Members
D 55
R 45
O 0

HOUSE .... 435 Members
D 258
R 177
O 0

ESTIMATED
POPULATION
245,021,000

Ronald W. Reagan
40th President
16th Republican

George H.W. Bush
43rd Vice President
Republican

UNITED STATES ECONOMY

GROSS NATIONAL PRODUCT ....$ 5,049,600,000,000
RETAIL SALES ....$ 1,968,972,000,000
EXPORTS ....$ 320,230,000,000
IMPORTS ....$ 447,189,000,000
FEDERAL GOVERNMENT
    EXPENDITURE ....$ 1,064,100,000,000
FEDERAL DEBT ....$ 2,601,300,000,000

Events

January • The U.S. Supreme Court rules that censorship of student newspapers by school officials is *not* unconstitutional.

February • Governor Evan Meachum of Arizona is impeached for high crimes and malfeasance. Meachum is the first state governor to be impeached since 1931.

March • The U.S. Senate ratifies an international agreement curbing global use of chemicals that deplete the earth's ozone layer.

March • Two senior Department of Justice officials and four assistants resign, claiming abuse of position and illegal acts by Attorney General Edwin Meese.

April • The Senate votes to grant $20,000 to each of the 60,000 Japanese-Americans who were placed in internment camps during World War II.

April • A federal law banning smoking on all airplane flights of two hours or less in the United States is enacted.

April • President Reagan's former deputy press secretary, Larry Speakers, admits that he had invented or "borrowed" statements attributed to the president.

April 18 • U.S. Navy Seals attack and destroy Iranian oil platforms in the Persian Gulf.

May 29-June 2 • President Reagan and Soviet premier Mikhail Gorbachev meet for the fourth time. The Moscow meeting will result in nine agreements, including the formal signing of the 1987 Intermediate-range Nuclear Forces (INF) Treaty on June 1.

July 3 • The USS *Vincennes* accidentally shoots down an Iranian commercial airplane, killing 290 civilian passengers.

July 11 • The U.S. ambassador to Nicaragua and seven other U.S. citizens are expelled.

July 19-20 • The Democratic National Convention nominates Governor Michael Dukakis (Massachusetts) as its candidate for president and Senator Lloyd Bentsen (Texas) for vice president.

July • Attorney General Edwin Meese resigns after a 14-month investigation of his activities in office.

August 8 • The United Nations (UN) imposes a cease-fire between Iran and Iraq. An eight-year war between the countries resulted in the deaths of more than one million people.

August 17-18 • Vice President George Bush is nominated for president by the Republican National Convention in New Orleans, Louisiana.

September 29 • The space shuttle *Discovery* is launched. It is the first launch since the January 1986 *Challenger* disaster.

October • Mikhail Gorbachev is elected president of the Union of Soviet Socialist Republics.

November 8 • Republicans George Bush and J. Danforth Quayle (Indiana) are elected president and vice president, respectively, but the Democrats retain a majority of seats in Congress.

December 15 • The U.S. government resumes relations with the Palestine Liberation Organization (PLO) after 13 years.

International and Cultural Events • British prime minister Margaret Thatcher introduces radical changes in British social welfare.

George H.W. Bush 1989

Events

January 20 • George H.W. Bush is inaugurated as the 41st President of the United States, and James Danforth Quayle is sworn in as vice president.

February 10 • Ron Brown is elected chairman of the Democratic National Committee, becoming the first African American to head a major political party.

March 10 • The U.S. unemployment rate declines to 5.1 percent, its lowest level since 1974.

March 24 • A tanker, the *Exxon Valdez,* spills 11 million gallons of crude oil when it collides with a reef in Price William Sound, Alaska. It is the largest oil spill in U.S. history.

May 4 • Lieutenant Colonel Oliver North is found guilty of three of 12 charges associated with the Iran-*contra* affair. His convictions will later be overturned.

May 31 • Following an investigation of financial activities, Jim Wright resigns as speaker of the House.

June 21 • In the case *Texas v. Johnson*, the U.S. Supreme Court rules that burning the U.S. flag is a legal form of political expression that is protected by the First Amendment to the Constitution.

July 5 • Lieutenant Colonel Oliver North is sentenced to a suspended prison term and ordered to pay a $150,000 fine for his Iran-*contra* affair convictions.

August 9 • Congress passes legislation bailing out the savings & loan industry at a cost of $166 billion over a 10-year period.

September 1 • The U.S. government discontinues its diplomatic relations with the Panamanian government and its leader, General Manuel Noriega.

September 21 • Hurricane Hugo, the worst storm of the decade, hits the eastern seaboard, devastating Georgia and South Carolina.

October 17 • Sixty people are killed and several thousand are injured when an earthquake strikes the San Francisco, California, area. The quake causes damage estimated at $5.6 billion.

December 3 • Presidents Bush and Gorbachev officially declare the end of the Cold War.

December 20 • U.S. military personnel invade Panama to arrest military ruler General Manuel Noriega and to restore the elected civilian government. The new government, headed by Guillermo Endara, will be installed during the U.S. occupation of Panama. Hiding in the Vatican's embassy, General Noriega will surrender to U.S. officials on January 3, 1990.

International and Cultural Events • Chinese authorities use brutal force against the pro-democracy demonstrators occupying Tienanmen Square.

101st CONGRESS

SENATE .... 100 Members
D 55
R 45
O 0

HOUSE .... 433 Members
D 258
R 175
O 0

ESTIMATED POPULATION 247,342,000

George H.W. Bush
41st President
17th Republican

James Danforth Quayle
44th Vice President
Republican

UNITED STATES ECONOMY

GROSS NATIONAL PRODUCT ....$ 5,438,700,000,000
RETAIL SALES ....$ 2,012,349,000,000
EXPORTS ....$ 362,120,000,000
IMPORTS ....$ 477,365,000,000
FEDERAL GOVERNMENT
    EXPENDITURE ....$ 1,143,200,000,000
FEDERAL DEBT ....$ 2,868,000,000,000

George H.W. Bush

Birth ....Milton, MA, June 12, 1924
Parents ....Prescott and Dorothy Walker Bush
Married ....Barbara Pierce
Home ....Houston, TX
Presidency ....1989 – 1993

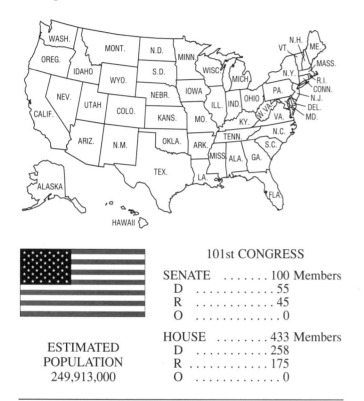

101st CONGRESS

SENATE .... 100 Members
D 55
R 45
O 0

HOUSE .... 433 Members
D 258
R 175
O 0

ESTIMATED
POPULATION
249,913,000

George H.W. Bush
41st President
17th Republican

James Danforth Quayle
44th Vice President
Republican

UNITED STATES ECONOMY

GROSS NATIONAL PRODUCT ....$ 5,743,800,000,000
RETAIL SALES ....$ 2,024,390,000,000
EXPORTS ....$ 389,307,000,000
IMPORTS ....$ 498,337,000,000
FEDERAL GOVERNMENT
  EXPENDITURE ....$ 1,252,700,000,000
FEDERAL DEBT ....$ 3,206,600,000,000

Events

January 18 • FBI agents and city police officers arrest Washington, D.C., mayor Marion Barry, Jr., after videotaping him purchase and then smoke crack cocaine.

January 30 • A federal judge orders former president Ronald Reagan to provide excerpts from his personal diaries for use in the trial of his former national security adviser, John M. Poindexter, who claims that Reagan authorized his activities during the Iran-*contra* affair. Reagan will later be ordered to testify in Poindexter's trial.

February 16-17 • In a videotaped testimony marked by memory lapses, Ronald Reagan reveals that he authorized the general policies of covert arms sales to Iran and economic aid to the Nicaraguan *contra* rebels in 1985 and 1986 but denies that he approved any illegal activities.

April 17 • A federal district court jury convicts John M. Poindexter of five felony charges related to the Iran-*contra* arms trade scandal, including obstruction of Congress and making false statements to Congress.

April 25 • The space shuttle *Discovery* launches the Hubble Space Telescope.

June 11 • The U.S. Supreme Court strikes down a federal law forbidding the desecration of the U.S. flag, calling the law a violation of First Amendment protections.

June 26 • President Bush announces a plan for deficit reduction that includes tax revenue increases, despite his campaign pledge of "No new taxes."

July 26 • President Bush signs landmark civil rights legislation, banning discrimination against people with disabilities in employment and public transportation and accommodations.

September 18 • Charles Keating, owner of Lincoln Savings & Loan Association, is indicted on 42 charges of criminal fraud by a California state grand jury.

International and Cultural Events • South African anti-apartheid leader Nelson Mandela is freed after 27 years of imprisonment. Iraq invades the Persian Gulf emirate of Kuwait. The invasion leads to the establishment of a coalition between the United States, Arab countries, NATO member countries and former members of the Warsaw Pact.

Presidents Reagan, Nixon, Bush and Ford gather at the Richard Nixon Library and Birthplace.

United States of America 1991

Events

January 12 • Congress votes to use military force in the Persian Gulf if Iraq refuses to withdraw from Kuwait by January 15, the date mandated by the United Nations Security Council.

January 17 • After Iraq fails to withdraw from Kuwait, U.S.-led coalition forces launch massive air strikes against Baghdād, Iraq.

February 24 • Approximately 200,000 troops began a ground offensive that lasts until February 27, when the first U.S. forces enter Kuwait City and President Bush announces the liberation of Kuwait.

February 28 • The end of the Gulf War is announced. The United States military reports an estimated 140 deaths, 450 injuries and at least 20 prisoners of war.

March 3 • Four white Los Angeles police officers are videotaped beating Rodney King, a black motorist whom they stopped for a traffic violation. On March 15, the officers are indicted by a grand jury for violation of King's civil rights.

June 17 • The body of the 12th U.S. president, Zachary Taylor, is exhumed from a Louisville, Kentucky, grave to determine whether he had died from arsenic poisoning. No trace of poison is found.

July 1 • President Bush nominates Clarence Thomas, a federal appeals court judge from the District of Columbia, to be the second African American to serve as a U.S. Supreme Court associate justice. Thomas was appointed to succeed Thurgood Marshall, who retired on June 27.

July 31 • Agreeing to reduce long range nuclear weapons by one-third, President Bush and Soviet president Gorbachev sign the Strategic Arms Reduction Treaty, (START).

October 6 • In a televised confirmation hearing by the Senate Judiciary Committee, Anita Hill, a law professor

President and Mrs. Bush.

102nd CONGRESS

SENATE	....	100 Members
D	....	56
R	....	.44
O	....	.0
HOUSE	....	435 Members
D	....	267
R	....	167
O	....	1

ESTIMATED POPULATION 252,650,000

George H.W. Bush
41st President
17th Republican

James Danforth Quayle
44th Vice President
Republican

UNITED STATES ECONOMY

GROSS NATIONAL PRODUCT	.... $5,916,700,000,000
RETAIL SALES	.... $1,974,351,000,000
EXPORTS	.... $ 416,913,000,000
IMPORTS	.... $ 490,981,000,000
FEDERAL GOVERNMENT EXPENDITURE	.... $1,323,400,000,000
FEDERAL DEBT	.... $3,598,500,000,000

at the University of Oklahoma, charges that Supreme Court nominee Clarence Thomas sexually harassed her. Despite Hill's testimony, the Senate, on October 15, confirms Thomas.

December 25 • The Soviet Union is officially dissolved.

International and Cultural Events • On June 17, the government of South Africa ends its system of *apartheid*, which had forced the separation of the races since 1950.

1992 United States of America

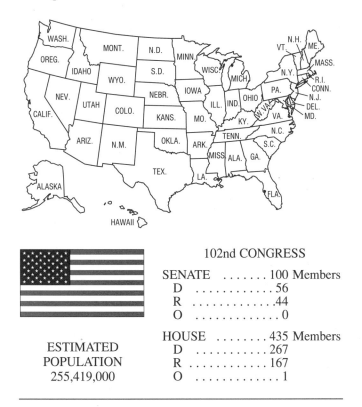

102nd CONGRESS

SENATE .... 100 Members
D 56
R 44
O 0

HOUSE .... 435 Members
D 267
R 167
O 1

ESTIMATED POPULATION
255,419,000

George H.W. Bush
41st President
17th Republican

James Danforth Quayle
44th Vice President
Republican

UNITED STATES ECONOMY

GROSS NATIONAL PRODUCT $6,244,400,000,000
RETAIL SALES $2,037,409,000,000
EXPORTS .... $ 440,352,000,000
IMPORTS .... $ 536,458,000,000
FEDERAL GOVERNMENT
EXPENDITURE $1,380,900,000,000
FEDERAL DEBT $4,002,100,000,000

Events

March 11 • Following a 1991 General Accounting Office (GAO) audit of the House Bank and a subsequent investigation by the House Ethics Committee, it is revealed that 355 current and former members of the U.S. House of Representatives have misused their bank accounts without consequence, often overdrawing their accounts by thousands of dollars. On March 13, the members of the House vote unanimously to release the names of all members who have overdrawn their checking accounts.

March 30 • Undeclared presidential candidate H. Ross Perot names retired admiral James Stockdale as his vice presidential running mate. (Twenty seven states require a vice presidential running mate for a presidential candidate to be included on the ballot.)

April 9 • In a U.S. district court in Miami, Florida, General Manuel Noriega of Panama is convicted of racketeering, drug trafficking and money laundering.

April 29 • Four white Los Angeles police officers are acquitted of criminal charges related to the March 3, 1991, videotaped beating of Rodney King. Riots follow.

May 7 • The state legislature of Michigan approves an amendment to the U.S. Constitution that bans midterm congressional pay raises. Michigan is the 38th state to ratify the amendment, giving it the required three-fourths approval by the states. The amendment, which had been introduced in 1789 by James Madison and was the second amendment sent to the states for ratification, is certified by the U.S. Archivist on May 18 and recognized by Congress as the 27th Amendment to the Constitution on May 20.

July 9 • Governor William J. Clinton of Arkansas, the front-runner for the Democratic presidential nomination, selects Senator Albert Gore, Jr., of Tennessee as his vice presidential running mate. On July 16, Clinton concludes the Democratic National Convention by accepting the nomination of his party.

August 24 • With winds up to 165 m.p.h., Hurricane Andrew is one of the worst natural disasters in U.S. history. The storm, which hit Florida and the Gulf coast states, kills at least 30 people and causes damage in excess of $20 billion.

October 2 • U.S. Senate approves the Strategic Arms Limitation Treaty (SALT).

November 2 • William J. Clinton is elected president, with Al Gore as vice president, defeating incumbent George Bush and independent challenger H. Ross Perot.

December 9 • About 1,800 U.S. Marines, U.S. Navy Seals and U.S. Army light infantrymen are sent to civil-war ravaged Mogadishu, Somalia, to aid in the United Nations' famine relief efforts. The mission is called "Operation Restore Hope".

International and Cultural Events • White South African voters grant their government authority to negotiate an end to white minority rule.

ARTICLE XXVII

Congressional Compensation

No law, varying the compensation for the services of the Senators and Representatives, shall take effect, until an election of Representatives shall have intervened.

William J. Clinton 1993

Events

January 20 • William J. Clinton is inaugurated as the 42nd president of the United States.

February 26 • The World Trade Center in New York City, New York, is bombed; five people are killed and several hundred are wounded. A Muslem fundamentalist is arrested on March 4 for the terrorist act.

February 28 • Agents from the Bureau of Alcohol, Tobacco and Firearms (BATF) attempt to arrest David Koresh, the leader of the Branch Davidian religious cult in Waco, Texas. The Branch Davidians resist, resulting in the deaths of four federal agents and the wounding of an additional 14 agents.

April 19 • The Stand-off at the Branch Davidian compound ends when agents of the Federal Bureau of Investigation attempt to storm the compound. A fire, started on the inside of the compound's main building, destroys the compound and kills approximately 80 people, including David Koresh.

June 28 • A U.S. missile attack on Baghdād strikes the Iraqi Intelligence Center. The attack was in retaliation for an April assassination attempt against former president George Bush while he was visiting Kuwait.

August 9 • The second-worst flood in U.S. history hits the Midwest, causing more than $12 billion worth of damage from North Dakota to Missouri. Along the Mississippi River, almost 70,000 people lose their homes. On August 12, President Clinton promises $6.2 billion in federal aid to flood victims.

December 7 • Astronauts successfully repair a malfunctioning mirror on the Hubble Space Telescope. The malfunction was discovered after the telescope was launched in 1990. On December 13, the astronauts safely return to earth aboard the space shuttle *Endeavor*.

International and Cultural Events • Residents of Eritrea vote for independence from Ethiopia.

William J. Clinton
42nd President
15th Democrat

Albert Gore, Jr.
45th Vice President
Democrat

103rd CONGRESS

SENATE .... 100 Members
  D 57
  R 43
  O 0

HOUSE .... 435 Members
  D 258
  R 176
  O 1

ESTIMATED
POPULATION
258,137,000

UNITED STATES ECONOMY

GROSS NATIONAL PRODUCT	$6,550,200,000,000
RETAIL SALES	$2,128,400,000,000
EXPORTS	$ 456,823,000,000
IMPORTS	$ 589,441,000,000
FEDERAL GOVERNMENT EXPENDITURE	$1,408,700,000,000
FEDERAL DEBT	$4,351,400,000,000

William J. Clinton

Birth .... .Hope, AR, Aug. 19, 1946
Parents ..... .Roger and Virginia Cassidy Blythe Clinton
Married .... .Hillary Rodham
Home .... .Little Rock, AR
Presidency .... 1993 –

Israeli prime minister Yitzhak Rabin and Palestine Liberation Organization (PLO) chairman Yasir Arafat agree to a peace accord.

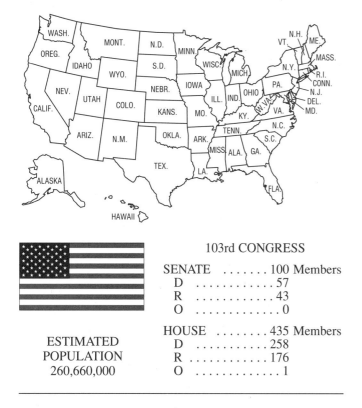

103rd CONGRESS

SENATE .... 100 Members
D 57
R 43
O 0

HOUSE .... 435 Members
D 258
R 176
O 1

ESTIMATED
POPULATION
260,660,000

William J. Clinton
42nd President
15th Democrat

Albert Gore, Jr.
45th Vice President
Democrat

UNITED STATES ECONOMY

GROSS NATIONAL PRODUCT $6,931,400,000,000
RETAIL SALES $2,256,981,000,000
EXPORTS ....$ 502,485,000,000
IMPORTS ....$ 668,584,000,000
FEDERAL GOVERNMENT
   EXPENDITURE $1,460,900,000,000
FEDERAL DEBT $4,643,700,000,000

Events

January 1 • The North American Free Trade Agreement (NAFTA) takes effect.
January 17 • An earthquake shakes Los Angeles, California. The quake, registering 6.7 on the Richter scale, kills more than 60 people and renders 25,000 others homeless.
February 21 • Aldrich Ames, a former chief of the CIA's

counter intelligence division, is arrested by federal agents. Ames and his wife are charged with spying for the former Soviet Union.
March 24 • Public allegations of financial mismanagement are made against President and Hillary Clinton. The charges are related to the failure of the Whitewater Development Corporation in Arkansas and the questionable investments and financial arrangements that led to the collapse of Madison Guaranty Savings and Loan.
April 19 • In a case heard by the U.S. Supreme Court, discrimination based on gender in jury selection is ruled as a violation of the 14th Amendment's equal protection clause.
April 28 • Aldrich Ames is sentenced to life in prison for selling secrets to the former Soviet Union.
May 26 • President Clinton renews the People's Republic of China's "most favored nation" status despite his ongoing criticism of Chinese human rights abuses.
June 6 • Former National Football League star and sports broadcaster O.J. Simpson is arrested in connection with the murder of his former wife, Nicole Brown Simpson, and her friend, Ronald Goldman. The arrest was made after a nationally televised police chase that lasts several hours.
August 11 • Cuban president Fidel Castro eases restrictions on Cubans who want to flee their country, resulting in a massive influx of Cuban refugees into the United States. President Clinton, in response, changes the criteria for the status of "refugee."
September 19 • United States military forces are sent to Haiti to enforce an agreement between President Clinton and the Haitian military rulers who have deposed democratically elected president Jean Bertrand Ariside. The U.S. forces will remain in Haiti to oversee Aristide's peaceful return to power.
International and Cultural Events • Nelson Mandela is sworn in as South Africa's first black president.

President Clinton signs the Community Development Financial Institutions Act into law at the Department of Agriculture on September 23, 1994.

United States of America 1995

Events

January 4 • The 104th Congress, which has the first Republican majority in 40 years, is sworn in and begins its first session.

March 23 • The U.S. Senate votes 69 to 29 in favor of legislation that would grant the president a line-item veto. This type of veto would allow the president to eliminate specific items in appropriations measures and special tax benefits in other bills. The House of Representatives had approved the same bill on February 6, 1995, by a vote of 294 to 134.

April 19 • At 9:02 a.m., a bomb explodes in front of the Alfred P. Murrah Federal Building in Oklahoma City, Oklahoma. The building, which housed the offices of federal agencies and a day-care center, is almost completely destroyed. More than 160 people are killed in the explosion. On April 21, Timothy McVeigh is arrested in connection with the bombing and is charged with destruction of federal property and malicious damage.

June 22 • The states get congressional approval to set their own speed limits with the passage of the National Highway System Designation Act. The legislation, which was signed into law by President Clinton on November 18, 1995, eliminates the national mandatory highway speed limits of 55 and 65 miles per hour.

June 29 • The U.S. spacecraft *Atlantis* docks with the Russian space station *Mir*.

August 10 • A federal grand jury indicts Timothy McVeigh and Terry Nichols on charges related to the April 19 bombing of the Alfred P. Murrah Federal Building in Oklahoma City, Oklahoma.

August 17 • A federal grand jury indicts Arkansas governor Jim Guy Tucker and two business partners of President Clinton on 21 counts of fraud, conspiracy and falsification of government documents in order to obtain millions of dollars in federally backed loans.

September 7 • Senator Robert Packwood (Oregon) resigns after the Senate Ethics Committee charges him with committing acts of sexual harassment and the misuse of campaign funds.

September 28 • President Clinton hosts a meeting of Israeli prime minister Yitzhak Rabin and Palestine Liberation Organization leader Yasser Arafat at the White House. The meeting results in an agreement for Palestinian self-rule in the Israeli-occupied west bank of the Jordan River and the Gaza Strip.

November 4 • Israeli prime minister Yitzhak Rabin is assassinated while leaving a peace rally in Tel Aviv.

November 15 • A partial government shut-down occurs as a result of the federal budget feud between Democrats and Republicans in Congress.

104th CONGRESS

SENATE	.... 100 Members
R	53
D	47
O	0

HOUSE	........435 Members
R	230
D	204
O	1

ESTIMATED POPULATION 263,034,000

William J. Clinton
42nd President
15th Democrat

Albert Gore, Jr.
45th Vice President
Democrat

UNITED STATES ECONOMY

GROSS NATIONAL PRODUCT	........$7,253,800,000,000
RETAIL SALES	....................$2,329,838,000,000
EXPORTS	.........................$ 575,939,000,000
IMPORTS	........................$ 749,363,000,000
FEDERAL GOVERNMENT EXPENDITURE	...................$1,350,600,000,000
FEDERAL DEBT	....................$4,921,000,000,000

November 23 • A judge overturns California's Proposition 18, which opposed immigration, stating that it is the responsibility of the federal government, not the states, to regulate immigration.

International and Cultural Events • O.J. Simpson goes on trial for murder in Los Angeles and the jury finds him not guilty. Professional baseball players end their 234-day strike.

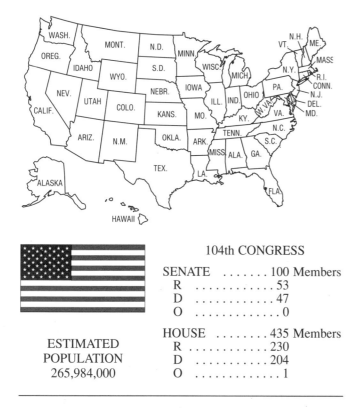

104th CONGRESS

SENATE .... 100 Members
R 53
D 47
O 0

HOUSE .... 435 Members
R 230
D 204
O 1

ESTIMATED
POPULATION
265,984,000

William J. Clinton
42nd President
15th Democrat

Albert Gore, Jr.
45th Vice President
Democrat

UNITED STATES ECONOMY

GROSS NATIONAL PRODUCT $7,545,100,000,000
RETAIL SALES (July) .... $ 206,304,000,000
EXPORTS (July) .... $ 351,746,000,000
IMPORTS (July) .... $ 458,993,000,000
FEDERAL GOVERNMENT
    EXPENDITURE $1,572,411,000,000
FEDERAL DEBT (September 30) $5,224,800,000,000

Events

January 6 • A 21-day partial government shutdown ends when President Clinton signs a spending measure that authorizes resumption of full government operations.

January 22 • It is disclosed to the public that Hillary Clinton has been subpoenaed by a federal grand jury to testify regarding her financial activities related to the Whitewater Development Corporation. Her testimony on January 26, 1996, marks the first time a first lady is called to testify before a federal grand jury.

February 24 • Two unarmed private planes belonging to the Cuban refugee aid association Brothers to the Rescue are shot down by Cuban fighter jets over international waters between the United States and Cuba. On February 26, President Clinton responds by increasing economic sanctions against Cuba and restricting flights between the two countries.

March 12 • Senator Robert J. Dole becomes the leading contender for the Republican presidential nomination by winning all seven states in the "Super Tuesday" Republican primaries.

March 19 • A federal appeals court judge in Louisiana strikes down the affirmative action-based admission policy of the University of Texas' law school. The court rules that a policy that allows admission of black and Hispanic students with lower grade point averages and test scores than white students is not justified.

April 3 • Secretary of Commerce Ron Brown and 32 other U.S. government officials and business executives are killed in a plane crash in Croatia. The U.S. Air Force jet in which they were flying crashed into a mountain during bad weather.

April 3 • Theodore Kaczynski, a Harvard University graduate and former professor of mathematics, is arrested as a suspect in the "Unabomber" case. He is under investigation for a number of serial bombings carried out over 17 years that have killed three people and injured 23 others.

May 11 • ValuJet Flight 592 crashes in the Florida Everglades after taking off from Miami. One hundred and ten people on board the Atlanta-bound flight are killed.

June 13 • The U.S. Supreme Court strikes down congressional districts in North Carolina and Texas, ruling that race-based electoral districts violate the equal protection clause of the 14th Amendment to the Constitution.

July 17 • TWA Flight 800 crashes off the coast of New York, killing 230 people.

July 27 • A bomb explodes at Olympic Centennial Park in Atlanta, Georgia, killing one person and injuring 111 others. The International Olympic Committee votes to continue the games.

November 5 • President Clinton and Vice President Gore win re-election, defeating their Republican challengers, Robert J. Dole and Jack Kemp.

International and Cultural Events • The Guatemalan government and rebels sign an agreement to end their 35-year-old civil war.

United States of America 1997

Events

January 2 • Six current and one former member of Congress file a lawsuit to challenge the constitutionality of the presidential line-item veto. This veto, which Congress extended to the president in 1996, allows the chief executive to cancel individual appropriations and tax measures. A district judge, on April 10, will strike down the law, arguing that it violated the Constitution by its delegation of legislative power to the executive branch.

January 8 • The White House Office of National Drug Control Policy announces that it will spend as much as $1 million to study the effectiveness of marijuana as a form of medical treatment. In November 1996, voters in Arizona and California approved measures authorizing doctors to prescribe marijuana for their patients.

January 20 • William J. Clinton and Albert Gore, Jr., are inaugurated for a second term as president and vice president, respectively.

January 21 • The House of Representatives votes 395 to 28 to reprimand Speaker of the House Newton Gingrich (Georgia). Gingrich is reprimanded for admitted unintentional violations of House ethics rules. The speaker is also assessed a $300,000 fine. In April, Gingrich will announce that former Republican presidential nominee Robert J. Dole will loan him the money needed to pay the fine.

January 28 • The Internal Revenue Service (IRS) announces that it will delay enforcing a regulation that would allow farmers to use commodity contracts that are deferred income payments as a tax deduction.

January 28 • The Federal Aviation Administration (FAA) announces that it will publish aviation safety information on the Internet. The agency notes, however, that the information will not include rankings of airlines by safety records.

February 27 • United States ambassador to Panama, William Hughes, announces that the United States and Panama have entered into discussions on maintaining a U.S. presence in the country after the Panama Canal reverts to Panamanian control in the year 2000.

March 21 • President Clinton and Russian president Boris Yeltsin met in Helsinki, Finland, to discuss a variety of strategic issues confronting the United States, Europe and the Russian Federation. President Clinton, with offers of new U.S. initiatives to help stimulate investment and economic growth in Russia, is unable to persuade President Yeltsin to accept the eastward expansion of NATO.

April 6 • Secretary of the Treasury Robert Rubin and Vietnamese minister of finance Nguyen Sinh Hung sign

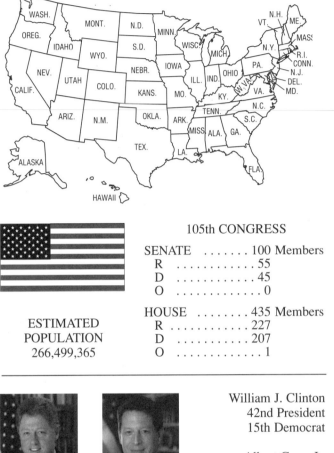

105th CONGRESS

SENATE .... 100 Members
R 55
D 45
O 0

HOUSE .... 435 Members
R 227
D 207
O 1

ESTIMATED
POPULATION
266,499,365

William J. Clinton
42nd President
15th Democrat

Albert Gore, Jr.
45th Vice President
Democrat

an agreement for the Vietnamese government to repay $146 million owed to the United States by the former Republic of Vietnam (South Vietnam).

April 17 • The Clinton administration announces a plan for the reorganization of the Department of State. Among its provisions, the plan would consolidate the Arms Control and Disarmament Agency and the United States Information Agency into the State Department over a period of several years.

April 22 • Vice President Gore announces that the United States will open "regional environmental hubs" in 12 embassies to address regional environmental problems. These hubs, the vice president says, illustrate how environmental matters have become an important part of U.S. national security.

International and Cultural Events • Peruvian soldiers storm the Japanese ambassador's residence, freeing 71 of the 72 hostages and killing all the *Túpac Amaru* guerrillas.

The Flag

☆ ☆ ☆ ☆ ☆ ☆ ☆ ☆ ☆ ☆ ☆ ☆ ☆ ☆ ☆ ☆

The History of the Stars and Stripes

The Stars and Stripes originated as a result of a resolution adopted by the Marine Committee of the Second Continental Congress at Philadelphia on June 14, 1777. The resolution read:

"Resolved, that the flag of the United States be thirteen stripes, alternate red and white; that the union be thirteen stars, white in a blue field representing a new constellation."

The resolution gave no instruction as to how many points the stars should have, nor how the stars should be arranged on the blue union. Consequently, some flags had stars scattered on the blue field without any specific design, some arranged the stars in rows, and some in a circle. The first Navy Stars and Stripes had the stars arranged in staggered formation in alternate rows of threes and twos on a blue field. Other Stars and Stripes flags had stars arranged in alternate rows of four, five and four. Some stars had six points while others had eight.

Strong evidence indicates that Francis Hopkinson of New Jersey, a signer of the Declaration of Independence, was responsible for the stars in the U.S. flag. At the time that the flag resolution was adopted, Hopkinson was the Chairman of the Continental Navy Board's Middle Department. Hopkinson also helped design other devices for the Government including the Great Seal of the United States. For his services, Hopkinson submitted a letter to the Continental Admiralty Board asking "whether a Quarter Cask of the public Wine will not be a proper and reasonable Reward for these Labours of Fancy and a suitable Encouragement to future Exertions of a like Nature." His request was turned down since the Congress regarded him as a public servant.

An Early Stars and Stripes

During the Revolutionary War, several patriots made flags for our new nation. Among them were Cornelia Bridges, Elizabeth (Betsy) Ross and Rebecca Young, all of Pennsylvania, and John Shaw of Annapolis, Maryland. Although Betsy Ross, the best known of these persons, made flags for 50 years, there is no proof that she made the first Stars and Stripes. It is known that she made flags for the Pennsylvania State Navy in 1777. The flag popularly known as the "Betsy Ross flag," which arranged the stars in a circle, did not appear until the early 1790s.

The claims of Betsy Ross were first brought to the

attention of the public in 1870 by one of her grandsons, William J. Canby. In a paper he read before the meeting of the Historical Society of Pennsylvania, Canby stated:

"It is not *tradition*, it is *report* from the lips of the principle participator in the transaction, directly told not to one or two, but a dozen or more living witnesses, of which I myself am one, though but a little boy when I heard it . . . Colonel [George] Ross with Robert Morris and General Washington, called on Mrs. Ross and told her they were a committee of Congress, and wanted her to make a flag from the drawing, a rough one, which, upon her suggestions, was redrawn by General Washington in pencil in her back parlor. This was prior to the Declaration of Independence. I fix the date to be during Washington's visit to Congress from New York in June, 1776, when he came to confer upon the affairs of the Army, the flag being no doubt, one of these affairs."

The Grand Union Flag

The first flag of the colonists to have any resemblance to the present Stars and Stripes was the Grand Union Flag, sometimes referred to as the Congress Colors, the First Navy Ensign, and the Cambridge Flag. Its design consisted of 13 stripes, alternately red and white, representing the Thirteen Colonies, with a blue field in the upper left-hand corner bearing the red cross of St. George of England with the white cross of St. Andrew of Scotland. As the flag of the revolution, it was used on many occasions. It was first flown by the ships of the Colonial Fleet on the Delaware River. On December 3, 1775, it was raised aboard Captain Esek Hopkin's flagship *Alfred* by John Paul Jones, then a Navy lieutenant. Later the flag was raised on the liberty pole at Prospect Hill, which was near George Washington's headquarters in Cambridge, Massachusetts. It was our unofficial national flag on July 4, 1776, Independence Day; and it remained the unofficial national flag and ensign of the Navy until June 14, 1777, when the Continental Congress authorized the Stars and Stripes.

Interestingly, the Grand Union Flag also was standard of the British East India Company. It was only by degrees that the Union Flag of Great Britain was discarded. The final breach between the Colonies and Great Britain brought about the removal of the British Union from the canton of our striped flag and the substitution of stars on a blue field.

Fifteen Stars and Stripes

When two new states were admitted to the Union (Kentucky and Vermont), a resolution was adopted in January of 1794, expanding the flag to 15 stars and 15 stripes. This flag was the official flag of our country from 1795 to 1818, and was prominent in many historic events. It inspired Francis Scott Key to write "The Star-Spangled Banner" during the bombardment of Fort McHenry; it was the first flag to be flown over a fortress of the Old World when American Marine and Naval forced raised it above the pirate stronghold in Tripoli on April 27, 1805; it was the ensign of American forces in the Battle of Lake Erie in September of 1813; and it was flown by General Jackson in New Orleans in January of 1815.

However, realizing that the flag would become unwieldy with a stripe for each new State, Captain Samuel C. Reid, USN, suggested to Congress that the stripes remain 13 in number to represent the Thirteen Colonies, and that a star be added to the blue field for each new State coming into the Union. Accordingly, on April 4, 1818, President Monroe accepted a bill requiring that the flag of the United States have a union of 20 stars, white on a blue field, and that upon admission of each new state into the union, one star be added to the union of the flag on the fourth of July following its date of admission. The 13 alternating red and white stripes would remain unchanged. This act succeeded in prescribing the basic design of the flag, while assuring that the growth of the Nation would be properly symbolized.

The Flag House

The Flag House is located on the northwest corner of Albemarle and Pratt Streets in Baltimore, Maryland. It was the home of Mary Pickersgill from 1807 to 1857, and it was where she made the original "Star-Spangled Banner," which measured 30 by 42 feet. The stripes were two feet wide and the stars were two feet from point to point. Mrs. Pickersgill was paid $405.90 for her services. The flag was delivered to Fort McHenry on August 19, 1813, a full year before the Battle of Baltimore.

In 1876, Caroline Pickersgill Purdy wrote a letter to Georgiana Armistead Appleton, daughter of the Fort McHenry Commandant, in which she recounted the details of the making of the flag. Caroline wrote:

"It was made by my mother, Mrs. Mary Pickersgill, and I assisted her. My grandmother, Rebecca Young, made the first flag of the Revolution under General Washington's directions, and for this reason my mother was selected by Commodore [Joshua] Barney and General [John] Stricker to make this star-spangled banner, being an exceedingly patriotic woman. This flag, I think, contained four hundred yards of bunting, and my mother worked many nights until twelve o'clock to complete it in a given time."

The flag bears the autograph of Lt. Col. George Armistead as well as the date of the British bombardment. The flag remained in the Armistead family for many years until it was loaned to the Smithsonian for an official display in 1907. On December 19, 1912, it was donated to the Smithsonian where it is now on permanent exhibit. In 1914, much-needed preservative work was done on the flag by Mrs. Amelia Fowler and several other restoration experts. Although the flag was reduced in size in order to repair it, the reinforcement technique used has preserved its existence.

The Flag House is a National Historic Landmark, and is operated by an independent non-profit association. The flag is flown over the house 24 hours a day.

Fort McHenry

Fort McHenry is located in Baltimore, Maryland. This low citadel overlooks the entrance to Baltimore harbor and it is where the Americans defended the city against British land and naval attack on September 13-14 in 1814. It was during this battle that Francis Scott Key began the draft to "The Star-Spangled Banner" after seeing the flag still flying after a day and night of bombardment.

The fort continued in active military service for nearly a century after the battle but changing technology eventually made it obsolete as a coastal defense system. Today the 43-acre fort is preserved as a national monument and historic shrine. The property is managed by the National Park Service and the flag is flown over the fort 24 hours a day.

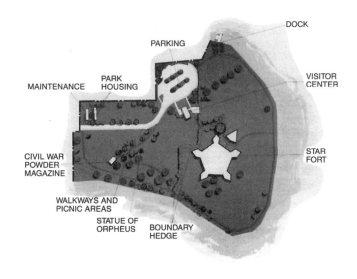

Fort McHenry National Monument and Historical Shrine.

Eventually, the growth of the country resulted in a flag with 48 stars upon the admission of Arizona and New Mexico in 1912. Alaska added a 49th in 1959, and Hawaii a 50th star in 1960. With the 50-star flag came a new design and arrangement of the stars in the union, a requirement met by President Eisenhower in Executive Order No. 10834, issued August 21, 1959. To conform with this, a national banner with 50 stars became the official flag of the United States. The flag was raised for the first time at 12:01 a.m. on July 4, 1960, at the Fort McHenry National Monument in Baltimore, Maryland.

Traditionally a symbol of liberty, the American flag has carried the message of freedom to many parts of the world. Sometimes the same flag that was flying at a crucial moment in our history has been flown again in another place to symbolize continuity in our struggles for the cause of liberty.

One of the most memorable is the flag that flew over the Capitol in Washington on December 7, 1941, when Pearl Harbor was attacked. This same flag was raised again on December 8 when war declared on Japan, and three days later at the time of the declaration of war against Germany and Italy. President Roosevelt called it the "flag of liberation" and carried it with him to the Casablanca Conference and on other historic occasions. It flew from the mast of the U.S.S. *Missouri* during the formal Japanese surrender on September 2, 1945.

Another historic flag is the one that flew over Pearl

Harbor on December 7, 1941. It also was present at the United Nations Charter meeting in San Francisco, California, and was used at the Big Three Conference at Potsdam, Germany. This same flag flew over the White House on August 14, 1945, when the Japanese accepted surrender terms.

Following the War of 1812, a great wave of nationalistic spirit spread throughout the country; the infant Republic had successfully defied the might of an empire. As this spirit spread, the Stars and Stripes became a symbol of sovereignty. The homage paid that banner is best expressed by what the gifted men of later generations wrote concerning it.

The writer Henry Ward Beecher said:

"A thoughtful mind when it sees a nation's flag, sees not the flag, but the nation itself. And whatever may be its symbols, its insignia, he reads chiefly in the flag, the government, the principles, the truths, the history that belongs to the nation that sets it forth. The American flag has been a symbol of Liberty and men rejoiced in it.

"The stars upon it were like the bright morning stars of God, and the stripes upon it were beams of morning light. As at early dawn the stars shine forth even while it grows light, and then as the sun advances that light breaks into banks and streaming lines of color, the glowing red and intense white striving together, and ribbing the horizon with bars effulgent, so, on the American flag, stars and beams of many-colored light shine out together . . . ."

In a 1917 Flag Day message, President Wilson said:

"This flag, which we honor and under which we serve, is the emblem of our unity, our power, our thought and purpose as a nation. It has no other character than that which we give it from generation to generation. The choices are ours. It floats in majestic silence above the hosts that execute those choices, whether in peace or in war. And yet, though silent, it speaks to us—speaks to us of the past, of the men and women who went before us, and of the records they wrote upon it.

"We celebrate the day of its birth; and from its birth until now it has witnessed a great history, has floated on high the symbol of great events, of a great plan of life worked out by a great people . . . .

"Woe be to the man or group of men that seeks to stand in our way in this day of high resolution when every principle we hold dearest is to be vindicated and made secure for the salvation of the nation. We are ready to plead at the bar of history, and our flag shall wear a new luster. Once more we shall make good with our lives and fortunes the great faith to which we were born, and a new glory shall shine in the face of our people."

The Flag Today

The flag of the United States of America has 13 horizontal stripes—seven red and six white—the red and white stripes alternating, and a union which consists of white stars of five points on a blue field placed in the upper quarter next to the staff and extending to the lower edge of the fourth red stripe from the top. The number of stars equals the number of States in the Union. The proportions of the flag as prescribed by Executive Order of President Eisenhower on August 21, 1959, are as follows:

Hoist (width) of flag 1.0

Fly (length) of flag 1.9

Hoist (width) of union 0.5385

Fly (length) of union 0.76

Width of each stripe 0.769

Diameter of each star 0.0616

"Old Ironsides" in the War of 1812.

Flag Anatomy

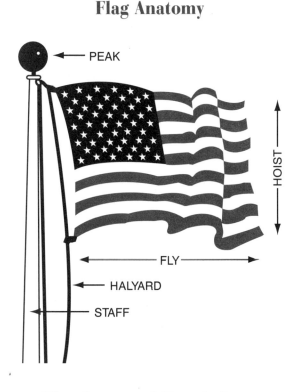

PEAK

HOIST

FLY

HALYARD

STAFF

Flag Laws and Regulations

The laws relating to the flag of the United States of America are found in detail in the United States Code. Title 4, Chapter 1 pertains to the flag and seal, seat of Government and the States; Title18, Chapter 33 pertains to crimes and criminal procedures; Title 36, Chapter 10 pertains to patriotic customs and observances. These laws were supplemented by Executive Orders and Presidential Proclamations.

Title 36, Chapter 10—Patriotic Customs

§171. National anthem; Star-Spangled Banner, conduct during playing

During rendition of the national anthem when the flag is displayed, all present except those in uniform should stand at attention facing the flag with the right hand over the heart. Men not in uniform should remove their headdress with their right hand and hold it at the left shoulder, the hand being over the heart. Persons in uniform should render the military salute at the first note of the anthem and retain position until the last note. When the flag is not displayed, those present should face toward the music and act in the same manner they would if the flag were displayed there.

§172. Pledge of Allegiance to the flag; manner of delivery

The pledge of Allegiance to the Flag, "I pledge allegiance to the Flag of the United States of America,

and to the Republic for which it stands, one Nation under God, indivisible, with liberty and justice for all.", should be rendered by standing at attention facing the flag with the right hand over the heart. When not in uniform men should remove their headdress with their right hand and hold it at the left shoulder, the hand being over the heart. Persons in uniform should remain silent, face the flag, and render the military salute.

§173. Display and Use of flag by civilians; codification of rules and customs; definition

The following codification of existing rules and customs pertaining to the display and use of the flag of the United States of America is established for the use of such civilians or civilian groups or organizations as may not be required to conform with regulations promulgated by one or more executive departments of the Government of the United States. The flag of the United States for the purpose of this chapter shall be defined according to Title 4, United States Code, chapter 1, section 1 and section 2 and Executive Order 10834 issued pursuant thereto.

§174. Time and occasions for display

(a) It is the universal custom to display the flag only from sunrise to sunset on buildings and on stationary flagstaffs in the open. However, when a patriotic effect is desired, the flag may be displayed twenty-four hours a day if properly illuminated during the hours of darkness.

(b) The flag should be hoisted briskly and lowered ceremoniously.

(c) The flag should not be displayed on days when the weather is inclement, except when an all weather flag is displayed.

(d) The flag should be displayed on all days, especially on New Year's Day, January 1; Inauguration Day, January 20; Lincoln's Birthday, February 12; Washington's Birthday, third Monday in February; Easter Sunday (variable), Mother's Day, second Sunday in May; Armed Forces Day, third Saturday in May; Memorial Day (half-staff until noon), the last Monday in May; Flag Day, June 14; Independence Day, July 4; Labor Day, first Monday in September; Constitution Day, September 17; Columbus Day, second Monday in October; Navy Day, October 27; Veterans Day, November 11; Thanksgiving Day, fourth Thursday in November; Christmas Day, December 25; and such other days as may be proclaimed by the President of the United States; the birthday of States (date of admission); and on State holidays.

(e) The flag should be displayed daily on or near the main administration building of every public institution.

(f) The flag should be displayed in or near every polling place on election days.

(g) The flag should be displayed during school days in or near every schoolhouse.

§175. Position and manner of display

The flag, when carried in a procession with another flag or flags, should be either on the marching right; that is, the flag's own right, or, if there is a line of other flags, in front of the center of that line.

(a) The flag should not be displayed on a float in a parade except from a staff, or as provided in subsection (i) of this section.

(b) The flag should not be draped over the hood, top, sides, or back of a vehicle or of a railroad train or a boat. When the flag is displayed on a motorcar, the staff shall be fixed firmly to the chassis or clamped to the right fender.

(c) No other flag or pennant should be placed above or, if on the same level, to the right of the flag of the United

With flags of two or more nations.

In a procession.

With another flag on crossed staffs.

On same halyard with flags of States, cities and organizations

Grouped with flags of other States, cities and organizations.

States of America, except during church services conducted by naval chaplains at sea, when the church pennant may be flown above the flag during church services for the personnel of the Navy. No person shall display the flag of the United Nations or any other national or international flag equal, above, or in a position of superior prominence or honor to, or in place of, the flag of the United States at any place within the United States or any Territory or possession thereof: Provided, that nothing in this section shall make unlawful the continuance of the practice heretofore followed of displaying the flag of the United Nations in a position of superior prominence or honor, and other national flags in positions of equal prominence or honor, with that of the flag of the United States at the headquarters of the United Nations.

(d) The flag of the United States of America, when it is displayed with another flag against a wall from crossed staffs, should be on the right, the flag's own right, and its staff should be in front of the staff of the other flag.

(e) The flag of the United States of America should be at the center and at the highest point of the group when a number of flags of States or localities or pennants of societies are grouped and displayed from staffs.

(f) When flags of States, cities, or localities, or pennants of societies are flown on the same halyard with the flag of the United States, the latter should always be at the peak.

253

When the flags are flown from adjacent staffs, the flag of the United States should be hoisted first and lowered last. No such flag or pennant may be placed above the flag of the United States or to the United States flag's right.

(g) When flags of two or more nations are displayed, they are to be flown from separate staffs of the same height. The flags should be of approximately equal size. International usage forbids the display of the flag of one nation above that of another nation in time of peace.

(h) When the flag of the United States is displayed from a staff projecting horizontally or at an angle from the window sill, balcony, or front of a building, the union of the flag should be placed at the peak of the staff unless the flag is at half staff. When the flag is suspended over a sidewalk from a rope extending from a house to a pole at the edge of the sidewalk, the flag should be hoisted out, union first, from the building.

(i) When displayed either horizontally or vertically against a wall, the union should be uppermost and to the flag's own right, that is, to the observer's left. When

On a wall.

Over the middle of a street
⟵ North or east ⟵

At an angle from a building.

Suspended over a sidewalk.

displayed in a window, the flag should be displayed in the same way, with the union or blue field to the left of the observer in the street.

(j) When the flag is displayed over the middle of the street, it should be suspended vertically with the union to the north in an east and west street or the the east in a north and south street.

(k) When used on a speaker's platform, the flag, if displayed flat, should be displayed above and behind the speaker. When displayed from a staff in a church or public auditorium, the flag of the United States of America should hold the position of superior prominence, in advance of the audience, and in the position of honor at the clergyman's or speaker's right as he faces the audience. Any other flag so displayed should be placed on the left of the clergyman or speaker or to the right of the audience.

(l) The flag should form a distinctive feature of the ceremony of unveiling a statue or monument, but it should never be used as the covering for the statue or monument.

(m) The flag, when flown at half-staff, should be first hoisted to the peak for an instant and then lowered to the half-staff position. The flag should be again raised to the peak before it is lowered for the day. On Memorial Day the flag should be displayed at half-staff until noon only, then raised to the top of the staff. By order of the President, the flag shall be flown at half-staff upon the death of principal figures of the United States Government and the Governor of a State, territory, or possession, as a mark of respect to their memory. In the event of the death of other officials or foreign dignitaries, the flag is to be displayed at half-staff according to Presidential instructions or orders, or in accordance with recognized customs or practices not inconsistent with law. In the event of the death of a present or former official of the government of any State, territory, or possession of the United States, the Governor of the State, territory, or possession may proclaim that the National flag shall be flown at half-staff. The flag shall be flown at half-staff thirty days from the death of the President or a former President; ten days from the day of death of the Vice President, the Chief Justice or a retired

A.M.   P.M.

Memorial Day

Draped over a casket.

On a speaker's platform.

Chief Justice of the United States, or Speaker of the House or Representatives; from the day of death until interment of an Associate Justice of the Supreme Court, a Secretary of an executive or military department, territory, or possession; and on the day of death, and the following day for a Member of Congress. As used in this subsection—

    (1) the term "half-staff" means the position of the flag when it is one-half the distance between the top and the bottom of the staff;

    (2) the term "executive or military department" means any agency listed under sections 101 and 102 of title 5, United States Code; and

    (3) the term "Member of Congress" means a Senator, a Representative, a Delegate, or the Resident Commissioner from Puerto Rico.

  (n) When the flag is used to cover a casket, it should be so placed that the union is at the head and over the left shoulder. The flag should not be lowered into the grave or allowed to touch the ground.

  (o) When the flag is suspended across a corridor or

When unveiling a statue or monument.

lobby in a building with only one main entrance, it should be suspended vertically with the union of the flag to the observer's left upon entering. If the building has more than one main entrance, the flag should be suspended vertically near the center of the corridor or lobby with the union to the north, when entrances are to the east and west or to the east, when entrances are to the north and south. If there are entrances in more than two directions, the union should be to the east.

§176. Respect for the Flag

No disrespect should be shown to the flag of the United States of America; the flag should not be dipped to any person or thing. Regimental colors, State flags, and organization or institutional flags are to be dipped as a mark of honor.

(a) The flag should never be displayed with the union down, except as a signal of dire distress in instances of extreme danger to life or property.

(b) The flag should never touch anything beneath it, such as the ground, the floor, water, or merchandise.

(c) The flag should never be carried flat or horizontally, but always aloft and free.

(d) The flag should never be used as wearing apparel, bedding, or drapery. It should never be festooned, drawn back, nor up, in folds, but always allowed to fall free. Bunting of blue, white, and red, always arranged with the blue above, the white in the middle, and the red below, should be used for covering a speaker's desk, draping the front of the platform, and for decoration in general.

(e) The flag should never be fastened, displayed, used, or stored in such a manner as to permit it to be easily torn, soiled, or damaged in any way.

(f) The flag should never be used as a covering for a ceiling.

(g) The flag should never have placed upon it, nor on any part of it, nor attached to it any mark, insignia, letter, word, figure, design, picture, or drawing of any nature.

(h) The flag should never be used as a receptacle for receiving, holding, carrying, or delivering anything.

Proper display of bunting.

Saluting the flag.

(i) The flag should never be used for advertising purposes in any manner whatsoever. It should not be embroidered on such articles as cushions or handkerchiefs and the like, printed or otherwise impressed on paper napkins or boxes or anything that is designed for temporary use and discard. Advertising signs should not be fastened to a staff or halyard from which the flag is flown.

(j) No part of the flag should ever be used as a costume or athletic uniform. However, a flag patch may be affixed to the uniform of military personnel, firemen, policemen, and members of patriotic organizations. The flag represents a living country and is itself considered a living thing. Therefore, the lapel flag pin being a replica, should be worn on the left lapel near the heart.

(k) The flag, when it is in such condition that it is no longer a fitting emblem for display, should be destroyed in a dignified way, preferably by burning.

§177. Conduct during hoisting, lowering or passing of flag

During the ceremony of hoisting or lowering the flag or when the flag is passing in a parade or in review, all persons present except those in uniform should face the flag and stand at attention with the right hand over the heart. Those present in uniform should render the military salute. When not in uniform, men should remove their headdress with their right hand and hold it at the left shoulder, the hand being over the heart. Aliens should stand at attention. The salute to the flag in a moving column should be rendered at the moment the flag passes.

§178. Modification of rules and customs by President

Any rule or custom pertaining to the display of the flag of the United States of America, set forth herein, may be altered, modified, or repealed, or additional rules with respect thereto may be prescribed, by the Commander in Chief of the Armed Forces of the United States, whenever he deems it to be appropriate or desirable; and any such alteration or additional rule shall be set forth in a proclamation.

Index

S

T